T0374292

Kashur

The Kashmiri Speaking People

Analytical Perspective

Mohini Qasba Raina

 # 258 Sector 17,

Panchkula 134109

Haryana, India

PARTRIDGE
A Penguin Random House Company

Copyright © 2014 by Mohini Qasba Raina.

ISBN:	Hardcover	978-1-4828-9946-7
	Softcover	978-1-4828-9945-0
	eBook	978-1-4828-9947-4

All rights reserved. No part of this book may be used or reproduced by any means, graphic, electronic, or mechanical, including photocopying, recording, taping or by any information storage retrieval system without the written permission of the publisher except in the case of brief quotations embodied in critical articles and reviews.

Because of the dynamic nature of the Internet, any web addresses or links contained in this book may have changed since publication and may no longer be valid. The views expressed in this work are solely those of the author and do not necessarily reflect the views of the publisher, and the publisher hereby disclaims any responsibility for them.

To order additional copies of this book, contact
Toll Free 800 101 2657 (Singapore)
Toll Free 1 800 81 7340 (Malaysia)
orders.singapore@partridgepublishing.com

www.partridgepublishing.com/singapore

DEDICATION

To young generation of Kashmiris who have only seen and read about turbulence and militancy that evokes the name of Kashmir now a days and know very little about the glorious past of their ancestors.

An appreciative effort and labour put in by the author in her research and in compiling an authentic account of the past history of the *Kashur* and their land. It should serve as an open window for our young boys and girls, who know very little about their past and shall greatly benefit from this book.

B.K.Kaul, Nazir Ex-Prof of Agriculture University Udaipore, Rajasthan, India

Having had to face the compulsive exodus and its trivialities that the Hindu Kashmiris have undergone, it goes to the credit of the author for having maintained an unbiased attitude through out the compilation and presentation of this classic: History of the Kashmiri speaking people.

V.K.Raina, ex-deputy Director General Geological Survey of India; author of *Glacial Atlas of India; Images Antarctica, and* under publication *Glacier Snout Monitoring in the Himalayas'*

Dal Lake

CONTENTS

Illustrations

Preface

This book—*Kashur* the Kashmiri Speaking People—is an analytical study of the ancient and medieval history of the KSP. Chroniclers and intellectuals have variedly defined the term History. Some believe history is supposed to record the inception, progress, or decay of organized communities, their movements, their land marks, and the personalities involved there in. For me, history simply means a record of events that have happened prior to the present moment. To record this history, humans have taken recourse to numerous means in accordance with the growth of intellect and the evolution of the times. Earliest means of recording history have been the stone implements, the rock paintings, seals, tablets, legends, myths, religious and social anecdotes carried down the age's- word to mouth-and so on, till finally the written word was discovered a few millennia's ago.

I believe without the knowledge of the past, present hangs in vacuum and the future can not be built on a swinging pendulum. Past is the scaffolding on which the present can be reconstructed and remodelled, and the future can be conceived and shaped. Due to an unexplainable indifference and unjustified modesty towards the past, barely any attention is paid to its authenticity. "Thanks to the culture of isms the true story of human experience and perception of heritage and inheritance has been disdainfully ignored. An enlightened yet critical view of how our ancestors coped with challenges and uncertainties have been replaced by either idyllic or prejudicial fantasies." Often biased facts are fed to belittle the achievements and accomplishments of our ancestors, and their eras. Some-how their accomplishments are not given due recognition; and it is with this aim of setting right what is wrongly detailed, the conceptualization of this book originated. I am aware of the fact that this is not the first attempt in this direction. Many an exhaustive publications have been compiled by chroniclers over time. Gen x for whose benefit this book is meant, does not have the time and patience to read those huge toms of History. Hence an attempt is made to present a concise version. The book is compiled in a lesson format, and each lesson in this capsule is individually devoted to one significant topic related to the history of the *Kashur*/ Kashmiri.

It aims to present an impartial and unbiased view on those aspects of the *Kashur* that appear very significant to me in the history of this small linguistic group numbering not more than six million in all. A number that does not have any numerical value in a vastly populated country as Bharata, or the *'Aryavarta'* as its Aryan ancestors would have preferred to call it. As is well known India is a land of thousands of languages and dialects. In this plethora of languages and dialects, 'Kashmiri' is recognised as one of the fourteen languages in the eighth schedule of the Constitution of India. In this book an effort has been made to study the history of those people whose mother tongue is this language.

The sole purpose of my writing this book is to record facts about the saga of this linguistic group that is now scattered all over the globe with major concentration in the state of Jammu and Kashmir. While recording the history of any people, their political set up plays a major role and impact on their historical evolution, hence an abridged account of the same is given at the end.

This linguistic group labelled *Kashur* in the native tongue, while otherwise better known as KSP (Kashmiri speaking people), originated in one of the most beautiful and the largest valley in the Himalayas, known by the name of *Kasheer* to the locals and Kashmir to the rest of the world. The valley that, right from the days of 'Neel Naga' to the scientific and space age of the present 21st century has been, often, referred to as the 'Abode of Gods.'

I have tried to trace the history of this KSP home land right from the very inception at the end of the Ice Age-fourth glaciation, when a very large water body-112km by 32km-gradually shrunk and desiccated and thus, came into existence smaller areas of marshes and lakes from which evolved the present valley of Kashmir.

It is the history of the KSP, from the earliest aborigines-the Naga tribes-to the advent of Pisachas from the dry cold deserts of Rajasthan, and finally till the coming of *Brahman*s from the plains and southern parts of India. That was the time when the dwellers of the valley had no longer to leave the valley during winter and travel to warmer plains. That was the time when Nila Naga accepted the Pisachas as equals and in order to retain the identity of his people, framed religious codes and laws, a constitution, named Nilamat Purana and made it compulsory for every inhabitant of this land to abide by it.[1]

This book tries to record the evolutionary history of these dwellers of Kashmir; their character, their culture; their failures and successes; their moments of glory and downfall; their religious compulsions and changes that have taken place down the ages in their lives; their adjustments and travails of the migrations; their habits, customs, and festivals.

During the march of their history covering a period of over six millennia's, these people experienced many an ups and downs. In the moments of glory they achieved eminence in every field and, these moments of glory are highlighted within the pages of this book.

It is the history of the people known for their literary genius from the days of antiquity. People that gave the country the literati like Bana, Panini, Aryabhatta, Vasudeva, Shombu Bhatta, Kalhana Pandit, Jona Raja, Shirivara Lal Ded, Habba Khatoon, Haider Malik, and many more in the earlier periods of history, and in the recent years personalities like Alama Iqbal, Jawaharlal Lal Nehru, Sheikh Mohamed Abdullah, Mehjoor, Nadim Kashmiri to name a few.

Many a religious currents and cross currents made inroads into their spiritual and religious codes that helped them to evolve new philosophies. This book records the efforts and achievements of the people who propounded, Mahayana Cult of Buddhism and the Tantra philosophy of Kashmir Shaivism. People, who, till very recent times, gave a very concrete and practical shape to Sufism and practiced it in their daily lives.

It is the history of the people who were known in far off lands like China and Tibet for their religious zeal, teaching institutes and collection and preservation of precious manuscripts, like the Gilgit manuscripts, about which the latest research studies have established that the "corpus of G.M. throw significant light on the evolution of Sanskrit, Chinese, Korean, Japanese and Tibetan literature"

It is the history of the people who, with their valour and wit could defeat even the great invaders like Mohamed of Ghazni and even successfully withstood twice the onslaught of the army of the Great Mughal king Akbar.

It is the history of the people who were known as great strategists and administrators by the Mughals. These people were successful mediators between the Nawabs and Rajas; for the Kashmiris, besides being fluent in Sanskrit and Persian languages, were also the early Indians to master English language. Learning has been their greatest weapon and asset, be it Sanskrit, Persian or English.

It is the history of those people, whose liberal social codes enriched by their philosophies, created a social order based on equality of gender and cast. From the times immemorial, their society gave equal status and respect to women; though, in between, the heinous practice of *Sati* was adopted, when the Kshatriya kings opted for this Rajput tradition, which was, however, abolished during the reign of the Mogul kings. Likewise the stringent Islamic laws, imposed by the Muslim rulers could not negate the social right that was granted to the KSP women. Yet the travails of time and circumstances thrust on them by the invaders compelled them to adopt, at times, some selfish and cowardly means for survival. These moments of shame, which were inflicted on them by the invaders, also find place in the book.

History has proved that the greatest undoing of these people was their tradition of hospitality, compassion and habit of granting asylum to those who sought it, without verifying their real worthiness and intent. This innate weakness of these people that time and again, made them to loose their independence, face immense hardships, changed the very nature of their destiny: political, religious or social has been detailed in this book.

This book '*Kashur* the Kashmiri Speaking People' is an effort to record the history of these people from the earliest eras of their existence to the middle of the 20th century that I have tried to compile and reproduce to the best of my ability, with the help of available records. And I did this after a thorough research of most of the available written material like manuscripts, their translations; treatises of the various historians; ethnologists, Indologists, geologists' and linguists'; archaeological findings and folklore, and even some of the major and minor journals.

Attention has been paid to the local sources, as a better source of information, as I believe writings of the indigenous people, who have not only been first hand witnesses to the occurrences but also have lived and shared the idiom and the environment of the place, whose history they have recorded is bound to be worthier than the random records of the casual visitors. Besides the information supplied by our local sources on the whole, belongs to dates of much earlier times as compared to what the Greek, Chinese, and Mohammadan notices or even what Indian classical literature provides. Hence the former sources deem to be more authentic.

I do not wish to shy away from the fact that I have quoted in extensor from the sources consulted: (a) for the benefit of the sceptics who are reluctant to accept the validity of KSP's glorious past, (b) to authenticate my observations and (c) to retain the original feel and flavour of the assessments recorded by different scholars, historians and travellers about the various aspects of *Kashur* over the last millennia.

I have mentioned, very briefly, the contemporary era in these pages, as I believe, to write about the contemporary era, the protagonist should have experienced the time concerned both by physical and mental presence. I have been out of the homeland since the middle of the last century, and did not have the luxury of that circumstance. There is a saying in Kashmiri *"bumsiney zaane satut's senz toph"* (only an earth worm can comprehend the peck of the

Hootoot). As such, I have neither been the victim in the real sense and nor the victor, though factually I am not qualified to make this statement; since, even I have lost eight members of my extended family to the terrorist mayhem besides loosing my home and hearth to vandalism during the contemporary era.

My book does not 'seek to rival the works of the professional historians'. I am not a historian, and I must confess, history was neither my favourite subject, nor a favourite pastime. Yet a perchance incident, at the most opportune moment of my life, led me on the path of historical research, not of the contemporary times, but of ancient history and its antiquities, out of a genuine desire to learn and trace the history of my ancestors, record their achievements, study their distinctive character and cultural excellences, and at the same time unravel their noble and ignoble passions for living. It is an effort of an amateur that can be found wanting in many aspects, though I have not spared any effort, on my part, to record facts. In this journey of our unknown past I have been greatly handicapped due to my inability to read the original Persian and Sanskrit manuscripts and hence have had to depend upon translations that can, at times, be a biased presentation, depending upon the translator's perceptions. The other handicap has been the present turmoil and upheaval in the state that did not permit detailed excursions to physically verify the authenticity of the places and other data.

THIS BOOK COMPRISES FIFTEEN CHAPTERS AS FOLLOWS:

First chapter: 'The Home land of KSP' is exclusively devoted to the detailed study of the origin and creation of the valley of Kashmir. Common legends and mythologies about the creation have been analyzed and tested on the basis of scientific data gathered from the science of geology and archaeology. In addition various names of the homeland are recorded.

Second chapter: Physical Landscape of the native land, deals with the, three gradient geographic levels of the valley and some prominent landmarks.

Third chapter: The *Kashur*-Kashmiri Speaking People (KSP) deals with the subject of the *Kashur* the people; their prehistory, origin, composition, character, classification, ethnic as well as religious, and also the subject of the inception of the tradition of surnames in the community.

Fourth chapter: The Evidences of various religious cults and faiths of the KSP, and their contribution to these religious streams; gives the history of the religious streams that have flowed through the lives of the KSP's during the last five thousand years not in strict chronological order. An attempt has been made to give due recognition to all the religious thoughts, their impact on the life of the people and the contribution made by the people of the land, towards enhancing the merits of almost all the religions practiced by the KSP willingly or under the force of prosecution

Fifth chapter: Rites, Rituals and Festivals observed by the KSP is a detailed study of the festivals and the rites and rituals of the *Kashur* ethnic group.

Sixth chapter: Social Order of the Kashmiri speaking people during Puranic and Medieval era is an exhaustive study of the social order of the society during the Puranic and medieval era, i.e. up to the end of 13th century AD

Seventh Chapter: Social order during and beyond Islamic era is a detailed record of the changes that the KSP society under-went with the arrival and acceptance of Islam. There after the social order is monitored up to the recent times.

Eighth chapter:KSP Cultural Heritage and Prowess is an elaborate study of the expertise and achievements of the KSP in various fields of learning, language and literature, medicine, art and aesthetics, their religious and missionary zeal, their contribution to the Sanskrit and Persian language etc.

Ninth chapter: Foot Prints of KSP Architectural Excellence is a concise study of the acumen and proficiency of the KSP architects. A brief account of a few important monuments is given to substantiate the arguments.

Tenth chapter: Some of the prominent KSP Chroniclers and their contribution is a detailed account of the local chroniclers and their chronicles that record the history of Kashmir and its people. Two main chronicles the Rajatarangini and the Nilamata Purana have been dealt with exhaustively, as compared to other chronicles mentioned in the chapter.

Eleventh chapter: *Kashur* the Language-The Single Binding Link is the history, growth and development of *Kashur* as a spoken language from a lay person's point of view, till its gradual evolution to a full fledged language used as a medium of expression in different forms of literature. An effort has also been made to record names of a sizable number of Kashmiri writers of repute and some of their compositions.

Twelfth chapter: Political Chronology is a birds eye view of the rulers who played an important role in the development of the valley as a whole and more so in the lives of this minor ethnic group. It does not happen to be a detailed study of the rulers as such, as this book is intended only to be, about the common people, and not of their rulers.

Appendix, Notes and References and Selected Bibliography forms the final three chapters.

I do hope this humble effort would in time serve the purpose for which it is conceived.

ACKNOWLEDGEMENT

I wish to acknowledge with gratitude the encouragement and the mental support of two women-one of whom has since left this mortal world-that gave me strength and courage to take up this stupendous task of compiling the history of my people. Two great ladies, who have meant a lot to me: Mata Ji-Chanda Maal Bamzai Raina-my late mother-in-law, who like a true representative of Kashmiri womanhood, showed the capacity, grit and determination to learn to read and write the Devanagri alphabet when she was an octogenarian. I am indeed obliged to her for encouraging me in-spite of all domestic hindrances and, for being an epitome of patience during my initial stage of research hunting in the libraries. Having discussed with her the material of the book, her constant reminder to me, day in and day out, used to be when are you going to publish the book? Alas! I had no answer then and now she is no more.

The other great lady that I am indebted to is my mother Shyam Rani Mattoo Qasba-Bhabi for all her children, a typical Kashmiri way of calling your mother. She is a role model for me. Her blessings, force of her will power, agility and alert senses in her early nineties-has acted as a power house for me and made me aware of my genetic capabilities and in turn assured me that "I can do it at seventies". I wish to gratefully thank her for sharing her fund of knowledge about the traditional beliefs, customs, rites and rituals of KSP. For her narration, touchingly, of the eye witness accounts of the penury conditions of the Kashur peasant class in the early twentieth century that was enhanced and caused by the callous behaviour and treatment of a few feudalistic employees of the state. I am also grateful to her for the eye witness account of the impact of the communal violence that took place in the Kashmir valley in the year 1931-the first and probably the only instance of confrontation between the native majority Musalman and the minority Bhatta. Its impact on the social order of the Bhatta, who being educated Brahman class, adopted other menial professions for the smooth and self sufficient functioning of their community as a consequence of these riots. Thank you Maa for your graces and blessings!

I acknowledge with grateful thanks the assistance, guidance and co-operation of the Chief Librarian and the staff of National Library Calcutta (Kolkatta) for enabling me to consult and scan books related to my topic from all sections, general, archival or rare books, and even from the section comprising the personal collections of late Sir Ashutosh Mukerji.

I acknowledge gratefully the help of the librarians of The Asiatic Society Library, Kolkatta; Adhiyar Library Madras, Chennai; State Library Chandigarh; Geological Survey of India Library, Kolkatta; Westchester District Library U.S.A. and the National Library Singapore.

I acknowledge my indebtedness to various authors whose works I have consulted and quoted. To the best of my knowledge full references have been given at the appropriate places.

I wish to acknowledge the help rendered by the J&K Academy of Arts, Culture and Languages for enabling me to acquire a copy of Nilamata Purana translated by Dr. Ved Kumari.

I acknowledge with thanks the efforts of Shri A.K. Raina (a colleague of my husband) for procuring the copy of M.E. Stein's translation of Rajatarangini Vol.1&11 for my use. And to my maternal uncle Shri J.L. Mattoo, I am thankful for gifting me a copy of R.S. Pandit's translation of Kalhana's Rajatarangini.

Three books: Nilamata Purana and the two versions of the Raja Tarangani procured as above have been a great source of information to me in my research.

I wish to acknowledge gratefully the efforts of late Shri Ram Ji Pandit for explaining some very archaic Kashmiri words and some Sharda sentences of yore.

I wish to convey my grateful thanks to Professor Dr. B.K.Koul (Nazir) for his guidance and suggestions regarding the reconstruction of the format in-order to improve the readability of the book. But for his appreciation, encouragement and faith in me, my task would have been difficult.

For a house wife the support and cooperation of her family means and matters a lot and I wish to acknowledge that support, how so ever small or great that may have been.

Abhinav and Rahul, my grand sons, who genetically being Kashmiris, were neither born in the valley, nor were able to visit their ancestral home till late in their teens, due to the political upheaval there. Yet they have always shown such eagerness and urge to learn about the valley and their ancestors that initiated me into this project to find answers to their queries. I am thankful to them.

I am thankful to my son-in-law Sunil Kaul for providing me opportunities to collect data from different libraries in the course of his postings to U.S.A., Singapore and different parts of the country.

I am thankful to my daughter Nishu for her help in my research work at the preliminary stage; for designing the cover page and formatting the manuscript and above all for encouraging and egging me on in my sombre moods.

Finally I would like to acknowledge with gratitude the support, co-operation, understanding, and patient guidance of my husband Vijay (V.K.Raina), during the compilation of the book ***'Kashur the Kasmiri Speaking People'.*** He not only read the manuscript but gave valuable suggestions and advice, and also spent his precious time explaining the geological aspect of the valley. Besides being an admirer and a constructive critic, he, all along, expressed full confidence in me and pushed me, at times, to the limits of nagging for completing my book.

Picture Credits-Pic nos, ,2,3,6,&9 by Abhinav Kaul and pic nos. 1,4,5,7,8,10 by V.K.Raina

Glossary

Names of the months of a year

Kashmiri version	Devnagari version	English version
Tchiter	*Chaitra*	15th March- 15th April
Vaihaik	*Vaisakh*	15th April - 15th May
Zyeth	*Jestha*	15th May- 15th June
Haar	*Ashaad*	15th June-15th July
Shrawun	*Shravana*	15th July-15th August
Bhădrapeth.	*Bhadrpad*	15th August-15th September
Ashid	*Ashvin /Assuj*	15th September-15th October
Kartik	*Kărttik*	15th October-15th November
Monjhore	*Marga*	15th November-15th December
Poh	*Posh*	15th December-15thJ anuary
Magh	*Magh*	15th January-15th February
Phagun	*Phalguna*	15th February-15th March

Manvantra is a time period of 300 million years plus

Kalpa is a time period of 4.320 million years

A *Yojna* is a measure of distance differently regarded as equal to as low as 5km to as high as 20km

Abbreviations

KSP Kashmiri speaking people

N.P. Nilamata Purana

R.T. Kalhana's Rajatarangini

Rajat Sitaram Pandits translation of R.T

masl Meters above sea level

BP Before present time

A.H Al Hijri (Muslim era)

D.O.V Daughters' of Vitasta

CHAPTER-1

KASHEER - THE HOMELAND OF KASHMIRI SPEAKING PEOPLE

THE STORY OF ITS ORIGIN

The phrase, 'home-land' touches an emotional cord and rings a sensual buzz of belonging, for it connotes that geographic land mass, where our ancestors were born; where we inherit the right of ownership and the natural right of living as its citizens; in short where a person feels at home. Every community and its people have an individual space identified as their home-land in the hypothetic global village of the twenty first century. Home land of the 'Kashmiri speaking people', the 'Vale of Kashmir' is a boat-shaped basin, 140 km long and 40 km wide, situated in the North-Western tip of the country India/ Bharata, between 74° to 75°-30'E longitude and 32° 30' and 34° 30'N latitude, within the confines of the Asian continent that forms a measure part of our globe.

The globe that according to earth sciences was shaped, in the bygone times, billions of years ago, at an unknown moment of time, when a fiery ball of gases parted the company of several such masses of its kind, either by accident or by intention, and fell far apart from the Sun. This fiery mass, with the passage of time, over billions of years, cooled down to a reasonable temperature to attain the present shape and form of the planet earth, i.e. a mass of land and water surrounded by atmosphere. Planet earth and its crust have under gone many a changes and upheavals where in continents and oceans have changed their relative positions. It was during this process of change, after many a great upheaval, convulsions and volcanic eruptions in the bosom of the mother earth, over millions of years that an idyllic piece of land came into existence: an abode of Gods-a paradise on earth- that is the valley of Kashmir. Though the authenticity of the concept of the paradise on Earth is a moot question, yet this epithet creates an aura about the land and incites an, 'emotion of pleasing expectancy and joy in the beholders eyes', be it the, 'apathetic eye of the *Brahman*, or the cold fixed thoughtfulness of the Mullah 'or the catholicity of a Christian priest.'

Baron Charles Hugel sums up this dilemma thus, "Whether Kashmir was that favoured spot where six thousand years ago, the Almighty Word called the human race in to being, whether it was the seat of that paradise which man forfeited by his disobedience to the first commandment ever given or whether as Hindu mythology pretends it was there that countless ages back, the world was again renewed by the creation of the present race, are questions which throw no light either on the history of mankind or of Kashmir itself . . . . Most assuredly there was an earthly paradise, what matters is where it was . . . . and the same fond fancy, that has persuaded even the Hindu, surrounded on every side by the magnificent scenery of his native land, that Kashmir was in truth the paradise of the newly awakened world . . . . . . This belief undoubtedly does invest it with peculiar charm, and expectancy when one gets the glimpse of this lovely valley . . . . . ."[1]

Be it a paradise or not, to acquaint our selves about the formation, physical features, and age of this stretch of the global village labelled as *Kasheer*, we have not only to study its geology and geography but also the legends and mythologies about its creation that are preserved in the oral traditions and in written literature.

Legends and mythologies are the only source of information left to us regarding that hoary past, as in the earlier eras of our existence this was the best option available to our ancestors. This was the only form of composition through which they could preserve the histories, the happenings and events of their age without adulterations and interpolations by later generations. As such we shall primarily find out what these legends state and try to deduce the crux of the theory of the origin of the valley and later verify it with the logical and scientific observations of geology, archaeology and anthropology.

The legends

Generally much credibility is not attributed to most of the legends and myths passed down by our earlier ancestors, while I believe that every composition, every myth or legend is always based on some truth; however, flimsy, distant or even irrelevant it may appear at times. After all, these very ancestors of ours laid foundations of all our institutions; they cleared the wild woods and mountain ranges, tilled the lands and gave us the science of agriculture. They introduced the system of community culture, organised the communes and then developed villages, townships and the tribal governing bodies. Above all they evolved the language system which has enabled us to question their actions. How can we imagine that they would have concocted baseless myths, without any underlying facts and truths? "However", writes Goethe the great German philosopher, "if our ancestors were great enough to invent myths like that we at least should be great enough to believe in them." The ancestors of the KSP with their fertile imagination and well developed powers of observation and perception, have compiled legends about almost every aspect of their life and living circumstance, be it social, religious, geographical or historical. These legends are interesting not only for their imaginative content but also for the fact that quite often scientific analysis corroborates in totality with their theme.

According to Nilamata Purana-our earliest source of information regarding the legend of the creation of the vale of Kashmir-the land of Kashmira was occupied, for six Manvantras since the beginning of the Kalpa by a vast lake by the name of *Sati Sara*, six yojnas long and three yojnas wide. In the 7th Manvantra, the water of the lake was drained off through an outlet made with plough by Ananta at the orders of Vishnu, who along with other gods and goddesses had come there to kill the demon Jalodbhava. The story runs further informing how, after the death of Jalodbhava, the Pisachas and descendants of Manu were settled there by Kashyapa to live in the company of the Nagas,-(the progeny of *Prajapati Kashyapa* and his wife *Kadru*-the daughter of *Daksha-*) the original inhabitants of the valley

It is this basic theme that the valley was a vast lake prior to human settlement that has been recorded by different people in different formats. There are a lot of similarities and differences in the given versions. Many chroniclers, travellers, scholars and pilgrims alike have reproduced it in their compositions, like the RajaTarangni, Nilamata Purana, the Mahatamyas, the records of the Chinese scholars, Muslim chroniclers and random travellers etc.

THE OLDEST HINDU LEGEND

One of the oldest Hindu legends—albeit mythological-about the origin of the valley recorded by Zadoo and Kanji lal,- two Kashmiri Sanskrit scholars- reads, "In the sixth Manvantra, of the *Chatur Yuga* the sage Kashyapa was on a pilgrimage to all the Tirthas of the earth. Nila his son went to meet him at Kankhal and prevailed on him to visit the *Tirthas* of Kashmir. Kashyapa on his way to Kashmir saw the ravages in the country of Madras (valley) and asked as to how this devastation was caused. Then Nila, his son, acquainted him about the existence of Jalodbhava in the lake of *Sati Sara* and how he had destroyed and devastated the valley by his spoils. Having learnt in detail about the cause of the destruction of the valley Kashyapa decided to help his son in reinstating the land and its inhabitants. They both went to the *Brahmaloka* to seek help of the divinities. All the gods and deities came to their help and met at the lofty peaks of *Kosarainy Kuther*, above *Konsarnag* or *Kramsara.* Brahma seated himself on the northern peak, Vishnu on the southern peak and Siva in between. Then Ananta cut off a path through the mountain banks of *Sati Sara* so that the water rolled off to expose Jalodbhava who was hiding in the water. Still the demon tried to create darkness, which Shiva prevented. Finally it was Vishnu who killed the *daitya* (demon) and the *Sati Sara* was turned into a happy valley. The goddesses watered it in the form of rivers and Nagas became the sources of springs. Then Kashyapa suggested that he would introduce humans (Saraswat *Brahmans*) into the valley. The Nagas did not accept this, so he cursed them to live with the Pisachas. Later, however, his favourite son Nila again entreated him and forced him to modify his curse by allowing the Pisachas to live in the land for only six months of winter, from *Kartica* to *Chaitra.* And thus the humans would inhabit and cultivate the land for the summer six months and evacuate it before the King of Pisachas would arrive. Later after four Yugas Vishnu granted the Nagas to live happily with the humans. When four Yugas had come and gone, one season, when the summer dwellers had left the valley as usual in *Asuj*, one old *Brahman* named Chandredeva, who was too old to travel decided to stay back in the valley. During this period Nila expounded to the old *Brahman*, a number of rites and observances calculated to free the country from the yoke of Pisachas and from the excessive cold. Chandredeva appreciated these rites and rituals of the Nagas. When after six months king Virodya returned with his men to the valley, the *Brahman* impressed upon him the efficacies of all the rites and ceremonies expounded by Nila. The king liked them and imposed the same on the migrant people who promptly and willingly accepted them. Since then people of all classes were introduced in to the valley.[2]

In the later eras when travellers and scholars like Hiuen tsang, Bedia ud-din, Forster etc visited the valley and got acquainted with the existing legends, they were so convinced by the validity of their theme, that they in turn compiled their own versions of the basic theme of desiccation with modifications to suit their audiences.

Hiuen Tsang in the Buddhist version has changed the name of the desiccator of water from Vishnu to Ananta. Yet in another place he writes; "This country was once a dragon lake instead of *Sati Sara.*"[3]

Mohammadan chroniclers have given their own version, in which Bedia-ud-din begins with the creation and brings Adam from Sarandip where all Musalman authorities place him after the fall of *Cashmere.*"[4]

Yet another Muslim version of the same fact as recorded in the Wakiat-I-Kashmir is almost similar to the version recorded in Nilamata.[5]

European travellers and chroniclers have put in their version, where Solomon is declared to have desiccated the waters.[6]

Despite all the variances and changes of format basic content of the legend is the same and it has survived, even in the oral traditions of the KSP; yes, with an effort to amalgamate all the versions according to the nature of the populace.

Lawrence in his book *The Valley of Kashmir*, records yet another version which is also prevalent and surviving in the oral tradition.(See notes.) [7]

It is really impossible to pin point as to what led to the generation of these legends, which have preserved both geological and geographic occurrences of that hoary past. Is it the basin like shape of the valley surrounded by high mountains or did this phenomenon—draining of the lake waters—occur due to some natural activity, which was observed by the aboriginal inhabitants of the valley and that has come down the ages, through word to mouth. Or is it a distant possibility that these inhabitants had the geological conception of the lake formation and its desiccation.

Well whatever the reason, we can certainly conclude:

a) The main protagonist of the legends is the water demon Jalodbhava a creature about whom many a conjectures have been forwarded and most common being an imaginative fib, but after the recent reported discovery of the fossil of fire emitting dragon, in the caves of Romanian hills, one is forced to ponder a while and accept that Jalodbhava, might have been in reality the water dragon, a counter part of the land dragon to whom a reference is made by the discoverers of the said fossil, which till recently existed only in the fairy tales.

b) The legends record that the valley was a huge lake till the seventh Manvantra of the *Chaturyuga*, and it was drained to make it habitable. It also evidences that the lake waters were desiccated not once but twice. Once prior to Kashyapa's arrival, that is why he enquires from his son about the destruction caused to the Madra Country thus, "O Nila, tell me—the inquirer- as to why this country of Madras has been deserted? This has always been charming, devoid of calamity of famine and full of wealth grains."[8] Second time the desiccation took place after Kashyapa's intervention.

c) For what so ever reason Kashyapa succeeded in ridding *Satisar*, "the Land of Virtuous Woman", from the shackles of Jalodbhava and made it worthy of human habitation. The people who settled there named the land Kashyapmar, and according to some chroniclers, in the course of time, the term Kashyapmar got transformed in to the name Kashmir / *Kasheer*.

Scientific Appraisals

Geologists' agree that the valley, for most of the time in its geological history, was a part of a large sea, and around 200 to250 million years ago it had under gone severe submarine and terrestrial volcanic activity. As a result mountain ranges that surround the valley, retain the core of the volcanic rocks known under the name of 'Panjal Trap'; Shankaracharya hill and Hariparbat hill-volcanoes of that era-stand as evidences of that terrestrial volcanic activity. The Himalayas, of which the vale of Kashmir is a part, originated from this vast sea around 60 million years back.

Geological science further postulates, that the "absence of the marine rocks younger than that of the Jurassic age (80 million years) in the valley proves that it had become a landmass with the uplift of the Himalayan mountain chain, or in fact just prior to it."[9]

We are, however, interested in the recent geological set up of the valley that is the *Karewas* or Wudders- for these flat lands originated by the desiccation of the vast lake and subsequently became the cradle of the earliest settlers of this valley. Geologists observe, "*Karewas* are the lake deposits that began to get deposited in the so called *Sati Sara*, the legendary lake from around 5million years back till the end of the Pleistocene age, immediately following the Ice Age (1.5 to 1.7 million years BP) of this planet over a time period of about four million years that is one *Mahayuga* of the Hindu calendar. The Lake apparently extended from the Pir Panjal Ranges in south to Baramulla in north."[10]

"Upper most loamy soil, which was deposited after the ice cover had withdrawn represents a time span of around 10-15,000 years and during that period while the upper reaches of the mountain ranges surrounding the valley, that is Lidar and Sind valley were occupied by the glaciers up to 3,000m above the sea level, Kashmir valley per—se was free of any ice cover; a phenomenon that the early humans of Kashmir valley must have witnessed and lived through."[11]

Further the geological history of the *Karewas* tell us that "a huge lake was formed covering a measure part of, what is today, the Kashmir valley, obviously by blocking the course of the *Vitasta*. And this lake, with tectonic ups and downs survived for about four million years, and towards the end of the Pleistocene era, with the continuous uplift of the Pir Panjal Range, the lake waters had shifted east and northwards and were being drained out through the Baramulla gap."[12]

The archaeological studies at Burzahoma and Sinthan have revealed that the humans of that era were cultivating wheat, barley and pulses as the grains of the same have been recovered from the site. This evidence and the very mention of the wealth of the grains by Kashyapa would mean that he entered the valley much after the Burzahoma culture dated at 5000 years BP. He could not thus have been a witness to an event that most likely took place around (10 to15, 000) years back. His description of the desolate nature of the countryside encountered by him while approaching the Kashmir valley and the subsequent lake burst is bound to be related to the desiccation that occurred second time.

On the basis of above mentioned scientific observations it is confirmed that the act of desiccation did occur twice as mentioned in the legends. The only difference being that the events have been presented and preserved in a rather confused form in the legends, most probably due to the time gap and antiquity of the event and its recording in a written format. Again the act of water gushing out through an out let is also confirmed by the tilt of the lake basin towards north and the possibility of waters draining out through the Baramulla gap. An act attributed to Ananta and other gods in the legends.

It is in reference to the later assumption that Bernier (a French Doctor who spent one whole year in the valley during Aurangzeb's rule) even after accepting the lake origin theory, does not agree to the fact that the process of drying up could have been achieved by the efforts of one single individual. He writes, "For my own part I am not disposed to doubt this country having once been entirely covered with water, as is affirmed of Thessaly and other countries, but I must confess, that I can with difficulty reconcile myself to the idea, that the opening for the issue of the water was the work of one man, since the mountain is of no ordinary extent and height. I should rather think that one of those violent earthquakes which are common to those places may have opened a subterraneous cavern, which swallowed up the mountain."[13]

As a befitting tribute to the scientific capabilities and imaginative genius of the earliest inhabitants of the Kashmir valley, to record the theory of creation and evolution of the homeland through interesting legends; I quote the remarks of a famous geographer Fredric Drew and V.K.Raina, a renowned geologist of international fame.

Drew records, "The observation of nearly every traveller to Kashmir has tended to show the vale was in late geological times completely occupied by a lake. The traditions of the natives—traditions that can be historically traced as having existed for ages—tend in the same direction and these have usually been considered to corroborate the conclusions drawn from the observed phenomena. Agreeing, as I do with the conclusion, I can not count the traditions as perceptibly strengthening it; I have little doubt that they themselves originated in the same physical evidence that later travellers have examined, they do not therefore afford independent support to the theory, but are valuable rather as showing in how early times some races of mankind had learnt to interpret aright the geological records of the history of their dwelling places. The existence of a lake over the whole valley of Kashmir occurred at no remote time, speaking by geological standards, but it was long enough ago to have preceded any of the monuments of man that have yet to be discovered." [14]

Raina writes, "Armed with the most modern dating technology, we know today that the Karewa group of rocks- period of the lacustrine nature of the valley- covered an epoch of four million years plus, that would mean one *Mahayuga* of Hindu calendar and not one Manvantra as depicted in the Purana. It is possible that our ancestors originally mentioned one *Mahayuga*, which, with the time, got corrupted to a Manvantra as the legends usually do? Be that as it may, one can not but appreciate the very concept of the logical interpretation- dating and classifying an entire sedimentary sequence when similar observations in the western world had not even been thought of, and also for giving a geo-chronological age to it. Thus Kashmiris deserve the credit of being the first to have conceived the concept of geology."[15]

The truth of these legends can be vouchsafed, as much as the truth of, other such legends in any other part of the world. They have one common peculiarity that the mythical description in its essence agrees with scientific discoveries. Analysing the case of the valley further, one can say that during the sixth Manvantra, there was a great effort made by a community of Supreme Deities to relieve the "valley of Gods" from the curse of the demon Jalodbhava. The name signifies a hurdle or demon born out of water or (as mentioned earlier the water born counterpart of the fire emitting dragon), while that in the logical and scientific language would be a large concentrated body of water that would destroy the valley whenever it overflowed its banks. This would happen very frequently since there were no outlets. It seems in due course nature broke through the mountains, in the vicinity of Baramulla / *Varah-mula* of the ancients that were blocking the water. With the release of the water the threat of regular floods would have receded and the marshy land all around would have dried up to be habitable for the people of that era.

To sum up, home land of the KSP- the valley of Kashmir- was born out of a vast lake known as *Sati*sar. Be it by the efforts of Vishnu; or Ananda the *Bhouda*, or *Aadam* or Solomon; or may be the lake was desiccated by a natural phenomenon like a catastrophic earthquake that opened an outlet at

Baramulla / *Varahamula* and dried this land mass to give birth to an idyllic spot, variously described and verily compared to the paradise on earth if there be one. Historians, travellers, pilgrims, poets and commoners have competed to describe this land and eulogise its natural bounties in most flattering terms. "It is such a beautiful country, blest with a fertile soil, glorious climate, grand mountains, fine rivers and lovely lakes, and with such charming flowers and delicious fruits that it once enjoyed a great fame as the seat of original paradise of the human race."[16]

The astonishing beauty of the valley of Kashmir has not only been lavishly praised by people of different times and nationalities; its grandeur, the awe inspiring scenery and beautiful mountains have been the theme of the lyrics, written by the ancient and modern poets of the land. They rightly believed that their country was specially created by Gods for their own exclusive use; truly—a heaven replicated on the planet earth.

Some Selected Eulogies

In the words of Mughal Emperor Jahangir, "Kashmir is truly a paradise on the earth, the paradise of which priests have prophesied and poets have sung."[17]

Pearce Gervis in his book, *This is Kashmir* (1954) records, "The vale is just like some huge flawed emerald—flawed by the rivers and the lakes and surrounded by close set pearls- the snow capped mountains are as though clasping it tight, as we cruised round for a while other colours appeared to frame first the emerald, the sapphire, and amethyst shading of the mountain slopes."[18]

Sir Francis Young Husband, who was a British Resident in Kashmir writes, in his book' *Kashmir*': "The beautiful Greece with its purple hills and varied contour, its dancing seas and clear blue sky, produced the graceful Greeks. But Kashmir is more beautiful than Greece. It has the same blue sky and brilliant sunshine, but its purple hills are on a far grander scale, and if it has no seas, it has lakes and rivers, and the still more snowy mountains. It has too a greater variety of natural scenery, of field and forest, of rugged mountain and open valley. And to me who have seen both the countries, Kashmir seems much more likely to impress a race by its natural beauty". He further writes The Valley, "nestled in the bosom of mighty Himalayas with its hill tops laden with snow, romantic scenery, bewitching landscapes, lovely serpentine rivulets, and unruffled lakes with crystal clear waters, deep blue skies, ever green forests, unending white sheet of snow in winter, fragrant flowers and succulent fruits in summer, besides the superb climate that enlivens the anaemic and invigorates the lethargic."[19]

KASHUR THE KASHMIRI SPEAKING PEOPLE

Lawrence, who was the Revenue Commissioner of the J&K state and a great admirer of the valley and its people writes, "In the language of the Orientals the valley is an emerald set in pearls, a land of lakes, clear streams, green turf, magnificent trees and mighty mountains- where the air is cool and waters sweet, where men are strong and women vie with the soil in fruitfulness."[20]

In all we can say, it is a veritable treasure trough of nature's bounties; it is equally blissful for the sick and the healthy. It is a school for learning and a laboratory for research, for every scholar and scientists respectively. Nowhere else do we find all the interests amalgamated and interwoven into one cast? Perhaps there is something unique about this small vale; might be it was really meant to be an abode of the gods. So much infinite variety in form and colour, an artist even in wildest dreams could not have exhibited, on a single canvas what nature has created in this oval shaped glen. Yet the history of this Valley bears it as a proof, as to what its inhabitants, would not have given to seek a different latitudinal and longitudinal geographic location, for this paradise of theirs, to live a life of peace and prosperity.

The Name Kashmir and its variants

Records and references prove that this single land mass has been verily named by people of different eras, origins, religions, countries and languages, and yet most of them some how or the other revolve around the name *Kashmira* of the Sanskrit origin. Now the question is why this valley is named Kashmira or *Kasheer* in the native tongue? And what other variations of the names are attributed to this valley and by whom?

As to why this name Kashmir or *Kasheer* was given to the valley is an enigma. Even "Linguistic science can furnish no clues to the origin of the name nor even analyse its formation."[21]

Nilamata records since *Prajapati* is called *Ka*, and Kashyapa is also *Prajapati*, so a country built by him is called Kasmira.[22] Besides there are many a suggestions given regarding the name Kashmir in N.P. The common one explains (Kasmira as "*ka-* water, *shmir-* to desiccate, Kasmira-land desiccated from water. *Ka*-water, *samara*-wind, (Kasmira land from which water has been drained off by wind.") [23]

Haider Malik Chadurah, Burnof, George Wilson and many others suggest that name Kashmira is an '*Apabhramsha*' (Contraction) of *Kashyapamar* wiz Sea of mountains of Kashyapa.[24]

Dr Ved Kumari who has translated Nilamata Purana into English, has given a very interesting conjecture that, "the valley was named after the goddess Kasmira whose worship is prescribed in the Nilamata and who was some hilly goddess identified with Uma The feminine form Kasmira, found in Nilamata and Rajatarangini indicates this".[25]

I am inclined to accept the given premise, because Kashmir in oral and literary tradition is mostly known by feminine names like *Sati Sara, Sati Desha*, and *Maej* (mother) *Kasheer*. It is known as Sharda *Peeth* (The seat of Goddess Saraswati) and Shakti *Peeth* again a feminine form. Written records can be erased or even destroyed but oral traditions remain etched in the memory and pass down the ages by word of mouth; that can not be wiped or mitigated. Like the Greeks, Kashmiris also believe that their land represented mother goddess Kashmira. Most of the shrines, which we can classify as belonging to the tribal era or to the aboriginal people, are dedicated to goddesses like the Sharika, Jwala, Bala, Sharda Devi etc. Most important shrines of modern era, in the valley, are dedicated to Maa Sharika and Maa Raginya. Besides in the Mahabharata also Lord Krishna refers to Kashmir as the land of Parvati. These examples do lead to the conclusion that the valley may have been named Kashmir after the goddess Kashmira.

Sufi, in his book . . .' *Kashir*' derives the name from *Kash*, *Kashan* and *Kashgar*. He also explains the word *Kasheer* as an extension of the native word '*Kash*' that implies a deep slash in the native dialect. [26]

Yet another nomenclature given in the Nilamata is *Vitastika* since the valley is situated on the banks of river *Vitasta.* [27]

In Sanskrit classical literature the valley has always been referred by its original Sanskrit form '*Kashmira*', from the earliest eras to the present times. The earliest references to the name Kashmir in Sanskrit classic literature has been found in the world famous Sanskrit scholar and grammarian Panini's composition '*Ashtadhyayi*'.

In Puranas it is described as *Gerek* (hill) nestled as it is in hills. In chapter viii of *Avanadikosha* the meaning of the word Kashmir is given, "land in which ruling is difficult."

Generally in the Hindu literature, like Vedas, Puranas, Mahabharata, Brhat Samhita etc, it is referred as Kasmira.

Some foreigners have named this beautiful land, according to their own linguistic norms. The Chinese traveller and famous Buddhist scholar Huien tsang calls it, "*Kia-shi-milo*" while as other Chinese accounts refer to it as, "*ki-pin*" and "*ache-pin.*"[28]

Snow Covered Mountains & the Valley

Thomas Walter named the valley *Ki-(Ka) - Pin*, because he gives another dimension to the etymology of word Kashmir, as he relates a fabulous Chinese version of extraction of water from the valley after lulling of demon/dragon by a Bodhisattva at the end of which people were afraid to enter the valley and asked each other *'Ki-pin'* meaning 'who will enter' in Chinese language, thus the name given was *Ki-pin.*[29]

Ladakhi and Tibetan accounts named the valley '*Khachul'* which means snow clad mountains in their language.

Greeks who are supposed to have largely influenced art and architecture of Kashmirian style have called Kashmir as, *"Kashyaptreras"*. Dr. Stein indicates that Herodotus and Alexander called Kashmir as, *"Caspapyrus"*[30]

Claudius Talmes, a Greek Geographers and Astronomer, in his works which surfaced in 139 AD names Kashmir as,'*Cashperio*' or *"Cashperia"*. Scholar Burnof thinks that these words are in fact distortions of *'Kashyaf-Mar'*

Reference to the Valley of Kashmir is also come across in the Greek classics of Ptolemy, Dionysios and Hekataios who lived between 549-486 B.C.[31]

In the light of above references we will have to agree that various scholars at different times have analysed and assigned varying inferences to the name of this valley. Outsiders have more than often quoted names for the valley which are very close to its original one, and keeping in view the fact that every *'Sa'* becomes a *'Sha'* in Kashmiri language, it can be comfortably concluded that the name, 'Kashmir' is indigenous and has been there since ages. Stein concludes "It has been the sole designation of the country throughout its known history. It has been uniformly applied both by the foreigners as well as the local inhabitants."[32]

One tends to agree with Stein, who writes, "Nature itself when creating the great valley of Kashmir and its enclosing wall of mountains seems to have assured to this territory not only a distinct geographical character, but also a historical existence of marked individuality. We see both these facts illustrated by the clearly defined and constant use of the name, which the territory has born from the earliest accessible period."[33]

What ever be the origin of the names assigned to the valley, the natives in their local dialect call it '*Maej Kasheer*' (the mother land) and it is known by this name traditionally among the Kashmiris as their home-land.

View Off Srinagar City

Chapter-2

Physiographic Landscape of the Valley

The valley appears to the naked eye like an elongated emerald green bowl surrounded by snow decked glistening mountain chain under the canopy of azure blue sky. The snow line followed, lower down, by green rolling hills and dales, spruced and bedecked with pine and birch grooves and colour full blooms accompanied by the music of the gurgling streams, roaring yet sublime waters and finally settling into a prosaic country side and a twentieth century town ship with all the facilities of modern life.

The Vale of Kashmir (*Kasheer*) is true to the geographic definition of the term valley. Its landscape is an amalgam of many a smaller clone of the same type. Poets, painters and travellers have tried to describe the physical features of this valley and yet have failed to do justice to this perpetual dream that is spread over an ethereal canvass, by the very hands of its creator. Using proverbial clippers, its physical landscape can well be described in three gradient levels in descending order, each vying with the other in beauty, charm and grace.

Level one

Level one determines the geographic boundaries of the valley measuring 114 km x 40km, which is surrounded by an unbroken ring of the perennially snow capped mountains of the Great Himalayan Range in the North-East and the Pir Panjal Range on the South-West. Immediately to the North of the valley is the Harmukh Range and in the East lies Mahadev. Further North and East are the lofty ranges of Kolahoi-Gwash Brari and the Amarnath peak.

The mountain ridges that surround the valley vary in height from around 6,000masl (metres above sea level) in the North East to the low of 3,000masl on the southern limit of the valley. They appear like Greek amphitheatres guarding the valley on all its sides, and are never monotonous. They stand like valiant sentinels draped in varying colours, some in sparkling white snow veil, while some in, "copper brown fatigue glistening like a wrestlers naked muscles" and others are draped in a mixture of white, brown and green.

The veil of white snow on these mountain tops, when shadowed with the bewitching hues of rising and setting sun creates an ethereal sight.

Baron Charles Von Hugel writes, "It's almost indescribable beauties are enhanced by the immense chain of snow clad mountains which encircle it, whose lofty peaks seem to pierce the clouds, and whose rugged sides grandly desolate, form a formidable rocky bulwark against northern foes, part of the chain of mountains have their sides bristling with bare crags and dizzy precipices, others are clothed with dense forests, gloomy and grand, both forming a vivid contrast to the happy smiling valley which nestles at their mighty feet. It might well indeed have been the Garden of Eden, and the lofty mountains, the angels guarding its portals."[1]

These mountains have often been quoted to provide a natural protection to the valley from the prying eyes of intruders and invaders. A glance in to the past history of the valley would hardly substantiate that. Narrow mountain passes in this security wall have proved a great fault in the natures design. On the one hand the walls isolated the valley, and on the other hand they roused the curiosity of prying eyes; thus making it a coveted prize to be possessed at any cost. In turn some pampered it and appreciated its beauty, while others desecrated it.

The passes especially the Zojila Pass in the North and the Banihal Pass in the South proved the infallibility of the wall, due to weak defence of these passes- During the Hindu period these passes were addressed as the drangas and the officer in charge was designated as the *Dvarpati* or *Dvarpalas*, who latter in the Mughal period attained Persian flavour and became the *Malik's*-. Though the passes were considered well protected, yet they allowed many an invaders, travellers, traders and runaway fugitives to enter and occupy the valley, be it the *Pisachas* from the plains of Rajasthan; the Saraswats from the banks of river Saraswati, (the 'Lost Tribes from 'The forbidden Land'), the Mongols, the Afghans, the Turks, the Huns, the Kushans, the Tibetans, the Sayyids from Iran, and the Mughals, a cascade of invaders who intruded on the lot and life of the KSP, the original inhabitants of this garden of Eden.

The high mountain ranges that surround the valley are symbolised by many a picturesque peaks like Tratekuti, Kolahoi, Harmukh, Amarnath and Mahadev etc, which not only add to its beauty but also have been, sacred to the Hindu Kashmiri speaking people right from the ancient times, and continue to be so even now. The reason being:

(a) Mythological explanation for the desiccation of the *Sati*sar as per N.P. and I quote "Later Brahma, Vishnu and Shiva allotted their names to these peaks that resulted in their sanctity"[2].

(b) In the primeval times humans preferred to select their dwelling places on highlands and hill slopes for these offered protection not only against the attacks of other humans and animals but also against the fury of violent natural elements like sudden and disastrous inundations, which have been a bane of the valley even in the civilised eras of it's history. Agreed, the mountains referred here are mostly very high inaccessible and inhospitable for living, but the lower slopes of these mountains would have been a safe option for habitation in the earlier times for the KSP. We have to bear in mind that humans of those eras were unaffected by the sensitivities of modern civilized environment, hence they must have been tough and sturdy physically, to live on these highlands in the earlier eras. It is quite natural that the *Kashur* would have built temples and Viharas on the lower slopes of these peaks in memory of that ancient past and hence they are still sacred to them.

(c) Natural beauty of these surroundings is so inspiring, that no wonder many a sages, saints and philosophers had chosen these inaccessible highlands and peaks for worship and deification; some of which like Amarnath cave are even today famous pilgrimage centres for the Hindus.(For details of this pilgrimage see Appendix iii)

Level Two

Descending down from the outer ring of high mountain ranges and ridges, we move to level two of sloping meadows of the grassy uplands called *Margs*. These are profusely covered with dense forests of birch, chirr and deodar in the higher reaches, and lower down carpeted with emerald green verdure interspersed with ravishing colours of wild iris, clematis and daises. To name a few of the *Margs*/meadows often visited by travellers and tourists, we have Khilenmarg, Gulmarg, Tangmarg, Sonemarg, Yusemarg, Nagmarg and many more picturesque spots. This gradient plain abounds in forests that are full of a variety of many species of trees and games where in we find many types of spruce, like blue pine, silver fir, Himalayan spruce, etc. Anchored along the lower reaches, these meadows pass down in to the relatively flat outer ring of the alluvial Wuddar plains (*Karewas*) of the valley. The *Karewas* are the deposits of the lake—clays, shale and loam, a typical landform, which is found in the valley only. They are supposed to have collected under the bottom of the legendry lake *Satisara*. Since the lake was covering the whole expanse of the valley these *Karewas* are found bordering the mountain slopes that gradually merge with the valley floor.

Sir Walter Lawrence giving a pictorial description of the meadows of Pir Panjal writes, "There are grand forests of pines and firs. Through these forests dash mountain streams, white with foam, pass in their course through pools of purest cobalt. When the great dark forests cease, and the brighter woodland begins, the banks of the streams are a blaze with clematis, honey suckle, Jasmine and wild roses which remind one of Azaleas. The green smooth turf of the woodland glades is like a well-kept lawn dotted with clumps of Hawthorn and other trees and bushes. It would be difficult to describe the colours that are seen on the Kashmir Mountains. In early morning they are often a delicate semi transparent violet relieved against the saffron sky, and with light vapour clinging round their crests. Then the rising sun deepens shadows, and produces sharp outlines and strong passages of purple and indigo in the deep ravines. Later on it is nearly all blue and lavender, with the white snow peaks and ridges under the vertical sun, and as the afternoon wears, these become richer violet and pale bronze, gradually changing to rose pink with yellow orange snow, till the last rays of the sun have gone, leaving the Mountains dyed ruddy crimson with the snows showing the pail creamy green by contrast. Looking down words the Mountain's the valley in the sunshine has hues of opal, the pail reds of the Karewa, the vivid light greens of the young rice, and the darker shades of the grooves of the trees relieved by sun lit sheets, the gleams of water and soft blue hays give combination of tints reminding one of the irresistibility of the changing hues of that gem. Few countries can offer anything grander than the deep green mountain tarn Konsar Nag in the Pir Panjal Range, the waters of which make a wild entrance into the valley over the splendid cataract of Aharbal, the springy downs of Raiyar are looking over the Sukh Nag, the magnificent scenery of the Sind and Liddar valleys, gentler charms of Lolab. Those beautiful stretches of turf which are ringed round with forest at an elevation of 7000 to 9000 feet above the sea level"[3]

Nature's bounties and charms are so abundantly bestowed in this land that one can muse for hours together, in solitary corners of the dense forests of Gulmarg and the meadows of Khilenmarg, sitting on stumps of pine and deodar trees, mesmerised by the hues of light blinking through the crevices and reflected often on the glistening waters of the mountain streams lost in an ethereal dream. I would often reminiscence, the prophetic words of Late Jawaharlal Nehru who wrote, "Some times I would lie under the pine trees and listen to the voice of the wandering wind, whispering many strange things to my ear, and lull my senses, and cool the fever in my brains."

Jahangir's in his memoirs has described these meadows as, "the pleasant meads and enchanting cascades of Kashmir (that) are beyond all description. There are running streams and fountains beyond count. Where ever the eye catches there are verdure and running water. The red rose, the violet and the narcissus grow of themselves, in the fields there are all kinds of flowers and all sort of sweet scented herbs, more than can be calculated. In the soul enchanting spring the hills and plains are filled with blooms, the gates, the walls, the courts, the roofs, are lighted up by the torches of the banquet adorning tulips. What shall we say of these things or the wide meadows and the fragrant trefoil?"[4]

Level Three

From the 'Rolling Meadows' we step on to the flat plains of the valley. The prime land mark of the flat planes of the valley is its capital city Srinagar. It is abundantly endowed with nature's bounties as well as human endeavours. It is a mini replica of the valley itself, both in shape and beauty. Low lying peaks of snow covered mountains surround it in the back drop of lush green skirt like projecting spurs slipping in to vast expanses of lakes and blue waters that surround the whole city barring a stretch in the Northern side. It is a heavenly sight, to witness the reflections, of the various hues of the rays of rising and setting sun, on the white snow clad peaks and crystal blue water bodies around and within the city. The breathtakingly beautiful Pir-Panjal snowy peaks peer over the city from the heights and lower down the green velvet plains and walled pines are lined the exquisitely designed Mughal gardens along the Boulevards of Dal Lake and, in between, are the mountain tarns, lovely lakes and swampy lagoons.

Amongst the lakes, the Wular, the Dal and Manasbal, are the most beautiful, owing to the varied scenery provided by the mountains, which surround them. Wular Lake is the largest fresh water lake in Asia. 'The old Sanskrit name of Wular was *Mahapadama sar* and latter it was named, '*ULLOLA Saras*', (the lake with high- going waves) It has a bad reputation among the boat men of Kashmir, for when gale blows over the quiet surface of the lake it suddenly changes into a sea of rolling waves which are dangerous for the flat bottomed boats of the valley. It is believed that under the blue waters of the lake is buried a wicked city which existed there long ago.'[5]

Manasbal is famous for its deep clear water, pink lilies and its grand mountain backdrops. It is indeed a heavenly sight that has no match even in dreams and what to talk of reality.

Dal Lake/ *Vitalin Marg*: Haider Malik Chadurah in his book, *History of Kashmir* translated and edited by Razia Bano (1991 p16) writes that when the city of Srinagar then named Pravarapura got burnt accidentally in around 500AD, the waters of the *Beth* flowed over the *Maraan* Mountain (Hariparbat) and the Dal Lake was a waste land without water. The natives called it *Vitalni Marg*. I believe that subsequent to this fire, during the rule of

Pravarsena, waters of the *Vitasta* were diverted in to the *Vitalini Marg* around the present times Sonawar, along the canal that is known as *Tchunth kol* today. Diverted waters so inundated the *Vitalini Marg* that it became a large expanse of water called *dala* in Sanskrit hence the name. At present it is perhaps one of the most beautiful spots in the world. It is lined by artistically designed superb gardens of Nishat, Shalimar, Naseem and Cheshmashahi. The waters of the Nageen lake that is a part of Dal Lake when bedecked by full blooms of lotus interspersed with the round fan like green leaves, is an unforgettable sight. Towards the west it has the famous floating gardens (gardens which can be shifted from one place to another with a pole stuck in and pulled along from one corner to the other at random. -an amusing sight-. These gardens are commonly used for growing vegetables and flowers. Famous Hazratbal shrine Mosque revered by the Muslim KSP, is situated on the periphery of Dal Lake.

The sky line of the city of Srinagar, besides the lofty snow clad mountains and the Mughal gardens, is also dominated by the remnants of two extinct volcanic cones; Shankaracharya and Hariparbat both venerated for the location of two most revered Hindu temples.

Other spectacular and charming features in the landscape of this plain are, the fabulous avenues of the highways guarded by the tall sentinels of the popular trees, the sprawling majestic chinar *"Buin"* trees of varying sizes, enhancing the beauty of the well laid Mughal gardens, campuses of temples, mosques and *Ziarets* dotting all over the country side. And finally the sleek, slim hanging branches of the willow trees adoring the embankments of rivers, streams, rivulets and the back waters of the lakes, caressing the flowing waters beneath complete this canvass. The Chinar[6]/ *Buin,* going by the fossil leaf found in the Karewas is probably one of the oldest trees found in the valley. Since Hirpur Formation has been dated 50,000 years old by the palaeo-botomists, it is obvious that the *Buin* or its ancestors must have appeared even prior to that age. There is a misnomer prevalent that the chinar was imported from Iran. Chronicler records belie this belief. Abul Fazal mentions in '*Akbar Nama*' about a Chinar tree, and I quote, "Thirty-four persons entered in to the trunk of a *cenar* tree which had been hollow for ages." He further writes "The tree had exceeded the age of the crows (supposed to be more than a hundred years) that twenty men found room in it and that 200 horsemen could be sheltered" apparently under the foliage of the tree."}[7] Presence of the Chinar tree thus predates the entry of Mughals in to the valley.

Visitors to this enchanted valley have often painted the word picture of its landscape. Jawaharlal Nehru, the proud son of this land, saw in it a synthesis of the masculine and feminine aspects of beauty. For him Kashmir was not merely a place for pleasure, it was an object of awe and wonder. "Like some supremely beautiful women, whose beauty is almost impersonal and above 'human desire, such was Kashmir in all its feminine beauty of river and valley and lake and graceful trees. And then other aspect of this magic beauty would come to view, a masculine one, of hard mountains and precipices, and snow-capped peaks and glaciers and cruel and fierce torrents rushing down to the valleys below. It had a hundred faces and innumerable aspects ever-changing, sometimes smiling, and sometimes sad and full of sorrow. The mist would creep up from the Dal Lake and, like a transparent veil, give glimpses of what was behind. The clouds would throw out their arms to embrace a mountain top, or creep down stealthily like children at play. I watched this ever-changing spectacle, and some times the sheer loveliness of it was over-powering and I felt almost faint. As I gazed at it, it seemed to me dream-like and unreal like the hopes and desires that fill us and so seldom find fulfilment. It was like the face of the beloved that one sees in a dream and that fades away on awakening."[8]

It is this veritable paradise, 'the face of a beloved that one sees' not in dream only, but in reality, that was and is, the aboriginal home of the *Kashur* as Kalhana wrote, "A country where the sun shines mildly, being the place created by Kashyapa, as if for his glory. High school houses, the saffron, the iced water and grapes, which are rare even in heaven, are common here. Kailash is the best place in the three worlds, Himalayas the best part of the Kailash and Kashmir the best place in the Himalayas."[9]

Apart from the mountain ranges, yet another most striking physiographical feature of Kashmir is the river Jhelum that flows through the valley and is navigable from *Khanabal* in the south to almost a distance of 150km to Baramulla (the legendry *Varahamula*) in the north. All the waters of the valley within the walls of this amphitheatre flow out through this one single outlet referred lovingly as *Veth*. This river travels South almost a course of 300km and then reaches the plains as the great river Jhelum that is also known as Hydaspes of the ancients, and the *Vitasta* of the Hindus.[10] Source of this great river is the spring (general belief) of the blue water at Verinag, which bubbles up underneath a steep scrap of rock clothed with pine trees. KSP believe that the actual source is *Veth Vatur*. Origin and name of this river has been discussed in detail in verses - 257-61 of Nilamata Purana.

SRINAGAR

To complete the physiographic landscape of the valley, detailing of the capital city 'Srinagar' an important land mark of human design and endeavour, is a must; for the history of Kashmir has always been reflected as it were in that of its capital. Srinagar is an extremely picturesque city built along the banks of the river *Veth/Vitasta/Jhelum* which flows along the centre of the city and for the purposes of communication across is spanned by nine bridges at present. As per Kalhana's chronicle the original name of the city was *Srinagari;* Emperor Ashoka was the founder of this city, and its location was in the neighbourhood of present Pandrethan. The present sight of the capital city has been there at least for more than thirteen centuries, as per Hiuen Tsiang who visited the capital city in AD 631, and he found it already in the position of the present Srinagar. During the Mohammadan rule, for some hundred years, the city was called by the same name as the country that is 'Kashmir'.[11] Even Forster, while writing about the capital uses the name, 'Kashmir' instead of Srinagar. It was renamed Srinagar by the Sikhs when they conquered Kashmir.

In appreciation of the feasibility of the location of the city, Stein records, "We can safely attribute this exceptional position of Srinagar to the great natural advantages of its sight. Occupying a place close to the true centre of the valley, Srinagar enjoys facilities of communication which no other site could offer. The river, along which the city is built, provides at all seasons the most convenient rout for trade and traffic both up and down the valley. The two lakes which flank Srinagar offer the same facilities for fertile tracts which lie immediately to the North. The lakes themselves supply an abundant supply of products which materially contribute towards the maintenance of a large city population. The great trade rout from Central Asia debouches through the Sind Valley at a distance of only one short march from the capital."[12]

Srinagar city does not follow any regular and planned format. There is nothing like a quay or an embankment, no line of regular buildings, but each house is built independently. The houses are of uneven height and form. The material used for construction is both wood and stone or either one of them. All have sloping roofs with eves extending and window space guarded by movable wooden lattices of elaborate patterns. The base of each house is a solid stone wall, some times of rough masonry and some times better built of cut stones. The continuity of these houses is some times broken by numerous stone Ghats and the stair-ways that lead either to the houses or the lanes or by-lanes of the streets. In the present times all types of material and architectural facilities are used while constructing most modern residential houses. Besides the independent residential houses, there are the public buildings like the temples, mosques, royal palaces, government offices bazaars and gardens built within the precincts of this city. Over all present format of Srinagar the capital city of the valley can match any modern town of the twenty first century.

KHEERBHAVANI / TULUMUL

Chapter - 3

The *KASHUR*—Kashmiri Speaking People

The term '*Kashur*' is a Prakrit word; a word that the aboriginal inhabitants of the valley would have innovated to address or refer to their group, prior to the inception of the Vedic Sanskrit. And in all probability, it is the derivation of the letter '*Kasheer*', the name of our homeland and as a term it is used to address both the people of the valley and their native tongue. In unison i.e '*Kashur*' means the Kashmiri speaking people (KSP)

Earliest reference, very similar to the word '*Kashur*', is found in the Greek travelogue of Pliny, where in he mentions about the existence of a tribe of Indian people namely *'Casiri'* in the North Western Frontier of India and he further adds that they were eaters of raw flesh. This is confirmed by the Nilamata Purana, which records the existence of a raw flesh eaters' tribe during the time when humans were living in the valley for six months only. Nilamata Puran does not mention any name for the tribe[1].

Grierson has compared the word *'Casiri'* with the modern Kashmiri adjective *Kasiru'* that connotes, "belonging to Kashmira."[2]. In this context we can definitely say that 'Casiri' were not the earliest aboriginal '*Kashur*' for the Greek observation does not refer to the inhabitants of the valley during primitive eras.

Earliest history of the *Kashur* is shrouded in mystery and like all ancient civilisations in mythology, it is distant and intriguing, to the extent, that one is tempted to believe the legend of Adam and Eve having committed the sin and when god punished them, he out of compassion, first created a valley as beautiful as heaven and then sent the two to live there.

History of this ethnic group does not begin with the coming of the Sanskrit speaking Aryans from the sweltering plains of India. It does, however, begin, with the creation of the humans, in the land, which as per some observations existed prior to the beginning of the Kali Yug and Dwaper Yug. It almost starts with the genesis during the era of the Palaeolithic (2, 00, 00,000, to 12,000B.C) and Neolithic age (12,000 -4,500B.C.), when the humans first made their appearance in the mountains, vales and lakes of this north-western limit of the Himalayas

To establish the presence of these humans and their relation if any, with the ethnic group named '*Kashur*', the signatures and evidences of their prehistory collated from the Archaeological and Anthropological findings are of great help. Hence an attempt is made to gather data from these primary sources.

PREHISTORY

Prehistoric evidences of the Neolithic and Chalcolithic (4,500-3,500B.C) inhabitants of the Valley

Prehistory defines that part of the history of humanity, which is available to us prior to the introduction of writing in any form. It is based on the study and interpretation of the various stone tools; implements and objects of daily use like pottery, weapons and dress; in short objects made by humans of those hoary days. This primarily is the domain of an anthropologist, - one who systematically collects and studies old objects- but needs the assistance of various other experts, like the chemist, archaeologist, palaeontologist and even a statistician to complete the research.

The range or scope of the prehistory varies from region to region, country to country, depending upon when the written documents were first available in that place. Prehistoric period was initially divided into three ages: The Stone Age, Copper/Bronze age and the Iron Age, implying the type of material that was used primarily for making weapons of day-to-day use. At the same time it indicates that during the Stone Age, other two were unknown; while during the Copper age, stone implements were known, iron was not known in any form. The Iron Age that corresponds to the discovery of iron roughly begins around 1500 BC. By this time the humans had learnt how to extract iron and copper from its ore and also the development of alloys.

The Stone Age is the oldest with two subdivisions Old Stone Age and the New Stone Age, based upon the type of the stone implements. Rough chipped flat stone tools belong to the Old Stone Age and partially ground and polished tools indicate the New Stone Age found in relatively younger geological strata. The preservation of stone implements is, to a large extant, encouraged or hindered by the climate and the terrain of a particular place. During the past half a million years Kashmir has experienced four glacial and three interglacial periods and these climatic phases have left their mark on the prehistory of the valley.

ARCHAEOLOGICAL EVIDENCES

Until recently it was thought that the early human had not lived in Kashmir valley during the Ice Age. Evidence now has come forth to show that they had lived on the banks of, what is now, Liddar at Pahalgam, apparently during the interglacial warm periods; presumably climate then was congenial for human habitation. Fossil evidence has indicated rich fauna and floral life in these forests and even trees like cinnamon, pine and oak grew in the valley at that time. This establishes the advent of the human beings in the valley, which, at that time, or about that time, as evidenced by the geological set up, was a huge lake

"The tools which indicate human presence, in this environment, are huge, massive flakes that have been carved out of the volcanic rocks- Panjal trap- that forms the major portion of the mountain chain surrounding the Kashmir valley. These flakes- stone implements- have been recovered from the boulder conglomerate beds of the Karewa Formation and probably represent the earliest human tools found in Asia. If, it is presumed, that these tools belong to the first Interglacial period of the Himalayas; these would then belong to a period of very, very distant past."

As mentioned earlier geologists tell us that the mountains surrounding the valley, especially the Pir Panjal Rranges, have risen considerably after the deposition of the beds in which stone implements are found due to tectonic activity. This would have been accompanied by severe earthquakes that led to the opening of the gap at Baramulla through which the lake waters were drained out, giving rise to terraces. It is possible that these terraces became the habitat of the humans of that Era and they would have carved the stone implements that have been found recently. These stone implements are, however, unlike the massive stone flakes referred to earlier.

Discovery of the two kinds of stone implements: the pebble tools and the stone flakes, had led the archaeologist to postulate, that the people who had made these tools may have originated from different places; but later discovery of hand axes in 1934, at Pahalgam, Kashmir, in a layer of brownish clay, just above the horizon where the massive flake had been found earlier, has contradicted this view.

This discovery, not only helped to remove the impression that there were human beings belonging to two different cultures namely as the "Chopper Chopping culture and the hand axe culture, former named after the inhabitants of Soan valley and the latter after Madrasian culture; it also established the existence of the humans during the Ice Age."[3]

G.E.L.Carter during his field excavations found a variety of stone implements and megaliths in various locations in the valley. Some of the places he highlights are, "*Pandrethan, Takht-I-Sulaiman, Yanderahom, Naranbagh, Arhom, Gãndarba*l. Carter even refers to having observed the cup markings on the plinth of the Hindu temple on the *'Takhat-I-Suliman,*(Shankaracharya Hill) He saw, "a labourer using a stone pickaxe, which he believed must have actually belonged to Palaeolithic tool category because it was so primitive. (It had been borrowed from the museum.)"[4]

P.N.Bamzai writes, "The fossil remains of *'Elephas hysudricus'* have been found in the lower *Karewas* pointing to lower Pleistocene age . . . . The Mesolithic or the proto-Neolithic period appears to be indicated by the findings of De Terra and Paterson in the Jhelum valley of Kashmir, . . . but in all these places it was certain that the flakes are associated with pottery-bearing layers of either Neolithic or historic date,"[5]

Sunil Chandra Ray records, "One of the two megalithic sites in the extreme north west of the Indian sub-continent was found at Burzahoma. We do not know the exact cultural horizon of the Burzahoma megaliths, nor the purpose for which they were erected, but the indications are that they were put in place towards the end of the Neolithic period at that site, partly buried and clearly moved from the place in which they were erected." He further adds, "While digging a trial trench at the site, De Terra found a highly black polished ware at about five feet in the section. Besides these polished wares, Paterson also unearthed at Nunar, 71/2 miles northwest of Burzahoma, a proto-Neolithic industry consisting of ground stone Celts, bone awls and pots. This industry, of an apparently great antiquity; is similar to that of Maski and Brahmagiri and shows a stone-axe culture starting perhaps as early as 1200 B.C."[6]

The Archaeological Survey of India began systematic excavations at this enigmatic site in 1960. Near about the silt bed, pits have been discovered in section, indicating a settlement of early pit-dwellers, whose date has been tentatively fixed at 3000B.C. This is perhaps the only known find of such a settlement in India and indications are that more valuable data will be found when extensive surface diggings are completed.[7]

Besides Burzahoma the only other places where a few ground and polished stone axes were found are Orangi near Karachi, Mohenjo-daro and Sirkap at Taxila. Very few such polished stone axes have been found in the northern sector of the country while they are found in abundance in the south of India. Thus giving an impression there must be some relation between this culture in the north and south of India. Gordon dates these axes between 2000 and 800 B.C.[8]

Dr.H.D.Sankalia in his review on visiting the site of Burzahom, Gurfkral and Martand with Shri T.Khazanchi and his colleague Shri Sardarilal (both reputed archaeologists) writes, "The Karewa terraces at Burzahom and Gurfkral are found strewn with huge stones, which are foreign and were certainly brought by man who had erected megalithic monuments. Not much is known about this man but of his predecessor(s) we have fairly good knowledge. Long after the last flat terraces—the *Karewas*-were laid, the men who appeared did not live on the shrinking river banks; instead they chose to live on these terraces. The evidence from Burzahom and Martand indicates that instead of building with mud/ clay or stone, the man preferred to scoop out earth from the *Karewas* and live in the dwellings that are called 'pit-dwellings'. The inhabitants of the *Karewas* primarily depended upon hunting and fishing and were naturally growing fruits, vegetables and eatable grasses the valley offered then. However, no exact idea of the animals can be had, unless the bones found in the several storage pits and on the floors of houses are studied. But the presence of ibex, wild dog or wolf and deer is suggested by the skeletons of these found buried in the pits. Even five human burials were also found. These were found buried in pits which were generally circular or oval on plan and in most of the cases narrow at the top and wide at the base. Their inner sides were often coated with lime. Four of the human skeletons were found buried in a crouched position. It is not clear as to which period they belong. Both the ground or polished stone and bone industries are rich and varied. They give an idea of the comparatively sophisticated or complex life of the inhabitants of these high, elevated places.

The tools discovered are polished broadly and are of two grades:

(a) heavy duty tools and

(b) light duty tools.

In each category, there are axes, wedges, chisels, adzes, hoes, perforated pick, harvesters, flake knives, mace-heads and double pointed poker.

"Though in the remains of the houses no grains or traces of clothes have been found, one can definitely postulate two things. The archaeological finds ascertain that the high Karewa inhabitant was not a nomad, living only on fishing and hunting. Though these arts for eking out a livelihood were practised, as the bones of the animals from the kitchen middens would testify, the- different kinds of ground stone tools particularly the large and small hoes, stone querns and the harvesters—show that the man needed these tools for various agricultural practices, such as digging, sowing, planting and cutting the grains which should be rice and millets. There are indications that the grain was pounded and also mixed with meat, cereals and vegetables. Another very important feature is the presence of large and small bone needles among the stone implements. These they must have used to stitch their clothes. The bigger needles (bodkins) must have been used for stitching the skins and other thick material, since they lived in a cold country."[9] *(For details refer Appendix IV)*

The prehistoric study of the *Kashur* thus far only establishes the existence of the humans in Neolithic and Chalcolithic era in the valley. Who were these people and where from did they come are questions to which nobody has as yet hazarded an answer? Much more work is needed before firm conclusions can be reached as regards the date and historical significance of these Neolithic and Chalcolithic people. Question arises were they the aborigines? Study of the prehistoric finds, definitely establishes the existence of the humans in the valley in the prehistoric era, but it does not identify them. It can only define them as the lake dwellers or the pit dwellers or even civilized humans. It does not qualify them as the Ahis or the Nagas; or the settlers from the plains of India. For that we require concurrent and uninterrupted testimony of creditable historians.

Prior to an in depth study of the observations of historians regarding the topic, if we peep through the key hole of the time capsule for the physical appearance of the *Kashur*, we witness a kaleidoscopic mosaic of different specimens, of varied colours, creeds and physique of a variety of ethnic backgrounds. Though majority of them are fair complexioned with Grecian pointed noses, lotus eyes, well built and tall like their Aryan ancestors, yet we have some brown complexioned, pug nosed and slit eyed specimens of the Mongolian breed, that represent the typical features of Turkish, Sakas, Hun and Tibetan origin.

The physical evidences demonstrate, the imprint left on the aboriginal *Kashur*, by all these later immigrant groups, who came to the valley as settlers, invaders or asylum seekers. From this chaotic kaleidoscope it is a tough ask to identify the original native of the land, especially, since, to my knowledge, no measure etymological survey of the Kashmiri speaking people has been carried out so far. Only an exhaustive analysis of the physical and physiognomic features of the majority of the Kashmiri people of different strata of the society can help to solve this riddle.

KASHUR THE KASHMIRI SPEAKING PEOPLE

To reach to a plausible conclusion an effort is made to enumerate various openions and arguments put forth by different chroniclers and researchers, to identify the aboriginal ancestors of the *Kashur*.

Nilamat Purana one of the earliest literary product of the valley records that the country was inhabited by the Nagas originally and they were followed by the Pisachas with whom they were not friendly, and last of all by the people who had migrated from the banks of river Saraswati. The Pisachas were at first hostile to them but afterwards they had to abandon the valley and leave it exclusively for the immigrants referred as humans in the Purana.

Even this premise can not be accepted fully that the Nagas were the original settlers of the land; because the Archaeological evidences prove the existence of humans in the valley prior to the Nagas. "Though the skeletal remains from Burzahoma have not yet been analysed, it is however to be noted that these people have been assigned to a period ranging between 2300 and 1500 B.C. on the basis of carbon 14 dating."[10] This date in all probability proceeds the period of the entry of the Naga ancestors and we could presume that they were the earliest known human inhabitants of the valley and thus they could be the original *Kashur*. Yet the prehistoric era finds of the pebble tools and stone flakes in the clay terraces and the hand axes at Pahalgam are proof enough to the existence of humans prior to the above mentioned group.

Logically the people responsible for shaping these tools deserve the right to be labelled as the autochthons. We gather evidences of the existence of these people from the Palaeolithic and Neolithic stone implements discovered in Pahalgam; also from the variety of wares, pottery and implements, the usage of ochre to colour the floors of their dwellings as discovered in Burzahoma, Gurfkral and Martand terraces. I, for all purposes of the historical documentation consider these autochthons to be the ancestors of the present *Kashur*.

The form of communication-a spoken word of distinct character-which these people would have used could be labelled as the first vocabulary of the Kashmiri language spoken by the '*Bhata*.' By *Bhata* I mean the people of the snowy mountains as it is even now referred to, in the Anglo-Norman language. Probably this is one of the earliest Kashmiri words that has passed down the ages and survived like some other words of similar meaning like, *Malla* and *Kolla*, (meaning the people of the snowy lands). I feel these people would thus be the earliest known ancestors of the Kashmiri speaking people, prior to the introduction of the tribal names like the Nagas, the Pisachas, Abhisaras, Vikarnas, Ahis, Gauda Dravids and finally the Aryans.

THE KASHUR—KASHMIRI SPEAKING PEOPLE

Trying to identify the people who were living in the valley soon after the desiccation of the lake second time, P.N.Bamzai writes that, "on the basis of the Archaeological discovery of the polished black stone axes found in Burzahom, and the same variety found in south of India, proves that people from south and some people from Daradistan and Ladakh region from north simultaneously came to live in the valley. The later stayed in the winter months only and the former in the summer months, till they got acclimatised and finally settled for good, driving away the trouble some tribes from the mountain regions to their original habitat."[11] These troublesome tribes were Pisachas and Yakshas, who used to migrate up north in summer and return to the valley in winter. In course of time they finally settled in the north.

There is a general agreement among scholars, Indologists and historians, about Nagas being the original inhabitants of Kashmir, on the basis of the information given in Nilamat Purana. Nila, a Naga was the ruler of the valley at the time, when due to natural calamity or due to a *Rakhsha's* attack the land was devastated and the people suffered. Besides, the Purana records a long list of 603 Naga chiefs and personalities from verse no., 915-980. The said Purana puts their number at thousands, *"nay Arbudas."*[12]. Some of the prominent names mentioned are the Mahapadma Naga, Sudangula, Shesh Naga, Naga-Arjuna, and Naga-Bodhi and so on.

Presumably the ancestors of these Nagas were the carvers of the stone implements and there by the original inhabitants of the valley. May be it is by virtue of that right only, they could protest against the intrusion of outsiders into their land, as revealed in the Nilamata Purana. We can also argue that the Naga king, Nila, by virtue of being the descendent of the original inhabitants of the valley, could impress upon Chandra Deva about the efficacy of the Naga rituals. He even was authorized by this right to allow the people, from the plains of River Saraswati (Saraswat, the fore fathers of present *Kashur*) to come and settle in the valley on the condition that they would uphold the traditions and rituals of the Nagas.

We are aware of the fact that nature has, indeed, endowed the valley and the neighbouring mountains with an abundance of fine springs. Each one of these springs has its tutelary deity' in the form of a Naga, and popular tradition looks upon Kashmir as the favourite residence of these deities. Besides these evidences chroniclers like Kalhana, and Hiuen Tsiang ascribed the superiority of Kashmir over other countries to the protection it received from a Naga. [13]

KASHUR THE KASHMIRI SPEAKING PEOPLE

The earliest written recorded history of civilized *Kashur* that is the Saraswat *Brahman*, available to us is through Kalhana's Rajatarangini, which he has compiled, after studying some previous eleven works of scholars containing the chronicles of kings, and the Nilamata Purana, besides the ancient coins and seals. He also has referred Kashmira as the dwelling place of Nila, the king of Nagas, and many others of his tribe. He frequently refers to sacred springs and *Tirthas of Papasudana* and *Tri-Sandhya, Sarasvati's* lake on the *Bheda hill*, the' self created Fire' (*Svayambhu)*, and the holy sites of *Nandikesetra, S'arada, Cakradhara* and *Vijayesha* whose origin is associated with the dwelling places/ springs protected by the Nagas. The Nagas are supposed to have come to Kashmir when Kashyapa, their father, had drained 'the lake of *Sati*,' and to have found there a refuge from *Garuda*.

This further adds to the validity of the argument that the primitive ancestors of the Nagas were the aboriginal inhabitants and in turn, ancestors of *Kashur* who settled in the valley after the desiccation of the waters of the lake second time. Having said so, there are still some contradictory opinions about the identification of the Nagas.

Ved Kumari writes, "The difficulty is about the identification of the Nagas as they are still behind the veil of myth and legend, peeping out at one time as reptile snakes and at another as human beings."[14]. There are many a scholars who do not believe the Nagas were humans; they consider them as serpents. Hiuen Tsang, like other Chinese pilgrims, calls the Nagas by the term of 'dragon,' no doubt because the popular conception represents them under the form of snakes living in the water of the springs or lakes they protect.[15]

Professor Herman Oldenburg reckons, "the Nagas belong to the class of demonical beings which is best represented by the ware wolves". Hendricks Kern believes, "the Nagas to be water spirits. They are personified as the five elements."[16]

Dr C. F. Oldham, however, states that the Nagas of Kashmir were human beings like the present Naga tribes of Nagaland. They were no serpents or demonical beings, even though there are references in R.T. to a particular king being cursed and reduced to a mere serpent. In Oldham's opinion the Nagas were people who claimed decent from the sun and had the hooded serpent for a totem.[17]

"The most plausible suggestion, therefore is that the Nagas were the aborigines inhabiting Kashmira and other parts of North India prior to the advent of Vedic Aryans." [18]

The Nagas of Kashmir were no serpents but were a predominant element in the population of Kashmiris when Buddhism entered the valley, and an old legend exists to the effect that the Nagas were the ones who first accepted Buddhism. There is no doubt about the significance of the legend, despite the miraculous element in it for in early Buddhist literature there are other references to the Nagas as paying homage to the Buddha's ? Naga-Arjuna is always referred to as a Siddha and so is Naga-Bodhi. Indeed, the Nagas and the Siddhas are often associated together in the ancient Indian tradition. This undoubtedly means that, besides Naga-Arjuna and Naga-Bodhi, there were many other Siddhas among the Naga people. One of them was Kapila, the reputed founder of the Sankhya system and he was in all likelihood, a Naga by race as is evident from Kapila's close association with Patanjali, who was unquestionably a Naga and also assured by the legend that Patanjali was the Shesha-naga incarnated.

Why were the Nagas deemed to be serpents ?

The Nagas of Kashmir should not be treated in isolation, in an era, when almost every other aboriginal tribal legend has some sort of important space reserved for the serpents. May be it was a psychological impact of their not being able to tame a serpentine creature with fire or any other stone implements, that made these aboriginals to assign the serpent a place of importance. For example the Nors in their mythology divide the universe in three regions, *Asgard, Midgard* and *Utgard. Asgard* is the abode of Gods and *Midgard* is the abode of men which is surrounded by the ocean, while in *Utgard* lays a huge serpent. This serpent is supposed to have come out of the ocean and spread over the world and thus sunk the earth into the sea. Like wise the Moweri tribes assign the serpent with super human strength. No wonder the Naga suffix was adopted by earliest humans in the valley, who in turn are accepted as the aboriginal people of the valley, hence the earliest *Kashur*. Yet there is a discrepancy for the letter *'Naag'* in Kashmiri language denotes, a spring and not a serpent, as in Sanskrit. May be the dwelling place of a serpent, would be the right origin of the letter '*Naag*' in Kashmiri. There is a distinct possibility that the valley prior to desiccation being a lake with numerous swamps around was inhabited by snakes. Hence the people who were living in the valley were referred as Nagas and for all practical purposes they were the aboriginal ancestors of the *Kashur*.

OTHER TRIBES THAT INHABITED THE VALLEY IN THE EARLIER ERAS

Nilmat Puran records that along with the Nagas, Pisachas, and Yakshas were also living in the valley and were later made to migrate to the higher reaches by the *Brahmans* from the plains. We also find the names of several sects namely *Nishadas, Khashas, Dards, Bhuttas, Da'mars, Tantrins, Ekan'gas, Bhauttas*, etc living around the mountain territories of Kashmir, who reportedly, constantly gave trouble not only to the rulers of the country but also to the *Brahmans*. Whence and where from they came is a long study in itself?

Prof. G.M. Rabbani writes, "The Kashmiris form a branch of the race which brought the languages of Indo-Aryan type into India, is a fact established by the evidence of their language and physical appearance. But the period of their immigration and the route they came by are still moot points."[19]

No historical work has dealt in a satisfactory fashion with the origin of the KSP. Some have discussed the origin of the community in legendary terms; where as some English ethnologists of the 19th century base their conclusions on facile physiognomic observations and agree, both on the antiquity of the community and its Aryan nature. In the words of Sherring, "Kashmir is one of the primitive homes of the Brahmins in India is beyond dispute". Like wise George Campbell portrayed the Kashmiris as "quite High Aryans in the type of their features, very fair and handsome with high chiselled features and no trace of intermixture of the blood with any lower race". While Peacock speculated on the possible racial links between the Kashmiris, the Greeks and the Persians, but these links would have been established at the time of Alexander's invasion and not in the earlier eras of their existence.

In the present era, on the basis of religion, Kashmiri speaking people can be classified into three groups:

a) *Pandit or* *Kashur* *Bhatta* (Kashmiri Hindu)

b) Musalmaan (Kashmiri Muslim)

c) Sardar (Kashmiri Sikh)

Besides there may be a negligent number of Christian and Buddhist Kashmiris

The origin of *Kashur Musalman* and Sikh belongs to a period of chronologically recorded history. We know for certain that the founder of Islam, Prophet Mohammed, was born in Mecca about 570AD and Sri Gurunank Dev, the founder of Sikhism, was born about 1469AD Majority of KSP today are followers of Islam and with a very minuscule minority as followers of Sikhism. We can chronologically date their history, as to when they adopted the new faith and new nomenclature. Yet these two subsidiaries of the original *Kashur*, though the inheritors of the same gene; can not in any way help to locate the autochthon, or the aboriginal ancestors, whose remnants are surviving as the Hindu KSP (the *Kashur Bhata*).

Conclusion

There is many a fault lines in the arguments put forth, yet an effort is made to draw a simple and plausible conclusion about the aboriginal ancestors of the *Kashur* ethnic race. One thing is certain that from the time of the chronologically recorded local *Sapt Rishi sanwant*, (era) that dates 5,086BP, the KSPs' who were the decedents of the 'Rishis', and the bordering tribes of the valley, were the earliest civilised settlers of the land. They were the followers of the *Sanatana Dharma*, the only existing *Dharma* at that time and KSP Hindus a very small percentage of their descendents still pursue the same *Dharma*.

To repeat, the general conception that the ethnographical analysis of the *Kashur*, can never be complete, unless and until, we take an account of their physical traits-both external and internal- or even to some extent their physiological characteristics is a valid argument. In fact only the statistics of a scientific physical examination of a large group of people of different strata of the society carried on in the same uniform method, can give us some solid foundation relying upon which, we can make out to a great extent the specific human races that entered Kashmir since the dawn of its history and also ascertain the degree of their intermixture up to the present times. I am sure such a study will be carried out in the near future to derive at a logical and a systematic identification of the aboriginal *Kashur*.

Let us try to analyze some of the prominent characteristics of the KSP community.

The Physical Appearance

Majority of Kashmiri speaking people are said to belong to the Aryan race by virtue of their physical features. They are generally of medium height, fair, and handsome, with aquiline Jewish nose, a typical characteristic of Aryan race, predominantly found among the Hindu Kashmiri who are the oldest and the original inheritors of this race. That definitely does not mean the Muslim and Sikh Kashmiris are bereft of these features. Yes due to later intermingling of people from different countries, nationalities and faiths as recorded earlier, one does not find pure specimens of the earlier race among them. As these people with a variety of racial and physical features and characteristics peculiar to them, would definitely have made inroads into the physiognomic features of the later *Kashur*. Thus we do come across occasionally KSP's of darker complexion and at times with slit eyes and pug noses, but such specimens are rare.

Be it as they are, Kashmiris as a whole are a very handsome, well proportioned, people with regular features, and of fair complexion. Especially the beauty and charm of their women folk has 'hardly any parallel. They are reputed for their fair complexion and charming demeanour. Their eyes are their prize possessions that are extremely beautiful, expressive and appealing. They generally posses a well proportioned and well shaped figure. Their figures are full and flawless and have been paid homage to by travellers to their land from the earliest times. Kaumudi writes, "The feminine beauty of a *Kashur* is, proverbial in the east, and seldom fails to impress the aesthetic eye."[20]

Tyndale Biscoe the founder of English system of education in Kashmir has recorded, "The Hindu women and boys have generally refined features, quite of Greek type. Many have rosy cheeks and pink complexions, and a few have blue eyes and auburn hair; but auburn hair is not a popular colour, and they dislike any remark on the fact."[21] Men as a whole are stout, well proportioned, well built, and sturdy. The villagers at times give the impression of being true specimens of the Greek patriarchs. M. Griffith writes, "The people of Kashmir belong mostly to the Aryan race. Tall and handsome, the Kashmiris possess a beautiful physique and a sturdy temperament. One can still find some ancient Aryan traits in the well regulated features of Hindu Kashmiri Pandits."[22]

The loveliness and beauty of the women of Kashmir often made them a prey to the ruler's lust. Bernier who accompanied Emperor Aurangzeb on the latter's visit to the Kashmir valley writes, "The people of '*Kachemire*' are proverbial for their complexion and fine forms? They are well made as the Europeans, and their faces have neither the Tartar flat nose nor the small pig eyes that distinguish the natives of '*Kacheur*' and which generally mark those of great Tibet. The women especially are very handsome; that nearly every individual, when first admitted to the court of the Great Mogul, selects wives or concubines that his children may be whiter than the Indians and pass for genuine Mongols."[23]

CHARACTER TRAITS

To enumerate numerically the specific character traits of a community belonging to a certain ethnic group, which has had the good or bad fortune of having under gone major religious conversions; willingly or forced is not so simple. It becomes all the more complicated because these people have had, the misfortune of having suffered the most inhospitable and unsympathetic political and administrative environment repeatedly over the millennia's of their long history. An effort has been made here to asses their character traits in the context of their reactions to different situations and on the basis of their achievements, successes and failures.

A KSP, like every human being, has certain specific, individual qualities as bright as the day and as dark as the night, if they suffer from 'faults and foibles' they also posses many a virtues and excellences.

A *Kashur* is a simple, god fearing, kind hearted and hospitable individual. Chakbast, a reputed poet of the modern era writes, "In Kashmir hospitality oozes even from the country rocks, what to talk of the people of the land." Alas! It is this hospitality trait and the habit to grant asylum to seekers, has cost the *Kashur* immensely, over the eras of its existence. Often it has changed the very course of a *Kashur*'s political, religious as well as social genre. Just to site a few examples. If Chander Deva the *Brahman* would not have been given asylum, may be the men from plains would not have come to the valley. The autochthons would have thrived. Instead of Sanskrit, Kashmiri language would have prospered and we would have had a well developed *Kashur* language with a perfect script. Had Madhyantika not been welcomed in and around 269 BC may be the Naga cult would have continued to flourish in the Valley. If the run away Sayyids, who tried to escape from their country Hamdan for the fear of persecution at the hands of Timur Lang, would not have been given asylum in the valley, may be it would have retained its exclusive Hindu nomenclature. If Simha Deva would not have granted refuge to Rinchin a Tibetan prince and to Bulbul Shah may be Islam would not have got a foot hold in the valley. Finally coming to the present century and that too the recent times, if the *Kashur* had not welcomed the *Wahabi Moulvees* and the *Jihadis* may be the *Kashur Bhata* would have been spared the shame of exile; mayhem and tyranny of fundamentalism and fanatic violence that they have been suffering for the last two decades.

Pt. Anand Kaul -a local historian of great value for his interest and insight in the life of a *Kashur*-describes, a *Kashur* as a simple breed, simple in food and simple in dress. Patience and resignation are writ large on his behaviour; he is law abiding, free from crimes against person, burglary and thievery. He is not even a compulsive or habitual drunkard.

Enumerating especially the character of KSP *Brahmans* he writes, "they believe in the law of phenomenal world namely Karma, that means each person receives exactly measured recompense of his good or bad deeds during his or her past life in happiness or misery. They guard with jealousy the pure traditions of Hinduism and take every care to preserve the integrity of their religion."

A KSP is an intelligent human being but at the same time shrewd and alive to comic touch and has a natural gift of repartee. Kaul narrates two interesting episodes to substantiate this. Once Timur Shah Durani in Kabul asked his courtier Diwan Dila Ram Quli Khan, "As to why the Tika mark was made by him on his forehead? Pat came the answer that it indicated God was one. Why on the ear lobes? These are the two witnesses to the said fact. Why on the throat? One who doesn't believe must be beheaded." The second instance quoted reads once Maharaja Gulab Singh said, "the Pandits are cowards and lack martial spirit hence they shirk taking to military services." A Pandit present answered, pray thank heavens, the Pandits do not take to military service, for do you not remember what one Brahmin Parsuram did in ancient times after he wore the belt and sword[24]

A KSP has a unique capacity to adopt and adjust in any environment and yet be very possessive of his/her own traditions, and to assert his/her individual identity. A KSP is usually loyal and faithful to his/her master and has a knack to adapt to changing circumstances and locale. It is this trait that has enabled a *Kashur* to adapt to the changing and evolving manner of dress, language, and outward physical appearances over the eras of its history. Their dress changed from two garments, upper one and lower one of the N.P. era.[25] to the Central Asian loose gown now known as Pheran imposed by the Mughal Emperor Akbar, and then again to the latest Punjabi Shalwar and Kameez or the western dress pant and shirt. During the Pathan rule they even wore a girdle round their waist, and a '*Chakma Dulak*' on their feet. During the Sikh rule they had long flowing beards and also long moustaches during the Dogra rule. With the advent of the British they began to shave the beard and even moustaches and dress and spoke English like them. At present, with the influence of the *Wahbies* and *Jihadis* they have started growing long beards and wearing *salwar*.

THE KASHUR—KASHMIRI SPEAKING PEOPLE

One would have been tempted to say that one of the great virtues of a KSP, was to be peaceful and live in harmony, in spite of following different religious faiths, but alas they seem to have surrendered this virtue to the travails of time. Still we can give a *Kashur* the credit for not following the custom of untouchablity in the rigid sense right from the *Puranic* era.

A KSP by virtue of the land of their birth; a land of par excellence beauty, in climate unparallel and rivalled for its antiquity, has imbibed beauty, art, aesthetics and grace in every day routine of their life. They are renowned as craftsmen and artisans. Like wise their philosophic, spiritual and monolithic architectural monuments, like the world famous Martand temple and hundreds of other temples, mosques, and Viharas stand testimony to the engineering skills of the *Kashur*.

Modern concept of animal lovers and environmentalist is ingrained in the every day routine of a KSP. Their day starts with feeding the birds and small minute insects like ants, worshipping and watering the plants, after paying obeisance to the various elements of nature.

The KSP as a whole are courteous, polite, and graceful to fault. They are fond of beautiful things and rich food. They live happily at home, take care of their families, respect their elders, and are kind to their wives. Till recently the evils of divorce and immorality in the homes were rare occurrences. 'A Kashmiri wife is a real helpmate, both in labour and interest of the family'. The ethics and values of the camaraderie between man and wife are very healthy. They have a highly developed moral sense; the traditions and family are a very important part of their life. They will go to any extent to maintain the dignity of their ancestors.

They have a unique sense of charity. Quoting an incident during the reign of Simhadev proves the extent of this sense of charity. "It is well known that they did not eat without a guest. Since, the arrival of a guest every day was necessary, it was decided that the Chandala women should come to the house of each of the residents every day before noon, and then the residents should give them food first and then eat themselves."[26]

Traditional and ritual art is an essential part of a KSPs life style. They have a good account head and their pronunciation in any language is distinct. Even with little knowledge they manage to do well.

Wakefield writes, "What ever he plans he executes. His judgement is sound and his council is pregnant with wisdom. A *Kashur* possesses self respect and in spite of poverty presents a glistening face to hide his real state."[27]

A KSP is essentially mystical and imaginative and has a strong faith in *Sufis* and saints. They are very tolerant, and superstitious. Unlike non-Kashmiri Muslims or Hindus they did not entertain a strict tenderness for the fundamentals of Islam or Hinduism and that is why Aurangzeb dubbed them (particularly the Muslims) as *'bapir'*/vicious) and, '*betamiz*', lacking discretion. They are very superstitious attaching much importance to quaint legends which are associated with *Asthans, Khanqahs* and springs writes Lawrence.

The Encyclopaedia Britannica records that the people of Kashmir are still strongly influenced by their ancient superstitions. Refuting or neglecting them is considered a sin, which hardly any Kashmiri dare commit. To most of the people, they are known as asthan parast, (worshipping the shrines of those saints, Sadhus and fakirs who are dead.) The Muslim *Khanqahs* and Hindu *Asthapans* are, therefore, a great rendezvous where members of both communities meet. On the occasions of *Oorus* (anniversary) of *Chararar-i-Sharif* and Shah Hamdan, they are seen associated with each other commonly enjoying the pleasant blessings of these national festivals. Common worships of the saints and sadhus, and common beliefs and superstitions were vital characteristics of Kashmiris till recent years, which distinguish them from co-religionists from the plains. Some centuries ago, the Muslims of the Valley were considered to be Hindus at heart and vice-versa. Jahangir was surprised to see such characteristics, and in his momentous work *Tuzk-i-Jahangiri* has recorded that the Muslims of the valley 'ally themselves with Hindus and both give and take girls'.

Irrespective of religion, cast, creed or gender, they always strive to achieve excellence in the task at hand and have left indelible stamp in all the fields of their state.

Faults and foibles

Every coin has two sides and so have the KSP. They suffer from an extended dosage of ego, snobbishness, conceit and cynical tendencies.

Thinking in one voice, for them and following one leader is almost a taboo. One of their major weaknesses is being envious towards the members of their community, with an in-verse ratio of distance in relationship.

They are susceptible to gossip and enjoy listening to sen*sati*onal political news. Lawrence observed: "*Kashur* always loves to over state his case. He is very loud and voluble. He is very persistent. They are very quick in argument, and they never abandon a case unless they are convinced that it is hopeless, and they always insist on knowing the grounds of a decision. The commonest *Kashur* can talk intelligently on most subjects, and they have a great aptitude for sarcasm. They believe that every man has his price but are quick to recognise ability in their rulers. A Kashmiri can turn his hand on anything. He has a considerable knowledge of both horticulture as well as the agriculture. In support of his system of agriculture and indeed in support of every act of his every day life he can quote rhyming proverbs. For every action of his there is a proper time, date and season, which he follows."[28]

Mild climate, fragrant flora and the enticing scenic environs have developed in the KSP's, the habit of lethargy and tendency to embrace idleness and hence shirk from taking risks in life. It has been asserted by many a foreign travellers and rulers that a *Kashur* is "a coward, a liar and a dirty fellow". The quality of tenacity, adaptability and elasticity in the character of a *Kashur* is construed to mean cowardice, but it is these traits that have helped him to struggle and survive the brutal activities of religiously fanatic administrators. He is a coward because long oppression has made him so. "The Kashmiri is indeed made of contradictions. He is timid yet persistent, degraded yet intellectual, mystical yet adventurous, shrewd and business like."[29] Again he is a liar because of the peculiar system of government, which encouraged the most elaborate system of espionage. Cowardice and lying have, in turn bred in him envy and malice, self praise and condemnation of others. Pessimism, lack of education, poverty- (not now) - and the severity of climate, has made him dirty.[30]

I wish to reproduce an interesting episode of the Nilamata era in this connection. When the land of *Satidesha* was made habitable, Kashyapa requested the Goddess Laxmi in the form of river *Visoka* to join the waters of *Vitasta* ahead of *Sati*, to purify the people of the valley of all their sins. Initially she was hesitant, as she thought, *Sati* had already gone there and she would take away all the credit. She changed her mind when Kashyapa convinced her saying, "It is you who are *Kashmira*, it is you who is glorified as Uma, and it is you who, O Goddess, are living in the form of all goddesses." When Laxmi changed herself into the form of river *Visoka*, Kasmira spoke thus, "Go soon before *Sati* reaches to wait for you. Kashmira whose speed is like that of the mind also told everything to *Sati*. Thus when *Visoka* (Laxmi) exited through a narrow hole, she saw *Sati* (*Vitasta*) waiting for her. The two waters joined and were named *Vitasta* because *Sati* had reached first. This invoked the wrath of *Visoka* (Laxmi) and she cursed Kashmira thus, "O wicked one, as I have been absorbed by you today by means of falsehood and you have informed *Sati* about my activities, so your people will be mostly liars, possessed of impurities, hired servants and dishonoured in the worlds" [31].

One wonders whether these curses fructified, or were the people of Kashmira able to seek forgiveness from Goddess Laxmi and undo the curse. But one thing is definite that the Goddess Laxmi has been very frugal in bestowing her benevolence on the *Kashur* who has always preferred learning to affluence Travellers like Hiuen Tsang (631 AD)Alberuni (11th AD) and other pilgrims from far of countries in different eras have always specified this characteristic of a *Kashur* in their observations.

CHARACTER OF A *KASHUR* VILLAGER

Sir Walter Lawrence in trying to give an over all picture of the character and disposition of a rural *Kashur* writes, "a Kashmiri villager is a nature lover, he loves flowers and fruits, leads a simple rustic life in his village, in his simple huts with barest possible furniture but the most essential part of his life is the Kangri. They have a keen intellect, but are very unstable and prone to give undue weight to rumours. They are emotional and ruled by sentiment. They will do excellent work if praised; they admire stern determination in their rulers. They are accomplished talkers but have an instinctive dread of their words being committed to paper. Writing in their opinion is a trap and a fraud. The dark side of a *Kashur* is revealed when in the presence of officials. He has had good reasons to hate and distrust them and his only weapon against them is deceit. His light side is seen when he is in his fields No interest is charged on loaned money. No contract is signed. Everything is on word and is never broken. Crime is almost non-existent in Kashmir. The crimes of dishonesty may be said to be absolutely non existent among the peasants. Property is entirely safe and during the six years of my stay in the villages I have never heard of theft or burglary being committed by the agriculturists. This surely points Kashmiris are not dishonest people as some have assumed them to be. A Kashmiri will rarely lie when he is confronted in his village by his fellow villagers but he will lie when he enters the murky law courts."[32]

I would say that his counterpart in the city is in no way different, only he is hardened by the complexities of city life.

Some Europeans, prior to Lawrence have described the character of a KSP in no flattering terms.

Moorcroft describes the Kashmiri as "selfish, superstitious, ignorant, supple, intriguing, dishonest and false, he has great ingenuity as a mechanic and a decided genius for manufacture and commerce; but his transactions are always conducted in a fraudulent spirit, equalled only by effrontery with which he faces detection."

Drew admits that they are, "false tongued, ready with a lie,' and given to various forms of deceit."

Barron Hugel however justifies this behaviour and writes, "Such was the oppression of the political class and the cruel and inconsiderate ruler that justice was practically non existent and the only weapon of safety and survival was deceit and cunning."

It would be unnatural to look for virtues among people as oppressed as a KSP over a long period of its history. People who had suffered the extortions of the Afghan and Pathan governors, and their exacting officers, who would go to any limit in the process of revenue collection, in order to please their bosses; least did they care for the farmers needs, who would be left with nothing to feed his family. People who had to pay a tax called Jazia in order to keep a tika on the fore head (the mark of their religion) or even wear shoes. People, who were tied in pairs in grass sacks and drowned in the Dal Lake. People in whose homes Afghan and Pathan soldiers would come in thundering on their steeds and carry the hapless maidens. Such people had to take shelter in such sly and mean tactics. They had to lie or cheat to survive, because they had to live under very trying circumstances for many centuries and hence their psyche suffered much damage. It is believed short term tyranny may prove a challenge but long term sustained tyranny tends to benumb and dehumanise.

Lawrence writes, "But when one reflects on what they now are, one can not help the thought that many races, had they lived through generations of oppression, like the Kashmiris, might have been more cunning and more dishonest."

The belief that a *Kashur* did not commit any crime because the punishments were so severe that they were scared to commit one if true, one wonders, what prevented the authorities to enforce such laws to ensure better sanitary and sewerage facilities, to help the people to be clean and they would have been spared to be labelled as, 'dirty'.

I feel the observations of the earlier travellers were based on their contacts with the lower strata of the *Kashur* community, especially the boatmen class, because others would not easily mix with them.

Possible reasons for the indifference could be:

I) The fear of being forced to convert to Christianity, as observed attempts were made in that direction by some Jesuit Missionaries or

ii) the fear to be contaminated by their religion, and

iii) finally the language barrier, both the subjects and the Europeans did not understand each others language; hence reactions and statements were often misinterpreted.

Having been a subject race for the last six hundred years, suffering untold miseries at the hands of Mughals, Pathans, Sikhs and Dogras they had to take shelter under subterfuge to save their family's honour and life. In turn they were vilified by outsiders as 'coward, shirkers, and cry baby' etc. To set the record right we know they displayed their military prowess in the times of Lalitaditiya, Jayapida, Avantivarman and Zain-ul-Abidin, Akbar the Great and others are a matter of history. But the manner in which the Kashmiris defended their freedom and homeland against an unscrupulous enemy in1947 has once for all buried this myth of their being a coward. To top it all a Kashmiri has shown the resurgence of his fighting spirit in the last two decades in such a violent form that one can never attribute timidity to their character.

Some mixed Observations

Abul Fazal Allami remarks in his book *Ain- I-Akbari* "The bane of this country is its people, yet strange to say, notwithstanding its numerous populations and the scantiness of the means of subsistence, thieving and begging are rare." [33]

Father Xavier who visited Kashmir towards the end of 16th century writes about the KSP, "The intelligence of the people, this applies especially to the Hindu *Brahmans* is note worthy and that the Muslims are out worldly very pious such as prostrating themselves in prayer at the appointed times, wherever they may happen to be."[34]

Bernier remarks, "The conquerors came in hordes but they scarcely touched the soul of the people. Kashmiris are celebrated for wit and considered much more intelligent and ingenious than the Indians. In poetry and science they are no inferior to the Persians. They're also very active and industrious. It is possible for a people to deteriorate under foreign yoke and that is why Kashmiri did not mind to speak a lie sometimes. Men and women generally dress' alike . . . their dress helps to breed cowardice in them. Without it they look like a fine race. Untouchablity between the two sister communities is quite unknown. However you may annoy him, the Kashmiri will never attempt to offend you. To provoke his neighbour is not in his scheme. Isolation from the outer world accounted for the stable unchanging nationality of the Kashmiris till Pratap Singh's reign".

Dr. Neve while describing the *Kashur* writes, "On the whole the Kashmiris are grateful to benefits. Their moral sense is fully developed. They readily distinguish between right and wrong. The intellectual superiority of the Pandits over the rest of the population must be admitted. They are quick of apprehensions and have good memories. One of their besetting faults is conceit. But some of them are very superior, trustworthy, honest, clear headed and industrious."

A French researcher M. Hicks remarks that "The Kashmiris are a race of most superior order in every respect they resemble the Konkanasthas and their countries also resemble as they both produce rice which accounts for their intelligence. But in two respects the two people differ. The Kashmiris are eaters of flesh from ancient times and have not given up flesh eating even now. The *Konkanasthas* appear to have been vegetarians from ancient days. The former again usually wear the beard but the latter do not (beard looks rare now). Beards in Kashmir are ancient and pre-Mohammadan as we have already seen from Kalhana's description of *Brahman*s collected for the election of a King".

The following passages from the book "*The India we served*" by Sir W. R. Lawrence who worked in Kashmir for many years must be read with great interest: "The Kashmiris are called *Hawabin* (who can smell the wind). Nowhere in the East have I met anybody of men so clever and as courteous as the Kashmiri Pandits. The people were, Kashmiris as they are, in spite of centuries of repression and wanton cruelty. Physically they were splendid, in spite of the effeminate dress which foreign tyrants, had imposed on them. As cultivators, as artisans and as artists they are unrivalled in the East and for brains the *Kashur* Pandit is hard to beat, as all India knows well. They are to be found in many provinces of British India and in the Indian States in the higher ranks of officialdom. And I say after careful examination that the Kashmiris are perhaps as great a people as any in the East, but they will beat all three-Rajput, Pathans and Punjabis as cultivators, artisans or as wits. I saw also the growth of self respect and of manliness . . They not only know the facts but had the most surprising genius for appraising the real value of other men's lands. They supported their valuation by most logical and convincing arguments and during my 21years in India I have never met the equal of these Kashmiri sages . . . . Kashmiris have easy and pleasant lives, in times of danger they show much courage and endurance. Physically they are among the finest people on the earth. Their, physique, their character and their language are so marked as to produce a nationality of its own. Intellectual superiority, keenness of perception, clearness of mind and ingenuity dominate their character. Their alert, intelligence, quick wit and artistic capabilities show in them signs of bright future. They are essentially of mild and cheerful disposition. Their, versatile genius wins laurels for them everywhere. They are extremely hospitable and carry the arts of civil life to perfection . . . . . . (.He adds to remind the reader.) A man who can be beaten and robbed by anyone with a vestige of authority soon ceases to respect himself and his fellowmen and it is useless to look for the virtues of a free people among the Kashmiris, and unfair to twist them with the absence of such virtues. The Kashmiri is what his rulers have made him."[35]

Prof. A. Foucher records, "The types of the old Pandits-these literati were, to be sure, excellent people and admirably versed in their Sanskrit texts but they were devoid of historical sense and their intellectual horizon was bounded by the narrow limits of their native valley . . . , but the race possessed exceptional intellectual qualities."

Prof. Jadu Nath Sarkar's remarks in his book 'History of Aurangzeb' (Vol,v p,415, indicate the other extreme, and he writes, "So backward were the people in civilisation that even the upper classes of Kashmiris were deemed unfit to be employed in the Imperial Service as *Mansabdars*, till near the end of Aurangzeb's reign. We learn that it was only in 1699 that the Emperor was first induced by the then *Subedar* to appoint people of Kashmir as *Mansabdars* in any appreciable number especially Kashmiri Hindu". G.L Kaul, (*Kashmir p 251*) contradicts Sarkar's claim of *Tarikhi Azmi* as the source of this (Sarkar's) information. Kaul writes, "This observation is misleading, biased and factually incorrect as the given quotation that is, recorded in the *Ruqat-i-Alamgiri* proves and I quote, "*Kashmiri-darin mulk nestand ki ma muqqarar kunem*" (The Kashmiris are not to be found here that we might appoint them in public offices).[36] Apparently Aurangzeb held them in high esteem and paid a compliment to the intelligence of the Kashmiris specially that of the Pandits. I wonder if Sarkar's biased comment is in retaliation to the episode during Lalitaditiyas reign, when the *Gauda* (Bengali) king was murdered in deceit and the troops who came to avenge his death were massacred by Kashmiri Troops.

It is befitting to conclude in G. L Kaul's words, "Kashmiri is too deep rooted in its tradition to wither away under the storm of foreign conquest. The old ascetic life has survived the shock of as many centuries of alien tyrannical cult. The people own prosperity, poverty, and religious strife, wars with invaders, shocks of earthquakes, floods, droughts, plagues and pestilences like many other people of this universe; and yet they have managed to retain the stamp of their originality."[37]

Original Classification of the KSP Ethnic Group

Classification of the ethnic communities, in reality, is culmination of a long and continuous process of human endeavour to fix an individual identity of a sect, as well as of an individual person, who combine to form that sect, in order to infuse a kind of discipline in the society. There is nothing enigmatic about this craving for individual identity. It is the law of nature; a law that has been followed in all kinds of creations, animate or inanimate, by the creator of this universe. Amongst animates, homo-sapiens, being the most advanced form of life; they divined innovative identities and classifications for their specie. The earliest as well as universally applicable identity and divisions of this specie were, super humans, sub humans and humans. To the category of super humans belong the divine angels/devas, who were assigned to the domain of heaven supposed to be some where above the stratosphere. The sub humans were the devils / *dhanavs*/ Satan and they were associated with *Patal*/ hell or what is termed as the nether world, which is at the bottom of the ocean. The third category was the human race /*manush* the inhabitants of the earth. Presumably this division was based on some genetic, ethical and moral codes of the earliest people. (Surprisingly even today when, a new born Kashmiri Hindu child's horoscope is cast, it is clearly mentioned as to which one of the above mentioned categories the child belongs to, that is *manush zaat*/ *deve zaat* or the *Rakshas zaat)* With the progress of culture and human civilisation these broad based classifications were further refined and their field was reduced and associated to the place, that is the country one inhabited and to the mode of worship. With this originated different categories of humans, as we place them on the globe or the physical map of the world. The search for identity did not stop there for this division was once again very broad based. The next step in this search was reached with the evolution of different religions. Human identities now were more compact and could be easily placed under different religious precepts, laws and codes. One of the major religions of the world is Hinduism and that religion is associated with the theme of this topic. The earliest Hindus worshipped the procuring Gods like the sun and the moon which provided them with light and energy and thus they classified themselves as Sun worshipers and the moon worshippers. This nomenclature is prevalent in the Hindu KSPs in the terms of the *Malmasis* and the *Banamasis*. The *Malmasis*' observe the Lunar astronomical calendar) where as the *Banamasis* observe the Solar astronomical Calendar.[38]

In the Vedic era this grouping further bifurcated in to sects worshipping different elements of nature. Moving away from the nature worship to the worship of deities and gods, the new identity assigned was Shavites for the followers of Shiva, Vaishnavite for the followers of Vishnu and Shaktas as the followers of the Shakti; the mother Goddess. These were further subdivided according to the intellectual calibre, physical strength and stamina, mental and genetic grouping which was also termed as division of labour and this system was called (*Varnaasramadharma*). This way the Hindus as a religious community were identified as:

(a) Brahman-one who dealt with learning and cultivating the art of learning;

(b) The Kshatriya-the warrior class,

(c) The Vaisya-traders and

(d) The Sudras-artisans and agricultural class.

Since, in the beginning, this division was not hereditary, it was so fluid that one could find all the classes existing in one clan or even in one family as well. Gradually this division of the society started attaining a rigid form as is evident from the records left by the Greek historians.

Megasthenes in his book Indika writes "The people of India were divided into about seven castes:

(1) The Sophists,

(2) The tillers of the soil

(3) The herdsmen-shepherds

(4) The handicraftsmen and retail dealers

(5) The warriors

(6) Superintendents

(7) Councillors of the state.

How Greeks came to the conclusion that people of India were divided into seven casts is beyond our subject. *(For details refer to Appendix VI)*

Megasthenes states that the custom of the country prohibited inter marriage between the casts and only the sophist could belong to any cast because the life of a sophist was not an easy one but the hardest of all.[39]

Due to the physical isolation and exclusivity of the valley, cast division *per se* was a late entrant in to the KSP ethos and the early records indicate that the Kashmiris had no state, no slaves and no private property. Theirs was a homogeneous society with no classes or castes. They worked collectively, produced collectively and consumed collectively. FM. Husnain writes, "There was no kingdom and no king, no punisher and no punished. By their very law of being, the people pooled their resources together and worked and produced collectively. They were divided into groups or tribes. Every one worked, not for himself, but for the benefit of all. Later there came into existence a division of labour. But this division of labour had no effect on the status of a person, because this was only a division of work and every one was still, the respectable member of the coherent society."

"With the increase of the Aryan population in Kashmir, the importance of the divisions of labour increased, and ultimately resulted in social divisions and castes. This is how the division of labour and, later, divisions in the society came in to existence in Kashmir. The early people were animal breeders and tamers. Then a section of them started agriculture, another restored to melting of metals and so on and so forth. This sharp division of the society shattered the concept of collectivism in production and gave rise to the institution of the ownership of property. Every one now worked for his self and for his own family."[40]

Nilamata Purana our earliest source of information regarding the classification of the KSP "does not discuss the origin of the *Varnaasramadharma* or describe it in any detail. It how ever casually refers to some *Varanas* and *Asramas* along with their main characteristics."[41]

As per Kalhana's R.T. we find that the KSP were classified on the basis of the nature of the profession/occupation they followed to make their living. There were no cast divisions during the N.P. era and even first three books of R.T. make no mention of casts like Rajput, or Kshatriyas. There was no formal cast system during the reign of Ashoka, Kanishka, Juska and Huska and yet we observe the Brahmin class existed as a distinct class. In the later books we do find mention of casts like Rajput and Kshatriyas and so on, [42] thus we can presume rigid rules of demarcation did not segment the early KSP's.

Expressing his views on the cast system in Kashmir, Ray writes, "Though the conception of the population as consisting of four traditional casts was not all together unknown, yet there was no such cast as *Kshatriyas, Vaisya,* and *Sudras* in early Kashmir. In other parts of India there were various intermediary castes between the *Brahmanas* on the one hand and the lower casts on the other. Curiously enough, so far as we can ascertain such intermediate castes did never exist in the valley".[43]

Krishna Mohan records that the rigid cast division may have been accepted theoretically but not in practice. "There is not any reference to the old spirit of cast segregation. We find much mention of the *Brahman* class in the Rajatarangini. The kings are referred as *Kshatriyas*, while we get a few references to *Vaisyas* and *Sudras*. The lowest order is that of the *Chandalas*."[44]

The people as reflected in the historical records seem to have been divided in minor classes e.g. *Brahmins, Kshatriyas, Kayastha*, Merchants, Agriculturists, *Chandalas, Shudras, Vaisyas* and *Mlechhas*. Among all these classes the Brahmin occupied the most prominent place.

Though the word *Brahman* as a cast is not used in the N.P. but the duties and the studies carried out by one sect of people in the N.P. era is a positive indication of the *Brahman Verna*.[45] They were well versed in history, astronomy, astrology, and in recitation of Puranas.[46] The kings were supposed to consult them at the time of their coronation and in turn the priest had to undergo fast and perform a *Yagya* and make the king to sit on the throne.[47] High respect was shown to this class in the society.[48]

The next division-the *Kshatriyas*-are referred as people with martial character, well versed in the art of weapons and worshippers of Goddess Durga, They were held in esteem in the society.

People occupied in the profession of agriculture, cattle rearing and trade were the *Vaisyas*.

Karmajivis and Silpis: The *Silpis* were the weavers, carpenters, blacksmiths, gold and silversmith, leather tanners and potters. Where as the *Karmajivis* acted as servants of the higher casts

Besides these groups, there were people occupied in various other occupations like *Aurabhrikas* (the shepherds) the *Mallas* (wrestlers), the *Natas* (the dancers) etc.[49]

Ksemendra's works belong to the 8th century AD and Kalhana's chronicle to11th century AD, and both agree that the people of ancient Kashmir were divided on the basis of various race, religious, and socio-economic factors. The majority of the KSP population were *Brahman*s and they occupied the highest place in the society People involved in the professions of agriculture, trade and industry were a separate class and the powerful among them were the *Dammars*. "The term *Kayastha* in the ancient Kashmir did not denote any particular caste. It was purely a term applied to the officials in the kings service,—what later in the Islamic era was converted in to the term Karkun.—this is evident from Kalhana's assertion that the *Brahman*s were *Kayasthas*."[50]

The career of the *Kayastha* seems to have been thrown open to all the members of the state. Even persons holding other hereditary occupations some times as lowly as the *aramika* /gardener could enter in to the rank of the *Kayastha*.[51]

A *Kayastha* holding a lower post could be promoted into a higher rank. Kshemendra says that it was the ambition of every *Kayastha* to become the *Grhakrtyamahattama* (highest administrative officer).[52] Both Kalhana and Kshemendra have written about the greed and corruption of this class of people. There is no mention of *Dammars,* in the first three books of R.T where as both *Dammars* and *Kayastha* classes appear in the fourth book as a separate class.

Besides the above mentioned classes, to run a society properly, there was need for yet other groups, who took up occupations like soldiers (the *Tantarians* and *Ekangas*), the administrative workers, promoters of cultural professions and the menial jobs. It is about the last group that is referred as the *Dombas, Chandalas,* and *Svapakas,* which are mentioned often in the Rajatarangini. These sections of the society are considered lower than the *Sudras. Chandalas* are referred as untouchables.[53] *Dombas* and *Svapakas* were ordinarily not allowed to enter the temples but the *Domba* singer with his daughters Hamsi and Nagalata were allowed to do so.[54] The occupations' of the *Dombas* were mainly singing, dancing, hunting, fishing, besides being buffoons and quacks.

There is a general belief that these people did not belong to the original KSP group and are supposed to have come with Kashyapa. They are the descendents of various races and communities who came to the valley in different eras of its history, as invaders and intruders from the surrounding countries and mountainous tribes. Aversion of the locals for some of these races like the *Yavanas*, the *Tartars*, the Huns, the *Kritikyas*, (Tibetan tribes) the *Nishadas* and *Svapaka* tribes from the surrounding hills, led, in due course, to declare them as untouchable *Mlechhas*.

Jyoteeshwar Pathik records in his book, *Glimpses of History of Jammu & Kashmir,* "In Kashmir castes came into existence at a later period. The process went on and in the rule of Jayasimha we find nearly sixty four castes in the society."[55]

To conclude, the chroniclers of early and medieval eras record that *Varnaasramadharma* was a very late entrant in the KSP fold, and the subsequent division on the basis of *Gotras* and Surnames followed in the process.

The *Gotra* and the Surnames

Prior to detailing the *Gotra* classification it may be pertinent to record opinions of a few eminent scholars about the *Brahmans*/*Kashmiri Pandit*, who observed this classification. Rev M.A. Sherring writes, "*Brahmans*, popularly called *Kashmiri Pandits*, form a distinct class of their own and are considered to be the purest specimens of the ancient Aryan settlers in the Valley . . . . . . That Kashmir, or as it is usually spelt, *Cashmere*, is one of the primitive seats of the *Brahmans* in India, is beyond dispute. Situated on the highway from Central Asia to India, it was only natural that the Aryan race should select this beautiful country, with its hills and valleys, for one of its first settlements. It is singular, however, that the only Hindu caste known to the province is the Brahmanical. While innumerable castes have sprung up on the plains, the *Brahmans* have appropriated *Cashmere* exclusively to themselves. This circumstance furnishes an argument for the original unity of the Hindu tribes. If this unity did not exist in very ancient times, it is difficult to account for the fact that only *Brahmans* have occupied *Cashmere*."

George Campbell, in his' *Ethnology of India*,' further adds "Kashmir is a Brahmin country. The lower classes have long been converted to Mohammedanism; but they seem to be ethnologically identical with the Brahmins; and tradition also asserts that they are of the same race. At the present day no other Hindu caste, save the Brahmin, is known; nor is there any trace (so far as I could find) that there ever was any other in the country. The Brahmin population is numerous; but it would seem as if, while the illiterate multitude adopted the religion of the ruling power, the better educated and superior class maintained their own tenets."

Abu-l-Fazal writes, "The most respectable class in this country is that of the *Brahmans* who, notwithstanding their need of freedom from the bonds of tradition and custom, are true worshippers of God. They do not loosen the tongue of calumny against those not of their faith, nor beg, nor importune. They employ themselves in planting fruit trees, and are generally a source of benefit to the people . . . of learning alight in Kashmir"[56]

Brahman/ *Bhata* / *Pandit:*

The original castes as well as the ones created by intermingling further sub divided on the basis of territorial distinctions, ethnological variations, tribal and clan distinctions. These distinctions led to the creation of titles and surnames.

The *Brahmans* of all tribes, according to Hindu writings and traditions, are believed to have originally descended from seven Rishis, or sages, held by Hindus universally in profound veneration as semi-deities of great sanctity and wisdom These, as given by the *Nirnaya Sindhu,* and also in the *Dharma-Sindhu,*

(TWO VENERATED HINDU *SHASTRAS*) ARE AS FOLLOWS:

1. Bhrigu,

2. Angirah,

3. Atri,

4. Viswamitra,

5. Kasyap,

6. Vashisht,

7. Agasthi.

Pt. Anand Koul Bamzai gives different names for the original six *gotras* of the KSPs and they are *Dhattatreya, Bharadwaja, Paladeva, Aupamanaya, Maudgalya* and *Dhaumyayana*. Each of these Rishis stands at the head of a great division; various members of which are further sub-divided into sections termed *Gotras* or classes. These *Gotras* are found, more or less, in all the twelve tribes of Hindus.

The Hindu KSP group primarily divided on the basis of the *Gotra* they belonged to and were addressed as, *Bhata* /Pandit/or *Brahman*, as barring a few exceptions they are all *Brahmans* as mentioned earlier.

The term *Gotra* has been given different connotations by different people. Common belief is that a *Gotra* is named after the genetic ancestor of a clan or tribe.

J. F. Hewitt gives a unique explanation, he writes "The *Gotamas* or the sons of cow (go) and the black cloud *Pusipan/ Pusupati* are the sons of the priestly caste of the Rigveda, and it is from their tradition that the Brahmins call the subsections of their caste *Go-tras* or cow-pens and they are the earliest professional priests."[57]

Pandit Anand Kaul Bamzai writes that *Gotras* are the names of the earliest Rishis or inspired saints of the tribal divisions of the *Brahman* community.

While I believe the term *Gotra* was initiated by the Hindus exactly as the Latin names are used to identify biological species and specimens even after all the mutations and hybridization processes.

GOTRA(GUTHUR) CLASSIFICATION

Kashmiri Pandits are broken up into numerous *gotras*, or tribal divisions. There are eighteen known *gotras* among the *Levite Brahmans* and 103 among the other *Brahmans* in Kashmir according to A, K.Bamzai; where as Dr.S.S Toshkhani claims the Pandits are divided into 199 endogamous *gotras*. Be it 103 or 199, now days Hindu KSP's hardly keep track of their *Gotra*, unless they need to pronounce it at religious ceremonies and practices.

Lawrence writes, "Though the name of the *Gotra* is repeated seven times by the Pandit as he performs his daily ablutions, the outside world rarely hears it mentioned, and they are known by their *Krams* or family appellation."[58]

SURNAME

The *gotra* division further led to yet another division on the basis of the Surname known as Kram (*Zaat* in the native tongue) this concept of Krams is a very recent one in the Hindu KSP community. It came into existence on account of certain unusual circumstances and quirks. It owes its origin mostly to the specifics of the habitat (place of residence of a clan), the occupation / profession followed by the ancestor of the clan, some peculiar eccentricity of the ancestor or because of peculiar circumstances which may have occurred to him.

Pandit Anand Koul Bamzai records one such example thus, "A man, named Wasdev, had a mulberry tree growing in his courtyard and, therefore, he was called Wasdev *Tul* (mulberry). He, in order to get rid of this nickname, cut down the tree. But a *mund* (trunk) remained and people began to call him Wasdev *Mund.* He then removed the trunk of the tree but its removal resulted in a *Khoud* (depression) and henceforth people called him Wasdev *Khoud.* He then filled up the depression but the ground became a *Teng* (mound) and he was called thereupon Wasdev *Teng.* Thus, exasperated he gave up any further attempt to remove the cause of his nick name and it continued to be *Teng* which is now attached to the names of his descendants."[59]

Some Krams are often the relic of a nickname applied to the ancestor of the subdivision. Here I record some examples to that effect. A *Sopuri-Pandit* points to the fact that the ancestor came from Sopore; *Bakaya* signifies that the ancestor was a revenue defaulter; *Khar* (iron smith) suggests that the ancestor was connected with the iron trade'; like wise *Toshkhani* meant in charge of treasury, *Razdan*-secret services and *Sultan* obviously indicated that the family had close relations with one of the first line of Musalman kings and so on.

Some Krams have originated by virtue of inter- community alliances between the descendents of foreign invaders and the local inhabitants, such as Nakashbandi, Raina, Shargah, Duranies and so on. Surnames like Kelam, Cheervo, and Qasba owe the origin to the names of particular villages and districts where the ancestors of these clans resided.

"In one *Gotra* there may be many Krams, as the following instances will show. Among the *Malmas Gotras* is one known as *Paldeo Wasgarge*, and this *Gotra* embraces families belonging to the following *Krams*, or tribal subdivisions:-*Sopuri-Pandit, Mala, Poot, Mirakhur, Kadlabaju, Kokru, Bangru, Bakaya, Khashu, Kichlu, Misri, Khar, and Mam. Among the Banamas Pandits there is a gotra known as the Dattatrye, and from this gotra have sprung the great families of Koul and others less known, such as the Nagari,(Jinse, Jalali, Watal, Neka, Sultan, Ogra, Amin, Moja, Bamjai, Dont, Tota, Sabin, Kissu, Manslal, Singari, Rafij, Balu, and Darabi. Among the leading Krams may be mentioned the following names: Tikku, Razdan, Kak, Munshi, Mathu, Kachru, Pandit, Sipru, Bhan, Zitshu, Raina, Dhar, Fotadar, Madan, Thusu, Wangnu, Muju, Hokhu, and Dulu.* Of these the members of the Dhar family have probably been the most influential."[60]

As a tradition all over India among the Hindus marriage is forbidden within the same *Gotra*, because their ancestors feared such alliance would lead to the birth of *varnesenkras* (one who suffers maladies of in-breeding). However, in recent times the *Gotra* marriage restriction is not so stringent, for now people have realised that this tradition has lost its significance. May be when our ancestors introduced this taboo there were only the primary seven *gotras* and their few descendents, so there was need for the restriction to spare their progeny from the maladies of in-breeding, as is advised by the modern medical science too. Under the present circumstance of the multiplicity of the *Gotras* and their descendents, this taboo for all practical purposes is irrelevant.

The earliest Surnames

Casting a glance down the pages of the Chronicles of Kashmir we find that the earliest surnames that we come across, as mentioned by Kalhana, are *Rajanaka (Razdan)* and *Kak* and these surnames have survived down the eras. Later in about the 12th century often recorded surname is *Bhatta* e.g. Vagha*bhata*, Mahadev Bhatta, Srikantha Bhatta, Prayagay Bhatta, and so on. The word *Bhatta* is a nomenclature which refers to the Kashmiri Pandit community as a whole unit within the valley. It is believed by some that this term is derived from the Sanskrit word *Bhattarika*. Others write, it is the Prakrit form of the Sanskrit word *BAHARIRI*, which means a scholar. While D.N.Raina in his book, "*Kashmir Distortions and Reality*', writes, "The appellation Bhatta is a reminder of the honorific that went with the degree' *Bhatta*' awarded to the graduates coming out of the portals of the prestigious Shraadha Peeth University situated on the banks of Kishenganga in the valley of Mount Harmukh".[61]

There is yet another explanation given about the origin of the word *Bhatta*. N.N.Mujoo writes "In ancient time's *yogis*, who have had excess to supernatural powers or *VIBHUTIS*, could create any kind of body they desired in *SAMADHI* (meditation). Due to lack of determination and decay of vibhuti the creation of divine objects by spiritual intuition were substituted by stone idols. A stone in primitive Kashmiri language was called *Vath* and therefore a worshipper of *Vath* was nick named as such, which in due course of time was altered as *Bhat or Bateh*."[62]

What ever be the origin of this word, we will have to accept that the surname Bhatt is one of the most common surnames of Kashmiri Pandits and especially of (Hindu KSP) who originate from the rural part of the valley.

Re-Classification of the KSP after the advent of Islam in the 13th/14th century AD

With the induction of the new faiths KSP's were reclassified as: Bhatta, Musalman and Sardar and this re-classification is detailed under.

Bhatta

During their numerous political vicissitudes the Hindu KSP suffered enormously at the hands of religious persecutors and the rulers of the land in the 14th century. The mayhem was so intense and deep that it resulted in complete religious transformation. Most of the Hindu KSPs were either annihilated, exiled, or got converted to Islam, and those few who were left still holding on to their religious faith almost lost the sense of the Gotra divisions. They were so few that they had to look for a classification of different kind. Subsequently, during the long and peaceful reign of Sultan Zain-ul-Abidin most of the exiled Hindu KSP, by virtue of the king's decree, returned to their original home-land.

With their return to homeland Bhatta got categorized in to two groups: *Banamasi* representing the immigrants and *Malamasi* were those who had not left the valley during the religious turmoil.

This primary division was further sub divided on the basis of occupation and proficiency in the Scriptural language (Sanskrit or Sharda) and the court language Persian. Since Sanskrit was no more the court language they had to study Persian language and, in course of time, some of them were able to regain their traditional occupation, namely, government services' Kashmiri Brahmins were now divided into three categories.

The *Karkuns*-Those who joined the administrative, services of the court due to their proficiency in Persian as well as Sanskrit. Vast majority of the Pandits belong to this class at present. In general they usually made their livelihood in the employment of the state, yet at the same time we do find they even took up a variety of other jobs for earning their lively hood. Since Karkuns could not attend to the religious and scriptural aspects of the society, a separate group was made responsible for such duties.

The *Bashabattas*-KSP's who were well versed in the scriptural knowledge were classed as the Bashabattas. Initially it was decided that the grandson from the daughter's side, would be responsible for performing these duties in every household. This was a simple arrangement which later on got sub-divided into smaller groups according to the gravity of the religious services they would be in charge of. These sub divisions were:

***Jyotish* class**-Those who were learned in the Shastras and expounded them to the members of their community were addressed as *Jyotish*. They drew up the community Almanacs/calendars, for the events of the coming year, details of various festivals, customs, rites and rituals along with prophesies. Various essential prayers and religious injunctions were explained in it. This Almanac still functions almost like a religious and social guide for the KSP Hindus. The Jyotish class cast and study the horoscopes of the new born KSP children.

The G*our or Guruji*: were that group of priestly class, who conducted the Karma kanda and other associated religious rituals.

Besides these groups, a small percentage of business class of *Kashur* came in to being after the 13th century AD who were referred as *Buhur* and *Purbi.*

***Buhur* clan-** There are many a versions about the origin of this class. It is generally believed that they were a small *Khattri* group, who were mainly engaged in trade of herbs and dry fruits. Some, however, classify them as the descendants of those KSPs who would travel to the plains for trade and would inter-dine with the non KSPs (people they traded with). Hence the king on the complaint of some orthodox Pandits promulgated them as a separate class. Initially they traded in herbs, dry fruits and dry vegetables but in recent times they have diverted to various other big and small businesses.

***Purbi* clan-** They are the descendants of those immigrants who came from Chamba valley (Himachal Pradesh) and settled in the valley.

MUSALMAN

Majority of the KSP's, after conversion to Islam in the 14th century, follow Islamic tenets. They are addressed as Musalman in the local language and are mainly categorised as *Sunnis* and *Shias*.

Sunnis are in majority, where as *Shias* are limited in numbers. The latter consider themselves to be superior of the two sects. Majority of the narrow-minded conservatives are *Wahabi Sunnis,* besides some *Imamis* and *Nur-Bakshis,* who are perpetually at strife with each other. However the Musalmáns are divided on the basis of their genetic ancestry. Like their Hindu counter-parts they are also grouped under different names that are:

***Sayyids and the Pirzadas*:** The decedents of the Sayyids from Iran are designated as Sayyid; they are the preachers of Islam and are responsible for preaching and proselytising the new faith. Sayyids and Pirzadas are considered to be Krams of respectability among the Muslims. The Pirzadas, who are descendants of zealous converts to Islam, consider themselves equal to the Sayyids

***Sheikhs*:**Great mass of the people who come under the head *Sheikh* are descendants of the original Hindus. In other words they are the progenies of the Hindus who converted to Islam.

Mullahs or priests: They are a class by themselves and they attend to the religious needs of the people and officiate at the birth, marriage or death ceremonies of the Musalman. Recently they have taken to agriculture also; but otherwise they live by the free gifts and grains bestowed on them by their followers

Khans and Sardars: The progenies of the Mughals and the Pathans are a separate section of Musalmáns. There are some settlements of Pathans and Mughals in certain parts of the valley, the appellation of Khan and Sardar represents their identity.

Bombas and Khashas: They are the inhabitants of Jhelum Valley below Baramulla and belong to the warrior class. They were a source of constant terror to the Kashmiri masses till Maharaja Gulab Sigh subdued them.

Dooms and Galwans: Dooms and Galwans are descendents of the tribes which were once considered inferior to others inhabitants of the valley. They have now acquired wealth and their social status has automatically changed for good

Chaupans: They are the hereditary shepherds; who tend the sheep and cattle of the villagers during, the summer months by taking them to green pastures on the various *Margs*/ meadows of high altitude? They are a class of cheery and active people strictly marrying among themselves. The Chaupans have some knowledge of simple herbs and bring them down for the poor villagers.

The Bands or Bhagats: They correspond to the Mirasis in India and carry on the profession of singing and dancing and sometimes go in bands to perform short comic plays in different villages. "They add piquancy and gaiety to the otherwise dull and monotonous life of the villagers and are in great demand on marriage and other festivals.'[63]

Hanji: It is yet another class among the Muslims, by itself, having a separate identity and heritage. They claim to be the descendents of the ancient race of the Nishads (the boatmen). Some claim Noah as their ancestor but it is generally believed that they were Kshatriyas before their conversion to Islam. They still disdainfully refer to a novice at boat craft as a Shudra. They are 'excellent boatmen 'and are ranked in the social order according to the category of the boat they own and ply and the wares they sell, e.g. green grocery, (*Dal Hanji*) trade and selling fish (*Gada Hanji*) etc. They generally reside in their boats, that are well equipped with facilities for every day needs. Their profession involves hospitality of tourists. Theirs' is a close knit group.

***Sufi*:** In addition there is a separate sect among the Musalmáns known as Sufi's. They stand apart from the rest of their community. They practice and preach the purest and truest doctrines of Islam and live the religion in their lives of complete self-abnegation and tolerance to the ideas and beliefs of others.

The Muslim Kram Names

"The Musalmáns of the Valley", says Lawrence, "may have retained for some time after their conversion to Islam, some of the Hindu customs of endogamy within the caste and exogamy outside the *Gotra*, but there is no trace of these customs now and the different tribal names or Krams are names and nothing more,"[64]

However, the social classification of Muslim KSP also is recognized by the *Kram* name affixed to the family. The criterion of their Kram is based on slightly different parameters than that of the Hindu KSP. Muslim KSP's despite change in faith continued to follow the tradition of surnames as their Hindu ancestors, which explain the original ancestry of the group. Some Kram names like Bhat. Dhar, Pandit, Kaul have thus persisted in spite of the change of faith. "Musalmáns of the Pandit, Koul, Bhat, Aitu', Rishi, Mantu, and Ganai Kráms are descendants of *Brahmans* who were forcibly converted to Islam in the fourteenth century. Other Krams are believed to have sprung from Khattri origin, as ancient history mentions that the bearers of these names in Hindu times were a military and warlike people. Among these Krams may be mentioned the Mágres, Tántres, Dárs, Dángars, Rainas, Rahtors, Thakurs, and Naiks. Only one Kram, the Lone is generally assigned a Vaisya origin and the Dámars are said to be descendants of Sudras, the lowest of the four Hindu castes."[65]

Lawrence records some very interesting anecdotes about the origins of some Muslim Kram names like *Chang*, and *Kanchattu* he states, "In Zaini gir I found a large number of families rejoicing in the Kram '*Chang*.'(Harp) Their ancestor was a man, who played on the Jew's harp so that led to the origin of the Kram. While Azad, the Pathan tyrant, sliced off the ears of an old and faithful servant because he was slow, and banished him to the Loláb. His descendants are numerous, and their Kram is *Kanachattu*, the 'crop-eared.'[66]. Like wise other surnames originated over the centuries and established in the Muslim order.

SIKHS

Sikh, the smallest class of KSP, are of a very recent origin,as a few hundred years-in the chronology of millennia's and can not be labelled otherwise. The Sikhs of Kashmir are few in number, and how exactly did they establish themselves in the valley is variedly written about. According to one version, most of them were originally *Brahman*s who came along with Raja Sukh Jiwan and were converted to Sikhism in the time of Maharaja Ranjit Singh. The Sikhs of Hamal always say that their ancestors came to Kashmir with Raja Sukhjewan.

Most people say that they came into Kashmir with the lieutenants of Ranjit Singh, but the Sikhs in Traal assert that they came to Kashmir in the time of the Pathans. This is confirmed by Vigne, who states, "the Sikhs came to Kashmir in the service of Raja Sukhjeevan, a Hindu of Shikarpur, who was sent as a Governor of Kashmir by Timur Shah of Kabul about AD 1775".[67] While others believe that there were Punjabi Brahmans already established in the valley, who later converted to Sikhism.

Suraj Parkash records, "there were Sikhs in Kashmir when Hargobind was their Guru," and this would show that the Sikh religion existed in Kashmir as far back as the time of Jahangir. Whatever their origin, Kashmiri speaking Sikhs are entirely different from the Sikhs of Punjab. Being such a small minority, they were an underprivileged class till recent times and survived mostly on agriculture. Before 1947 they were chiefly concentrated in small pockets at Muzafarabad, Tral and Skardu.

Initially they existed as a single unit but slowly, the gradation of class according to the profession adopted by them came into being in their society as well.

1. **The Gyani's and Granthies** constitute those who are learned in Sikh scriptures and carry out and supervise the religious and social ceremonies in the Gurudwaras.

2. **The Kshatriya class** practice the military profession.

3. **The Trader class** is the largest group among this community, for they are successful entrepreneurs and believe in dignity of labour

Theoretically there is no cast division in their society, but one can not deny the fact that it exists nominally in practice.

To conclude it can be authoritatively stated that, due to environmental and social exigencies, many a changes have occurred in the practice and format of the classification of the *'Kashur'*, as a whole in the present era

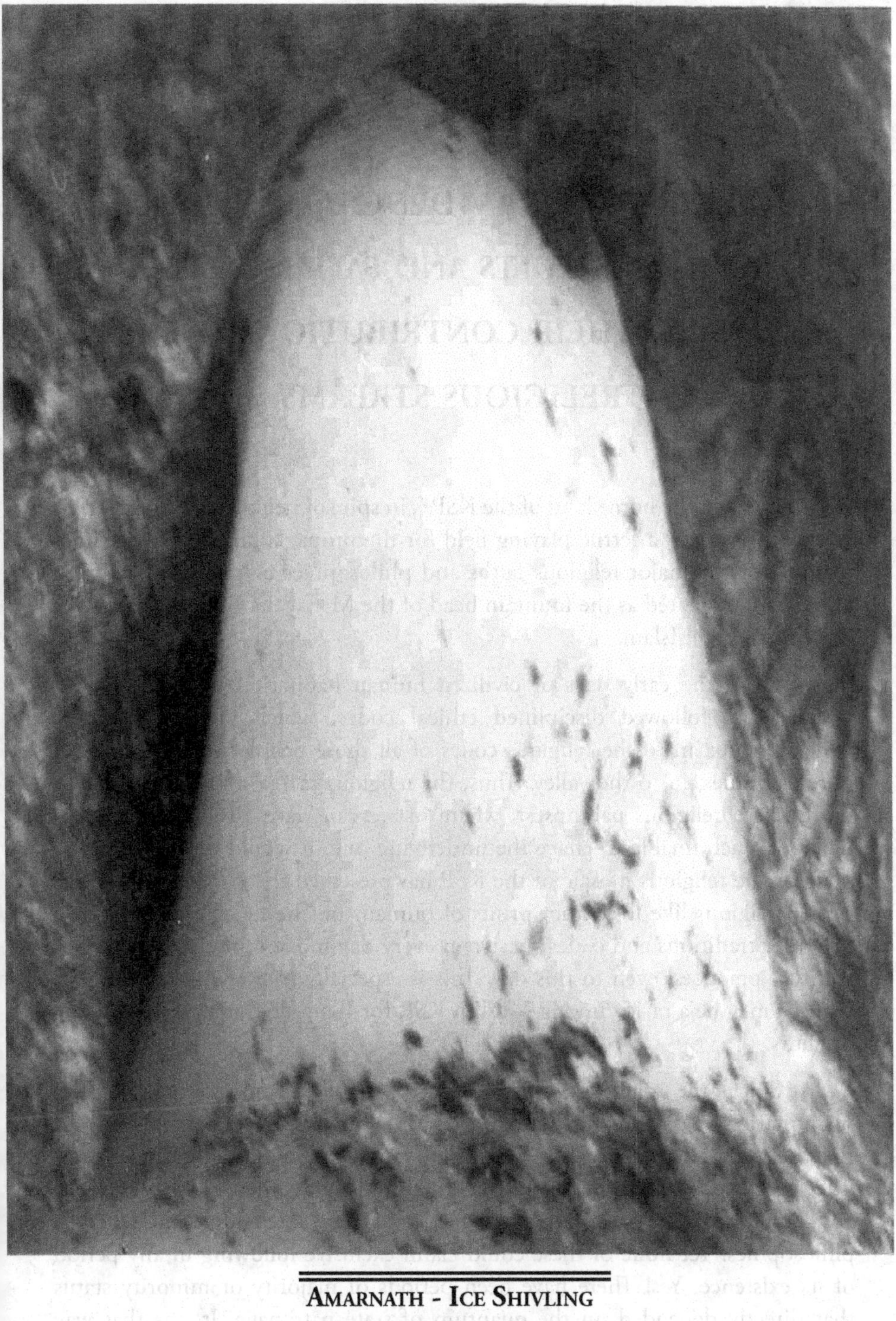

Amarnath - Ice Shivling

CHAPTER-4

RELIGION-THE EVIDENCES OF VARIOUS RELIGIOUS CULTS AND FAITHS OF THE KSP, AND THEIR CONTRIBUTION TO THESE RELIGIOUS STREAMS

Kashmir valley-the home land of the KSPs', in spite of being a small geographic territory, has been a fertile playing field for the propagation and perseverance of some of the major religious faiths and philosophies of the country. It has also been designated as the fountain head of the Mahayana Buddhism, Tantric Saivism and Sufi Islam.

From the early days of civilized human habitation in the valley, its people have followed disciplined ethical codes, which gradually evolved and integrated in to the religious codes of all those people who migrated, at different times, in to the valley. Thus, the religious scenario of the KSP looks more like a religious palimpsest, where in we can trace layer upon layer of religions; each unable to efface the underlying one. It would not be wrong to say that the religious mosaic of the KSP has preserved the evidences of all the earlier religions like fossil foot prints of humans on the sands of time. Traces of earlier traditions and codes survive in every day mode of their religious and spiritual practices, even to this day. This is especially true of the Hindu KSP, while it may be a rarity among Muslim KSP, for Islam does not permit mixing of faiths.

Since the dawn of history, innumerable people-conquerors and missionaries-have come and settled down in "this country taking this soil for their adopted home" and a welcome home for their religious faiths and creeds. The KSP, over its long history of recorded and unrecorded eras of existence has had the distinction of having practiced many a religions and religious philosophies. Yet none of these could claim exclusive following in any period of its existence. Yes! There have been periods of majority or minority status that directly depended on the quantum of state patronage. It was that way right from the days of organised Kin ship and through the eras of monarchy. Be it Nila the profounder of Naga cult; Ashoka the patron of Buddhism; Lalitaditiya the follower of Shaivism, or Rinchina the initiator of Islamic faith, religion of the ruler always flourished. The subjects adopted the ruler's faith to the extent that they could integrate it in their existing faith, unless they were forced to do otherwise as in the case of Islam.

Dr. S.S. Toshkhani writes, " Early Kashmiri derived its attitude to life and approach to reality, from a sense of harmony with nature. This gave rise to a spiritual and cultural climate in which different religious faiths flourished side by side without any antagonism. Thus, even before history was recorded, we find the religious fabric of Kashmiri life woven out of mature strands of Vaishnav, Shaiva and Buddhist, traditions with patterns of other heterogeneous modes of worship like that of the Naga cult revealing themselves on the margins. Not only did these different forms of worship co-exist peacefully, they also influenced each other, through a process of osmosis of concepts and ideas. In the age of Nilamata, some of these cults are centred on Vedic Gods like Vishnu, Rudra and other deities, for instance, we notice popular Naga deities' like Nila, Ananta (*Shesha*), "*Takshaka, Sushruvasa* etc. entering the Hindu pantheon. We also see Buddhist deities like *Avalokiteshvara* and *Tara* assume qualities and attributes of Hindu gods like Shiva and Durga. At a later stage, the Buddhist term of *shunyata* (nothing ness) entered the lexicon of Kashmir Saivism, though with a different interpretation. In the same manner, the Shaiva concept of universal consciousness provided the basis for the concept of reality in the Buddhist school of *Yogachara*."[1]

MAJOR RELIGIOUS CULTS

Major religious cults practiced by the KSP are basically off-shoots of the Sanatan Dharma (Hinduism). Hinduism is one of the oldest and the earliest faiths and is an unusual combination of many a subsidiary and corollary sects and cults. "It is a stupendously complex phenomenon. It could be said that there are more religions within Hinduism than out side of it. It has never discarded or excluded any thing, giving each teaching its particular niche within an ever expanding framework of ideas, beliefs and practices. In this way, Hinduism has been able to assimilate alien ideas and practices without fore going its own fundamental teachings. The more it has changed, the more it has remained the same."[2] Amongst the KSP, it has evolved chronologically from the primitive cults of polytheistic Ardnareshvera, to nature and elemental worship, to Naga cult, to the worship of Vishnu and the Vaisnava faith; to the cult of worshipping river goddesses, to the worship of the triad of the Hindu pantheon, to the worship of Siva Rudra, to the sophisticated Tantric Saivism, and most importantly introduction of Shakti worship. It has existed in all these forms at some time or the other in the religious stream of the KSP. Evidences and traditions prove that all these religions were, and are, even today, part and parcel of the religious culture of the KSP. We shall try to study and prove by recorded facts as to how and when these faiths evolved, established and flourished in Kashmir under the patronage of various rulers of different faiths, and also what was the contribution made by the Kashmiri speaking people to these great religious faiths and philosophies.

Naga Cult

In this chain the Naga cult /Naga worship or the snake cult, is deemed to be the earliest organised religion of these people as its practitioners the Nagas are the earliest recognized inhabitants of the valley. When exactly did the aboriginal KSP switch over from the primitive cult of nature and elemental worship to the Naga cult is difficult to establish with certainty, since this change over happened prior to the eras of recorded history. However there are recorded evidences, which point to the existence of Naga cult in the valley prior to third century BC, when Buddhism was ushered into the lives of the KSP and efforts were made to over shadow the existing Naga cult and convert the people to the new faith.

Evidences of the Naga Cult and Contributions of the KSP towards this cult:

Nilamata while describing the event of desiccation of the waters of the Lake Sati Sar and creation of the valley by Kashyapa mentions that the land was left under the care of Nila, the Naga king, by Lord Vishnu. It also elaborates as to how the emigrants were allowed to stay permanently in the valley on the condition that they would follow and observe Naga worship in their daily routine. From then on wards the people who settled in the valley accepted the cult of Naga worship, as they were given to under stand that the same was ordained by Lord Vishnu. They were already familiar with Vishnu, Shiva and other Hindu gods, and goddesses, so they willingly accepted this cult as one of the modes and offshoots of Hindu ethos. More ever to grant gravity to the Naga worship, the Naga deities of the Nilamata era (6th-7th century AD) are accorded to have had miraculous powers over rain, storm and snow, and their dwelling places are generally denoted as various lakes, pools and springs. It is while referring to such super human traits that the Naga king Nila is spoken of as the sender of water, and snow showers. The Naga Sadangula is stated to have turned the city named Candrapura into a lake.

Such emulations of these deities helped in the acceptance of Naga cult by the *Kashur*/KSP.

Dr. Ved Kumari records, "Kashmir was one of the principal centres of serpent worship in India. Though detailed evidence is lacking, there is no doubt that snake worship prevailed in the valley from a very early period. Regarding the exact date when the snake cult was prevalent in the land, no direct testimony is available. But there are reasons to believe that in the 4th and 3rd century B.C., it might have been the principal religion of Kashmir. In the Mahavamsa, (xii.3) it is said that Asoka's adviser Moggaliputta Tissa sent Majjhantika to preach Buddhism in Kashmir. When the *Sramana* reached the valley . . . . the King of the Nagas Aravala together with his followers submitted before the monk and accepted Buddhism. This was followed by the conversion into Buddhism of a large number of Naga worshippers of Kashmira-Gandhara."[3]

In the absence of written word, the impact, prevalence and the spread of any faith or religion is generally assessed by the number of temples built in honour of the faith; the festivals and rituals celebrated to commemorate it, and by the size of the population following its injunctions.

The elaborate and detailed account of some of the Naga deities, temples, festivals and modes of worship recorded in Nilamat Purana, compiled almost one thousand years after the inception of Buddhist faith in the valley, is proof enough of the existence of Naga worship in the earlier eras of the aboriginal KSP.

A detailed account of some of the festivals celebrated in honour of Nila the Naga king and even the time and mode of their celebrations is recorded in the N.P. and that is proof enough to the following of this cult. "Among these festivals, the main ones are the *Navahimapatmahotsava*, the *Iramenanjeri puja* and the *Varunapancam*i festival."[4]

The Puranic version of the celebration and worship of these three main Naga festivals is quite elaborate in comparison to present mode of celebration. I have quoted the details about these festivals as given in Dr, Gai's translation of N.P in the notes[5]. Among these festivals the festival of *Navahimapatmahotsava* (the festival of first snow fall) *Nav Sheen* as it is termed in the native tongue now, is celebrated by the KSP still. This festival marks the first snow fall of the season, and on this occasion Nila as well as the local Nagas were worshipped with offerings of flowers, fruits and incense of bdelliums during the Puranic era. Tradition of celebrating this festival, in a very short and symbolic form, continues even to this day or should I say till the exile of Hindu KSP from the valley in the year 1990. I remember during my days in college, we would eagerly look forward to this event and would feel elated to be the first to report the good news of the first snow fall by shouting '*navsheen mubark*'. Usually the first snow fall would happen during the night time, as if nature also conspired to contribute to the surprise element of the event. As a celebration a non-vegetarian feast, would be cooked and served. The menu specially included—Pachen-nadur dish. (Wild duck and the lotus stem cooked together).

Besides the festivals the names of some six hundred prominent Nagas, who were worshipped in the land of KSP during that era, are recorded in the Nilamata Purana. The names of the guards of the mountain passes of the valley, [the four *Dvarpalas (dikpalas)*] recorded are Naga Bindusara in the east, Naga Elapatra in the west, Naga Srimadaka in the south and Naga Uttarmanasa in the north connoting the importance of Naga cult.

The Nagas are presumed to have resided in the lakes and springs or more likely along the banks and Ghats of these water bodies, hence quite a few temples and pilgrimage centres had come up in these areas. Even now names of places like Verinag, Anantnag, Vecharnag etc. are famous religious centres and, if not any thing else, these places speak of their Naga origin by virtue of their name. Kalhana in his chronicle of Kashmir at the very out set recognises the valley as the land protected by Nila the lord of the Nagas.[6]

RajaTarangni was compiled in the eleventh century AD, when Buddhism had undermined the Naga beliefs and to some extent even Buddhism had started loosing its grip and under such circumstances if Kalhana records some Naga events it shows the importance of the cult in the KSP religious life. Kalhana narrates:

a) The stories about kings who were still sympathetic to the faith and describe their individual contributions to keep the faith alive.

b) Kalhana's detailed description of Susrava Naga and his alliance with a Brahman.[7]

c) The Naga Ancestry of king Durlabavardhana.[8]

d) The account of Naga Mahapadma, the tutelary deity of the Wular Lake. These evidences are enough to prove the importance and influence of the Naga cult that continued even in the 11th century.

Further the KSP's celebrated a great festival in honour of Taksaka Naga on the 12th day of the dark fortnight of the month of Jyaishta up to 11th century AD.[9] Both Ksemendra (8th century) and Kalhana (11th century) have given a detailed description of this festival of the 'Taksaka Yatra'.

RELIGION-THE EVIDENCES OF VARIOUS RELIGIOUS CULTS AND FAITHS

In addition to the local sources of information we also have records about the existence of Naga cult in the valley in various external sources especially in the classic literature, like Mahavamsa; that has recorded as to how the local inhabitants of the valley, who were followers of the Naga cult repulsed the efforts of the Majjhantika to convert them to Buddhism initially in 3rd 4th century B.C.[10]

Records preserved in the Chinese *Vinaya* of *Mula-Sarvastivadin* sect, state that Hiuen Tsang the Chinese traveller cum scholar, who visited the valley in 7th century AD, gives a detailed account of how the arhat Majjhantika rescued the valley from the Nagas and established Buddhist faith in the country. Even the Tibetan scholar Boston in his book History of Buddhism writes about subduing of the tough trouble some Nagas and converting them to the new faith.[11]

Abul-Fazal who came to the valley during the reign of Akbar, (1556-1605AD) records the numerical strength of the places of worship of different faiths in Kashmir. As per him, "there were 45 places dedicated to the worship of Siva, 64 to Vishnu, 3 places to Brahma, 22 to Durga but there were 700 places in the valley where, there were carved images of the snakes which the inhabitants worshipped"[12]

This scenario prevailed in spite of the fact that by 16th century AD Buddhism was already replaced by Brahmanism and Shaivism; along with it Islam was also accepted as one of the main religious faiths by the majority KSPs' of the valley. This proves how Naga cult was assimilated and accepted by the Hindu KSP as a part of their religious life.

Nilamata records that in 6th and 7th century the cults of Vishnu, Siva, and other Brahmanical and folk deities, along with Buddha and the Nagas were flourishing side by side in Kashmir. While analysing this scenario, Ved Kumari writes, "The influences which each cult received from the others are discernible throughout the work and many verses reveal the spirit of compromise and synthesis in the field of religion. The Brahmanic deities, the Nagas, the Pisachas' and Buddha, all receive their due share of worship from the inhabitants of Kasmira."[13] This aspect is further substantiated by the fact that many a religious ceremonies, worships, festivals and traditions of the Naga cult like the festival of *Khichri Amavasya, Gadha Batta, (Gare Devta pujan), Asarhastami, Kavpunim* etc. are still surviving and are celebrated with due sanctity by the Hindu KSP of the present era,

Buddhism

Buddha the founder of Buddhism is introduced as the incarnation of Vishnu in the Nilamata Purana and It is believed that, Buddhism, obtained a footing in Kashmir in the 3rd century B.C.as it "was in vogue there from the time of Surrendra, the earliest Buddhist ruler of Kashmir, who ruled about a century ahead of the time of Ashoka (273-232B.C)"[14]. Yet it flourished only after Ashoka's patronage.

Ashoka, who ruled the Kingdom of Gandhar and Kashmir along with the rest of Bharata, in the third century B.C, was a staunch Buddhist. During his rule Majjhantika revived Buddhism in the valley and was able to convert large numbers to the new faith under the patronage of the King. Being a staunch follower of Buddha philosophy he spared no effort in spreading the new faith in every nook and corner of the valley.[15]

Since Buddhism did not follow the policy of vehement force and conversion it was able to make peaceful inroads in to the religious regimen of the KSP. It could spread smoothly by its non-interfering religious policy. Thus Buddhism thrived along with the existing kind of Saivism and the haphazard polytheistic religion the Naga cult that was prevalent in the valley. In his efforts to cultivate his faith the emperor built numerous Stupas and Viharas in the valley there by trying to lay a solid foundation of the new faith in the valley. Yet it was not accepted by one and all. As is evident from the fact that after Ashoka's death his successor Jalauka followed the Shaivite religion and mostly the reluctant converts reverted back to Shaivism. So we can safely assume both religions existed side by side till the arrival of the Turuska Kings in the 1st century AD.

During the reign of Kushan kings i.e. Hushka, Jushka and Kanishka; whole valley was under the possession of Buddhism. Numerous Viharas, Mathas, and caityas were built all over the place. People practised the faith of Baudas and achieved a mark of excellence in every aspect and nuance of the new faith. It was due to the interest of the rulers and efforts of the people, that Kashmira was recognised as a great centre of Buddhism under the rule of Kanishka. Fourth Buddhist council was organised in the valley, to "revise, review and reinterpret" the Buddhist texts so that the purity of its canon could be preserved. It was a monumental event at which eighteen different sects accepted the conclusion of the Council, leading to the emergence of the Mahayana school.

Hiuen Tsang, the Chinese pilgrim, visited Kashmir in about 631 AD and stayed on for nearly two years to study and gather knowledge of the prevailing Buddhist scriptures. He was accommodated at the famous; "Jayendra Vihara" and the king provided him twenty scribes to copy the sacred manuscripts and scriptures. He enjoyed the liberal hospitality of the Hushkapura monastery for several days and was escorted with honour to the capital where he found numerous religious institutions attended by five thousand monks. Hushkapura -modern small village named Uskur- was founded by Hushka, and occupied a place of great importance as a Buddhist centre. It was known as the eastern gate of the valley. He spent his time in studying the "*Sutras*" and "*Sastras.*" He has left an authoritative account of his researches in theology and the sciences. He has recorded in detail the fourth Buddhist council and it's achievements, where in he writes, "Several commentaries were written, on the *sutra, Vinaya and Abhidharma*; in the said council. The original text and its explanation came to be known as *Upadesha Shastra,* and *Vibasha Shastra*. Kanishka had these treatises engraved on copper plates and deposited them at a Stupa apparently in Kashmir."[16]

According to Yuan-Chwang-the Chinese authority and contemporary of Emperor Kanishka-the king got all the Buddhist treatises discussed at the Assembly. The assembly was also responsible for the preparation of three authoritative volumes of Buddhism which had far-reaching effects on later-day Buddhist thought and philosophy.

This council was a new landmark in the History of Buddhism. Hiuen Tsang writes about the above mentioned inscriptions, "Kanishka raja forth with ordered these discourses to be engraved on sheets of red copper. He enclosed them in a stone receptacle; and having sealed this, he raised over it a Stupa with the scriptures in the middle. He commanded the Yakshas to defend the approaches to the kingdom so as not to permit the other sects to get these *Shastras* and take them away, with the view that those dwelling in the country might enjoy the fruit of his labour". [17]

From the available records of the Chinese and Tibetan travellers abundant information is preserved about the places of importance in the spread and extent of Buddhist faith in the valley. Besides the given references and details in R.T. about places like Pandrethan, Kanishpura, Harwan, Hushkapura, the archaeological discoveries at Pandrethan, Paraspora and Gilgat throw enough light on the state and spread of Buddhism in the valley, the religion followed by KSP till almost the end of 8th century.

Buddhism flourished in the valley in the 7th century, and while enumerating the number of Buddhist establishments Hiuen-Tsang records, "Buddhist monasteries, over 100 in number, and there were 5,000 Buddhist brethren; and there were four Asoka topes each containing at its top a *Sheng* or pint of the bodily relics of the Buddha".[18] Where as Ou-Kong who came later to Kashmir towards the end of the 8th century records that the number of Buddhist monasteries was more than three hundred.[19] He lived in the valley for four years as a Buddhist Bhikshu, visiting holy places and shrines associated with Lord Buddha's name. Like Hiuen-Tsang, Ou-K'ong too made an extensive study of Sanskrit works and Buddhist scriptures and literature at its fountain-head.

From the accounts of these two Chinese scholars we gather that, "The Buddhist-cum-Hindu society had begun to succumb to stagnation and ritualism" hence Buddhism was losing ground in the beginning of the 7th century when Hiuen Tsang, visited Kashmir, where as at the time of Ou-Kong's visit in 759-63 AD, Buddhism had apparently started flourishing again. This undoubtedly indicates a rise in the popularity of Buddhism in the valley during the period of the Karakotas."[20]

Though the supremacy of Buddhism lasted mainly till the end of 8th century AD, yet the importance and influence of this faith continued in the religious stream of KSP. Kalhana records not only did the Kushan kings patronise this faith, local rulers like Meghvahana, and Pravarsena also gave their full support to it by:

1) **Prohibiting animal slaughter for sacrifices;**

2) **Building Viharas for the Buddhist monks' and**

3) **Erecting the statues of Buddha.**[21]

The rulers of the Karakota dynasty, who ruled the valley after the Kushans, were followers of Hinduism and worshipped mainly Hindu Gods and Goddesses like Shiva, Vishnu, Surya, Saraswati, Lakshmi and Ganesha etc. and yet they continued to pay respect and support to the Buddhist faith.

There are umpteen references in Kalhana's chronicle about the acts of patronage of Karakotas towards the religion of the Buddha. At Hushkapura, a colossal copper image of Buddha was made by Lalitaditya Muktapida. At Parihasapura, Cankuna, a Tukhara minister of the king erected the Cankuna Vihara, built a Stupa and placed there in a golden image of Jina, (Buddha).[22] Second Vihara, together with a caityas was built by the minister at Srinagara and in this Vihara the minister put a brownish image of Buddha Sugata, which was brought from Magadha on the shoulders of an elephant.[23]

Jayapida Vinayaditya, another celebrated monarch of the Karakota family, set up three images of Buddha and a large Vihara at his newly founded town Jayapura.[24]

Kalhana's records in his chronicle are duly supplemented by the Archaeological discoveries. Excavations carried out at Parihasapura, the city founded by Lalitaditya, have brought to light Buddhist Structures: a Stupa, a monastery and a caitya. The Stupa has been identified as the Stupa of Cankuna, the monastery with Rajavihra built by Lalitaditya and the large caitya said to have been founded by the same monarch. Among the sculptures discovered at Parihasapura, are the two images of Bodhisattva and Buddha.[25] These go to prove the popularity of Buddhism in the days of the Karakotas.

Buddhism, however, seems to have been overshadowed by the end of the Karakota period by Vaishnava and Saiva faith that became predominant in the valley in the centuries following this period. The Utpala dynasty supplanted the Karakotas about the middle of the 9th century AD Founder of this dynasty, Avantivarman (AD 855/56-883) was a staunch Hindu and the architectural remains that have been discovered from the site of Avantipura, the town founded by this monarch, include images of Vishnu, Shiva, and other gods of Hindu pantheon. Not a single figure of Buddha or Bodhisattva has been reported from these temples.

"The opinion cherished by some scholars that from the middle of the 9th century on till the advent of the 11th century, the Buddhists fell on evil days and all the kings were anti-Buddhist in spirit, is an extreme view, yet to be established."[26] Except Kshemagupta (AD 950-958 and Harsa (AD 1089-11(1) no king of this period is known to have cherished any anti Buddhist feeling. Kalhana records that Kshemagupta burnt down a Buddhist monastery named Jayendra Vihara.[27] From this decaying vihara, he took away the brass image of Buddha Sugata and the stones of the temple, which he utilized for a Siva temple in his own name.[28] Ksemagupta, further confiscated thirty-two villages which belonged to the burnt vihara and gave them to the Khasa ruler.[29]

Yet the wrath of a cruel eccentric king against a single particular Buddhist monastery would not be taken as an instance of systematic policy of religious persecution adopted by the state against the Buddhist religion. The same can be said about Harsha who in his periods of rage and lust did not spare any images and temples, be they of Buddhist, Hindu or any other faith.[30]

We find Kings who ruled even after the 11th century venerated the Buddhist faith and one can definitely assume that all through and till the last days of Hindu period, Buddhism was held in high honour in Kashmir and it has left an indelible mark on the every day life-religious and spiritual activities-of the Hindu KSP permanently. We can attribute some character traits of the KSP, like contentment, simple living high thinking, laid back attitude, offering the other cheek instead of reacting with violence, happy to live in a state of penury, the culture of painting and ritual arts and so on as the residue of Buddhism in their life.

J N Ganahar writes, "The place of Kashmir in the history of Buddhism was great indeed. From the moment Buddhism was preached in the valley, Kashmir became the mistress of the Buddhist doctrine and particularly the citadel of the Sarasvativada School. She played a great role in the spread of Buddhism beyond India to Kandhar and Kabul and Bactria and thence to Central Asia and China. Tibetan Buddhism also drew its inspiration from Kasmir."[31]

An event of great significance in the history of Buddhist learning, the fourth Great Buddhist Council as mentioned earlier, was held in Kashmir in the Kundlavana-vihara, near about the present Harwan water-reservoir, in Kanishka's time in the first century AD.[32]

The greatest contribution by the KSP towards the Buddhist faith was the creation of Mahayana School of Buddhism: a philosophy that raised the status of its followers from the state of '*Arhat hood*' (good of the self, preached by the *Hynyan* school) to the state of '*Bodhisattva*' (good of the humanity at large).

Nagarjuna, the great Buddhist scholar came to Kashmir and, stayed to study the scriptures and in consultation with Kashmirian scholars and thinkers, he established, 'the radical school of Mahayana Buddhism.' Kalhana writes, "And Bodhisattva lived in this country as a sole lord of the land, namely the glorious Nagarjuna, who resided at Sadarhadvana." As per H.H.Wilson, "It was he who denominated the Saka era now in vogue in India."

Buddhism continued to occupy an important position right up to the advent of Islam. Rulers kept providing liberal patronage to it, by building Viharas and Stupas. Toshkhani writes, "At a time when the barbaric hordes of Mahmud Ghazni were putting thousands to the sword, Kashmiri artists were painting murals in Western Tibet."[33]

Shaivism/ Saivism

History of the beginning of Saivism in Kashmir is lost in the maze of antiquity just like the story of the origin of the KSP. It is believed that prior to the induction of Naga cult as well as the Buddhist faith, the KSP in the aboriginal state of their existence worshipped Shiva, who either originated in the valley or entered it from some where, at an earlier period along with other Brahmanical Gods and Goddesses of Hindu pantheon. Shiva the primeval god of creation as one of the triads of the Hindu pantheon occupies the place of ultimate spiritual awakening in the life of his worshippers. When exactly did Shiva worship become part of the KSP's culture is difficult to pin point. Was Siva one of them or was he an immigrant. The former perception, in a way, is authenticated by the miraculous phenomenon of the formation of the ice lingam in the cave abode of Shiva along the banks of Amravati stream consistently for almost last two millennia's'. In the lighter vein one is tempted to believe as if the lord by the perpetual formation of the lingam wishes to proclaim His ownership right or as per the law of the land renew His state subject certificate.

One thing is certain that Saivism was not a late entrant in the religious culture of *Kashur*. Shiva in some form or the other was worshipped by the KSP right from the creation of the land of Satisar. In the earliest chronological records Siva is known as *Rudra, Sarva, Mahadeva, Bhava Hara Mahesvara, Sambu*, Siva etc. and his abodes mentioned are *Amaresvara, Vijayeshwara*, and Amarnatha and so on. The physical description and the ensemble of Siva given in N.P are similar to what we come across in the present times. The importance of *Bhutesvara and Kapatesvara*; the two shrine temples built in honour of Siva are given in detail in the same Purana. There are some references to the non Vedic nature of Siva. He is associated with the *Pisachas* and *Raksasaas a*nd that is why on Siva Chaturdasi he is worshipped by the Pisacha chief Nikumba along with his followers. Ved Kumari observes, "Thus N.P. has preserved the tradition of Siva's savage associations, which induces us to see in him some non Vedic divinity, identified with Vedic Rudra."[34] That in turn substantiates the Antiquity of Siva worship in the valley.

We have evidence of Siva worship prior to the Buddhist faith in the form of shrines and temples existing much before the days of Ashoka's reign. Kalhana records in R.T. that even Ashoka had built two temples of *Siva-Ashokeshvara.*[35] and was a devotee of Siva in-spite of his having spread Buddhism as the main faith in the valley.[36] His son Jaluka and other rulers that followed: Damodara1, Huna chief Mihirkhula, Gokarna, Tunjina, Pravarsena I, Pravarsena II, Meghavahana, Samdhimat *(Aryaraja)* and Ranaditya were votaries of Siva and erected temples and shrines in honour of Siva, prior to the reign of Karakotas.

From the Karakota dynasty onwards Saivism thrived under the royal patronage of Kings like Lalitaditya who consecrated a lofty temple of Siva *Jyestharudra* and offered a large sum of money, land and villages for the maintenance of the temple and the shrine of Siva Butesa.[37] Like wise, the kings, queens and important personages of the Utpala dynasty and the two Lohara dynasties also patronised Saivism. Temples and shrines were consecrated to Siva and some of the destroyed and demolished temples were reconstructed during these periods. Among the famous ones recorded by Kalhana are the *Siva Avantisvara* built at Avantipura by Avantivarman[38] and Siva *Ranesvara* by the Lohara King Samgram Raja.[39] Temple of *Siva Avantisvara*, founded by Avantivarman, with massive walls now stands sadly mutilated just outside the village of Avantipura. The temples of *Samkaragaurisa* and Sugandha have been identified with two ruined temples of Patan. Temples at Naran nag has been identified by Stein with the, *Jyesthesa temple* of Lalitaditya and another large temple in the same site with Bhutesvara.[40] Most of the Saiva images whether in his phallic or in his human form have been destroyed. Yet, among the few early sculptural representations of Shiva that have survived till date, mention may be made of the following: seated figure of *Lakulisa f*orm of Siva at Pandrethan, several sculptured reliefs' of Siva at the temple of Payer including Siva seated cross-legged on throne under the canopy of an overhanging tree and surmounted by votaries; Siva Bhairva pursuing a human being; six-headed dancing Siva; three-headed Siva seated cross-legged; a large human faced Siva-Linga at Baramulla; a three-headed Siva image and a three-headed Siva alto-relievo from Avantipura.[41]

KASHMIR SHAIVISM AND THE *TRIKA* PHILOSOPHY

Earliest form of Saivism followed in Kashmir was dualistic and hence, there was a clash and confusion on account of the meditative Buddhist beliefs in the society. It was based on a number of Tantras and seems to have preached a dualistic doctrine. From the 8th/9th century, however, the Saiva system of Kashmir assumed a new character. Based on pure *Advaita tatva*, it henceforth began to preach a sort of idealistic monism. The Kashmiri thinkers of monism believe that Shiva and Shakti are not two separate entities or polarities. They are one and only one. Shakti is the power within Shiva that helps him to act or perform any *Kriya* (action). Without Shakti, Shiva would be powerless in simple parlance. "The Kashmiri Shavites believe in the combination of the *Jnan* (knowledge) and *Kriya* (action) unlike the Vedantists. This new system took the name of Trika Sastra. The founder of this new doctrine was a holy sage, named Vasugupta, who probably lived in the early years of the 9th century AD in Kashmir."[42]

S. Shukla writes, "When in the 8th Century AD Saivism had its epoch in Kasmira, it had before it the tremendous task of establishing itself over Buddhism and a haphazard polytheistic religion prevalent in those days. This was possible only when Tantric Saivism could prove itself as powerful and unique in itself. The Tantric Saivism flourished with both these qualities. It not only imbibed the meditative and philosophical aspect of Buddhism but also the ritualistic aspect of a mixed religion which had eventually developed by the mixture of the local polytheistic religion and Buddhism. Another reason for the rise of the Tantric Saivism was that it had scriptural support as against this mixed faith which had no such authority. This was a very important factor which could attract the common people and therefore they accepted it as their ancestral faith, This Tantric Shaivism due to its popularity in Kashmira was later on called Kashmira Saivism. KSP brought out a more logical and correct path consistent in all respects. The conflict in different ideologies was removed by it by finding out harmonious principals."[43]

Trika

To enumerate further we can say the Shaivism of Kashmir is a distinct philosophy in its own right, which originated in Kashmir, though it may have some connections with similar philosophies elsewhere. This original philosophy, which is generally called the Trika philosophy by the Kashmiris, is of divine origin and as such they refuse the authority of the Vedanta philosophies. The Trika is the fundamental science of three most vital facts of universal experience, namely: (a) Human being, (b) universe and (c) adjustment

"While all these three are dealt with in the Trika, it is the human who is its primal as well as final concern, so much so that the Trika Shastra might as well be called the science of humanism. The Trika does not just stop here, but analysis a human being's entire construction: physical, mental and spiritual. In addition to the analysis of the human form it also analysis universe into thirty six principles, and gives us, in detail, the exact method of knowing these principles in direct experience and realising them as positive facts. Trika is meant for all human beings without any distinction of sex, creed, caste or colour."

Three Divisions of its Literature

Trika has a very extensive literature, comprising three different divisions, namely:

(a) The *Agama Shastra*,

(b) the *Spanada Shastra* and

(c) the *Pratyabhijna Shastra*[44]

The *Agama* literally means what has come down from remote antiquity. The *Spanada* literally means energy and it has reference to the fact that the whole universe in all its aspects, physical, psychic and spiritual, is nothing but a play of energy or vibration manifested. The *Pratyabhijna* primarily means the recognition of one's own-self that means the recognition of Shiva.

SHAIVIC TREATISES AND THEIR COMPOSERS

A legend associated with Vasugupta and his Siva-sutra is that Lord Siva instructed Vasugupta in a dream to go to Mahadev peak in Kashmir to find the sutras inscribed on a stone slab there, and propagate them among the people. The legend goes that Vasugupta, as instructed by Siva, went to the mountain and found the sutras accordingly. The purport of the legend, if interpreted rationally, would be that Vasugupta received the non-dual Saiva philosophy in a state of spiritual inspiration and then presented it in the form of sutras.[45]

As per records, in the 8th century AD Vasugupta expounded the Shaivite teachings extensively. He also composed an authoritative treatise the Spanda-Karika on the subject of naed; and in the 9th century AD Kallata Bhatt wrote another treatise, namely the *Spanda Vriti*. Soma Nand further elaborated the system and explained its intricacies in *Shiva Drishti*.

In the tenth century AD, Upal Deva wrote some authoritative treatises, which are still considered as the basis of the Monistic Shaivite Yoga philosophy of Kashmir. But the greatest authority on Kashmir Shaivism was Abhinavagupta of the 10th century AD, who wrote many an imperishable works on Saivism and the most outstanding among them is *'Tantraloka'*

Ksemendra, Kshema Raja and Yoga Raja are the three outstanding names in the history of Kashmir's Shaivism, who, besides elaborating the fundamentals of the system, were instrumental in spreading its philosophical message far and wide. The lamp of Saivism burnt in the valley through out the period of Hindu rule and even afterwards, and as late as the 18th century AD a work on the Pratyabhijna Sastra was-composed by a writer named Sivopadhyaya. In the 20th century this work was continued by yet another great scholar and teacher of Shaivism, Swami Lakshman Joo, revered as "*Param Shaiva Trikacharya*" by the devotees of the Trika Darshan Philosophy around the globe. "Swami Ji was instrumental in enlarging the boundaries of Kashmir Shaivism to the Western world." [46]

RELIGION-THE EVIDENCES OF VARIOUS RELIGIOUS CULTS AND FAITHS

With the untiring research of these Shaiva philosophers and scholars, Kashmir became the fountain-head of Shaivite philosophy, and scholars and philosophers came to its centres of learning from the rest of India, to study the latest developments in Shaivism. It was in this quest that Shankara, the great Shaivite teacher from the south, travelled to Kashmir towards the end of the 9th century AD and preached his monistic doctrine from the famous, "Gopa Hill"/Gupkar, opposite the Dal Lake. This hill later received a new name- "Shankaracharya hill"-after this great teacher "Shankara", and the temple at the top of this hill built earlier by King Gopaditya in the 4th century B.C., is celebrated as the "Shankaracharya Temple".

It is said that this great teacher who did not otherwise believe in the divine powers of Shakti became conscious and realised the importance of Shakti in the realm of creation when he visited Kashmir. The story details that when he along with his troop of followers came to the valley, locals aware of his anti-concept of the powers of Shakti provided them with all the necessary facilities for survival on the mountain top, except the means to light fire to cook. This continued almost for a month and his men had to literally starve all this while. This was his first lesson to realise the power of energy / Shakti. The second incident recorded by scholars is that when he had a *Shastraarth* (discussion) with the Saiva philosophers of Kashmir he was defeated by the great philosopher Madan Misra's wife, when she asked him questions regarding *Kama* (sexual aspects of life). He was dumbfounded and accepted the powers of Shakti. It is after this incident that Shankaracharya composed his famous treatise: *Soundriya Lahri* in honour of Devi / *Shakti.*

In the 11th century AD, yet another great religious teacher of the south, Ramanuja, who was the head of the rival Vaishnavite sect, travelled to Kashmir to study the rich Shaivite scriptures / *Tantras*, the source and the basis for Kashmir Saiva philosophy- since Kashmir Saivism is the culmination of the Tantric traditions- the central philosophy of Tantrism.[47]

While Kshemendra (10th century) has recorded that Saivism and Buddhism were the chief religious faiths followed in the society, we have no hint of the Trika system In Kalhana's Rajatarangini. If he is to be believed, then in the 11th century AD and even afterwards the old traditional Pasupata Saivism prevailed in the valley. At the same time simultaneously Vaisnavism was also gaining ground because the Saiva teachers and the Buddhist monks instead of following the path of religion showed a bent of mind towards corruption. They showed signs of all kinds of disrespect to the religious dogmas either because of ignorance or due to an inability to follow the philosophical and ethical theme of the idealistic monism of the *Trika* system. Hence people preferred to seek solace under the precepts of Vaisnavism.[48]

Vaisnavism

Vaisnavism occupies an important place in the Nilamata. As per Puranas and Brahmanas, Lord Vishnu, one of the triads of the Hindu pantheon, occupied a very important place in the KSP religious ethos from the earliest eras. The importance of Vishnu cult and its antiquity during the Nilamata era can be gauged by the very fact that the creation of the land and draining of the Satisar Lake was initiated by the orders of Vishnu and also by the mention of Vishnu more than any other deity in the festivals elaborated in this Purana. Besides, the detailed description of Vishnu's appearance, ensemble and modes of worship along with the different Avatars (incarnations) of Vishnu like *Matsya, Kurma, Varaha, Hamsa, Asvasiras,Narasimha, Vamana, Rama, Madhusudana, Buddha* and so on given in the Purana, prove that the KSPs were practicing Vaishnavism in the Puranic era. The Purana also records, that Vishnu as Varahaavatara (boar incarnation) lifted the earth with his tusk and tore the mountain to pieces.[49] and the *Varahatirtha* is mentioned frequently and people would visit this place as it was considered as good as performing a *Rajasuya* sacrifice.[50]

Ved Kumari writes, "The popularity of the Vaisnava cult in early Kashmira, as indicated by the Nilamata, is corroborated by the Vishnu Dharmotttara Purana mentioning Kashmira as a seat of Vishnu in the form of Cakrin."[51]

As a rule the supremacy of a faith ascended or descended according to the extent of patronage received at the hands of the rulers. The same pattern followed in case of Vaisnavism after the Nilamata era.

Rajatarangini refers to many Vishnu images, shrines and temples consecrated by various kings, queens and other personalities of importance, during their rule that are detailed here in a chronological order.

In late 6th century AD Image of *Vishnu Jayasvamin* was consecrated by king Pravarsena [52], and an image of *Vishnu Ranasvamin* was consecrated by king Ranaditya near his capital Pravarapura.[53] Jayanta Bhatta confirms the consecration of this image in *Agamadambara*. Mankha refers to his father's worship of Ranasvamin.[54] Jonaraja also mentions Ranasvamin Vishnu in his commentary and describes it as *'Sripravarapurapradhanadevata* (the supreme devta).

In the 7th century AD, When Karakotas' ruled the valley, Vaisnavism gained ascendance as Vishnu was the adored deity of the family. Karakotas built many illustrious shrines and temples of Vishnu all through their period of reign. King Durlabavardhana's son Malhana built a shrine of *Vishnu Malhasvamin*, [55], while the king himself consecrated at Srinagari the shrine of Vishnu Durlabhasvamin.[56]

Candrapida, (8th century AD) consecrated the shrine of Vishnu *Tribhuvanasvamin*. Lalitaditya who was a great devotee of Lord Vishnu built a shrine of Kesava Vishnu at Hushkapura; he also built a splendid shrine of Vishnu Muktasvamin.[57] At Parihasapura, which is supposed to have been constructed by the king in honour of his adored deity Vishnu, he built the glorious silver statue of Vishnu *Parihasakesava* and yet another famous image of Vishnu *Muktakeshva*, was made out of gold at Hushkapura.[58]

The Utpala dynasty that succeeded the Karakotas followed in the same vein. Avantivarman (AD 855/56-883), the first king of the dynasty, built the shrines of Vishnu Avantisvamin. His brother Samara founded Kesava in his quadruple form in a temple called *Samarasvamin*. Suyya, the irrigation minister of Avantivarman also built a temple of *Hrsikesa Yogasavamin* at the confluence of Sindhu and Vitasta.[59]

Besides these temples and idols, "The popularity of the cult of Vishnu in the happy valley, during the 8th and 9th centuries is further attested to by a large number of images discovered from various ancient ruins. These include a few busts and heads of Vishnu which have been recovered from Vijabror, three-faced Vishnu figures carved on the walls of the Martand temple; relief sculptures of *Caturbhuja Vishnu* and Vishnu seated between consorts hailing from the ruins of Andarkoth, and four-headed Vishnu images from Avantipura and the surroundings."[60]

Kalhana has recorded in chronological order the progress of Vaisnavism in Kashmir, from the 10th century onwards, in the Rajatarangini in a great detail. He records the names of all those Royal personalities who patronised and built monuments to the glory of Vaishnavite faith. Queen Sugandha (AD 904-906) built a temple of Vishnu Gopala Kesava and her daughter-in-law Nandi founded a temple of *Nandikesava*. A temple of Vishnu *Meruvardhanasvami* was built by Partha's minister (AD 906-921); Yasaskara (AD939-948) started the construction of a temple of Vishnu Yasaskarasvamin, which, when he died, was left incomplete. The construction was completed by Parvagupta (AD 949-950). About the same time, Bhima, the illustrious monarch of the Sahi dynasty, who was the maternal grandfather of Ksemagupta's queen Didda, built a high temple of *Bhimakesava*.[61] About the end of the third quarter of the 10th century AD queen Didda, founded a series of Vishnu shrines like the *Abhimanyusvamin* temple, the shrine of *Vishnu Simhasvamin* and two temples under the name of Vishnu *Diddasvamin.*[62]

In the 11th century when Harsa the iconoclast destroyed a large number of Hindu and Buddhist images, one among them was the famous shrine of *Parihasakesava,* which was later replaced by king Uccala, who reigned in the early years of the 12th century AD[63] Uccala also restored the decayed temple of the ancient shrine of Vishnu *Cakradhara.*

Vaisnavism was popular even after Uccala's death. Ratnavali Jayasimha's queen established V*aikunthamatha* and other pious buildings in honour of Vishnu.[64]

Jonaraja mentions that Ramadeva, renewed the Vishnu temple at Utpalapura and Udayanadeva, donated all golden ornaments in his treasury to this temple. [65]

S.C.Ray writes, On the whole, "In the Vaisnavism of Kashmir, we find a synthesis of the different Vaishnava cults, which were current in ancient India. In it seems to have mingled, the faith of the Vedic Vishnu, the system of the *Pancaratra* School, the religion of the *Satvats* and the faith in the cowherd god *Gopala Krsna.* Rama was worshipped as an incarnation of Vishnu but there is no definite evidence of the existence of Rama-cult in early Kashmir. Rama seems to have been worshipped only as an incarnation of Vishnu. The same impression is gathered from the information given in the N.P. were it is mentioned that Buddha was worshipped as an incarnation of Vishnu and no mention of Rama is given. Systematized *Avataravada* (Prophet Cult) is believed to have come to the people of the valley by 11th century AD among the various incarnations of Vishnu, *Varaha* (boar), *Krsna,* and *Nrsimha* (man-lion) were most popular." [66]

MINOR GODS AND GODDESSES

Besides the main religious philosophies and faiths illustrated above, many a minor Gods and Goddesses amalgamated in the religious stream of the KSP. Though Siva and Vishnu occupied the most important and prominent place in the Kashmiri cults of worship, yet there were many a minor gods and goddesses like *Surya, Ganesha, Agni, Lakshmi, Durga, Sharika and Raginya* etc. whose worship was common among the KSP. Many a literary and archaeological evidences exist to support the said fact. One among them is the world renowned Martand temple, an archaeological wonder, which was dedicated to the worship of Aditya/ Surya, (the sun god)

Ganesha

Ganesha, one of the most popular minor gods of the Hindus, was worshiped in the valley from the days of antiquity. Vinayaka Ashtami in the month of Asadha is dedicated to the worship of Ganesha. This tradition continues even at present. Every ceremony, be it religious or social, begins with the invocation of lord Ganesha, both in the form of a puja or any other event with the recitation of Ganesh mantra, seeking blessings for the successful culmination of the ceremony. Lord Ganesha is known by many names, like *Vinayaka, Heramba, Ekdenta, Lambodra, Vignesh, Ganapati, and Gajanana* and so on. There are many temples dedicated to lord Ganesha and one of the oldest and most famous is the rock Ganesha at the base of the Hariparbat Hill, locally known as *Ganishun.* Here 'Ganesha is represented by a massive vermilion-smeared bossy, bumpy rock formation symbolizing the elephantine head of the venerated god that is facing towards the east of the city in order to have a better view of the city built by Pravarsena.' Offering obeisance at this temple is a must in the ritual process of the Parikrama or circumbulation around the holly shrine of Shri Chakreshwera at the Hari Parbat. N.P records that the worship of Vinayaka / Ganesha, was essential to be performed on the eve of the anointing ceremony of the kings. Kshemendra mentions that bowls of sweets offered to lord Ganesha were sold later in the market.[67] Images of Ganesha along with the Ardhanareshvera have been reported from amidst the ruins of Avantipura dating back to 9th century AD

Agni

Agni /fire occupies a very essential and sacred place in the present form of Hindu religious code, be it the every day puja, a Mahayagnya or any of the twenty four essential ritual ceremonies prescribed by the scriptures to be performed by a Hindu during his life time. Worshipping fire in the form of an invocation of Shakti and a peaceful adieu of the same powers is a must for all the rituals. Reference to the existence of the Fire god/ Agni in the earlier eras of the K S P's is the presence of the Svayambhu shrine of fire/Agni in the Village Suyam about half a mile (one kilometre) from the present village of Nichhom,[68] and the temple of the Goddess of fire known as J*awalaji* at the village Khrew.

Laxmi

By tradition the Hindu KSPs pay scant attention to the worship of Laxmi the goddess of wealth; instead they prefer Saraswati the goddess of learning and knowledge. Yet it would be incorrect to presume that Laxmi was not accorded rightful place in the KSP religious ceremonies. The festival of *Sukha Suptika* (Deepavali in the present times) is dedicated to the worship of Lakshmi the goddess of wealth since the Puranic eras as recorded in the N.P. besides the images of goddess Lakshmi found at the historic town of Vijabror, and also in the ruins of the *Avantiswamin* temple-both belonging pre 9th century establishes the practice of Lakshmi worship.

Shakti Cult

The manifestation of Shakti as a supreme power side by side with Shiva the male representation of the supreme, go together in the realization of the ultimate. Hence their worship and importance are held in equal esteem in the Hindu KSP's religious belief; to the extent that the bride and the bride groom are worshipped as Shiva and Shakti prior to the final union of the two. Shakti the goddess of energy plays a vital role in the religious calendar of the Hindu KSPs right from the Ardhanareshvera days. She is worshipped in various forms, like Sharda, Durga, Sharika, Raginya, the Sapt matrikas, and even in the river forms like Ganga, Vitasta, and so on. So much so that in the present era the Hindu KSP is generally grouped as the follower of the Sharika cult or the Raginya cult: the two main representations of the principle of energy.

Sharda and its Chronology

Goddess Sharda is believed to be the earliest representation of Shakti in the valley, which is embodying three separate manifestations of energy, i.e. goddess of learning, fine arts and beauty. Goddess Sharda is the presiding deity of Kashmir and that is the reason why Kashmir is referred as Sharda desha and also Sharda peeth (seat of Sharda). The significance of this deity and its pilgrimage is given in the Sharda Mahatmya in Bhringish Samhita. From times immemorial KSPs have worshipped this goddess of learning in different manifestations of her powers and achieved excellence in different fields of culture and learning. Not only KSP Brahmans worship her, every orthodox Brahmin in the South after rising from his bed in the morning with folded hands offers salutations to goddess Sharada reciting, *"Namaste Sarada Devi Kashmira mandala vasini."* -Salutations to Goddess Sarada who resides in Kashmir.

A few sculptural evidences of the deity that were recovered from the mutilated ruins of Sarda temple are still preserved in the museum at Lal Mandi, Srinagar

As per a legend given in the Sarda Mahatmya Goddess revealed herself to Muni Sandalya when he was practicing penance for her darshan at Sardavana in the upper Kishenganga Valley of north Kashmir. The Mahatmya says, "Special holiness accumulates at the tirtha . . . The sacred spot where the goddess appeared in her divine form is marked by a stone slab seven feet long, six feet wide and half a foot thick. The stone is supposed to cover a *Kunda* (spring cavity) from where the goddess rose. The slab has ipso-facto become the sanctum sanctorum of the temple. The temple is a dilapidated ruin now."[69] Alberuni (l0th century AD) describes its location as, "inner Kashmir about two to three days journey towards the mountains of Bolor" (upper Indus between Gilgit and Ladakh). He speaks of the shrine as much venerated and frequented by pilgrims and mentions it along with the most famous ones of those days like Surya at Multan, the *Vishnu Chakraswamin* of Thaneswar and the Linga of Somnath. [70]

Bilhana (11th century) mentions the tirtha of Sharada, in his description of Pravarapura or Srinagar. According to him it is because of Goddess Sharda that the valley claims to be the centre of learning. The goddess is said to resemble a swan, carrying as her diadem the glittering gold washed from the sand of river Madhumati.

As per yet another legend the temple of Sharada figures in a story related to the great Jaina scholar Hemacandra (1088-1172 AD), in the *Prabhavakacarita.* When king Jayasimha of Gujarat Commissioned the scholar to compose a new grammar, he requested to be supplied with necessary material in the shape of the older grammars which could be found complete only in the library of Sharada in Kashmir. Jayasimha sent his envoy to the temple of the goddess for the same. The manuscripts were delivered to the king's-envoys who brought them to Hemacandra, who, after perusing the same, composed his own grammatical work, the *Siddhahemachandra.*

Reference to Sharada Peeth is also come across In Jonaraja's chronicle where in he mentions that Sultan Zain-ul-Abidin visited the shrine perhaps in 1422 AD to witness the miraculous manifestations of the goddess.[71]

Even in the 16th century the temple of Sarada must have enjoyed considerable reputation in Kashmir as is evident from Abul Fazl's following note, "at two day's distance from Hayahom is the river named Madhumati, which flows from the Darda country. Gold is also found in this river. On its banks is a stone temple called Sharada, dedicated to Durga and regarded with great veneration. It is believed that on every, eighth tithe of the bright half of the month, it begins to shake and produces the most extraordinary effect."[72]

This temple lost the royal patronage with the advent of Islam i.e. (1st quarter of the 14th century) but the flow of pilgrims was quite sizeable even during the rule of the Sultans, Chaks and the Mughals. Fortunately the destructive hands of Sikandar Butshikan did not reach the shrine and its temple because of its location at an isolated spot where perhaps his writ did not run. As the shrine falls in Pakistan occupied territory of Kashmir, it is out of bounds for the Hindu KSP but the veneration of the Goddess Sarda in its different manifestations of Shakti continues.

GODDESS *SHARIKA*

*Chakreshwera i*n Srinagar is the most famous extant temple of Goddess Sharika. Sharika Mahatmya records that it originated with the arrival of humans in the land of Kashyapa. It is not a man made structure but a natural formation. The deity is represented by a huge *Shila* (boulder) with naturally engraved Sri *Chakra* (circle) in the centre of the boulder, representing the cosmic circle. It is believed that the Sri Chakra is a symbolic representation of the cosmic union of the Lord Shiva and Shakti. As per a legend when the gods tried to kill the demon Jalodbhava, who had made life impossible in the Satisar, the demon hid in the lake and they could not reach it. Hence the goddess Sri /Haeri in native tongue) was approached to solve the problem. She took the form of a bird and dropped a celestial pebble over the huge torso of the demon. This pebble by the spiritual powers of the bird enlarged in size so big that the demon was crushed under its weight. The site was named Hari parbat after the bird *Haeri/ Meina* and the hillock/ parbat. Since then this temple continues to be part of Hindu KSPs religious pantheon. This event is believed to have occurred on the ninth day of the solar fortnight of the month of Ashad, hence this day is dedicated to the goddess Sharika and a Mahayagnya is performed on this day every year. On every Tuesday and Saturday and on her birthday specially, her followers whose presiding deity she is, make offerings of *Taher* (yellow coloured salted turmeric spiced cooked rice*)*, *Charvan* (cooked liver) and the sacrificial offering of lamb or goat heart along with lungs, amidst ringing of bells and conch shells and singing of devotional songs and mantras. Sharika/ Durga are basically of Saivite origin and hence animal sacrifice plays a very important role in it. (R.T.111, Verse 83) As per tradition the heart and lung are to be torn with bare hands and fed to the kites hovering over head and the cooked prasaad is partaken by every one present at the venue. Level plateau at the foot of the this temple site, locally known *as Devi Aangan* (*Devi's* courtyard) is supposed to be an abode of almost all the Hindu deities and has been a venerated place of the Hindu KSPs, both in faith and practices in spite of the injustice inflicted jointly, by history and politics, on them and on their sights of veneration.

Goddess *Raginya*

The second most important manifestation of Shakti in the present era is the Goddess Raginya. She is of Vaishnavite origin, so unlike Sharika the offerings are exclusively flowers, milk and milk products and sugar candy. Usage of any kind of non-vegetarian preparation is strictly forbidden in the precincts of this shrine popularly known as the shrine of Khirbhawani situated in the village of Tulamulla, within a pious and miraculous spring. Traditionally it is believed that this goddess is not a native deity and is supposed to have come to the valley from Lanka, as recorded in *Raginya Pradurbhava*, (a section of Bhringish Samhita). It records that during early period of the Epic Age, King Ravana ruled Lanka, an island to the south of India. King Ravana in order to gain temporal power and glory worshipped goddess Parvati (Shama) who manifested herself to him in all her nine aspects. For sometime he remained sober in thought and deed and worshipped the goddess with utter devotion. When Shri Rama King of Ayodhya invaded Lanka and his generals Sugrev and Hanuman killed Kumbakaruna his brother and Megnad his son, he was kindled with rage and tried to invoke the blessing of the goddess by offering her various kinds of sacrifices. The goddess, was angry, she cursed him and ordered Hanuman to take her to Sati Sara (Kashmir) on her vehicle along with 360 Nagas. Hanuman selected a spot in the northern side of the valley within the space surrounded by the villages of Borus *(Bhawanish*), Ahatung (Tungish), Ladwun (*Labdawan),* Wokur (*Bhageh).* Here he installed the goddess with all her satellites. She is called Khir Bhawani, exclusively preferring milk, sugar, rice and all vegetarian forms of offerings. Raginya is a manifestation of a form of Durga and inhabits in the sacred spring of Tulamulla referred as *Tulamulaka.* [73] (Abu-l-Fazl and Srivara mention about the location of Dudorhom /Dugdhasrma in close vicinity of the village of Tulamulla.)

Raginya is worshipped by the Hindu KSP and also by the Hindus at large all over the country. The venerated spring of Shakti exhibits miraculous changes in the colour of its water, which are ascribed to the manifestations of the goddess. The colours usually witnessed are, light green, rosy pink, grey, milky white, and at times of dark blackish hue. Latter, as per the devotees is a warning about an impending disaster. What ever the reason for the changing colours that I have personally witnessed many a times over the years, the faith in the miracles of the deity reins supreme in the minds of Hindu KSPs'

To conclude the detail about the religions so far mentioned, it would be fair to say that the Hindu KSP right from the beginning and through its religious evolution followed with equal respect and devotion all the cults and religious philosophies that happened to represent various Gods and Goddesses of Hindu Dharma. That led to a spirit of compromise and synthesis in their religious regime. People were absolutely free to worship and obey their own dictates and deities, and there by an atmosphere of unity in diversity existed in the religious pattern of Hindu KSP. What Ved Kumari derives after the study of the Nilamata, applies aptly to whole of the religious environment of the KSP. She writes, "The various cults of Vishnu, Siva, other Brahmanic and folk deities, Buddha and the Nagas, flourished side by side in Kashmira. The influences which each cult received from the others are discernible throughout the work and many verses reveal the spirit of compromise and synthesis in the field of religion. The Brahmanic deities, the Nagas, the Pisachas and Buddha, all receive their due share of worship from the inhabitants of Kashmira."[74]

Islam

Islamic faith was a very late entrant in to the religious calendar of the KSP. It was neither a subsidiary nor a corollary of Hinduism; it stood at variance with all that represented the earlier faiths. It was imported from foreign lands and as usual the broadminded Kashmiris accorded their hospitality to its exponent, the great Shah Hamadani, with open arms, but alas this innocent hospitable act, led to a volcanic eruption, which descended on the religious life of the KSP. It changed the very nomenclature of the majority of KSP's from Bhatta to Musalman; and Bhatta the original KSP was reduced to the barest number of less than 5% of the total population, with the incursion of this faith.

How did Islam as a religion secure a foot hold and spread so extensively in the valley like a deluge is the first step that needs to be illustrated?

For once we do not have to dig the archives, look for the archaeological proofs or rummage the classic literature to trace the beginning of Islam in the KSP fold. Its' beginning is recent and belongs to chronologically recorded era, i.e. about seven centuries ago, during the reign of Rinchin (1320-1323), Islam got its foot hold in the religious calendar of the KSP, of course, as usual, with the state patronage.

Kashmir's high walled security is always mentioned in the annals of its history by almost every chronicler and yet it seems to have always failed in-spite of all the precautions taken by its people. After the invasions of Mahmud in the rest of India the KSP took all the steps to block the outsiders. Alberuni writes, "the people are particularly anxious about the actual strength of their country, and therefore take always much care to keep a strong hold upon the entrances and roads leading into it. In consequence it is very difficult to have any commerce with them. At present they do not allow any Hindu whom they do not know personally to enter much less other people."[75] Yet these precautions did not prevent some individual Muslim travellers, from visiting the valley and also some invading armies to come up to the outskirts of this territory.

CHRONOLOGY OF EVENTS RELATED TO INTRUSION OF ISLAM IN THE KSP FOLD.

"Islam in fact came to exercise its influence on the Kashmir Court from about the middle of 8th century." In between some Arab attempts were made to spread this faith in the outskirts of the valley without any success. The settlers in one of the colonies whom Kalhana' in a derogatory reference calls *Mallechas* (people who did not follow Hindu rituals) almost proves that there were a few Muslims in the valley during the period 7th to 11th century, but no measure assault or willing conversion of the religious faith of the KSPs took place during all these centuries.

According to some evidences it is revealed that in the year (677AD 97 A.H.) a person named Hamim, the son of Sama, a Syrian Muslim was the first of this faith to enter the valley in the company of Jaisiya. The ruler of Kashmir as per the inherent culture of hospitality bestowed a place named Shakalha to Jaisiya. After Jaisiya's death his accomplice Hamim took over full control of Shakalha, converted a few locals to Islam and founded a masjid there. Hindu majority declared them as untouchables and hence they were forced to live separately. They were called *Mallechas.* The king of Kashmir gave him and his co-religionists (*Mallechas*) a colony to settle in a part of Srinagar which was known as *Mallechamar*-(Ali-Kadal of present Srinagar). Services of these Muslims were called for by the Hindu rulers of Kashmir such as Harsha, who used them for breaking the idols in his revenue collection drive, and also to cater to his whims and extravagant habits. They were even employed in the army, and the war prisoners were sold to them whom they would convert to their faith i.e. Islam forcibly, as is but a natural behaviour between a master and the prisoner/slave.

As per Rajatarangini, we discern first evidence of the Muslims in connection with the Valley, when Candrapida (711-719AD) and Lalitaditya Muktapida (725-753AD) seek help from the Chinese Emperor for fighting against the invading Muslims, who were actually based in Multan. Rulers like Vajraditya Bappiyaka. (754 to 761AD) sold many men to *Mallechas* Harsha Dev (1089 to 1101 AD) who did not trust his own army employed Turkish (Turushkas /Muslims) soldiers in the army and put them in charge of groups, (in Kalhana's terminology as "captains of hundreds",)because he feared that Hindu soldiers did not agree with his anti Brahman codes. During the reign of Biksacara (1120-21AD) Muslim soldiers were recruited and sent on an expedition against Sussala in Lohara (modern Poonch and Rajori).

Marco-polo, the Venetian traveller, refers to the presence of Muslims in the Valley before the end of 13th century. In his reference to the non-vegetarian habits of the KSP, he has noted that they would employ the services of Saracens (Muslims) to kill birds and animals, if they wished to take meat. This group lived as the butcher class in the society. These Saracens could either be the emigrants from far off lands or the converts from among the locals or those who came from the surrounding hill tribes.[76]

The questions arise as to how was the Islamic faith introduced in Kashmir and why did it spread like a deluge? Generally the followers of the said faith and some liberal researchers have written that the KSP were fed up of the ritualism, dogmas and sacrificial dictums of the conservative Brahmanism, the philosophical monistic Shaiva Tantras and the resultant confusion that they were looking for avenues to seek peace and love, which Islam was able to provide. So they adopted the faith. Some even write that like the previous faiths in the valley Islam was accepted as yet another flower of knowledge added to the garden of supreme love, learning and beauty.

Stein in his introduction to the English version of Rajatarangini writes, "Islam made its way into Kashmir not by forcible conquest but by gradual conversion for which the influx of foreign adventurers both from the South and from Central Asia had prepared the ground."[77]

Rabbani one of the reputed Muslim scholars of the present times, while analysing the cause of the KSP compulsions to accept the new faith writes, "As for the earliest colonisation of Kashmir by Muslims, historical evolution had to play its natural role. The original creeds and the communities of the valley had grown so sterile, stale and unresponsive that they needed to be revolutionised. The revolution from within was impossible at the stage. A spark from outside was required to ignite the explosives accumulated in the course of centuries. Many local inhabitants and their leaders did not abhor Muslim ways and virtues. Hence the followers of Islam were accommodated."[78]

We have to accept that the social environment and the political upheavals, and invasions of the marauding forces that descended upon the country like a swarm of locusts in the beginning of 13th century destroyed the religious, social and economic fibre of the KSP to the extant of annihilation of the people in spite of all the walled barriers.

Mongols under the leadership of Zuljoo and Qaan descended on the valley like locusts and played havoc with the Kashmiri population. These Mongols were brutes and savages. They devastated peaceful villages and prosperous towns of the valley, killing thousands of innocent civilian with utter disregard for human values. "They repeated the invasion, destroyed the standing crops and houses, looted property and killed old and young indiscriminately. Rama Dev the ruler could not survive the catastrophe. Within a short period after Cann, yet another Mongol invaded the valley. Zuljoo the grandson of Halaku came with an army of 70,000 troops who captured and tortured everyone who came in their way."[79] It is the general belief among the KSP that after this event, almost whole KSP population was annihilated, only eleven families of Kashmiris survived in the valley and this belief survives in the given native phrase (*Kasheer gaye kahai ghare*) The invader in the month of November, 1318 A.D carried with him 60,000 captives, and all of them were destroyed in the bitter cold caused by the heavy snow-storm, while crossing the High Lands of Devsar at Batapora (now known as Batot).

The effect of these Mongol invasions was most adverse both on the land and its people. Moulvi Ghulam Hussain Gamru, as quoted by Rabbani, on the authority of authentic evidence bewails the consequences of loot and destruction, thus, "After the annihilation of these vicious invaders, the survivors in Kashmir came out from their hideouts in the hills and found no relative or friend alive. Only a hundred men were seen living in distress. These men rebuilt their fallen habitations, while there were only eleven families who resumed the work of reconstruction in the city."[80]

Jonaraja, the 15th century historian in the same vein laments and writes, "When the violence caused by the Rakshaa Dulchu ceased, the son found neither his father nor the father his son, nor did brother meet his brother. Kashmir became almost like a region before the creation, a vast field with men without food and full of grass".[81]

Rabbani records, "It can well be imagined how tragic the aftermath of the terrible calamities could be. In sum, Kashmir was in a hopeless state. The effect on the minds - of the survivors was deep. The man in the street and the tiller in the country-side felt him-self resource less both materially and spiritually. Disappointed with his lot, he had turned to be depressed within and demoralised without. When tragedies overtake families, they find people to sympathise with them. But there was none to help keep up their spirits. For them, it was the question of how to adjust in bewildering conditions and start the new chapter of their life. They and their immediate forbears had seen much of religious practice and lived according to the tenet of the indigenous religions. In their state of confusion it was Islam and its votaries which came to their succour and freed them from their collective numbness. And as they had already experienced the sweetness of contact with Muslims most of them welcomed to get Islam. But astonishingly, the process of conversion began with the ruler of the kingdom and not the people he ruled, and this by all estimates was a miraculous event in the annals of Kashmir"[82]

While I agree with Rabbani that the murderous assault, loot, destruction and dance of savagery of the forces of Qaan and Halaku Khan did prepare the ground for the spread of Islam in the valley, yet it certainly was not responsible for the deluge or say the complete metamorphosis of KSP faith. After all we can not deny that Islam was in no way a subsidiary or a corollary of the previous faiths of the people there. It was a complete change over. I agree the intellectual, and spiritual philosophers of the valley must have accepted Islam, as yet, another flower of learning but not the masses, who as records prove had not accepted Islam, even in small measures over the last six to seven centuries since the inception of the faith in the valley around seventh century AD, because the masses are usually prone to be more conservative in matters of faith. Hence we will have to accept that Islam, as well, came on the vehicle of the ruler's patronage, for the process of conversion began with the ruler of the kingdom and not the peoples he ruled.

Rabbani himself corroborates that Rinchin the Buddhist king of Kashmir was the first to convert to Islam. Later the kings who followed in their eagerness to spread the faith used all the means at their disposal to spread the new faith to such an extent that 99.05 % Hindu Population was reduced to less than 5% and the rest adopted the new faith willingly or by force. Let us enumerate some of the ways and means adopted by the rulers of the valley to patronise the new faith.

Methods Adopted to spread Islam in Kashmir

In case of the religious streams discussed above we found that the building of viharas and temples, compilation of religious treatises and philosophies; and celebrations of the festivals and pilgrimages to the centres of the concerned faiths, were successful, means of spreading it and gaining the acceptance of the society. But, these methods were untenable in the context of Islam: One, because there was no willing and knowledgeable work force available and two, it was considered an alien and anti faith as against the prevalent one. Hence the patrons of Islam had to devise different methods to achieve the popularisation and acceptance of the new faith.

Initially, the new converts came to be looked down by their old compatriots and found no place in the society. They were even rejected the privileges enjoyed by them earlier. This created a gulf and a sense of inferiority complex in the new converts to Islam. Worst sufferer was one Suha Bhatta. Tradition has it that he was seriously taken ill and completely emaciated thus to recover his health; he on the advice of a mullah took chicken soup which was strictly forbidden in the Hindu fold during those times. For this act he was ridiculed and labelled as an outcast, and this incident led to his conversion to Islam in the reign of Sikandar; he took the Islamic name of Saif-ud-Din and became the leader of the new converts, and as it is well known, a convert always suffers from the complex of having 'a holier than thou attitude', Saif-ud-din proved to be a perfect representative of this attitude and is believed to have converted and tortured maximum Hindus under the patronage of his ruler Sikander.

"Both Sikandar and Saif-ud-Din planned the extirpation of the Hindus and obliteration of all traces of Hinduism from Kashmir. Saif-ud-Din had his own axe to grind but Sikandar wanted thereby to consolidate and strengthen his rule."[83]

The methods adopted by Sikandar may well be given in the words of Hassan who writes, "This country possessed from the times of Hindu Rajas many temples which were like the wonders of the world. Their workmanship was so fine and delicate that one found himself bewildered at their sight. Sikandar goaded by feelings of bigotry destroyed them and levelled them with the earth and with their material built many mosques and khanakahs. In the first instance he turned his attention towards the Martand temple built by Rama Deva on Mattan Karewa. For one full year he tried to demolish it but failed. At last in sheer dismay he dug out stones from its base and having stored enough wood in their place set fire to it. The gold gilt paintings on its walls were totally destroyed and the walls surrounding its premises was demolished. Its ruins even now strike wonder in men's minds. At Bijbehara three hundred temples including the famous Vijayeshwara temple which was partially damaged by Shahabud-Din were destroyed and with the material of the latter a mosque was built and on its site a Khanakah which is even now known as Vijayeshwar Khanakah."[84] After having described the destruction of many temples the ruins of which even now bespeak a fully developed architectural grandeur and massiveness Hassan further writes, "Sikandar meted out greatest oppression to the Hindus. It was notified in the city that if a Hindu does not become a Muslim, he must leave the country or be killed. As a result, some of the Hindus fled away, some accepted Islam and many Brahmans consented to be killed and gave their lives. It is said that Sikandar collected by these methods about three khirwars (six maunds) of sacred threads (from Hindu converts) and burnt them. Hazrat Amir Kabir who was witness to all this orgy of brute passion and vandalism at last advised him to desist from the slaughter of Brahmans, and told him to impose Jazia instead of death upon them. All the Hindu books of learning were collected and thrown into Dal Lake and were buried beneath stones and earth."[85]

Having almost annihilated them, he allowed the surviving Hindus to live only on payment of Jazia (a tax to be paid for retaining non-Muslim faith).The governmental coercion, coupled with brisk proselytising activities indulged in by the Muslim preachers, and also the privileged position which the fresh converts secured, succeeded in bringing about a mass conversion.

Sikandar was succeeded by his son Ali Shah who also appointed Saif-ud-Din (Suha Bhatta) as his prime minister. In his short reign of about six years the persecution of the Hindus continued with greater vigour. This persecution of the Hindus or more particularly of the Brahmans has been born as testimony by almost all the Muslim historians. Hassan and Fouq, two great Muslim historians, have condemned these excesses in un-scathing terms. Thus during Sultan Sikandar's reign, the propagation of Islam in Kashmir received a strong impetus and he has been rightly blamed for his bigotry in the persecution of the Hindus of the valley.

G.M.Sufi writes, "I am afraid it is based on considerable misrepresentation, on more fiction than fact, and a number of non-Muslim chroniclers one after the other have heaped their quota of abuse on the head of the Sultan the calumny has been perpetrated to such an extent that we now find Sikandar as an abominable personification of ruthless destruction of all noble edifices, erected to the Hindu deities. Sikandar in his zeal for his own religion may have transgressed the limits of moderation but it is unquestionably a false charge against him that he broke down all Hindus temples in Kashmir and cruelly persecuted every Pandit"[86]

Sufi, interestingly, goes on to state (page 73 of his book 'Kashir') "He (Sikandar) seems to have possessed a passion for enforcing religious law in all state affairs. [87] Being himself a rigid Mohammadan who carefully observed all the practices of his religion, he put an end to all practices which were contrary to the Shariat of Islam, the sale and distillation of wine, suttee, gambling, prostitution and music were all tabooed. The tangha tax was abolished and Islamic courts of justice were established."[88]

In this process of proselytization Sayyid Mir Ali Hamdani played a major role. He came to Kashmir with about seven hundred Sayyids, followed by his illustrious son who brought additional three hundred followers,[89] they stayed in Kashmir under royal protection and took to the proselytization of the local people. They secured many converts to the new faith. Even, "The Sultan became one of his disciples and was now fired with zeal to change the character of his rule into purely Islamic administration and a considerable advance was made in this direction. As his orders in this behalf were carried out either by Mohammadan Converts or the other officials, the Sultans object could not be achieved without the destruction of some idols and temples which wounded the susceptibilities of the Hindus."[90]

In the context of the Sikandar's patronage of his faith, Jonaraja writes, "Then came the most fanatic and religious despot of Kashmir-Sikander who not only massacred the Hindus, he got all the books on philosophy, theology, and art in Sanskrit destroyed by flames even as fire burns grass. All masterpieces of architecture produced by the Kashmiri shilp Shastras demolished and pillaged. There was no city, no town, no village, and no wood where the temples of gods were un-broken. Hindus were neither tolerated nor allowed to escape. Struck by fear some Brahmans killed themselves in water, others again by falling from a precipice and others burnt them-selves."[91]

After Sikander his son Ali shah seems to have continued the process of proselytising with the help of Saif-ud-Din (Suha) as is evident from Jonaraja's account. "Suha passed the limit by levying fine on the twice born; this evil-minded man forbade ceremonies and processions on the new moon. He became envious and apprehended that the twice-born who had become fearless would keep up their caste by going over to foreign countries he therefore ordered all the guards on the roads not to allow passage to anyone without a passport. Then as the fisherman torments fish, so this low born man tormented the twice-born in this country. The Brahmans burnt themselves in the flaming fire through fear of conversion. Some Brahmans killed themselves by means of poison, some by the rope, and others by drowning themselves . . . others again by falling from a precipice . . . The country was contaminated by hatred and the king's favourite (Suha) could not prevent one in a thousand from committing suicide . . . A multitude of Brahmans who prided on their caste fled from the country through bye-roads, as the main roads were closed, even as men flee under ground when the doors of their houses are closed. Even as men depart from this world, so did the Brahmans flee to foreign countries, the son was leaving his father behind and the father leaving his son . . . The difficult country through which they passed, the scanty food, painful illness and the torments of hell during life time removed from the minds of the Brahmans the fears of hell. Oppressed by various calamities, such as encounter with the enemy, fear of snakes, fierce heat and scanty food, many Brahmans perished on the way and thus obtained relief. Where were then their bath, their meditation, and their austerity and where were then their prayers?" [92]

The role of a historian is to impartially record facts and not to justify or feel apologetic about the acts of a ruler or a despot just because he or she belongs to a common faith. I do agree the noble and ruling class would have not been extensively persecuted because they had to run the state Government, but I wonder how complete transformation of Hindu administration and law to Islamic tenets could have been possible without force and coercion in a country dominantly populated by the Hindu KSP. Islam was a very recent faith introduced into the valley in the early fourteenth century and the opinions of some observers and researchers of the given period quoted here do substantiate the view that coercion was adopted to achieve the end.

Newall records, "Sikandar destroyed all their (the Hindu) sacred places." [93] Sufi writes, "Yes in a country where temples and Viharas were built in such number that even a seed of seism could not fit between the two, to destroy all would be impossible." He further adds Sikandar partly under the influence of Timur and partly prompted by the fanatic Muslims who had lately entered his country was instigated to religious persecution and he began to force his subjects to abjure idolatry and thereby acquired the surname Butshikan or Iconoclast.

Adoption of the new faith was not result of any abrupt acceptance due to frustration and disgust of the existing faith but it was a result of a slow coercion or a fate accomplice. A decade or two ago, people like me, would have considered it an exaggeration or an impossibility, but not now, after witnessing the events and happenings in the valley, where, within a duration of about just three months, the Muslim Kashmiri speaking people urged and egged by the fanatic Muslims who had lately entered the valley, turned a peaceful, prosperous land of love, brother hood, cultural and religious tolerance into a veritable hell, for the Hindu KSP. Latter, as a result had to leave their homes and hearth within a short period of three months, in order to save their life and honour, that too during the times when the country boasts of a democratic and secular system of governance. Imagine, what would not have been possible for a fanatic despot to achieve in a period of twenty five years? Yes even today G.M. Sufi would be within his rights to say that all the Hindus have not migrated, for out of a population of about 3,00,000 Hindu KSP there are still 10 thousand odd Hindus in the valley living a life of abject misery. Any way G.M. Sufi justifies Sikandar actions in the given statement, "In fairness to the Sultan we must not however, omit to mention that his age was the age of religious persecution, and again that the king ordered the destruction of temples, forbade the use of the Tika on the head and abolition of Suttee (which existed till the 18th century) at the instance of his minister Saif-UD-Din who was a recent convert."[94]

Yet, as soon as a considerate ruler like Zain-ul-Abidin ascended the throne, things changed. He adopted certain laws relating to the Hindus, which vouchsafed to them a just administration and a trial of their cases according to their own laws. The odious persecution measures instituted during Sikandar's rule were revoked and a general toleration of all religions proclaimed. Hindus especially the Brahmin class who had migrated during the last reign were recalled, complete religious independence was granted and some of the temples which had been demolished were rebuilt and permission was accorded to erect new ones. The sultan remitted the Poll-Tax and granted Jagirs to Hindus and did away with the custom of killing of cows. If the KSP's had been willing converts there would have been no need for all these changes and concessions.

During the reign of this benevolent ruler the fair and humane face of Islam was discovered with the massive efforts of some saints and seers. It was the time when the KSP were facing an identity crisis as for as the religious identity was concerned. Confusion and chaos reigned supreme in the social melee. Sages and seers came out of hibernation to rescue the confused masses from the most unsettling mess of religious confrontations and guided them to a middle path of adjustment, path of peace and mutual trust, by giving birth to the cult of Sufism. Abu- l-Fazl describes this sect as, "A very respectable and inoffensive order in his time, some 2000 in number, living up on fruits and berries and abstaining from sensual delights."[95]

The greatest proponents of this cult were Lalleshwari and Nur-ud-Din Noorani. Rabbani writes, "synthesis of Hindu and Islamic religious thought found its greatest exponents in Lalleshwari and Sheikh Nur-ud-Din in the darkest periods of religious persecutions by ignorant and fanatical foreigners, the people of Kashmir lived like brothers, giving what little solace, shelter and comfort they could, to their brothers in distress."

Mohamed Azim the historian enumerates many worthies of this sect and their deeds. These learned doctors seem to have fixed the religion of the country, and to have built the Ziarats and shrines all over the country including the Jamma Masjid.

Unfortunately once again for a few years from 1752 the valley became subject to one of the cruellest and worst rule of the Pathans. The Pathan rulers and governor were ferocious and brutal in their methods of governance as well as in methods of patronage of their faith. They inflicted heart rending brutality and cruelty on their subjects. For Hindus shoes were forbidden, and the tika was interdicted. Jazia and poll tax was revived, thus many either fled the country, or were killed or got converted to Islam.

Even the Mughal ruler Shahjahan, the ardent lover of the heavenly beauty of Kashmir, gave only two options to the population of the conquered territory of Ladakh either convert to Islam or be ready to die. The brutal means adopted by the rulers of the valley in their jihadi zeal to spread their faith has only one equivalent in the present era, and that is the Talibani system of imposing Sharia laws. One shudders to think what the Hindu KSP would have faced in the 16th or 17th century monarchy rule, comparing it to the Taliban savagery against their co-religionists in the modern era of the 21st century. Under the given circumstances the KSP had little option but to accept the new faith of Islam.

ISLAM IN A MODERATE FORM

The KSP as in the case of earlier faiths and religions modified and changed the fanatic Islam to create the Kashmiri version of Islam. A Muslim Kashmiri continued with the manner of prayers to his Prophet, as his Hindu ancestors had taught him. The cult of Sufism that may have been a derivative of the Greek Sophists or the product of native Islamic Sufis, resurfaced as KSP Islam. In spite of all the atrocities and pressures of the foreign preachers and sympathisers of the new religion, the Kashmiri Islam is of its own kind; bereft of the Fatwa raaj (decree]. "A Kashmiri did not adopt the religion as preached by its founders, rather introduced certain practices which would appear today to be un-Islamic. Such as the Buddhist Muslims of the valley continued to follow their own style of architecture and added innovations,"[96] Sultan Qutab ud Din, in spite of being a Muslim King, would visit in the morning a temple called Alaudinpora. He had still two wives who were sisters, which is un-Islamic.[97] Strict Sharia laws were not imposed or followed. They preferred Sufi Islam; one that taught them to believe in Rishis and Pirs. There was no compulsory *Purdah* system for the common women. "The innovation of the period is the imprint of a foot in a stone which is revered by the Muslims as *Kadam-I-Rasul (Vishnu Paad Foot),* and by the Buddhist as *Sakyamuni Paad* (Buddha's foot print). Even now we find people like to gaze on the saints old clothes and turban and to examine the cave in which he spent his ascetic life." [98]. Thus Islam attained the status of a humane faith of mutual love and peace in Kashmir by virtue of the Sufi tenets

K.N.Dhar writing in his book, 'Hindu Historians and Muslim Kashmir' states, "Some chroniclers have not been able to extricate themselves from the cocoon mesh of personal likes and dislikes, their subjective involvement has gone a long way in tarnishing the inherent image of this period in Kashmir".

One wonders why some Muslim historians skirt historical facts of the forced conversion imposed by Rinchin Gyalpo and his convert minister Suha Bhat /Saif-ud-Din after he accepted Islam, and later to be continued even more cruelly by Sikander Butshikan and Shah Mir. Why not record the truth instead of presenting distorted facts like: 1. Rinchan brought Islam to the willing masses." 2) "The Muslims have had to use force on certain occasions but, as for Kashmir, no force was used to convert non-Muslims to Islam." and 3). "Rather influxes of saints, scholars and adventures continued, who by their piety and scholarship attracted the people to Islam" etc. Why do they try to justify the means and methods of conversion to their convenience and not record it as it happened; however brutal or barbaric it was? It is an accepted fact of history for which they are nowhere to be held responsible. Dictators, throughout the world history, and fanatic bigots of any country, creed, caste or religion are known to have taken recourse to most ruthless means to obtain their ends; the ends that they tried to justify as being the worthy ends for the good of their religion. Were not the early Christians burnt alive for following a particular creed; were not the Jews, in very recent times, subjected to one of the worst holocausts of the human history, did not Mihirkhula slaughter millions of people for being Buddhist.

The Aftermath

We have to accept that Kashmir was not only an abode of Gods, a simple residence but a sadhana Peeth; (a place of worship and meditation), with very congenial surroundings to be able to communicate with the inner self and the Parmartha (Supreme Being) in their own Shaivite manner of worship. This was deprived to them by the repeated assaults of Islamic proselytisers. It is a fact that the KSP had not confronted for the first time the religious change over. They had earlier incorporated, Naga faith into their process of Nature worship, and later imbibed Buddhism and amalgamated it with their Shaivite and Vaishnav Philosophy, but this change was not an amalgamation. It was conversion of faith, that shook their very basis, and it was also a violent change over, under any pretext or garb. Some may try to give it a sugar coating; but those who faced it have had to chew a bitter pill.

Yet while turning to the other side of the coin, the advent of Islam in Kashmir has been at least good for those KSP's who accepted the new faith of Islam that spread and flourished well in the valley. Befitting the number of the followers of this faith, symbols of Islam like Masjids, Darghas and Khankhas, are spread all over the valley in large numbers. To name some of the illustrious and famous ones are: the Dargah of Mukdham Saheb at Hari Parbat hillock, Hazratbal shrine along the banks of Dal Lake and the venerated shrine of Chrari Sharif. Besides every district, every village and every mohala has its own masjid. At present Islamic faith is observed by almost 95% Kashmiris. Such an achievement for this faith is almost unparalleled in the religious history of any country.

Sikhism

Towards the end of Muslim rule yet another religious faith seeped into the KSP religious calendar. As it was a corollary of the Hindu system it did not involve any conversion or force. One can say it was a self willed invite. The Kashmiris, fed up with the Pathan rule, its travails and hardships that they suffered till 1819, thought of seeking help from the Sikh ruler Ranjit Singh, to relieve them of their miseries. As they, themselves, were reduced to such a state of in-action, starvation and poverty, that they had no capacity to revolt on their own. When the ruler came to help he was accompanied by his people, his soldiers and commanders, who followed a new faith and that was Sikhism.

Initially only a few hundreds of them settled in the valley and practiced their faith. Later, during Raja Sukh Jeevan's time who was the governor of the state, thousands of Sikhs entered the state as soldiers. These Sikhs settled permanently in the valley in areas, like Tral, Naogam and Kruhin. In 1890 as per the census there were 4,000 odd Sikhs in the valley. These numbers have since increased and at present there are said to be about 80,000 Kashmiri Sikhs residing in about 116 villages across the valley.

The symbols of representations of the Sikh faith are the Gurdwaras. Some of the famous Gurdwaras constructed by them are at Mattan, Anant Nag, Avantipur Bandipura, Pahalgam etc. All these Gurudwaras were built during Gurunanks visits or in memory of his visits to these places[99] The famous Gurdwara of Chatti Padshahi near Hari parbat fort in Srinagar has been built to commemorate Guru Har Govind Singh's visit to the valley. However, on the basis of references in the history books, Sikh literature and on construction details of the Gurdwaras, it can be said that people who have faith in Sikh religion are living in Kashmir since the inception of Sikhism by Sri Guru Nanak Dev Ji in 1469 AD Sikhs are part and parcel of Kashmir in all aspects, living and sharing things with their Kashmiri brethren; one needs, however, to record that this section of Kashmiris do not use *Kashur* language as a medium of everyday conversation amongst each other; instead they mainly speak in Punjabi language.

SOME OBSERVATIONS ABOUT RELIGIOUS PRACTICES AND THE DAILY RELIGIOUS ROUTINE FOLLOWED BY THE KSPs IN THE PRESENT ERA

KSPs of different faiths follow different laws and practices, yet one common factor pervades in their society, and that is, they do not practice their religion strictly according to given fatwa's and edicts. In the present era though Islam dominates, yet its Wahabi cult has not been able to overshadow its Sufi culture. Pearce Gervis writes, "There does not seem to be a very great percentage of either of the faiths who practise their religion in the really orthodox fashion and live their lives as laid down by the books. Few fail to observe their own festivals though, while many also enjoy those of the other religion, and when you attempt to discuss their professed religion or way of life with them, it is surprising how little they really know of it in the Valley."[100] "Religion generally was practiced by the senior generations of both Hindu and Muslim KSP . . . Though Ramzaan was a must for a Muslim, but Friday was never kept as a day of rest, only seniors would go for Friday Nemaz. Hardly any one would go to Mecca, as compared to the numbers they are. The festival of Eid was celebrated with pomp and gaiety along with neighbours and friends Ziarats and Dervishes were venerated by one and all Mohammedans and Hindus".[101] It, however, is a fact that this culture of religious practice has under gone a marked change in recent years.

KSP Hindus used to follow a very elaborate process even during the recent centuries as recorded by Lawrence in great detail.[120] (See notes and references)

I am sure these details would sound Greek and unimaginable to the present generation of Hindu KSP's. For river Ghats and banks nowhere figure in her or his ambience at present. They are only familiar with rationed water flowing through the municipal taps. These are bygone stories for them rather fairy tales. Yet in-spite of these handicaps some of the elders follow this routine in their solitary corners.

CONCLUSION

Moving away from this diversion one can authentically state, till about last two decades religion, faith and its observances were a private affair for the KSP. Religion was never worn on the sleeves and broadcast on the pulpits. Unfortunately they had suffered immensely on account of the faith they followed, who ever they be and which ever faith that be. Religion for the Hindu KSP was mostly home bound. Every Hindu home had a room designated for worship, and it was called *thoker kuth* (prayer room) The seniors would perform daily routine puja, they would go daily for a *Parikramaa* (Circumbulation) of the Devi at Hariparbat, that served both as an exercise as well as prayer. The juniors were free to do their biddings as per their personal beliefs. There were no compulsive laws to bind them to the faith. Few days of religious significance were ear-marked for yegnayas, for which the Musalman would supply flowers, fruits, milk, wood and other essential items needed for the puja. The festival of Shivaratri was a major festival of the Hindu in the valley, the gaiety and celebration lasted almost a month and on the culmination the Muslims would equally dance, sing and join in wishing well to their Hindu acquaintances and get the Salaam *Nekh Namal Hairath Kharach* (pocket money)

KSP Muslims would perform their regular Nemaz at the mosques and also visit the Darghas and Ziarets. Youngsters and juniors were not obliged to religiously accompany the elders. Selected few went on a pilgrimage to Mecca. Special days were earmarked as vorus (anniversary of the saints and Rishis) wherein Hindus donated and had the *tobruk* /prasaad. Eid was their main festival and Hindus would receive portions of the sacrificial offerings, and wish Eid Mubarak to them.

Same applied to the followers of Sikh faith. They visited the Gurudwaras, as a routine without any untoward pressures. Mostly seniors joined the recitation of Guruvani and Kirtans. Baisakhi was their chief festival and all KSPs' would have picnics in the lovely Mughal Gardens and in the blooming almond orchards.

The recent atmosphere of fanatic mayhem and militant orgies is bound to have damaged this ethos and religious amalgamation. Yet some optimists like, Riyaz Wani-a journalist- write, "Inspite of the upheaval, the valley has exhibited a remarkable continuity. Shrines continue to be the destinations of a large population of the faithful; belief remains suffused with Sufism.—the valley collectively has successfully resisted efforts at a radical overhaul of its traditionally tolerant cultural and religious ethos"

To say the least the KSPs' in-spite of following many a faiths, religious philosophies and cults, they do not over ride each other, they are free to adopt their own norms, and to worship their respective deities. It is often observed that the beauty of their religious faith is that, even the deities of the various religious faiths not only compliment each other but also accept and honour each others existence irrespective of their origins and other variances.

SHANKRACHARYA TEMPLE

CHAPTER 5

RITES, RITUALS AND FESTIVALS OBSERVED BY THE K.S.P'S

Humans in-spite of being descendents of a common family of the homo-sapiens, have an urge, to establish individual, or group identities. These individual identities do not cease at the level of religion, race, or class to which they belong, but extend even to the manner of performing rites and rituals in their life time. This identity is the bedrock of individuality that flourishes and breeds on the mode of set customs and traditions of a civilized society. Most encouraging and satisfactory part of being a KSP is their uniqueness of origin, culture, civilization, social and ritualistic structure. Their religious dispositions have not obliterated, even though for centuries, "time has behaved with the KSP like a bitter enemy."

The KSP of different faiths having originated from the common stock, lived in similar physical environment and undergone similar political upheavals, it is but natural to expect many a similarities in the rites, rituals and festivals of the people of the valley. Having said that, we can not deny that many differences have occurred in this ancient ethnic community's set of rites and rituals under the influence of the different religious faiths that they followed. Besides, their ceremonies and rituals have had to adapt to changes under the impact of modern education, economic strains and stresses and the horrifying experience of forced exoduses because of religious persecution. Again, the rituals and ceremonies of people who were residing and continued to reside within the valley, due to physical isolation and climatic environment, often differ from people who have been migrating to and fro from the valley.[1]

Social customs and rituals of the KSP are mostly associated with the three stages of the life of a person: birth, marriage and death. Over the millennia's the basic rituals have been mostly retained, yet, in the course of changes in the living conditions, and environment of the society, these rituals have also undergone perceptible changes so for as the religiosity and the detail is concerned.

Rites and Rituals of Hindu KSP's

Maharishi Laugakshi as per scriptural references was nominated to prepare a detailed religious code for the inhabitants of the valley, who in the earlier eras of their existence were the followers of Hindu faith. Laugakshi was a great scholar of Sanskrit and Sharda language and an accomplished spiritualist. "He compiled a comprehensive treatise on *Karma Kanda*"[1] titled "*Logathe* and also known as The *Laugakshi Grihyasutra.*"[2] This treatise covers every stage and every event from pre-natal to post-demise involvements for an individual of Hindu faith. It lays down, in detail, the directions and practices to be followed, while observing and performing the rites and rituals, ceremonies and sacrifices by the Hindu KSP. Till date, all Hindu KSPs' adhere, in the performance of all dispensations, to this treatise faithfully. The *Laugakshi Grihyasutra* is believed to have been compiled some where between 500-200 B.C.

The KSP calendar that is supposed to be five thousand years old, (5086 *Samvat* at present) enlists all the rites, rituals and festivals as recorded in the Nilamat Purana. How ever, it can not be denied that most of them are just symbolic references of the past. In the recent times especially, after the inception of Islam, barring the life-cycle rituals, the performance and celebration of most other rites and rituals have been considerably reduced in number and also altered according to the faith followed by the people concerned.

"Every ritual has been evolved with a great deal of thought and experience, in order to enhance physical and mental well-being that will contribute towards spiritual uplift. One can say the rituals are supposed to solve our problems in the life, as the technological rituals are there to solve our technical problems in the operation of technical devices."[3]

The ritual activity of the KSP can be classified as 1) Life cycle Rituals or Samaskars and other domestic ceremonies. 2) Puja or Worship rites. 3) Shaiva and Shakta rituals

Samskara is a term that is used to explain the life-cycle rituals as performed at different stages in an individual's life, from cradle to the cremation ground.

Puja rites are related to the rituals of the cult to which a person or his family belongs. and the worship of the God head.

THE CONSTITUENT ELEMENTS

Essential elements that play a very dominant role in the performance of Hindu KSP's rites and rituals are:

Fire: It is the first and most sacred of these elements, being worshipped as the "chief domestic Deity" since Vedic and perhaps pre-Vedic times. At every religious rite, Kashmiri Hindu makes offerings into sacrificial fire and through it to the Gods. They burn bdellium and sesame or mustard seeds in a *kangri'* (fire-pot) on almost all auspicious occasions and ceremonies to scare away evil spirits.

Water: It is the next important constituent used for its purifying effects and powers to ward off evil influences and for removing physical as well as moral or spiritual impurities. A Kashmiri Hindu considers bathing essential before every rite, be it marriage, sacred thread investiture, tonsure or any other religious ceremony. Sprinkling of water over the head or on the ground is considered essential for success, happiness, and fame. Even *aachman* (sipping water prior to breaking a fast and or at the end of the meal) is considered essential for physical purification.

PRAYERS, ENTREATIES AND BLESSINGS

Prayers for success, health, material prosperity, long life, happiness, obtaining children, spiritual salvation and even for seeking blessings of Gods, elders, teachers, spiritual personalities etc. are a common feature of their rituals. Blessings are invoked at birthday ceremonies for fulfilment of desires and wishes and for spiritual and material progress.

BALI OR OFFERING

The term *Bali* stands for sacrifices of various nature and items made by the humans to propitiate and please the Gods and supernatural beings. A number of occasions and festivals have been set apart for this purpose, when the deities are invited, and feasted for gaining their favours in return. The offerings are usually made through the medium of fire during *Hawans and Yegnayas* where in barley, rice, sesame seeds, different kinds of dried fruits, molasses, clarified butter or ghee, milk etc are offered. Besides there are non-fire sacrifices like the traditional offering of *tahr* (rice cooked with turmeric powder and smeared with ghee), *Khichri*, offered to appease Kubera on *Yaksha Amawasi* and or fish and plain rice (*Gad batta*) to the *garadivta (grihadevata)* or the protector deity of the house. Mutton dishes, liver and lungs of a lamb are offered as sacrifice to deities like *Bhairava, Kali, Tripura* and *Jwala*. Special days are dedicated to their worship. To Goddess *Khir Bhawani (Raginiya)* only milk and *khir* (rice pudding) are offered while sweet bread-cakes are offered to Ganesha and Lakshmi.[4]

Rituals

Hindu KSP's follow a package of 24 rituals in their life time that can be categorised as:

a) life cycle rituals

b) death rites.

Life cycle rituals:

These rituals begin with the prenatal stage of an individual and of all the rituals of this stage only one namely *Dhod Duen* still survives in some sections of the society.

Dhod Duen (curd ceremony)

As per tradition it was usually performed in the seventh or the eighth month of the pregnancy, when the would be mother, came from her parental home on an auspicious day to her in-laws house with gifts of large pots of curds garnished with saffron, cardamoms and almonds. This was distributed among the local neighbours and near relatives of the in-laws. It was believed to be a discreet manner of announcing her would be motherhood by the daughter-in law.

After the birth of a child very careful note of the time of birth is made and the same is conveyed to the family astrologer who later compiles the horoscope of the child for future references.

Truy

On the fourth day after the birth of a child the *truy* ritual is performed. A special mixture of sesame seeds, sugar crystals, almonds, and walnuts is prepared by the in laws and it is distributed amongst friends and relatives. Especially a large quantity of it is sent to the mother's parental home for distributing among their relations, neighbours and friends. I think it is very much akin to distributing sweets on the happy occasion of a child's birth. Only speciality about it is the fixed day that is the 4th day after birth.

Shran-Sondar

It is a ritual bath given to the mother and the child after the sixth day of the delivery or on any auspicious day following the date, fixed according to convenience. On the *shran-sondar* day, ladies assemble in the confinement room of the mother and after the ritual bath; lighted pieces of birch bark are rotated round the head of the baby and all those who are present. "While doing so they sing a song with the refrain, *'shokh ta panasund'*. It is not clear as to what these words exactly mean. Some people think, *'panasund!*, is the distorted form of, *'punah santu'*, meaning, "May you have more children". While others believe it is a distorted form of, *'pumsvan'*. Both interpretations seem to be only conjectures. It seems that, "*shokh ta 'panasund'* is the remnant of a forgotten hymn or mantra and has been distorted to an extent that it is difficult to make any sense of it now. All the ceremonial acts related to *shran-sondar* have since been discarded as most children are now born in the hospital under the care of an obstetrician. An interesting feature of the *shran-sondar* ceremony had to do more with the ritual art than the religion. A *vyug* or circular design would be made with lime and colour on the porch of the house and the new born would be placed on it."[5]

Shishur

This ritual is supposedly performed to protect the child and the mother from the evil influence of the demons and goblins during winter months, when they are believed to be frequent visitors. To ensure the protection of the mother and the child a tiny pouch of cloth is stitched on to the headgear of the mother and her baby. The pouch is filled with lime and turmeric powder to act as an antidote against the evil spirits. The origin of this ritual is unknown, though presumably it must have been a part of some ancient magic rite,- now forgotten- for protecting the child and the mother from infection of sorts. Turmeric and lime powder are generally used as a curative for cuts and aberration of skin and thus serve as a disinfectant. (home remedies) and that could be the reason of its usage. On this day, *Keliya- (a* mutton dish in which turmeric powder is an essential ingredient)- is specially cooked along with pan cakes to be distributed among the relatives, friends, and neighbours and also sent to the mother's parental home.

Annapravish

This ceremony celebrates the event of feeding the child with solid food for the first time. On an auspicious day in the sixth month after birth the new born child is fed some cereal for the first time.(In the recent times the doctors have considerably brought forward the date and time of feeding any type of solids to the babies.) It is an invocation to the Gods to bless the child with good digestive powers. Traditionally the solid food included a little mincemeat-along with a little *khir* /pudding, in the belief that this would give the child nourishment as well as mental strength. It is also believed to be the indicator of the weaning time for the mothers, a warning to stop suckling the child. Generally an elderly person in the family, grandfather, grandmother or any other elderly relative, male or female is asked to feed the child on the selected auspicious day

Zarakasay (Tonsure)

This ceremony indicates clean shaving of the head, prescribed to be done when the child is three years old. The procedure followed traditionally was first to give a ritual bath to the child while sitting on a wooden seat as in the case of *Divagon* ceremony. Child would then be adorned with newly stitched clothes. The barber was sent for and asked to be present at the auspicious moment fixed astrologically by the family priest. The barber would then be asked to shave off the hair on the child's head, taking care to preserve the *tchog* (a tuft of hair at the centre of the skull,) The reason given for keeping the tuft is that "Inside the head, near the top, is the point of *Sira* (artery) and *Sandhi* (a critical juncture).There in the eddy of hairs is the vital spot called *Adhipati* (overlord). Any injury to this part causes sudden death. The tuft performs the function of a helmet. Even science today gives credence to the belief that the top knot is a lightning conductor. It is a preventive measure against external lightning and a stabilizer and controller of inner electric currents."[6] The cropped locks of hair are collected on a piece of new cloth. This piece of cloth, some cash, besides gifts in kind are given to the barber after he has performed his act. Later the cropped hair is gathered in a deep earthen plate filled with water and walnuts. A close relative of the child takes the gathered hair and the walnuts and buries them beneath a tree in the courtyard of the house.

Kahnether, (*Namkaran Samaskar*- Naming Ceremony)

This ritual used to be performed on the 11th day of the birth of the child. As per scriptures, Hindu KSP believed that till this ceremony, the child belongs to the gotra of the family of his/ her previous birth and, hence, has to be initiated into the gotra of the present family where he/she has taken the birth. In recent times hardly any one follows the traditionally prescribed day or spirit. Basically it is a purification ceremony that essentially follows *shran sondar. A homa of great* religious *significance* is performed and the mother goddesses are worshipped to seek their blessings for a long and prosperous life of the child. *Khir* (milk and rice pudding) is offered to the Deities and distributed as *naivedya./prasad* after the purification *homa* and initiation of the child in to the family Gotra. Following Laugakshi's instructions, while performing the ceremony the child's father dips a gold ornament, preferably a gold ring, for the purpose, in clarified butter kept in a bronze vessel and feed the child little clarified butter attached to it with the belief that this will increase the child's intelligence. The ring is then worn round the child's neck and the child is also given a name. The ceremony ends with a feast given to the presiding priest and other guests. It has become more of a social than a religious function now and is rarely performed at the prescribed age.

All the above mentioned rituals are prescribed and performed irrespective of the gender of the new born.

Mekhala

The last of the child hood ceremonies is *Mekhala* i.e. the sacred thread ceremony, also known as *Upanayana* in the general Hindu lore. This ceremony, as per traditional practice, is meant only for the male child, though the Vedic scriptures do permit even the girl child to under go the ritual. It is to be performed between the age of fifth and the seventh year of a child as per the scriptures, but once again this practice has fallen victim to space age, dearth of time, faith and finances, with the result it is often performed along with the first adult hood ritual named *Vivah,* i.e. marriage. The thread ceremony is one of the most important *samskars* of the child as it is the beginning of the educational life of a child when he is sent to study under the guidance of a teacher. As per primary injunctions a student is symbolically expected to collect his educational expenses from all his relations and well-wishers before proceeding to the Gurukul/Ashram (boarding house.) It is an elaborate ceremony that extends over a period of five days. The preliminary ceremonies performed prior to the final i.e. *Upanayana* are : 1) *Liveyun* or cleaning of the premises, especially the kitchen, 2) the *manziraat* (Mehandiraat), i.e. applying henna paste on an auspicious day followed by a grand feast and celebrations through out the night with singing and dancing, 3) *Divagone-* is a religious ceremony of high sanctity, performed to invoke the presence of Gods especially the Ganesha and the *Saptamatrika* (seven mother goddesses) to bless the initiate, and is followed by 4) *upanayana Yagniya*, a day long *Havan* ceremony performed by the family *Jyotishi* as well as the family *Guru* (priest), who invoke the protection of sixty four deities. In the process of the ceremony a sacred thread of three strings is placed round the initiate's neck that confirms his stature to undertake performance of Hindu rituals.

SIGNIFICANCE OF THE (*YOUNIA)* THE SACRED THREAD

"The three strings denote that one should be *Brahmachari* in thought, word and deed. Each thread represents a Veda viz, Rigveda, Yajurveda, and Samveda. It also represents Brahma; Vishnu and Shiva. The knot in the middle represents the formless Brahmin, the supreme principle. The three knots represent *Satva* (truth), *Rajas* (action), and *Tamas (*inertia) of three fold *maya*, ("*trigunatmika maya")* . . . Three strands also remind the wearer, that he is to honour his parents and elders; he is now in a position to participate in family rituals and prayers and is allowed to chant the Gayatri mantra."

This scriptural ceremony is followed by dancing and singing. A *veyug*, a circular ritual design is made either of flowers or colours on the ground and the *mekhla maharaz, / the* initiate is made to stand on it, while women sing and bless him and celebrate the moment. Later he is carried in state to the nearest river, where he performs his prayer ceremonies and congratulations are offered all around.

Finally on the following day a small *homa-(Koshal hom* in the native language 'or Sanskrit *Kushal homa-* is performed to thank god for satisfactory culmination of the event.

KHANDER VIVAH/ MARRIAGE

"(HINDU RELIGIOUS ORDER IDENTIFIES AS MANY AS EIGHT TYPES OF MARRIAGES; THE ONE INHERITED BY THE HINDU KSP IS THE BRAHMAN MARRIAGE)" 7

Hindu KSP's marriages are generally, as in the rest of the country, arranged marriages and are preceded by examination of the horoscope (birth chart) of the boy and the girl. To obtain the same, traditionally services of a *manzim- yor (*professional match-maker) who could be of any faith, Musalman, or Hindu, were utilized. Once the birth charts of the two is found to be matching-study generally is carried out by the family priest or any reputed astrologer employed by the girl's family-the girl's parents who have the first right to sanctify the relationship send a token *shagun/* good omen- to the boy's family conveying their acceptance. After the recent exodus role of the match maker has been replaced by advertising in matrimonial columns of the community newsletters and or in national news papers. Rare option is the self selection of the boys and girls by mutual consent termed as love marriage, where in the restrictions like that of economic or social status of the families or the restrictions of Gotra and cast are mostly overlooked.

Once the auspicious day for the wedding is finalised, the bride's parents formally convey marriage details on a scroll called *Lagan Charika* / modern *Lagan Cheer* to the groom's family, which is presented by the priest (*Guru ji)* of the brides family. On the wedding day the groom, richly attired, and decked with garlands sets out for the bride's house in a car now a days; previously it was either a *shikara or a tonga* (horse drawn carriage common means of transport in the valley till the end of twentieth century).KSP groom termed *Maharaza* does not cover his face with *Sehra-a* common tradition in north India- instead he is followed by a member of the family holding a colourful often flower decked umbrella over his head. During the Pathan rule, when child marriage was the routine a tradition had been adopted to have another boy decked in the same fashion as the groom-termed *pote maharaz* generally a near relative to accompany *barat* so that if some untoward event should happen to the bridegroom-common occurrence during the Pathan rule-the so called *Pote Maharaza* would take the place of the groom.

The wedding process by itself is an elaborate affair extending over a week at least. All the ceremonies that are performed prior to *Mekhla* are like wise observed prior to the wedding ceremony itself; i.e. *livun, manziraat, and devgone,* followed by the main wedding ceremony known as *Lagen* ceremony. On this occasion the groom along with the *barrat* is welcomed ceremoniously by the bride's family, their relatives and friends. As a first step the groom and the bride are made to stand on a well designed floral *rangolli* (mural art) and an *aarti* is performed by the grand mother or mother of the bride. Then both are led to the main door step where a short puja *(dvaar puja)* is performed by the fathers of the groom and the bride, seeking blessings for the successful completion of the *Lagan* ceremony.

During the *lagan* ceremony the bride and the bride groom are symbolised as Shiva and Shakti and worshipped along with other religious performances by the bride's and the groom's families. After lagan there is satraat i.e. a special feast for the bridegroom in the evening following the wedding day. Very close relatives of the bride also participate in this dinner. After a day or two, on an auspicious day the bride and the bride groom is invited by the brides parents and this function is known as *phirsaal or phir lat* i.e. return invitation to the couple. Finally the two families invite each other on two different dates to a sumptuous feast, for an informal gathering to introduce all the family members and their relatives to each other in order to build a good relationship. This ceremony is known as *Ghar Achun.*

The KSP Hindu wedding is an agreement between the families, and un-like Hindus in the rest of the country where the groom bestows upon the bride the so called marriage symbol *(suhag ke nishani)*; in a Kashmiri wedding, the groom does not play any role when the bride wears the *dej-hore-* sign of marriage. As a matter of fact, the groom is no where near the scene of action. This ornament has two units, one is *dej-hore* given by the parents to the bride during the *devgone* ceremony, and the other half namely *ath-hore and ath,* is given to the bride by her in-laws, when she accompanies the groom to her in-law's home after the wedding ritual. Two units of *dej-hore* are joined together usually by the *Buwa* (paternal aunt) and then threaded in to the brides upper ear lobe, which is pierced earlier during a ceremony called *Kan chomben (piercing the ear)* at a very young age.

Yet another peculiarity of KSP wedding ritual is that the mother-in law is the first person to lift the conventional veil of the bride to have a glimpse; and the bride gives her a gift *maete-moor* (either an ornament or cash). The bride receives blessings and gifts from all relatives and friends on the first sighting. This is called *gule muth*.

WITH THIS ENDS THE PHASE OF THE LIFE CYCLE RITUALS OF THE HINDU KSP.

ANTHYESHTI (HINDU RITUALS CONNECTED WITH DEATH AND THERE AFTER)

Having enjoyed the blessings of life, death is the ultimate goal, hence there are a set off rituals to be observed, as designated in every community.

"Most of the Hindu rituals performed after the death of a person are an out come of their conception of life after death, the mixed feeling of dread and love for the departed, desire for an easy and peaceful passage from the world of mortals, ensuring for the departed a fit place in the company of manes and the Gods, and the motive of securing the final liberation of the soul from the cycle of births and deaths." [8]

THE PROCEDURE TO BE FOLLOWED FOR THE FINAL SAMSKARA OF LIFE:

For a Hindu final Samskara of life is the *Shrada* ceremony, a rite performed in the memory of the departed souls. KSP Hindus perform a small rite known as ***antedaan*** prior to laying the body on a straw bed, where in rice, salt and money are placed in a plate by the side of the dead person and mantras are recited. These offerings are later distributed among the poor. Next the children and grand children offer a few drops of *Ganga jal* to the deceased person in the mouth. Traditionally, the body is laid on a straw bed of Kusha *(darbha* grass) that is supposed to be born from Vishnu's hair and sesame seeds are spread on the floor and a lighted earthenware oil lamp is kept near the head be it night or day. A plate full of sesame seeds with a few coins is also kept next to the body (as that is supposed to destroy evil spirits),) This is followed by the ***Shraan deuen***-traditional bath following which the dead body is wrapped in what is called *kafan* (shroud) comprising a loose toga, cap, and *sranpat (*a piece of cloth about two yards long and a quarter of a yard wide to cover the lower abdomen.). A short shrada ceremony is performed followed by *aarti* prior to the body being carried for cremation ground. Dead body is carried to the cremation ground preferably on a wooden plank borne on the shoulders of close relatives and friends. The funeral pyre may be lighted by the son/ daughter/ husband /wife and even by the closest relative of the deceased. If the deceased is a woman one or two ornaments are left on the body, which are recovered from the fire by the *kawuj-* the professional cremator of the corps. A day or two after the cremation, ashes and a few bone remnants *(astruk)* that the fire has not consumed are carried for emersion in a river preferably Ganga. In earlier days tradition was to bring the ashes home where these were kept till immersion in a sealed container in a hole made in the wall at the entrance of the house. In recent years facilities for keeping the ashes till immersion in the lockers are available at the cremation grounds and are being utilised. Previously in the valley, the ashes used to be taken for immersion to the holy lake of Gangabal at the base of Harmuk peak or at *Sangam-* confluence of *Veth* /Jhelum and Sindh at Shadipore in the valley. Now a days with the easier travel facilities, these are generally immersed in the Ganges preferably at Haridwar or any other sacred *ghat* (bank) of the river Ganges.

Since the Hindus believe in re-in-carnation of the soul, general belief is that, on the death of the physical body, the astral body leaves the physical frame and hovers around for some period till the spiritual forces guide it to another physical body. KSP's believe that for ten days after the death in the family the house of the deceased is unclean (*honch*) and hence, while the soul of the deceased is on its journey, rites for the dead *(kari karni)* are to be performed on the riverbank-a practice hardly followed now days. As a part of this belief, the son or daughter of the deceased person comes out on to the house threshold every day from the 2nd to 9th day after the death, before the sunrise, and calls up on the departed soul a couple of times loudly *(bochh ma lajiy babo/maji?) are* you hungry Father /mother?); *(Tresh ma lajiy babo/maji?) Are* you thirsty Father /mother? *(tur ma lajiy babo/maji?)* Are you feeling cold Father /mother?)

Deceased's son shaves his head and beard, on the completion of the tenth day, at the river bank and performs a *Shraddha.* At the end of the *Shraddha* ceremony either at the river bank or at the entrance to the house, the accompanying mourners draw themselves into two groups on either side while the deceased's son is made to walk in between without looking back. Only then do the accompanying mourners take their leave. Women mourners do not attend the ceremonies on the river bank, but visit the mourning family. On the eleventh day the shrada service is performed for the deceased and for ancestors up to the seventh generation. The family mourns the loss of the dead person for a period of 12 days initially. The daughter or grand daughter of the deceased performs ***noon Shraddha*** i.e. (offering salt to the cows) in memory of the departed soul. On the 11th and 12th day an elaborate *Shraddha* is performed for the whole day. The *purohitas-* the learned priests recite Vedic mantras, and receive cash and kind offerings from the family of the diseased. On the 11th day, yet another *Shraddha* ceremony termed ***Teel dyun*** is performed. On this occasion mustard oil is poured in a large number of earthen lamps with a cotton wick and lighted and placed at different corners traditionally meant to light the path for the astral body. Sweet pudding and pan cakes *(halwa and puri*) are prepared in large quantity and distributed among neighbours and friends. Tradition states that in earlier days fried fish instead of *halwa* was distributed.

Shradas are also performed every fortnight-***pachvarr***-for the first three months, and subsequently for the rest of the year every month- ***maasvaar.*** At the end of the sixth month- ***Shadmose-*** and at the end of one year ***Veharver* shradha** is performed. Both these rites are very elaborate affairs. After this it is a routine to repeat the *Shraddha* rite on the death anniversary every year and once during the *pitrapaksh*-the dark fortnight specially meant for offering our respects and remembrances to the departed souls.

Besides there is a daily ritual of ***tarpan*** (gratification*) i.e.* offering water to the deceased parents, and generations of grand parents every morning? In local language it is called ***tresh deun.***

Most of these rituals have been reduced greatly in their detail in the recent times.

Rituals of Muslim KSP

Muslim rituals are also as elaborate as that of the Hindus' and follow the same processes but in numbers they are comparatively very few.

Childhood Rituals

Azzan and *Takbir*

During the earlier eras a Muslim baby as per tradition used to be born in his mothers parental home, as the mother would feel free and comfortable in those surroundings. She would face less restrictions and taboos that would be good for the child to be born. In the recent times no such tradition is followed, and more often than not the delivery takes place in a hospital with all technological facilities in case of emergencies. When the child is born, a Mullah comes and whispers into the right ear the word *Azzan* welcoming the child into this world and his faith; he then repeats into the left ear the *Takbir*, adding the warning that death is the end of all living things.

Sundar

On the seventh day of the child's birth, both mother and the child are given a bath and the child is given a name by the Pir (Muslim priest) of the family. The name he suggests usually has some connection with the month the child is born or any other auspicious Islamic event, like for instance—the boy born in the month of *Ramzan* will most likely be given that name. After the naming ceremony, later the same day a barber is called who shaves the child's head. This double ceremony day is celebrated by feasting with the relatives and neighbours.

Khatanhal (Circumcision)

At the age of four or five the child is circumcised and this is an occasion of great rejoicing. Friends are invited, and the child's feet and hands are stained with the red *mehndhi* dye on *the manziraat* night and he is decked out in bright apparel. For seven days before the ceremony there is nothing but singing and feasting, and on the day of the circumcision *{khutnhal*) the child is placed on a basket under which a cock' is cooped, the perquisite of the barber who performs the circumcision. All friends and relatives kiss the child's hand and give him money (*guli-muit*), and enjoy a great feast.

Khander (marriage) *Nikah*

The Mussalmans generally marry within their near relatives or even within the extended family relations and in case no suitable boy or girl is available within their fold, then only do they go looking for other options. They also use the services of the middle men / women like the Hindu KSP, and follow the same process while selecting a bride or a groom. Once the match and the family is finalised the betrothal day is decided according to the advice of the mullah. Gifts are given by the boy's parent to the girl in the presence of the priest, who at the same time fixes the date of the wedding. The date is conveyed to the girl's family by the boy's family with the details of the family pedigree, the guest list, the accompanying paraphernalia and the time and date of the ceremony.

In the Muslim wedding ceremony mehandiraat and the *Baraat* are two main celebration events. A day before the marriage, the boy's family sends *mehndi* a dye to the bride's house; with this she decorates her hands and feet. On the day of the marriage, the groom dressed in all his finery sets out either riding a pony or now days in a car. On way to his in-laws house, in earlier eras he would visit a nearby shrine to offer his prayers and would also pay a visit to the grave of his ancestors, to pay his respects to them. Following that he would head for the bride's house, sending ahead of him the presents and the palanquin in which she would return. These practices have changed now. As the *barat* (grooms party) approaches, the women folk of the bride's family and friends come out, and standing in a half circle facing the men sing songs of welcome, describing the qualities of both the bride and the groom. Near the main door of the reception hall, a jar filled with water is held by one of the bride's family members and the groom's representative tosses a silver rupee in it. This custom is known as *adbul* and it is repeated when the groom takes his bride away. Then the wedding party along with the groom who specially sits on cushions like a Maharaja enjoy a sumptuous feast.

Wedding ceremony begins with the fixing of the *mehr* (dower) suitable according to economic viability of the two parties followed by the *Nikha-Nama* (marriage contract). After seeking the ascent to the contract of both groom and the bride, the *Kazi* certifies the *Nikha.* Earlier, traditionally the bride used to be carried either by her brother or her maternal uncle to the palanquin in which she proceeded for her in-laws home. On reaching the in-law's house, she is carried from her palanquin to a room which has been prepared for her, where like the Hindu KSPs her mother-in-law lifts her veil; at the same time taking from the bride's handkerchief some money which is her perquisite and known as *hash kant.* Female guests of the groom's family kiss the bride's hand, placing silver rupees or any other gift called *Glue muthe* in her hand as is the tradition with Hindu KSPs, obviously both these practices have been retained by the Muslim KSP's even after conversion.

The bride remains for seven days in her husband's house whence she visits her parents. Like the Hindu KSP' rituals many a changes have occurred in the marriage rituals of the Muslim Kashmiris, as well.

Death Rites

KSP Muslims or the Musalmáns as they are better known, have the tradition of, "laying a person, on the verge of death, on the floor give a last drink a *sharbat (*a sweet drink) made of honey and water, and those around call on the name of God, till he or she breathes his or her last." The corpse is then bathed and wrapped in a cotton cloth and placed in a *tabud (coffin)*, wooden box which is always in readiness at the mosque. The body is taken to the *mazaar (*graveyard), and relatives and friends repeat the funeral service.

The gravedigger and the priest fling a cotton pall over the dug up grave. The corpse is removed from the box and is buried in the cotton cloth. The assemblage one by one fling a hand full of clay on corpse till it is fully buried. On the day of the funeral, and for three days after, the guests and priest are feasted by some relative of the deceased, as no food is cooked in the deceased's house. On the fourth day (*chaudas*) a big feast is given, and on the Friday following the death all go to the graveyard to offer Nemaz.

For forty days prayers are offered for the deceased and food is distributed among the priests and the poor. For one year presents must be given every month to the priest, and here after on the anniversary of a man's death the priest receives a gift.

With the evolution of age, and environment it will not be wrong to say that in spite of their strict vigil quite a few changes have incurred in to the ritual system of all Kashmiri speaking people, and there is every chance many more changes will occur in future too.

Festivals of KSP's

The festivals celebrated by the KSPs-Hindus or Muslims are governed by their own calendar and do not match the Georgian calendar. While the Hindu festivals are to a great extant fixed according to the lunar calendar, Muslim festivals, likewise, are controlled by the sighting of the moon.

Festivals observed by the Hindu K.S.P's.

Festivals celebrated by the KSP, like the rituals, have undergone lot of changes in the manner of celebration and quite a large number have almost gone extinct over the past few centuries. For a broader perspective I have tried to describe the festivals under three eras i.e.,

1: Puranic era,

2: Medieval era,

3: Post Islamic era.

Available Information points to the fact that Hindu KSP celebrated quite a large number of festivals to mark different occasions of festivities in the ancient and medieval eras. These were labelled as social, seasonal and religious festivals, and for every occasion there were set guidelines for how, why and when. These would serve the purpose of interaction; socialisation, entertainment and religious identification besides enhancing the flourishing culture of pilgrimages, or say modern tourism.

In the Puranic era, as per Nilamata, the KSP were celebrating almost sixty five festivals in a year. Nilmata Purana describes in detail the instructions given about all the practices and taboos meant to be followed by the people of the valley during the celebration of these festivals that were grouped as the V*ratas* and *Utsavas.*

*Vratas i*nvolved fasting and restrictions regarding food and behaviour; *Utsavas* on the other hand were celebrations and commemorations of events and individuals like seasonal festivals and social festivities. Fasting, singing, and merry making are common to both. (D*etailed list of the festivals as recorded by Dr Ved Kumari has been reproduced in the Appendix 1.)*

A few words may be said about the nature and significance of these V*ratas, Utsavas* and other religious practices. In these festivals we discern the gradual moving away from 'Vedic ritualistic cult' to 'Upanishadic philosophy'. Ved Kumari records, "The Vedic ritualistic cult has been replaced here by the cult of *Vrata, puja, japa* etc. The replacement, however, was gradual and necessary. The influence of Upanishadic philosophy had long ago begun to modify the religious outlook of the people. Buddhism, Jainism and some other popular faiths were offering to the masses, substitutes of ritualism, which promised the act of thanksgiving, consisted in partaking of new grains only after those had been offered to the deity. The only method by which Brahmanism could attract the masses, under these circumstances, was to give some cheaper, easier and less violent replica of the sacrifice with the same conception of alluring rewards."[9]

The detailed list and description of the festivals celebrated in the Puranic era as recorded carries an impression of a society that used to follow set disciplinary religious instructions and injunctions, amidst all kinds of celebrations. They would fast, pray and at the same time sing, dance, drink, give away gifts and make merry. Great importance was given to the impact and influence of the constellations and stars; the victories of the kings, were commemorated along with the foundation days of the land and their deities. Pilgrimages were also part of the festivities. Historical event like the ouster of Pisachas from the valley was duly celebrated.

These practices under went a remarkable change slowly with the invasion of foreigners like Kushans, Huns, Turks, Moguls and Afghans. With the change of religious faiths, and especially with the forced or willing conversion of the majority of the people to Islamic faith, the number of the festivals was considerably reduced. Because the new faith did not permit observance of the existing festivals, and the chaos and confusion in the social set up was not congenial for celebrations and festivities. Result being that all through the medieval era the festivals celebrated gradually went on reducing both in scales of festivities and in numbers.

Most of the Hindu KSP festivals mean observation of a fast, and the peculiarity of these fasts is that a one-time cereal meal is allowed unlike the rest of the Hindu fold. Very few fasts *like Ikadashi, Shiv Chaturdashi, Krishna Janamashtami* are *nirahar* (without partaking any cereals). These are named as *kaishfakeh*. The genesis of this sort of choice is rather difficult to explain. Moreover, there are pointing differences in the intake of edibles on such occasions. Most of the vegetables like spinach, carrot, beans, etc. are a taboo on fast days. All this is contrary to the practice prevalent in the rest of the country.

Shri Anand Koul Bamzai has listed the festivals celebrated by the Hindu KSP during the medieval era in his book,' *Kashir*' (see *Appendix* 11)

The details of the individual festivals given by him are in some instances unfamiliar to the present generation. Quite a number of festivals recorded by him have gone in to the oblivion during and after the late twentieth century. They are mostly now labels printed annually on the Hindu KSP community almanac. Main reason for this change and neglect is inability to understand the significance and the complexities of the local calendar followed in the mentioned almanac and the exile of Hindu KSP from their home land. Besides these factors, one of the main reasons is the change of the physical environment for which these festivals were delegated.

A few festivals like: *Kechrii Amavas*, *Gada-Bata, Kawa Punim* and even *Herath* and *Zangatry*, according to some versions, have their origin attributed to the era of Nagas in Kashmir, that have managed to survive through the changing times in the KSP festival calendar. They are religiously celebrated, even today, by the dwindling senior generations of the Hindu KSP's. How far the young will carry these forward, only time can tell ? The festivals that are still observed are categorised as religious, seasonal and social festivals as follows:

Religious Festivals

Kashmiri Hindu community is predominantly Shaivite, i.e. believers in Shiva and Shakti. Latter's manifestations in the valley are grouped according to the affiliation to three different forms: those of *Maharagyina, Sharika and Jwala*. And the three famous shrines dedicated to these deities are situated at Tula Mula, Hari Parbat in Srinagar and at the village Khrew respectively. It is noteworthy that the festivals in the honour of these deities are held in the month of Ashada. On *ashtami (*8th day) is the festival at Tula Mula for *Maharagyina* the Shivas consort; on *navami* (9th day) is the festival at *Chakreshwara* for Sharika (Hari Parbat) and on *Chaturdashi,* (14th day) it is at Khrew to worship Goddess Jwala. Besides in the month of Ashada-H*aar* in Kashmiri-we have *Hara Satam* (The seventh day of the bright fortnight). On this day, the courtyard, the front door and the gallery called the *Vuz* are decorated with *Hare Mandul-rangoli* (circular design made of multicolour powders) to greet the goddess to grace the houses by her presence.

Jeyesht Ashtami

This festival is celebrated at Tulamula where the temple dedicated to the Goddess Raginya is situated within the Sanctum Santorum made of white marble built in a 'L' shaped spring. It has been observed that the water of this spring changes colours as referred earlier, and as per the traditional belief, this change indicates the overall health of the times and the society. Green, pink and sky blue colours stand for prosperity, happiness and health; where as dark grey and ink black fore warns adverse times. This temple is amply provided with rest houses for the stay of the pilgrims, meditation Halls and *yegnaya kunds* for the devout seekers. The ambiance of this place and the feel of the spiritual calm that pervades all around is a unique experience. Adherence to strict vegetarian diet is a must in the vicinity of the temple and this taboo is strictly adhered to by all KSP's including Muslims and Sikhs.

Shravana Punim

Sharavana punim—Sharavan Purnimasi is celebrated through out India as the 'Raksha Bandhan' day and also for the pilgrimage to the Amarnath cave to pay obeisance to the ice lingam that has been forming annually at least for the last two thousand years as per the records. (*For details of Amarnath refer to Appendix111.*) KSP Hindus do not celebrate Raksha Bandan as is done in the rest of the country where a sister ties the sacred thread of *rakhi* on her brother's wrist; instead they go on pilgrimage to Amarnath cave or visit the temple on top of the Shankaracharya hill. Elderly people go on fast and make *Partheshwaras* (*lingas*), from the clay collected from the said hill, for their puja.

ZARMA SATAM /JANAM ASHTAMI

Zarma satam (birth day of lord Krishna) is a day of fasting for the Hindu KSPs. The fast is broken at the midnight hour when the moon appears and is visible to the worshipers. Cereals are forbidden in this fast; only fruits, fried potatoes and milk or curds are permitted. Fast and the celebration in rest of the Hindu fold is held on the *Ashtami* (8th day of the fortnight) in honour of the birth of Lord Krishna; where as in the valley KSPs have it a day earlier on *Saptami* (7th day of the fortnight) prior to the birth of the lord, as would befit the culture of sages and saints to prey for the safety of both mother Deveki and her child, for she was delivering within the prison walls beyond which she had been put under the express orders of her brother Kansa. People take out religious processions through the cities singing and chanting praises of the Lord Krishna. Skits and plays replicating the scenes from Mahabharata were a very common sight in the valley during this festival.

KAW PUNIM

The full moon of the lunar fortnight of *Magha* is known as *Kaw punim*. It is on this day that Kashmiri specific yellow rice called tahri is cooked to be offered to the crows in a contraption made of two sticks tied in the shape of a cross and on the open ends of the cross, grass is woven to make a long handled flat spoon and after a little puja the tahri is served on it to the crows. "While the ceremony is on, children sing in chorus . . . . . . (0h clever crow,0! The lover of *khichri* come to our new house along with your spouse; be seated on the threshold of our roof and partake of the salty pudding." This festival is indicative of the love and care that the Kashmiri's bestowed on the birds.

HERATH- SHIVARATRI

There are varied assumptions about the origin of the name Herath. According to one version, it is associated with the successful attempt of the Nagas in draining the water out of the valley. J.K.Jalali writes, "when the water started flowing and the land was sighted by the Naga inhabitants, they were thrilled with joy and celebrated the event with singing, dancing and feasting for several days and thus began the festival of *Herath,* commencing from the first day of the dark fortnight of *Phalguna* (February) and extends over a fortnight. On the Herath, as the Nagas did, so do the present Saraswats offer fish, mutton, forest fowl meat, and even liquor to the *Bhairavas*".

Yet another version states that the Herath is a day of great feasting in Kashmir because it signifies the holy marriage of Shiva and Parvati known to have been conducted in this part of the Himalayas.

The most tangible explanation would be that word *Herath* is the derivative of the letter *Hara ratri* (Shiva's night). Herath or Shiva-ratri for certain is observed as a festival of great importance by the Hindu *Kashur*, who celebrate this festival a day earlier than rest of the Hindu fold as they believe that the time of platonic union of Shiva and Parvati was at *pradoshakala* (*the* twilight hour of the dusk on the *trayodashi* (13th day) of the dark fortnight of *Phalguna.*

Which ever explanation may be correct, it is a fact that the nomenclature '*Herath*' was not in vogue till the time Nilmata Purana was composed. In this Purana it is referred by the name Shivaratri celebrated by worshipping the Siva Linga on the dark 14th of *Phalguna.*

Shivaratri / *Herath* festival is the most important festival of Hindu KSP. One can say it is the 'crown' of the Hindu Kashmiri festivals that can be easily compared with Durga puja in Bengal, Ganesha Chaturthi in Maharashtra, *Navaratras* in Gujarat or the *Dashera* in the North of India, to quote a few. It is a socio-religious festival celebrated over a period of one whole fortnight in the *Phalguna*-February-March month. It involves a complete session of spring cleaning that begins with the first day of the fortnight-*Hurya Okdoh*- and carries on till the seventh day inclusive-*Hurya Satam,* the day of washing, cleaning and collecting the required items for the main puja. Eighth day-*Hurya Aetham*-is meant to be celebrated in honour of the presiding deity by singing devotional songs and by performing a *Havan /yagnya* at Hari Parbat. This is followed by *Hurya Navam*, (9[th]day*) Dyara Daham* (10[th]day) *and Gada Kah.*(11[th]day) *Vager Bah (12[th]day), Hereth Truvah(13th day).* The prefix Hurya in the native tongue denotes the process of mopping in other words spring cleaning. From the 11th day onwards starts the religious and spiritual part of this festival that involves elaborate and detailed pujaas of various Devatas and Bhairavas based on conventions strictly assigned to every clan and family of the Kashmiri Hindu fold. Puja on the 13th day is known as *Vatuk Puja.* On this occasion a Kalasha-metal pot-and a few other pots and pans,according to the family traditions, are filled with water and dry walnuts that are the main components of the puja. Kashmiri Hindus use walnuts almost for every auspicious occasion either because it was the commonly available dry fruit in those eras or may be due to the significance attached to the four distinct sections of the kernel of the fruit which some believe to be representing the four Vedas or even the cycle of life as per Hindu belief. Special items of the menu cooked for the auspicious occasion are also offered to the *VatakNath the god head* (Shiva personification*)*. Next day follows *Shiva Chaturdashi.*- popularly called '*Salaam*'-perhaps because on this day friends from the Muslim community come to felicitate Kashmiri Pandits. Also beggars, bards and street dancers (*baands*) would come for their due on this festive occasion, and greet the head of the family with the word *Salaam.* Children get *Herath Kharach* (pocket allowance) from the elders and relatives. Usual pastime is a game of covery shells, which creates a lot of enthusiasm amongst the children. On the *Amavasya* (15thday), pooja is performed with walnuts and small size flour pancakes (T*chochewoer)* and *prassad* distributed amongst the family members. Soaked walnuts are distributed among friends, relatives and neighbours. Paraphernalia associated with the puja like the grass seats of the *Vatuk,* flowers and *Naervan* tied round these pots and any other remnant are immersed into the nearby river on the *Tila Ashtami,* which marks the finale to this great festival. KSP believe that the Shivaratri symbolises wedding of Shiva and Parvati his consort.

An interesting finale of the celebration, observed in older days, when the last day's puja, referred above, used to be performed on the river ghats, could be termed as '*Dub Dub'*/ Knock, knock. Member returning from the ghat after the puja was debarred from entering the house. Finding the door closed he would knock and a conversation followed: "Who are you?" "*Ram bror* and I have come with wealth, riches, good wishes for health and happiness, food and means of livelihood and all the good things for the family". The door is then opened to receive him and his good wishes.

In the recent history of this festival an incident during the Afghan rule is worth recording for its impact on the Hindu KSP society. As per records during the reign of an Afghan *Sobedar* Jabbar Khan, the Hindu KSP's, who decided to stay on in the valley, in spite of all the tortures and coercions by the Afghans, were ordered to celebrate the festival of Shivaratri in the hot summer-month of *Har (Ashad*, June)-instead of the month of *Phalguna* (February/March). For the Sobedar believed that the Hindu KSP's faith in the sanctity of the Shivaratri festival was to a great extant associated with the snowfall that invariably used to take place during this festival. Jabbar Khan hence advised the change in the date of the festival. But, as the fate would have it, it snowed heavily that year on the day of Shivaratri even in the month of *Har* /June.The Sobedar Jabar Khan was humbled and his men aghast at the phenomenon and exclaimed 'Hairan/Herath' (Persian word for wonder). As per some observers, this remark led to the name Hareth. Memories of this incident survive in the local tradition in the medium of a saying, "*wuch toan ye Jabar janda Hars te korun wanda*" (behold the Jabaar rag-man who converted the summer month of June into severe winter).

Gurutoo Sect

This act of Jabbar Khan the Afghan governor was, responsible for the creation of a new sect among the Hindu KSPs namely the Gurutoos. P.N.Bamzai writes, "Hindus who had survived the conversion would live in Tolas, and a few Tolas, with the help of neighbours and good relations with the recently converted neighbours, could avoid meat eating on this day and adhere to their customary practice by completely remaining imprisoned within the four walls of their dwellings without allowing anybody to come to visit them. They remained almost incognito and survived on what ever little they had available in their larder. That is why even now their menu is very scanty unlike the rest of the fold. These Tolas subsequently became Gurutoos". Over the years this section was looked up on with awe for their courage and allegiance to their faith. No body would visit these homes during the festival puja days, for the fear of defiling their premises. As a matter of fact this tradition still continues on and the Gurutoos are proud of their ancestor's courage and the ingenuity to create a delicious menu out of minimum grocery items like moong Dal (pulses), radish, lotus stem and dry spices. I feel the top of the cake so far as their ingenuity is concerned is the dish v*arichatin* a *hot* sauce made of dried spice cake called *ver.* and other spices, which they must have created to provide some sort of variety and tang to other wise limited flat vegetarian menu.

Seasonal Festivals

Some seasonal festivals still celebrated are the *Navreh, Navroze,* (Kashmiri New Year), *Sonth (* spring), *Vyatha Truvah* (The day of beginning of life in the land of Satidesha).

Vyatha Truvah

Vitasta, the river Jhelum holds an important place in the KSP's religious and cultural ethos. Most of the famous temples of the valley are situated on its banks, noteworthy being Ganesh temple, Mahakali shrine, Somayar (the temple of the Moon), *Raghunath Mandir*, *Batayar, Bokhatakeshwar Bhairav* etc. KSP's celebrate the *Pradurbhava* divas (the appearance day of this life line of Kashmir) on the thirteenth day of the bright fortnight of *Bhadrapada*. All the *ghats (*banks*)* of this holy river are sacred for performing Sandhya (a form of meditation) to offer puja. This puja is carried out by offering water, milk oblations, vermillion, raw rice and flowers into the flowing waters of the river while reciting *mantras i*n praise of the mighty river Veth/Vitasta. Annual pilgrimage to its source at '*Vyatha Votur'* and Verinag used to be a must for the KSP in the bygone days and even so up to the last exodus of the community in the early nineties of the twenty first century.

SONTH AND NAVREH

Sonth heralds the spring season and *Navreh* the New Year and both are equally important for the KSP. A unique custom for these two occasions is *thal Barun* (to set a large metal plate) over night filled with rice along with cups full of yoghurt and milk, and also nuts, bread, flower, pen, gold coin, v*hy(*a herb root), picture of a deity or goddess, barring one variation and that is to place the new Panchang (only on the occasion of *Navreh)*. This plate is kept covered overnight and early in the morning every member of the family views the contents of the plate and seeks blessings for the year to follow. It is considered as an omen of prosperity, happiness and knowledge. In earlier times people would go to the river bank, take a dip and throw these nuts in the water then offer puja at homes or in temples. Since *Navreh* signifies New Year and also the beginning of the *Navratra* puja, KSPs dressed in new clothes used to celebrate the day by having picnics in the beautiful almond orchards of the valley. *Sonth*, on the other hand, is relatively a quite affair.

NAV SHEEN

It is yet another seasonal festival of sorts celebrated by the Hindu KSP from the earliest eras. The name of this festival given in the Nilamat Purana is *Himpathmhautsava*. Details of this festival have been recorded earlier in the book.

SOCIAL FESTIVALS

PUN

It is one such festival that is eagerly awaited by the members of the family, their friends and relatives for the delicious *prassad Roth (*sweetened crisp bread cakes deep fried in pure ghee). The genesis of this ritual is difficult to locate. Some link its relation to *Vinayaka,* as this particular fortnight is the period of celebrations in piety of Lord *Ganapati. Vinayak Chaturthi* and *Ganesh Chaturdashi* both fall in this fortnight. According to the native belief, it is held in propitiation of Mother Shakti, to be precise, *Beeb Garaz Maej* who is the deity for this ritual. Whatever might have been the reason, fact is that this ritual is observed, even today, with the same religious spirit and caution as before. During the whole bright fortnight of *Irapad,* this ritual is performed on any day of the selected *tithi* (date*)* as an individual choice. Sweetened breads are made in ghee. The lady of the house adorns a cotton thread on her ear, which used to be got spun by a pre-pubertal girl, hence the ritual is called *Pun*-thread. This festival known all over country as *Vinayaka Chaturthi* is celebrated in this unique way only in Kashmir valley. On the morning of the auspicious day, a metal pot filled with water is placed at a suitable place, generally in the kitchen for the puja. Sweet pancakes called '*Roth*', decorated with poppy seeds are prepared: number depending upon the size of the family. Puja ceremony is preceded by reciting the story of the *Beeb garaz Maej* by the lady of the house while rest of the members or guests sit around the metal pot. The story deals with a king who had been dethroned and imprisoned by an invader for his having committed an act of sacrilege and, thereafter, how his queen along with the princess, in exile and in distress, helped him regain his lost glory by performing this ritual with utmost faith. Moral being that by performing puja of Ganesha on this day, preparing sweet pancakes and offering the same to the deity, poverty and the miseries of the person are removed and one lives a pious life full of comfort. The story is very similar to the one narrated on the occasion of the *Satya Narayana Puja*. After listening to the story, offerings of flowers and a specific variety of green grass which they hold in their hands throughout the narration of the story are made by the family members to the sacred pot representing the deity. The sweet pancakes prepared are distributed after this puja, as *prasaad* among relatives, friends and neighbours.

GAAD-BATTA

Gaad- batta literally, means fish and rice. It is one of those festivals that are affiliated with the Naga era. During that era there was a valley-wide belief of the presence of a holy spirit who acts as a caretaker of the house. This ritual is in appeasement of this deity-the *Ghar Devta* (Deity of the House) who is propitiated by offering cooked rice and fish curry along with one whole raw fish placed on top of the offering plate smeared with vermillion and flowers on any saturday following the *Posh* dark fortnight. The tradition of using only fish and no mention of mutton must be because fish was readily available everywhere due to abundant water resources in Kashmir in the earlier eras. This festival on the side line also indicates that the KSP were non vegetarians from the earlier times.

The celebration of these two festivals is not mandatory on every Hindu KSP family, in stead there is an option of individual choice, but once opted for it literally binds the family for eternal commitment.

KHECHRI AMAVASYA

This ritual falls on the Amavasya of *Paush* every year. Like the festival of *Gaad- Batta* it is yet another festival that has come down to us from the very beginning of the settlement of humans in the valley, only difference being that unlike *Pun* and *Gaad Batta*, this festival is mandatory for every Hindu KSP. As per the legends and myths, when the humans settled in the land of the Yakshas there was a mutual undertaking-a sort of treaty-that on certain fixed occasions in the cold freezing wintry months, the humans would offer a sumptuous non vegetarian feast to the Yakshas who in turn would not trouble them. Yakshas by nature were believed less ferocious but more powerful with divine inclinations, unlike other hilly tribes. In keeping with the spirit of honourable promise, made by the ancestors, Hindu KSP has treated it and is honour bound to execute the ritual by offering Khichri (yellow coloured rice cooked with lentils) and non-vegetarian dishes on this day to the Yakshas. This ritual, without exception, is still observed on this Amavasya-dark fortnight of *'Paush'* dedicated to the '*Yakshas*'- every year, with sanctity, even after the recent migration and settling down in other parts of the world. Offering is made by placing the stuff on an improvised plate made of dry grass, which is then placed on the compound wall. The kitchen stone mortal (*kajwath*) is placed, by the side on a circular base *aer (*ring made out of hey), and worshipped as a symbol of the cosmos and decorated with *sindoor* (vermilion), sandal paste, raw rice and flowers. Some households also serve fish on this day. During our childhood, we used to be tempted and advised to keep a watch for the Yaksha's arrival for he would be wearing a red cap while partaking of this *Khichri* and, whosoever was able to snatch away his cap would be bestowed with riches. A myth that continued to remain a myth and the Yaksha's cap eluded everyone.

GORA- TRAI

Gora-Trai or *Gauri Tritya* is celebrated on the third day of the bright fortnight of *Magha* in honour of the Goddess Saraswati, the goddess of learning. In the by gone days, this festival was earmarked as the day of convocation, when students were issued certificates on the completion of their education. On this day the family priest brings a portrait of the goddess of learning with some sacred shalokas printed on it. Whenever a child is born or after a wedding the family priest of the bride's parents brings a special portrait and in return gets honorarium from the boy's family.

ZANGTRY

Celebration of this festival is exclusive prerogative of the ladies, especially the married ones. On this day they visit their parental homes and enjoy an outing or have fun and frolic with parents and their family. In the evening they return with gifts of *choch*i (bread) salt and *atgat* (cash) as a good omen for the members of her family

(For detailed studies refer to Dr. S.S. Toshkhani's Book '*Rites and Rituals of the Kashmiri Brahmins*')

MUSLIM FESTIVALS.

ID-UL-FITR

There are two Eids in the Muslim calendar. One is Id-Ul-Fitr which follows the thirty days of the fast known as Ramzaan and the second one is Eid-ul-baqr which follows two months and ten days later. During Ramzaan, barring very old and sick persons, pregnant ladies and children, all Muslims observe fast from sun rise to sun set for a period of thirty days The fast starts with the dawn and breaks at dusk. During that time they are supposed to be pious in thought and deed. Main rituals that make the fasting complete are: ***Tarweeh*** *(*special prayers every evening; ***Iftar*** collective breaking of fast, and ***Zakat*** (donating a certain percentage of ones property). Muslims go to the mosques especially on the Friday's, listen to recitation of Quran and try to observe very clean, disciplined and spiritual routine. Ramzaan is the spiritual aspect of this festival and *Eid Ul-Fitr* is the culmination when the Muslims celebrate thanks giving day. In Srinagar they assemble at *Eidgah* and in various other open grounds in the valley to offer *Eid* prayers facing towards Mecca, expressing their thankfulness to the Allah for His Benevolence. During Ramzaan people donate freely at the mosques and also distribute food preparations among the poor. They greet every one with *Eid Mubarak*, hug each other and socialize freely, gifts are exchanged and the atmosphere of joy and merriment prevails on the day of *Eid.* Hindu friends and families wish them *Eid Mubarak*; we can say used to, for there are hardly any Hindus in the valley at present.

Id-ul-Zuha

Id-ul-Zuha is probably the greatest of all Muslim festivals. It commemorates a great event in the life of Prophet Abraham, the occasion when he was about to sacrifice his son to the glory of God. That is why it is obligatory on all Muslims who are able to afford it, to sacrifice on that day an animal; in Kashmir it is usually a sheep, goat or chicken. Animals to be sacrificed are selected after great care many a weeks or even months in advance. They are well fed and tended with love and care, till the moment it is offered as a sacrifice. On this day, all men folk and boys dress in new attire preferably white garments and go for community prayers in the open *maidan* or a large hall or any other place big enough to accommodate the congregation. At the end of the prayer an Imam, delivers a sermon. Purport of the sermon is the significance of the day and God's message of peace and good for the humanity. The women folk generally pray at home, though on rare occasions they might sit together behind the great crowd of men. Purpose of community prayers is the demonstration of the brotherhood of all Muslims, irrespective of rank or station in life rubbing shoulders with beggars and men of poor means at least theoretically. End of the sermon is the signal for each of the congregation to turn and embrace the man nearest him then move among the crowd embracing all and sundry.

Returning to their homes, they carry out the ceremonial sacrifice of the animal, which has been given a bath that morning and often has splashes of yellow here and there on its coat. The sacrifice is performed, in the tradition that of Abraham, usually by the head of the house or some elderly relation. Portions of the meat-mutton or chicken meat, of the traditional sacrifice animals in Kashmir, are distributed with due ceremony to relations and friends, and the rest is cooked and served in many dishes of grilled and roasted meat that are common amongst the Kashmiri Muslims.

Miraj-I-Alam

Miraj_I-Alam, the anniversary of the night on which the Prophet ascended from Jerusalem into Heaven is yet another important festival for the Kasmiri Muslims.

Id -I-Milad-ul-Nabi

It is the anniversary of the Prophet's birthday.

Muharram

The Shia Muslim community observe this day to mourn the martyrdom of Hussein the grand son of prophet Mohamed. He was killed at Karbala and his followers mourn his loss vehemently by beating their breasts in some cases with iron chains and blood oozes from their frame. Mostly professional *marsias* (mourners) are hired for the purpose. The respected class just use a white handkerchief in place of the chains. All are dressed in black clothes. The long processions carry *Taziyaz* (a palanquin type decorated coffin made of tinsel paper and sticks). This procession is as usual composed of men only as women mourn at home.

The Sikh Festivals

Sikhs celebrate the Diwali, Baisakhi (New Year) and Raksha bandan along with the rest of the Hindu KSP. Besides these festivals there are also Sikh centric festivals like the birth days of their Gurus:

Guru Hari Rai Ji (31st Jan)

Guru Angad Dev and Guru Teg Bahadur (18th April)

Guru Arjun Dev (2nd May)

Guru Hargobind (5th July)

Guru Har Kishen (23rd July)

Guru Ramdas (9th Oct)

Shri Guru Nanak Dev Ji (10th Nov)

Guru Govind Singh Ji (31st Dec, 11th Jan)

These days are celebrated with great devotion and piety in *Gurudwaras. Akhand Paaths, Shabads a*nd *Kirtans* are recited by the *Granthies (*priests) and the congregation participate in the recitations. They organise *Langars,* (free food) where in every one irrespective of class creed and colour performs *Kar seva* (Self service). Ladies work in the kitchen and men are involved in serving free prasaad to the congregation.

Conclusion

The entire genre of the festivals celebrated by the KSPs, in the recent eras, is more or less ritualistic. The celebrations lack the fun, the frolic and the festive spirit of the earlier times. There is only symbolic reference to dancing, singing, musical events, dramatics or any such entertainments that were part and parcel of the festival celebrations of the Puranic and medieval era. In the later eras these celebrations are dominated by religiosity and ritualism. Be it the Shivaratri, the Eid or Gurunank's Birthday, the same attitude prevails in the society. The religious guide lines at present are not powerful stimuli for the Gen **X** to retain and continue the practice of celebrating the existing festivals. The twenty first century provides many a diversions hence the above given list is bound to dwindle and reduce further in number, even if we wish other wise.

CHINAR /BWOONE TREES

Chapter-6

Social Order during the Puranic and Medieval era

Social order of a community always rests on firm scaffolding of the religious faith it observes, the civil and social laws it obeys and the environment it lives in. Generally the laws and practices imposed on the people by various agencies influence their thinking and mannerisms, yet it is the religion that exercises a measure influence over the lives of the people, their philosophy, their habits and their thought process; in short their social organisation. KSPs' are no exception to the rule. Their social order too is religion oriented.

The social order of this ethnic group has been active, alive and evolving continuously. Like any other ethnic group, it has grown from the aboriginal roots, gone through change from a liberal and free society (as depicted in Puranas), adopted conservative norms of the medieval era (under the Kushans, Sakas and Huns), hand cuffed in iron jackets by the Afghans and Pathans, till it finally shaped and established itself to the twentieth century cultural norms. These transitions have not been always smooth; resistance and opposition to the change, as a mark of human intellect, have often been exhibited by the KSP.

To asses the social order of any society the main parameters are its class and cast divisions; its literary and artistic achievements and composite progress; yet the study of simple factors like family, its every day behaviour, dress, cosmetics, other physical embellishments, food, entertainment, modes of transport, games, and even vices of the society enable us to frame a complete picture of the social order of a community or a race.

Keeping these basic factors in mind while analyzing the social order of the KSP, during the chronologically recorded eras, I have preferred to describe it in two phases: a) Puranic and Medieval era, b) Islamic and Post Islamic era.

SOCIAL ORDER DURING THE PURANIC AND MEDIEVAL ERA

PHASE 1

PURANIC AND MEDIEVAL ERA

Plethora of the literary as well as archaeological evidences provides authentic information about the KSP society in the changing eras of its existence. Nilamata Purana, as in case of religious, geographic and traditional details acts as the mirror of the social order prevalent in the earliest periods of the KSP society. Besides the Purana, other literary sources that provide information about this period are Kalhana's Rajatarangini book 1, 11, 111, and Ksemendra's Narmamala. Quite a number of archaeological finds belonging to the period have since been unearthed and these further help us to enumerate the various parameters of the KSP social order.

1. Classification and Cast divisions

(*Classification of the KSP society has been given in chapter 3, yet a detailed study was deemed necessary to have a clear picture of their social order in different eras.)*

Study of its classification and cast division deserves to be the first on the list. In order to get an accurate picture of any society. For it not only delineates the various status disparities if any, followed by the society and the variety of the means of lively hood under taken, but also throws light on the subject of sanctions and taboos imposed by whom, on whom and how.

In the normal course, a Hindu society was classified on the basis of *Varnasramadharma* in to four divisions but in Kashmir it was so only theoretically. As per chronicler records, the KSP social structure in Puranic era was grouped on the basis of intellectual calibre, physical valour and environment, as well as artistic and manual capabilities. In the order of preferences, intellectual excellence was given the first place of merit. This group of the society was engaged in self study, contemplation, performance of sacrifice, penance and study of *Vedas* and *Vedangas.* They were supposed to preside over performances of sacrifices, *Homas*, coronation of the Kings, narrate Vedic and Puranic stories and receive gifts. This class was later to be labelled as *Brahman* class. The illiterate and ignorant Brahmans were not supposed to be given any gifts, only those Brahmans who were acquainted with history, astronomy, and astrology were eligible to gifts from the donors. No where in the Purana is it mentioned that highly expensive gifts like *Hiranyagarba*, *Brahmanda* be given by the donor to any Brahman for his services. *Brahman* as a *purohita (priest)* held important place viz a viz the ruler.[1] Kings paid respect to this class of the society as is evident from the treatment given to Chander Deva by Nila the Naga King and to Mahapadama by Visvagasa. [2] This section of the society was an important and respected limb of the early social order and were part and parcel of every occasion be it religious, social, ceremonial, festive or other wise, a tradition that has continued till date. There was no rigid cast system during the reign of Ashoka, Kanishka, Hushka and Jushka. Brahmans, however, did appear as a distinct class, but this division was not hereditary and any one capable of achieving excellence in the above mentioned attributes had the right to be included in this class.

A small section of the community was involved in the art of weaponry and martial services and they were known as *Kshatriyas.* Nilmata commenting on the origin of the *Kshatriyas*, records, "these people, who were afraid of Rama, sought refuge in Kashmir and lived equitably with the Brahmans."[3]

People who were engaged in the profession of agriculture, trade and cattle rearing were termed as *Vaisyas.* They formed the largest section of the society.

For the smooth functioning of the society there were people involved in services like artisans, weavers, carpenters, silversmiths, blacksmiths, potters and other self mastered professional services and were a respected limb of the society.

There is mention of some *varnas (classes)* who served in the homes of higher *Varanas* and they were given sympathetic treatment by their masters. They even participated in the coronation ceremony of the Kings. They were not considered debased.[4] Besides these groups there are references about people engaged as *Mallas* (wrestlers), *Natas (*the actors) *Nratakas* (dancers) etc

Aboriginal tribes that were bordering various peripheries of the valley were not given the privileges and the luxury of exalted status even in Puranic era. Casts, like the *Nisadas, Kiratas, Dombas, Chandalas /Svapakas* were placed at the lowest wrung of the society. The *Nisadas* were supposed to earn their living by hunting and fishing. (The *Nisadas* are the modern boat men.)The *Kiratas* lived in the jungles and lived by the jungle products. The *Dombas* and *Chandalas* were supposed to be very fierce and cruel fighters. They were the menial class as per Kalhana's description.[5]

With this type of division of labour, the majority in the society presented a picture of happiness and contentment. People of all professions were a happy lot. Impression gathered is that the tillers of the land were probably the owners of their land, or they had to pay minor amounts as revenue. In the early eras there is no mention of the *Damars* that is the feudal landlords whom we come across in the later part of the history. The celebration of many a seasonal festival on the occasion of harvesting or sowing of crops is an indication of flourishing agricultural society. There is no mention of the breed of corrupt officials who were labelled as *Kayastha* in the later historical records. The trader class gives an impression of being highly organized, and were involved in export and import of goods. References have been made to *ciamuskas*, i.e. silk imported from China as well as to the *Lavanasarani* (salt route) through which salt was imported. Even Saffron was one of the most important items of export from the valley, those days. Dr.Ved Kumari also mentions that from the study of epic literature the items exported from the valley included fabrics made of wool, of *ranku* deer's hair, of silk and fibre, pelts, woollen blankets and other smooth textile pieces manufactured from cotton, lamb pelts and soft skins.[6] One wonders if the Pashmina shawls were also an item of export during the era under reference.

It can be said that during the Puranic era there was no water tight compartmentalization of the society as prescribed in *Manu's* code. It was classified on the basis of learning and labour, with varying degrees of respect for all components of the society that was well equipped to run the established social order. Ved Kumari writes, "The humane treatment meted out to the servants is a pleasant feature of social organization of Kashmir revealed by the Nilamata."[7]

Even during the early medieval era, KSP society was following the practice of loose class less divisions as is confirmed by some of the observations of researchers and chroniclers. Dr. S.C. Ray writes, "The concept of four traditional casts was not altogether unknown to the people of the valley . . . There was no such cast as *Ksatriya, Vaisya*, and *sudra* in early Kasmira."[8] Even Kalhana in *Rajatarangini* has prominently displayed the non adherence to the injunctions of the four divisions of the Hindu *Sastra* in the valley. The majority of the people in the society are referred as *Brahmans* and, some kings as belonging to the *Kshatriyas*, and there are also a few references to the *Vaisyas* and *Sudras* besides the *Chandalas* and *Dombas*.[9] In another place there is a reference to sixty four intermediary casts on the occasion of a feast of "excellent food given to the sixty four casts at a sacrificial feast" by Rilhana, one of the ministers of King Jayasimha (AD1128-49). [10]

Following nature's laws of evolution and progress, the KSP society underwent quite a few changes both good and bad in the medieval era. Most of these changes were the end result of the nature of governance of their rulers; their philosophies, their individual belief systems and the social practices imposed by them. It is well said *yatha Raja tatha praja,* (the subjects are the mirror image of the king who rules them). The maxim: people are what their environment and their rulers make of them, applies nowhere as aptly as it does to a KSP born almost in an ethereal paradise and yet victim of the perpetual miss-management by the monarchs and their underlings, especially after the initial phase of their history. Historical books or treatises record in detail this aspect of their history. Right from the times of Kalhana it is the same 'lamenting tale'. There has never been any long durable period of peace. Not only are the rulers the culprit, even nature has contributed to this. Though nature has been so lavish in its abundance, yet it has in many ways played a very important role in shaping the life and behaviour of the KSP through the vehicle of natural disasters like floods, famines and draughts, resulting at times in devastation of the land and its people, particularly the aboriginal tribes and races. Seductive beauty of the land has also been the greatest source of attraction for people of far off lands, and hence instigated them to attack, grab and adopt this valley; irrespective of it's tallest and safest mountain frontiers.

Ruling class during the medieval era could be grouped as two types based on their concern and impact on the society in various aspects of their life. Barring the exception of the intruder Hun King 'Mihirkhula', the rulers were very patronising and well-wishers of their subjects' during the early phase. They were patrons of learning, arts, sculpture, philosophy, and so on. After the Karakotas and Utpalas', we again have instances of the savageries and brutalities of some of the mean and lowborn adventurers, who came to Kashmir before the 10th century. To what extent they could degrade them selves can well be illustrated by what the historians wrote about some of them.

The king Unmattavanti who ruled in the years 939-944 AD was so wicked that he would practise the use of arms splitting with throws of daggers in the hollows between the breasts of naked women. He would rip open the abdomens of pregnant women in order to see the foetus.[11]

Like wise King Harsha-eleventh century AD- otherwise known for his patronage of arts and learning, because of his (kings) spendthrift nature was involved in debt. So to collect the revenue, he went to the extent of imposing taxes even on night soil thus causing immense hardships to the people.[12]

This tale of idiocy and oppression by the rulers continued intermittently throughout the history of Kashmir. Having said all this, the life of the KSP never stagnated and the historians among them left an unbiased and unflinching truthful record of the changes that their compatriots under went in every field. Kalhana, Ksemendra, and Damodara Gupta have given us detailed account of the changes that took place in the social order of the KSP during the period AD 500 to AD1300.

THE *BRAHMANS*

As in case of the earlier eras topped the hierarchy and were the most respected class. The learned and well read in scriptures were held as superior to the ones engaged in priestly duties. Being learned in almost every field they were concerned both with religious and literary duties. They were well versed in *Dharmsastras,* and on occasions acted as ministers and councillors. On several occasions they also took up the military profession and took active part in battles as soldiers and chiefs of the army.[13] For example the *Brahmana* Mitrasarman was the *samdhivigrahika* (minister) of king: Lalitaditya. Jayapida's minister was Devasarman and his chief councillor was Damodoragupta.[14] Bhatta Phalguna was the minister of king Ksemagupta and queen Didda.[15] and so on. Bhujanga, the son of a Brahman Samanta fought with Samgramaraja.[16] Kalhana's father Canpaka was the dvarapati of Harsa.[17] Ajjaka, the Brahman minister of Salhana died in the battlefield while fighting against Sussala.[18] Kalyanaaraja was a Brahman, and yet a soldier well versed in military exercises.

Brahmans even interfered in the political matters; they were the king makers and hence were respected and at times even feared by the kings. They enjoyed special privileges and immunities in the society. They were exempted from tax regime in the earlier parts of this era, though later Harsha is supposed to have introduced levying of tax on them. Brahmins were excluded from the capital punishment how so ever great the crime might have been, especially if he would be engaged in his spiritual and religious duties. We have a reference in R.T. in AD 939-48 where King Yasaskara, punished a Brahman ascetic named Cakrabhanu, by branding him with a dog's foot on his fore head for his improper conduct. [19]

Though many Brahmans adopted political and military vocations, the majority of them earned their livelihood by performing religious rites, by serving as priests, and by teaching the sacred texts. For providing them with honourable sources of income, besides the sacrificial fees, donations were frequently made to them.[20] Kalhana often mentions that *agraharas* were donated by the king to the Brahmans. [21]The priests of the temples had other sources of income too; they enjoyed the revenue of the villages which belonged to the temples. [22]

As per records, *tantric* influences in the priestly class had started seeping in to the daily practices with the result sorcerers also formed a miniscule minority towards the end of this era. They were even shown to possess miraculous powers of causing natural and elemental changes.

Kayastha

The term Kayastha referred to people working in the administrative departments of the crown at any level from the highest bureaucratic post to the lowest. They did not denote any particular cast, as is evident from Kalhana's assertion that the Brahmans were Kayasthas.[23] It was a class open to all the members of the society. They were the paid employees of the state and their most attractive job was collection of revenue. Kalhana and Ksemendra have recorded in detail about the corrupt practices of this class, their greed for money and their inhuman and dishonest ways of collecting money. Both Rajatarangini as well as Ksemendra's 'Narmamala' gives us a detailed account about the different posts held by this section of society and the rise of their importance during and after king Anantas' reign.

Even though there were a few Brahman feudal chiefs, the land by and large belonged to the peasant class, about whom Lalitaditiya had instructed his officials to leave only that much crops with them as would suffice them for the year, lest they became powerful and rise against the administration. That is exactly what happened, when the **Dammars** (feudal land lords) rose in power and became a very strong wing of the society. They interfered in important political affairs of the state. By the 12th century they had become powerful enough to have their own private armies and being wealthy, they controlled important places in the valley.[24]In major skirmishes for power, only that party would expect victory which was supported by Dammar chiefs. They built high and magnificent well fortified mansions to live in. They did not belong to any particular tribe or cast. One can say, they belonged to a class of riches, who were usually hereditary. They could marry in royalty. Their importance as a class came into existence in the 8th century and reached its zenith after the 10th century. Main reason for the rise of this class given by the historians is that, "the commercial activities of the valley ebbed with the fall of the Kushans and the rise of the Hunas and ultimately closed the overland roots." Being a land locked territory Kashmir had to engage her whole attention solely on agriculture. Ou-Kong and Alberuni testify to the closing of some of the existing trade routes. [25]

The *Vaisyas*

This cast included the traders and agriculturists and the peasant class. The latter class, barring a few feudal land lords, irrespective of their tribe or cast alienation, were the most oppressed class in the society. Such oppression has been the fate of the peasant class all through in KSP society. It is the same story of the bureaucracy and the land lords demanding the lion's share of the produce for the state and for their own coffers, and leaving hardly anything for the producers of the bulk of wealth that is the peasant. Kshemendra records in detail as to how some kings would collect whole harvest continually for three years at a stretch leaving nothing for the farmer. [26] He writes, "while the courtiers ate fried meat, and drank delightful light wine, scented with flowers and deliciously cooled, the cultivators of the villages had to take rice or dry barley in husks, and a wild growing vegetable of bitter taste called *utpalasaka*."[27]

The traders or the merchants, as per Kalhana, were yet another rich class of the society up to the early 9th century. They owned palatial houses with all the comforts, and riches.[28] This was the period when the Kashmiri rulers had enlarged their kingdom by annexing the neighbouring areas and hence leading to greater demand of the products of the state. However from 10th century onwards their importance as commercial traders started veining and they took over mainly monetary transactions and in order to make money they adopted dishonest and deceitful means.[29]

There was no restriction binding them to their occupation. With merit they also rose to high positions. Such as Haladahara, son of a watch man rose to the position of prime-minister in the court of Queen Suriyamati in AD.1028-63.[30]

There seems to be a little contradiction regarding the status of lower casts like ***Sudras, Chandalas, and Dombas***. While on the one hand they were considered untouchables and not allowed in to the temples but, at the same time, a Domba girl named Hamsi was raised to the status of the chief Queen by the King Cakarvarman.[31]This could have been an exceptional case? Sudras generally took the profession of hunters, butchers, quacks, fishermen and watch men etc.

References to a separate area being assigned to this lowest class of the society indicates the sense of strict *Varna Ashram* had started making inroads in to the literally class less society of the Puranic era. We also find the aboriginal tribes were being gradually pushed to the status of an untouchable class towards the end of the era. The change in the social behaviour had set in, and the community no longer belonged to one strata. Separate groups and casts had been created even within the bounded walls of the vale, as ordained by the early founders of the *Varnasramadharma* system.

2. Family life

Family is a mini replica of any society, be it of any cast or class. It is an important limb of the social order. Its composition, status and mode of functioning acquaint us with the economic, moral and ethical standards of the society. The evolution and changes in the format of the KSP family unit is the proof of its adaptability to the times and environment. Nilamata uses the terms like '*parivara*' or '*kutumba*' and '*grahastha*' (the householder) to represent this unit. The unit constituted of father, mother and children. There is no mention of extended family members in the early eras, or about the size of the family. Where as later in *Kathasaritsagara* we find stories about the joint family system and the status of the daughter-in-law there in. Wife and children are equal participants in all the rites and ceremonies that a householder is supposed to perform. Birth of a son was a moment of great rejoicing for the family. The son showed respect to his father by touching his feet and in turn father would express his affection by smelling the head of his son.[32] This practice of touching the feet, so prevalent all over the country, is, some how, nonexistent in the present KSP society. Eldest member of the family enjoyed full authority over the rest of the members who were supposed to obey the dictates of the elders, a tradition that has survived in KSP society up to the very recent times.

3. Food Habits

Survival of every member of a family and in turn of the society as a whole is directly proportional to the type, quality and quantity of food they consume. The food habits of the KSP not only acquaint us with their culinary skills, ingenuity and creativity in their art of cooking, it also serves as a data bank of the agricultural produce, like crops, pulses vegetation, fruits and dairy products, poultry and animals found in the valley.

The KSP's, down the ages, have been connoisseurs of good food. The essence of good food-both vegetarian and non vegetarian-for them is the standard of taste, flavour, variety and colour. The menu is always thought fully planned to accommodate different colours and varying flavours in order to avoid monotony of similarity and every dish has a specific spice to identify its flavour. It is almost a labour of love. Kashmiri cuisine has a unique characteristic: every dish can be cooked in vegetarian as well as non-vegetarian format, with ingredients of identical variety, barring the main one i.e. mutton, fish or poultry for non-vegetarian dishes and vegetables for the vegetarian variety. Besides the quality of cooking the number of dishes is a huge list. It begins with the wild herbs and grasses of the earliest eras and carries on to the latest delicacies of culinary art. The best thing about it is that there is the same continuity in the Kashmiri cuisine as it is in its various other art forms and cultural trends. Even the petty wild vegetation like *Hand/sanda, or upalhaak (Utpalasaka)*-a wild herb- finds its place in the sacred as well as social gatherings along with the delicate *shupta- (*miniscule fried pieces of *paneer-* fresh cheese cooked along with a variety of dry fruits and sugar cubes) or the famed *roganjosh* (red chilly based dish comprising chunks of meat fried and cooked on slow heat) and *kabargah-* sheep's rib cage cooked in milk till tender then marinated in curds and spices and finally deep fried in pure ghee, served decorated with silver leaf- of ancient times

There are no means of asserting whether all this would apply to the early part of food culture of the KSP, we do however know that the staple food of the Kashmiris then as of now was rice (husked *Dhanya or Sali*).[33] The KSP even now use both these terms to denote un-husked rice. As per the Purana, rice was cooked in various forms like simple boiled rice or converted into sweet porridge along with milk. Any scarcity of rice would create famine sort of situation in the state thus emphasising its importance as the staple food of the people. Barley was consumed along with rice as is given in the Purana that *apupa and pistaka* (bread and cakes) were made of barley. [34] The terms used for edibles in the Nilamata are, *Sasya* i.e. all cereals and pulses, *saka* i.e. all green vegetables, besides there are references to spices, sweetmeats, fruits, roots and medicinal herbs.[35] Green vegetable that a KSP likes the most is *Hak-saag* probably a derivation of the word *saka* a name quoted in N.P. for every green vegetable. Some of the items mentioned in the long list of consumables given in the Nilamata, are in vogue even at present e.g. *gorasa/Gurus), ghrta, payasa*(Rice and milk pudding), krsara (Kheer-pudding made of rice and milk), saktu (sot), *utpalasaka (upalhak)* etc. A type of herbal grass named *kachaguhha or hund,* was consumed as vegetable by our early ancestors for want of variety. These wild herbs still find place in the Kashmiris cuisine on some auspicious occasions, like *utplasaka* is a must for the *devgone* ceremony.

Since the country was abundantly rich in fruits like plums, grapes, apricots and peaches people regularly consumed them. Drinking of wines was a common practice as it was specially advised on certain ceremonial occasions and on festivals as recorded in the Purana.[36] A variety of pulses consumed included *kulatha, cana masura and mudga.* Rice and pulses were cooked together to prepare *Khiccari,* especially on some religious occasions. This dish is even now a days prepared on the *Yekcha Amavasiya.* Yet another preparation named *parpata or papara* was cooked by mixing the pulses and rice.[37]In the later eras there is mention of onions and garlic being used. Onions were regarded as a nutritious vegetable food.[38] (Garlic was a taboo for certain orthodox sections of the society°[39] Milk and milk preparations like, *Ksira (kheer), dadhi,* (curds,) and *ghrata* (ghee) were common; *maksika* (honey) and *sarkara* (sugar) were used to sweeten the food. Among the spices used were black pepper, ginger and asafoetida. Salt is supposed to have been very scarce and hence was used by the rich and the nobles' alone [40]

The strict instructions about no usage of meat on the days of Vishnu worship and the practice of animal sacrifice and offerings of non-vegetarian food to the Goddess *Bhadrakali,* to *Pisachas* and to *Chandodeva,* is proof enough to the fact that meat also was one of the items of their diet at least from the time the Nilamata was compiled about 6th to 7th century AD onwards. Often aspersions are cast that in spite of being Brahmans the Kashmiri Hindus consume non-vegetarian dishes. If one ponders a while and muses why Eskimos eat seal meat? The simple answer would be, because they do not grow any vegetables in Alaska. It is snow and ices every where; like wise Kashmiri Brahmans did not have any vegetation in the beginning eras and the abundance of wild foal, fish and other animals were their saviours. "Fish was very common". Meat was an important item of diet. Fowl and goat (*kukuta and mesa)* were also served.

Marco Polo writes that the food of the valley was, flesh with rice and other grains.[41]Meat was generally fried and highly spiced. Fish and fish soup was considered a very healthy tonic.[42] Wines especially made from grapes and sugarcane was a common drink. And it was distilled in the valley itself. It might surprise modern KSP that Kashmiris were very fond of betel leaves (*Parana or tambula)* and betel nuts. The conception that the habit of eating and offering *paan (*betel leaves) was picked up during the Mughal rule is a misnomer. Rich people had their own betel bearers who regularly supplied them with these.[43] Kalhana also refers to the habit of chewing *potasa* a sort of camphor. [44]

4. Entertainments and modes of recreation

A well-fed and healthy society is bound to be happy and contented. The state of their happiness, contentment and prosperity can always be measured on the benchmark of the freedom it enjoyed to entertain, and the frequency of the festivities and celebrations it was permitted to conduct. We find abundance of both in the early eras of KSP society. Music happened to be one of the prominent modes of entertainment on each and every ceremonious occasion be it religious, social or seasonal one, like the festival of new snowfall. It included both vocal and instrumental music. A variety of musical instruments *vada, vaditra, and vadya Banda* are mentioned in the Nilamata. Dancing both individual and in group was always part of the celebration. Archaeological discoveries of the tiles from Harwan belonging to the 4th century AD depicting female musicians playing on a drum, and also female dancers surrounded by the musical instruments like flute, cymbal and a pair of drums certify the veracity of the custom and popularity of singing and dancing in the society.[45]

Mention of the theatre halls and the word '*Prekasadna*' (theatre performances,) in N.P. is an indicator of yet another means of entertainment of the society, e.g. drama and dramatic performances that are very highly appreciated by the Kashmiri poet Bilhana.[46] Literary evidences as well as the archaeological evidences of the tiles of that era prove that society also resorted to many other sports, namely, garden sports,[47] water sports[48], wrestling,[49] gambling, [50] hunting,[51] and playing with toys[52] etc. Regarding the custom of gambling on Deepavali, it is prescribed in Nilamata as a measure to know the goodness or otherwise of the coming year for the players.[53] We do find reminiscences of most of these sports and modes of entertainments like dancing and singing, existing even in the present era despite the detrimental and fanatic restrictions imposed on the society during the Islamic era. Among the Hindu KSPs, dancing and singing on the occasions of Shivaratri, marriage, and *Mekhal* (thread ceremony) etc and among the Muslims, on the occasions of wedding receptions, or during the sowing and harvesting seasons are reminiscences of that culture. The custom of gambling on the festival of Deepavali no longer exists as a must in present times, and this festival, by itself, has lost its place in the list of essential festivals of the Hindu KSP.

In the Medieval era the means of entertainment continued to be the same as depicted in the early Puranic era. Damodaragupta writes, "Dancing and music must have been cultivated by rich and noble class as well as by ordinary. Bharata's *Nātyasastra* was highly honoured and was part of the curriculum and according to an authority was one of the approved texts of studies. There were luxurious theatre halls in his native valley, fitted with leather-cushioned couches. But these luxury-houses were probably meant for the rich alone."[54]

Kalhana also was aware of the precepts of Bharata on dancing and singing. It is highly probable that many of the dancing performances of early Kashmir were strictly in adherence to the school of Bharata.[55] A passage in the *Rajatarangini* tends to show that common people would witness theatrical performances under an open sky, when caught by a downpour; they had to disperse in all directions.[56] Another interesting item of amusement was puppet-play. A writer of the ninth century refers to *daruma yiva pratima* (wooden-dolls which were made to dance with the help of a *yantrasütra*-mechanical thread)[57] Besides we have references in the R.T. about people indulging in games like dice (a game of chess)

5. Arts and Crafts Era

The cultural stature of a happy and healthy society finds expression in its artistry and craftsmanship. Nilamata records that the society was proficient in the arts of painting, sculpture, architecture, and handicrafts like image making, spinning weaving, dyeing, and washing, pottery work, wood work, leather work, polishing of metals like gold and silver, and art of jewellery making. Architecture happened to be one of the specialities of the KSP's and they were reputed as the builders of the Buddhist *Caityas, Viharas* and temples of high quality, like the ones at Harwan. (Refer to the chapter-10, Foot Prints of Architecture)

6. Transport and communication

Mobility of a community depends chiefly on the modes of transport available to its members. There is a general misconception that horses and elephants were not known to the early KSP society, and their only convenient mode of transport was water transport i.e. boats. This misconception arose because of Alberuni remarks, "The inhabitants of Kashmir are pedestrians; they have neither riding animals nor elephants. The noble among them ride in a *Katta* carried on the shoulders of men."[58]. Due to his observation KSPs have been thus type caste as 'pedestrians only'. While I would agree that masses would have been generally pedestrians as the distances were small and may be the environment encouraged that habit, yet his observation that horses and elephants were not known to the early KSP's is belied by the references given here. Nilamata records that horses, elephants and bulls in that era were referred as means of conveyance and the horses and elephants formed important part of king's army. Besides there are special rites prescribed for the training and safety of the horses and the elephants (Ved N.P.Vol. 1, p124.) Again a vivid description of the reception given to Hiuen Tsang (7th century A.D) in the Chinese record states that when he entered the valley the king had specially sent horses and carriages to escort the pilgrim to the capital.[59] Even Kalhana records that horse was one of the important conveyances of his times and he has written about the march of mounted troops (*asvavara)* in the chronicle. He refers to the stables of horses and elephants.[60]. There is evidence in the form of figures of elephants on the tiles of Harwan that confirms elephant was used as a means of transport; [61] It is thus obvious from these facts that horses, elephants, carriages, palanquins and boats were among the early known means of transport and conveyance of the KSP. Boats no doubt formed the most important and common means of transport in the valley by virtue of the navigable character of the river Vitasta. Hence all internal trade and travel would be mostly carried by means of water transport.

Kalhana refers to it as,' coming and going of ships.[62] Since Alberuni could not physically visit the valley, there is hundred percent chances that he was misinformed and hence this inadvertent observation was recorded by him.

7. Position of the women

Women, in terms of numbers and impact, are a dominant factor and play a major role in monitoring the health and growth of a society. Hence their position, their rights, their liabilities, and contributions to the KSP social order during the Puranic and Medieval era deserve a detailed study.

The women of Kashmir played a very crucial and significant role in shaping and modulating the social structure of Kashmir. As per N.P. it is gratifying to note that they were highly respected in the KSP society unlike the rest of the country. R.S.Pandit, the learned translator of Kalhana's *Rajatarangini,* observes, "That the ancient system of the Aryans in India who, like the Ionic and Doric races and the Lacedaemonians, recognised the freedom of women prevailed up to the twelfth century in Kashmir."[63] Possibly, the high mountain walls guarding the vale spared its women from the depraving faiths and beliefs prevailing in the rest of India. She was not referred as "the living torch illuminating the way to hell or the devourer of the intellect of men."[64] "The genuineness of the account given by the Nilamata," writes Ved Kumari, "is proved by the corroboration it receives from the works of many a Kashmiri writers like Bilhana, Damodara Gupta, Kshemendra, Somadeva and above all Kalhana." [65]

Nilamata gives a detailed description about the respect, freedom and the rights of equality enjoyed by the women in the earlier eras. There were no fetters placed on her, there is no mention of any veil that she was supposed to use as in the later periods. She participated in each and every religious ceremony in the company of her husband and children. She had the right to perform some religious ceremonies all by her self on some chosen days. The women were free to participate and witness, musical as well as dramatic performances, in company of their family and friends during the night time. Enjoy community feasts on the ceremonial day of ploughing the fields and sowing the seeds, singing and dancing in the fields, as we witness her doing even in the present times.

N.P. records, "The ladies of Kashmira are not denied any means of merriment. The young maidens should play in the waters during the *Sravani* festival. Women were allowed to play with men dressed in best attire, perfumed with scent and decorated with ornaments on the last day of the celebration of the *Mahimana* festival."[66]

As already stated the prominence of the Goddess cult during the Nilamata era and other such evidences are proof enough to the respectability granted to the women in the society. [67]

A woman as a wife and mother was respected, honoured and loved by her husband and children. They were educated and trained in fine arts and special honours were bestowed on them on a few auspicious days like, the first snow fall day, *Magha Chaturthi, Madana Triyodeshi, Dipamala* and so on. Nilamata does not any where mention about the custom of Sati that we come across in the later part of Hindu rule. [68]

On the whole, position held by the women was very exalted and loving, free from any restrictions or what is termed as, 'under tutelage'. They stood tall on the pedestal of equal rights with male gender, unlike their counterparts in the rest of Hindu society. There is nowhere any mention of *Purdah* system in the medieval society. The status of birth and caste was no barrier in their advancement.

Women continued to enjoy this dignified existence till late medieval era. They were duly nurtured and prepared for the tasks ahead in life. P.N. Bazaz writes, "Broadly speaking, from early times down to the thirteenth century a Kashmiri women enjoyed remarkable freedom, wielded ample power and exercised responsibility which gave them high status in the society."[69]

Education is a powerful tool to make a capable social being, and that was granted abundantly to the women of Kashmir in this era. Prior to marriage a girl was well versed in a wide range of subjects. Krishna Mohan writes, "Regarding the position of women in early Kashmir, we learn that the first part of a woman's life was spent in her father's house when liberal education was imparted to her and the same attitude towards her continued in the medieval era. The curriculum of studies in the 9th century AD included the sexual sciences of *Vatsyayana, Dattaka, Vitaputra* and *Rajaputra; the Natyasastra* (treatise on dance) of *Bharata, Visakhila's* treatise on art, *Dantila's* work on music, *Vikasayurveda,* painting, needlework, woodwork, metal work, clay modelling, cookery, and practical training in instrumental music, singing, and dancing." [70]

Their knowledge and proficiency in *shastras* and philosophy is often referred to by historians and travellers. Lila Ray writes, "In the eighth century, Shankaracharya, having defeated, in heated disputations, many Buddhist savants in various parts of India, arrived in Kashmir, then the renowned seat of learning and culture. He challenged Mandan Misra, the recognised local authority on religion, for a discourse. When the historic debate started, the two intellectual titans could find no better referee to judge between them than Ubhayabharati, Mandan Misra's wife, which is a conclusive proof of her ability and impartiality. Misra lost the debate but his gifted wife took up and forced Shankaracharya to plead for postponement so that, to continue the debate, he may acquire the requisite knowledge and experience which he lacked."[71]

Ubhayabharati was not a solitary instance of her kind in the old and medieval Kashmir. Among the Brahmans and other high caste women literacy was common and many of them were well versed in scriptures and literature in general. In his semi historic work *Vikramankadevcharita* (The Deeds of *Vikramana*), which deals with the life and adventures of the great Chalukya Emperor Vikramaditya VI (c.1075-1125 AD), Bilhana, who was the poet laureate at the court of Kalyan in the Deccan, (11th century), gives, in the last canto of his book, a brief account of his motherland and its people especially the women, he extols them for their learning, which allowed them to speak fluently both Sanskrit and Prakrit.[72]

Kalhana and other writers too have succinctly alluded to their scholarship and erudition. R.T, records that the learned women of Kashmir had already emerged from the domestic on to political stage, they owned immovable property, managed their own estates and even led their troops into the battle.

Perhaps the ladies of the royal family were given a bit of administrative training, for that might be the reason of the great success with which Kashmirian queens like, Sugandha and Didda governed their domains. Queen Kalhanika went at the head of an emissary to bring rapprochement between Bhoja and Jayasimha. Even women of a lesser status took leading part in the political activities of the State of which we have several examples in the pages of Kalhana.

The remarkable contribution made by the queens, queen consorts, women regents, diplomats and commanders on the battlefront till the beginning of fourteenth century is significant and note worthy. Their contribution to the political, social, religious, economic, military, architectural, and cultural life of Kashmir can be traced and discerned from the references, intentional or otherwise, available to us in various chronicles of the land. They ruled their kingdom as justly and as efficiently as that of the kings of the stature of Lalitaditya', Jaluka, Asoka and Avantivarman. It was due to such capabilities that Queen-Regent Yashovati merited the remark by Kalhana, "People looked up on this mother of her subjects as if she were a goddess." They ruled the state, they fought wars, lead their forces in the battlefields and were able to thwart the attempts of the enemy as well as control the rebels.

During the two decades- 1112AD to 1128 AD- when King Sussala secured the throne of Kashmir after murdering Harsha, a civil war ensued in the state as Harsha's grand son tried to reclaim his throne. Kalhana records practically every adult living in the valley was engaged, directly or indirectly in this warfare and women also actively participated and fought in the battle field. Among them was Silla, whose stout heartedness, presence of mind, and valour was praised and recognised by all.

Women of Kashmir have equally contributed in creating the architectural edifices like temples, *Viharas, shrines* and convents in their country. Names like that of queen Amritaprabha, Ranarambha, Bimba Kalyandevi and Ratnadevi stand out as prominent instances in this sphere. Kalhana writing about the building activities carried out during King Laltaditya's reign, records, "by the ladies of the royal house hold, the councillors and the rajahs who were in his service hundreds of sacred foundations were made which were the marvels of the world".

During the medieval era we find many a Manuistic, if I may use the expression, codes and customs had started finding place in the society. This change is primarily discerned in Ksemendra's critical analysis of the society of his era. Apparently by the time this great social critic arrived on the scene, the out look of the society towards the woman had vastly changed. He portrays a different picture of the state of a daughter in her family. That is the reason he writes in *Deso-upadesa* that the status of daughters was considered lower than that of the son. Naturally, therefore, they did not occupy an important place in the family and were regarded as a burden. To have sons instead of daughters was considered a good fortune.[73]

8. Marriage norms

No positive reference to the accepted norm about the marriageable age of a woman is come across. However, from casual references in the R.T. one gets the impression that early marriages were not in vogue in ancient Kashmira. A story related in Desopadesa may indicate that the girls were married at a mature age. The people always had the fear that daughters would stain the family reputations if they ever chose to engage in pre-marital relations and therefore it was a common feature to marry a girl with an old man in the absence of a suitable match.[74] Kshemendra has severely criticised and ridiculed such marriages with severe sarcasm and contempt and pitied the fate of those girls who are married to old men.

There are references to the custom of inter-caste marriages and polygamy in KSP society as it was practised by the royals, nobles and the rich class and hence carried the stamp of approval. Usually the ruling princes and the men of upper classes had plurality of wives. Rajatarangini mentions about kings who possessed more than hundred beautiful damsels in their harems. King Harsha outdid all others, says Kalhana. "In his inner-apartment over three hundred and sixty women of pure character were openly admitted by him whose mind had become infatuated. Nobles and grandees too married many girls as they could afford to maintain. There were practically no restrictions on the liberty of man in this behalf. Often, most of these unfortunate ladies survived the death of their husbands. They were not allowed to have another partner in life as remarriage of widows was forbidden. Worse still, the widows of the princes and upper class men were burned with the dead bodies of their husbands on the funeral pyre."

9. Property rights of the women

Women in Kashmir in this era are shown to have had some property rights. There is a reference to a woman who instead of her son inherits the immovable property of her husband after his death. In another case a woman is shown as the owner of a landed estate. Even Ksemendra describes in Samayamatrika how a prostitute, who was the mistress of a rich man, becomes the legal owner of his property by virtue of the law.

10. The practice of *Sati*

There is no mention of the custom of Sati in the Nilamata, but we have many instances in Kalhana's chronicle about it amongst the royalty. Queen Surendravati and two other queens of Samkaravarman cremated themselves along with the King. Like wise Queen Trailokyadevi, Bhiba, Suryamati, Mammanika Jayamati committed *sati*. In some cases, queens did not self immolate. We have instances where sisters, courtesans and even mothers cremated themselves on a brother's, son's or master's pyre. (Gajja cremated herself with her son Ananda; Vallabha with her brother-in-law Malla and Dilhabatrika with her brother. Even prostitutes have been shown performing Sati.

R.S.Pandit traces the origin of this pernicious custom and its spread, in many Asian countries and India being one of them. He writes, "The history of Kashmir helps us to trace the growth of what has been called Sati. Sati, (Sanskrit. *Anugamana*—following to death) grew out of a custom of Scytho-Tartars among whom it was usual for vassals and liegemen upon the death of their lord to kill them selves. The custom survived during the age of chivalry in Kashmir for several centuries as it apparently still does among the Japanese. A woman of quality gave up her life for the sake of a principle of honour. A knight was expected to die fighting and his lady and vassals to remain true to the traditions of Ksatriya chivalry. The honourable end was the one thing which could not be taken from a person of high birth. In course of time, the custom, which at first was confined to the martial invaders, spread among the higher classes—like the *Purdah*. *Anugamana* was denounced as futile by Bana in the seventh century in his novel the *Kddambari*. It is interesting to note that the first king who made his best effort to suppress Sati was Akbar, the descendant of the people from whom India had borrowed the custom in the past."[75]

It is on account of these details that we can definitely assume the practice of s*ati* was a latter adoption of the KSP society. Why this abhorrent custom was adopted by the KSP nothing is clearly mentioned. Could it be for the fact that the remarriage of widow was generally not countenanced and the death of the husband meant social ruin for the widow? Her position in society became miserable. Hence a widow was supposed to live a life bereft of all types of luxury, entertainment and out ward rich embellishments. If she was dissuaded by her family at the last moment, she could escape social censure otherwise it was preferable to face the flames and end the life in honour.

On the position of a widow in contemporary India Alberuni remarks: "if a wife loses her husband by death, she can not marry another man. She has only to choose between two things either to remain a widow as long as she lives or to burn her self and the latter eventuality is considered preferable, because as a widow she is ill-treated as long as she lives. As regards wives of the kings, they are in the habit of burning them whether they wish it or not, by which they desire to prevent any of them by chance committing something unworthy of the illustrious husband. They make an exception only for women of advanced years and for those who have children; for the son is responsible protector of his mother."[76]

Most scholars believe that the practice of *sati* was mainly a medieval development and became more frequent in Northern India during AD700-1100. Altekar and Mojumdar have tried to explain as to how this custom began to be followed by a few Brahmin families soon after AD 1000. [77](See *note)*

All the evidences agree on the point that it was the degraded and miserable plight of a widow in Hindu society which encouraged this practice widely in India. It is also evident from the Rajatarangini that those ladies, who did not immolate themselves on the death of their husbands, led a very simple and austere life; for example even a queen like, "Mallarjuna's mother wore no ornaments on account of her widowhood".

Bazaz writes, "Despite the heinous custom of sati and ban on remarriage of widows, a Hindu woman had the right to freely choose her own partner in life. The institution of *swayamvara* (*self* selection) was as well known in Kashmir as in the rest of India. How far it obtained in the lower classes is controversial; but among the higher castes and wealthy sections, especially the Rajputs, it was a common practice. Love marriages are frequently mentioned in the annals and other literary works. A woman also enjoyed the right of separation and if dissatisfied with the marriage on rational grounds she could, through mutual agreement with her husband, obtain a decree of divorce. Such a course was neither disapproved nor looked down upon. Even kings are known to have married divorced women and the progeny of such marriages have subsequently ruled the land as monarchs in their hereditary right. The most distinguished of the Hindu rulers, Lalitaditya Mukhtapida, and his brother Chandrapida who succeeded him, were King Pratapaditya's sons by a divorcee, a *banya* woman, it is, however, important to remember that cases of divorce or remarriage of widows were exceptions than the rule, in ancient Hindu society."[78]

Bazaz further writes that the women of, "Kashmir loved to be dressed in shining costumes and participate in social festivals. Dancing and singing were their common pastime, in which ladies of respectable families had attained high proficiency."[79]

To wards the end of the medieval era the society appears to have undergone some kind of moral degeneration and it is evident from the changed format of the practice of *Devdasi* cult as it prevailed in the early eras; when it was restricted to singing and dancing activities alone. The works of Kalhana, Ksemendra' and Somadeva evidence this change thus, "The practice of *Devadasi,* which existed earlier in its puritanical form, had degraded and the sexual aspect had seeped into it. The temple girls were accepted as property of the royalty and they could be absorbed in to the royal Harems e.g. Sahaja taken by Prince Utkrasa."[80] Kalhana in his chronicle R.T and Kshemendra in *Desospdesa, Naramala, and Kutanimata Kaviya* describes in detail the immorality and laxity of character of some classes of women in the middle eras. Alberuni also records that honest and pure minded people expressed there objection especially to the *Devadasi* system as it existed in the late medieval era.

11. Dress and other accomplishments

The fashion trends and tastes of a society that enlists the innovations of its members are always depicted by the dress they cover their bodies with, the fabric they use and the colours and patterns they fuse in the fabric. The ornaments and the cosmetic preparations used to beautify themselves showcase the progress of a civilised society. There are many a references available to us about this aspect of the *Kashur.*

N.P. while referring to the dresses worn or donated on various occasions, always uses the term pair, which points to the fact that the dress worn both by men and women comprised two pieces, the upper garment and the lower garment. The fabric used was both wool and silk from China. The dress worn by the male population was a lower garment *(adharansuka),* an upper garment *(angaraksaka)* and a turban (*sirhsata).* Rajatarangini, on the other hand, refers to a long cloak *(pravara)*,[81] worn by both men and women very similar to the *pheran* the principle type of dress worn by all classes of people in Kashmir today.

As per Hiuen Tsang, the dress worn by the people is very much akin to the Central Asian dress. He writes, "In the North India, where the air is cold they wear short and close fitting garments, like the Hun people."[82]

From the tiles recovered in Harwan, male figures are seen dressed in loose fitting trousers and Turkoman caps; where as female dancer is shown wearing tight fitting trousers, a transparent robe, a tight fitting turban and large ear rings. However, the image of Goddess Lakshmi on these tiles is seen wearing a saree.[83] In the later era the dress of a woman was mainly sari and jackets, while during the reign of Harsa fashionable ladies dressed themselves in jackets which covered but half the length of their arms and 'wore long lower garments, the tail end of which touched the floor. Sometimes a veil was used to cover the face. [85]

Regarding the dress worn by men, the terra-cotta tiles of Harwan in Kashmir (third century AD) depict knights on horse back, with bow and quiver of arrows, wearing long "frock-coats" with the fluttering edges of the "*Virapatta*" as recorded by Kalhana.[86]

The tile-paved courtyard of Harwan is extremely interesting on account of the portraits of ethnic types, which are Central Asian, as well as the style of dress and ornaments of the men and women of that age. Some of the figures and attitudes are Pompeian; a few of the women appear to be in Greek dress while others are dressed in central Asian style, which is still the dress of the Hindu women of Punjab.

Rich urban people would usually use woollen blankets made of fine fibre where as the plebeians had to keep themselves warm with cheaper woollen goods such as skins of black antelopes (*krsnajina*) or coarse woollen cloaks (sthulakambala) which were sometimes distributed to them by charitable people.[87]

Bazaz in his book *'Daughters of Vitasta'* writes, "In the matter of personal adornment and the ways of living Kashmiri women of the early times were no less remarkable. They loved to be gaily attired and had invented styles in dress and in make-up of hair which indicate a high level of culture. In sculpture as well as in literature they are often depicted wearing jackets and bodices which serve as an evidence that during those days the art of sewing must have been known. Like the women of the south who remained uncovered up to the waist, the women in the valley and other parts of the north were dressed using bodices or jackets to protect them selves against severe cold. The lower parts of the body including the legs were wrapped up either in a piece of long cloth which was tied to the waist or in a sewn garment not very different from that which is used by rustic womenfolk in India today. Wearing of shirts and trousers seems to have become common in medieval times in the valley as in Gandhara (North Western Frontier and East Afghanistan). The trousers were probably first introduced by the Kushans as they were in vogue among the ruling classes under them. Generally, women are shown wearing head veils or simple flare-like head dresses, sometimes they are depicted bare headed with the hair made up in a variety of fashions. On battlefield the Kashmiri women wore red trouser uniforms like other Kashmiri soldiers in arms. Occasionally, some care-free maidens took fancy to be dressed in the garb of men and moved about thus attired in the streets and public places of entertainment. No eyebrows were raised in astonishment, no accusing fingers pointed at them."[88].

In N.P. we have references to names of ornaments like ear-rings, bracelets, diadem, and jewels worn by the people and also cosmetics like perfumes, flowers, sandal paste, Collyrium and the combs, staff and shoe wear.

In the Medieval era both men and women wore ornaments gold, silver and precious stones of every available description were in demand for embellishment of the body. The women wore chains or necklace (*hāra,. srñkhalā, sütrikā, mālikā*).[89] Women of ordinary means wore ornaments of shells and silver *(vidrumarnālikā, tadiyugamarajatam)* while women of poor classes wore earthen ear-rings. During Harsa rule (AD 1089-1101) ladies twined golden strings in the ends of the locks, in their hair-braids they had golden tilaka-leaf ornaments and on their foreheads pendants, which made their forehead marks unsteady. In *Samayamatrika*, Ksemendra uses the term *stridhana* for ornaments. [90] Bazaz writes, "The Kashmiri women wore heavy rings and other large ornaments in ancient days, as now. They wore jewelled ornaments on their forehead and along the parting of the hair. Ornate necklaces were worn. Bangles and armlets were popular as also anklets often set with little tinkling bells to produce melodious sound while they walked. Among the ornaments, pride of place was given to *deji-hor*, an egg shaped solid but intricately engraved two piece set hanging from both ears with the support of a strong thread *(ata-hor)* which was fastened to the head with a pin and was covered with smaller differently designed hollow ornaments . . . . In the Srinagar Museum there exists, among the few surviving pieces of sculpture, one, belonging to the later 10th century, in which the birth of Buddha is depicted with the mother Mayadevi and another lady both wearing *deji-hor* just as it is worn today."[91] With the passage of time this ornament gained sanctity and was considered an important symbol of married life of a Kashmiri woman and she carries it on her person without fail.

According to Kalhana, ornaments used by the male population of Kashmir consisted chiefly rings, ear-rings, necklaces and brace lets; men wore wristlets (kañkana), armlets - (keyüra bracelets (pārihārya), ear-rings (*vailyayugaIam, taddiyugam, tādidala, karnikā, karnakundala.* girdles (*Kancimekhalā)* and anklets (*nüpura).*[92] Men wore leather shoes which some times had steel-made soles and floral decorations outside. Kalhana refers to a particular kind of footwear called peacock-shoe (*mayuropäna*t) which was a fashion of his day. The use of wooden sandals was also in 'vogue. A cane-stick in the hand and a dagger or sword at the waist, were other accessories.[93]

12. Cosmetics

Various unguents for decorating and perfuming the body were saffron (*kumkuma*), camphor *(karpüra)* and sandalwood paste (*candana).* The use of saffron as an unguent is repeatedly referred to as a royal privilege.' Collyrium was used for the decoration of the eyes. The ladies of King Harsa seraglio made the line of Collyrium (*añjana)* to join the corners of the eyes to the ears.' Women's feet were coloured with red lac (*yāvakaharinau pādau).* They also made forehead marks (*tarnālapattra)*.[94].

Beauty aids were various and commonly used by the women of cultured classes to look pretty and attractive in social gatherings. A paste made of finely ground dust of sandal-wood was smeared over the whole body or applied with varying patterns frequently coloured with dyes. This goes to show, as pointed out by R. S. Pandit that the art of making up the face-(Beauty Parlour)-must have been in vogue in Kashmir even in those days.

Even Kalhana refers to painting with the sandal paste and other emollients of the faces of ladies

Describing the personal appearance of women in King Harsha's days, Kalhana writes, "Set off with golden leaf of *Ketaka* the bun coiffure was decked with long flower garlands: the tremendous blossoms of the tilaka embraced the lovely forehead patch; the line of Collyrium joined the corners of the eyes to the ears; bows of string woven with gold were tied at the end of the tresses which were worn in plaits; the long tail-end of the lower garments kissed the surface of the floor; the brassiere which traced the curves of the breasts concealed the upper half of the arms; when they wore men's dresses they bore the charm of the god of love in disguise." [95]

There were many fashionable ways of hair make-up, which are mentioned in the contemporary literature and represented in the sculpture. The most popular coiffure with the Kashmiri women was a large bun at the nape of the neck often ornamented with a fillet or string of jewels, the pig tail was common through all times among the unsophisticated sections, elderly ladies and unmarried girls of all classes. Even the poor women who could not afford gold or gems loaded themselves with jewellery of silver, brass or other baser metals. All classes adorned their hair, ears and neck with fragrant and beautiful flowers which the valley provides in abundance. Interestingly Kalhana states that until the rule of Harsa, the common people of Kashmir wore their hair loose and carried no head dress or ear ornaments, it was only the privilege of the King.[96]

Even men for beautifying themselves used to apply *kumkuma* on the hair, *aṅgarāga* on body, white mustard on forehead and saffron pomade on beard. The sculptures and their fragments do confirm that the people of all classes according to their economic status, both men and women used jewellery as an embellishment.

13. Learning, Language and Literature

The touch-stone of any robust, active and civilized social order, is the quantitative and qualitative intellectual calibre, and the academic and philosophic achievement of its people. And one can proudly state that the valley was renowned as a place of learning and knowledge all along its history. It was not only celebrated as *'Firdos bar ru.i-zamin'* (Paradise on Earth), but also as *'Sharada Peetha'* (the seat of the Goddess of Learning).

True up to the 6th century AD we have no written records to prove this greatness, for what ever was written or compiled till then has been destroyed by fanatic zealots and the cruel natural elements. All we have are names of some composers like Vasunanda, Candaka, and some of the names of chronicles that have been used by Kalhana as his sources of information while compiling the *Rajatarangini.* Despite the absence of the early records the general consensus of scholars is that the proof of their excellence survives in the highly developed literary style found in the literary works compiled from the 8th century A.D onwards. The language of the Sanskrit literature of this period is so well developed that one is bound to accept it the outcome of centuries of evolution in the language system.

The medieval era was the golden period of the KSP society so far as learning, literature, arts, crafts, philosophy, and architecture are concerned. It is in this era that the fame and essence of its cultural achievements was at its zenith. This claim has been duly recognised by the natives of the land over the millennia's of their existence and also by foreigners be they litterateurs, pilgrims or commoners. The learned traditions upheld in Kashmir, even to this day, are very much the by- products of this era. During the period between ninth to the twelfth centuries AD, the KSP's composed the scriptural literature of Kashmir *Saivism-* the *Tantras, Agamas and* various philosophical treatises of Shavism, A galaxy of famous writers' scholars and philosophers like Abhinavagupta, Vasugupta's disciple, Bhatta Kallata, etc flourished in this land of cultural eminence during the medieval era.

People, at large, had developed a common language, which they had evolved them selves for communication; however, Sanskrit, the language of Brahmans and' upper cast continued to be the literary language patronized by the ruling classes. This era can boast of many litterateurs, poets, astronomers, experts in medical science, political analysts, and chroniclers. (*For details refer to chapter on KSP. Culture*)

Rajatarangini and the other Kashmirian sources give ample evidence of the scholarly education not only of the Brahmins who attained high proficiency in all the branches of the literature but also of men of other castes. Krishna Mohan writes, "Kashmir in medieval times, in the case of education as of kingship and the offices of state, the field was not limited to specific castes. Anybody who could prove himself competent enough could rise to any position. It appears that the study of Vedas and its teaching may have been limited to the Brahmins while there was no restriction for anyone to study and teach secular subjects." [97]

It is on account of this proficiency that foreign observers like Hiuen Tsang noted that the people of Kashmir loved learning and were well instructed. [98] Like wise, Alberuni (AD 1030), noted that Kashmir was the centre of Hindu learning in his time. He also praises the skill of the Kashmiri scholars in taking in hand any difficult task, even such as that of committing the Vedas to writing.[99]

Bilhana in his *Vikramaṅkadeva Carita* praises his motherland (Kashmir) for its holiness, for the sanctity and learning of its Brahmins and for the beauty and learning of its women.[100]

Dr. Suryakanta writes "Among the greatest luminaries of the age was Kshemendra who tried to write in every branch of language and literature, conforming to his own ideals of the branches of learning, a scholar was supposed to know of, and touching all the varied fields and aspects of the society of his day. His works also show that the great teachers of those days did not-believe only in textbook theories, but tried to encourage originality."[101]

He is said to have studied rhetoric under great teachers like Abhinavagupta, the author of *Vidyavivrti,* and Gahgaka and Somapada. Dr. Suryakanta's suggestion that Ksemendra may have had other teachers as well, under whom he may have studied different branches of literature appears to be possible, because Ksemendra shows himself to have been concerned with the stages of learning where pupils were in the making as poets and not as students in the early stages.

We do not have any clear reference to elementary or secondary education system in this era. Suryakanta observes, "The general schools arranged by the householders must have been concerned with teaching the students, ordinary reading and writing, while great scholars like Ksemendra's teachers and Kshemendra himself must have been concerned with learning in its higher forms. Whether they had special organised schools for this level or took individual students under their tutelage is not clear from our sources, nor is it stated anywhere whether the scholars were paid by pupils or imparted education for the sake of the dissemination of learning. As the kings also patronised learning in Kashmir these scholars might have possibly depended on the grant of agrahara lands and their produce. Kshemendra, Bilhana, Kalhana, Mankha and Abhinavagupta, to cite a few examples, do not in any way appear to be connected with *Viharas* and *Mathas*."[102] The proficiency attained by the scholars in different fields of learning, is in itself, evidence of the stature and curriculum, that may have been prescribed for the students at that time in Kashmir

Conclusion

To repeat myself we can thus conclude that the KSP society as a whole during the earlier centuries of the Puranic era was liberal and democratic, devoid of gender bias, respectable to the female sex. It was not a strict follower of the Varna Ashram division. The society was well educated, and well versed in the arts of ethics, philosophy, administration, scriptures, music, etc.

It flourished in the same line even in the medieval era, yet we can not negate the prevalent weaknesses and corruptions that had seeped into the whole social order due to certain lampoon elements both from within and outside the valley. Kshemendra who was not only the representative of the shiny face but also a ruthless social critique, has exposed these ungainly and 'diseased' limbs of the society with no holds barred in his works. "He presents the vicious customs, opprobrious characters of his time in true colours. The lechers of the society; various kinds of people like the poet beating after his peccant poetry; the knave in the form of a teacher; the charlatan; the corrupt 'bride: the vicious priest; the turbid and deceitful grocer; the beggarly gambler; the hypocrite pupil; the imposing player of the lute ignorant of the method playing on it; the insidious physician; the fraudulent scribe; the chicaning Siva mendicant and the incestuous widow."[103] May be the picture presented by Kshemendra is one-sided or satirical, but evidences prove a huge degree of corruption, deceit, and dishonesty had crept in to the society by the end of the 13th century. The rulers were lax and least cared about the welfare or good will of the subjects. They were cowardly and unable to grant security of life and property to the state and its people. All around degradation of the social order had started to set in towards the middle of the 13th century AD The veneer of the KSP liberal and just society, free from the clutches of cast divisions and gender biases, and enlightened by the scholastic achievements of its people had lost quite a bit of its shine, and it was a trailer of what was destined to happen to the KSP social order in the 14th century and after. Even the prophets of doom in their wildest dreams could not have dreamt of the approaching change. (*Refer to the next chapter for details*).

CHINAR & GLACIER - TWO FEATURES OF KASHMIR

CHAPTER-7

SOCIAL ORDER DURING AND POST ISLAMIC ERA

Advent of the Islamic era, beginning from early 14th century, was one of the most important landmarks in the history of the KSP social order. A land mark that defies the simple qualification terms like positive or negative. Its impact on the composition, culture and moral ethos of the society, can be genuinely compared to the impact of a massive volcanic eruption on a geographic land mass.

TWO MAJOR CAUSES OF THIS ERUPTION WERE:

One the whirl wind assault of a faith that was neither subsidiary nor intermediary to the existing religious faith of the society at that time. As a matter of fact it was both anti and alien, belonging to an exclusively different genre, ethos and philosophy.

The second important factor was the cult of non-stop despotic, autocratic and fanatic impositions of the rulers and their underlings, who occupied the valley for nearly whole of the last millennia. Most of them being asylum seekers and invaders; hence were always eager to achieve their goals, irrespective of the consequences. Yes, there were, in between, a few decades of peace and progress, well worth being labelled as an oasis in the vast eras of marauding deserts.

To present a picture of the state of affairs during the era under study, reference to the observations of some chroniclers about certain events and occurrences is made, herewith, as a background, prior to assessing the social order with regard to the set parameters.

Change of government, which took place in Kashmir at the end of the Hindu period, affected significantly some of the original characteristics of the KSP. As with the advent and also along the whole duration of the Islamic era the KSP had to suffer the misery of arson and loot of the Mongol marauders; the fanatic tyranny and repression of the Afghans, Chaks; the Mughal impositions and the Sikh brutalities. People were grappling with the changes thrust upon them due to conversion of faith, change of language from Sanskrit to Persian, change of social norms and customs and even change in elementary activities like, the methods of worship, the formats of address and even personal hygiene. To site a simple example, the Pandit begins his ablutions from the left leg and the Musalman from the right leg. All these changes resulted into complete confusion and chaos in their social order. This phenomenon is well explained by, Baron Charles Hugel, who writes, "Subjugated in succession by the Mohammedans from Central Asia, who subverted their ancient and patriarchal institutions and government by the emperors of Delhi, who brought among them, in their search of new pleasures voluptuous and luxurious court, abandoned to pomp and prodigality by the fierce Afghans and finally the half civilized Sikhs; who now dwell in those long deserted imperial halls. What can remain of originality to these inhabitants of the valley after so many changes of the rulers, each in turn eager to destroy the works of his predecessor? It is however important to notice that Hinduism, once obeyed is hardly ever to be eradicated from the minds of its followers, even though they may be compelled to exchange their faith for another."[1]

As in the earlier periods, the rulers of this era too, were responsible for the metamorphosis of the people, at every turn, of the events that befell on the masses. In the middle of the fourteenth century came the most fanatic and religious despot of Kashmir, who not only massacred the Kashmiris (Hindus), but also got all their books on philosophy, theology and art written in Sanskrit destroyed by flames. Jonaraja writes "Even as fire burns grasses, all masterpieces of architecture produced by the Kashmiri *Shilpa Shinas* / architects were destroyed and pillaged. There was no city, no town, no village no wood where the temples of the gods were unbroken." [2] Even in the times of the famous humane King Zain-Ul Abe- din, who is Known to a Kashmiri as *Badshah the pathshah* (the most benevolent king,) temples were demolished to construct the king's mother's mausoleum and to rebuild the banks and bunds of the Vitasta.'

Measures adopted to change the prevailing social order

From the very origin according to scholars well imbued in the Koranic/ Quranic laws and dictums, the aim of the proselytisers was to purify and wipe out the, "infidels and idol worshippers from the face of the earth." Hence the target in the valley was the religious faith of the KSP's, who at that point of time, were exclusively followers of Sanatan dharma and its traditions. These people were neither tolerated nor allowed to escape.

Shirivara records in his R.T. about Haider shah's Barber Riktatara- who was his favourite for his notoriety- how he killed innocent people by torture. His victims were high and humble, poor and wealthy. "The relentless and sinful barber cut off the *Thakuras* and the courtiers of the king's father by the saw, and then left them on the roadside for days shrieking till death relieved them. Nonedeva, Shikhajada and others . . . had their tongues, noses, and hands cut of. Jaya the son of an *Acharya,* as also a Brahman, was maimed, and they struggled and threw themselves into the Vitasta."[3] There is no reason for us to doubt the credibility of what Srivara wrote in the 15th century, as we have, in the recent times, witnessed almost similar behaviour of the Islamic fundamentalists in Kashmir, who in their fanatic frenzy did not hesitate to behead and slice a few Hindus mercilessly.

Pir Hassan Shah writes, "The Mughal governors became despotic and sectarian. People were raised to extreme poverty. Yet the worst was to come during the reign of the Afghans in the 18th century. It was a period of anarchy, savagery, and inhumanity to the limit, and the victims were Kashmiris of all the hues, without any distinction of cast, class or faith. Yes the worst sufferers were the Pandits, the Shias and the *Bombas.* The Pathan governor Asad khan used to tie up the Pandits, and drown them in the Dal Lake, where as Mir Hazar yet another governor used leather bags instead of grass bags to drown both Brahmans and Shias."[4]

It is no great surprise that the very ambience of the KSP social order under went a humongous change with the 'advent of Islam' during the 14th and 15th centuries. Only thing that has survived this onslaught, till date, is the KSP's tradition 'of love and tolerance.'

Sayyid Ali Hamadani the great proselytiser, in his zeal to convert the liberal Hindu society decided that the change should be initiated by involving the ruler, so that his efforts receive more authority and credibility in the eyes of the converts.

Sayyid Ali's proselytizing activities, writes Prof. A.Q. Rafiq, "are highly extolled by: both medieval and modern scholars. But none of them gives any details of the method adopted by him at his work . . . There is no doubt, however, that Islam received great impetus because of Sayyid Ali and his followers. He left his deputies at a number of places which were great Hindu centres of those days, such as Pompar, Avantipura and Vijabror. These followers of Sayyid Ali established Khanqahs and the network of branches which gradually emerged or became important centres of preaching and proselytization." Thus the religious aspect of the KSP society was being moulded by the efforts of such foreign preachers.

SOCIAL ORDER DURING AND POST ISLAMIC ERA

The society was divided into two categories, "Muslims and Kafirs-and accordingly a list of twenty most humiliating and degrading rules for the infidels, to comply with absolute obedience were framed. The non Muslims were forbidden to construct any new places of worship, reconstruct any existing place of worship that may fall in to ruin; ride horses with saddle and bridle; carry any weapons, wear signet rings and practice their customs and usages. Hindus were forbidden to carry their dead near the graveyards of Muslims, mourn their dead loudly, build their houses in the neighbourhood of Muslims, and to prevent Muslim travellers from staying in their place of worship or temples. They were required to receive any Muslim traveller in to their houses and to provide him with: hospitality for three days and to wear humble dress so that they may be distinguished from Muslims and if they infringe any of them then Muslim had a right to kill them."

If there was some semblance of humane proselytizing in the beginning of the fourteenth century it reached a crescendo in Kashmir during the reign of Sikander Butshikan the Iconoclast under the patronage of Sayyid Muhammad Hamadani, who came to Kashmir in 1393. Sultan Sikandar let loose a reign of unprecedented terror against the Hindu population. "To him" writes the author of Baharistan-i-Shahi, ':goes the credit of wiping out the vestiges of infidelity and heresy from the mirror of the conscience of the dwellers of these lands," adding that, "immediately after his arrival, Sultan Sikandar, peace be on him submitted to his religious supremacy and proved his loyalty to him by translating his words into deeds". It is during his rule we are introduced to the first most pivotal neo-convert named Suha Bhatt prior to his conversion and Malik Safu'd-Din afterwards. Sikandar and this neo-convert are attributed to have committed the most barbaric atrocities on the Kashmiri Hindu society giving them no option but to accept Islam, exile or death. Hassan writes, "Sikandar meted out greatest oppression to the Hindus. It was notified in to the city that if a Hindu does not become a Muslim, he must leave the country or be killed. As a result, some of the Hindus fled away, some accepted Islam and many Brahmans consented to be killed and gave their lives. It is said Sikandar collected by these methods about three *khirwars* (210 kilograms) of Hindu sacred threads and burnt them . . . All the Hindu books of learning were collected and thrown in Dal Lake and were buried beneath stones and earth."[5]

The orgy of violence and proselytising frenzy continued unabated into the reign of Sultan Ali Shah (1113-1120 A.D). The renegade Suha and the 'demoniac *Sayyids* went berserk in their attempt to destroy Hinduism from Kashmir valley, root and branch. The whole Valley was bathed in the blood of the innocents. Jonaraja draws a heart-rending picture of the plight of Hindus, in particular Brahmins of Kashmir, comparing them to fish tormented by fisherman in a closed river. He says that their religious ceremonies and processions were banned and heavy taxes were levied on them; and to starve them their traditional allowances were stopped, forcing them to become beggars. For a mouthful of food, "they went from house to house, lolling out their tongues like dogs Some roamed in the streets in the disguise of Muslims to save their emaciated families from the hunger. To escape oppression and to preserve their religious identity, many of them ran away from their land through bye-roads as the main roads were closed; the son leaving his father behind and the father leaving his son. But not all succeeded in escaping. Passing through difficult terrain, many of them died of scorching heat and illness; of starvation due to scanty food. Many of those, who remained behind, committed suicide by taking poison, by drowning, and self immolation, by hanging, or jumping from precipices. And numerous Hindus were killed brutally while many were forced to convert to Islam."[6]

Degree of the inhuman treatment meted to Hindu KSP during this period can be assessed from the fact that as an amusement, a pitcher filled with ordure was placed on the Pandits head and the Musalmáns would be asked to pelt stones on the pitcher so that it would break and unfortunate Hindu get blinded by the filth. In those days any Musalman who met a Pandit would jump on his back and forcibly take a ride and, as the saying goes "*Buta chuk tu khosa dita*", meaning, since you are a Hindu you must give me a ride.

The Pandits were forced to grow a beard and wear a turban. Shoes were forbidden, and the tika was interdicted. Madad khan's agent was an old woman named Koship, and she was the terror of the Brahman parents, who rather than allow the degradation of their daughters destroyed their beauty by shaving their heads or cutting off their noses

The Impact of these fanatic interventions on the KSP social order

Cast and class divisions

The stunning impact was the complete change over of the religious format of the society. Up to the beginning of the fourteenth century, practically entire population of the valley was Hindu; and by the end of the century, the majority of the people were converted to Islam. Tradition affirms that the persecution, of the Hindus was so keen that only eleven families of Hindus survived in the valley. This number gradually increased to around

28,000 in the early 18th century during Ranjit Singh's reign (if rightly recorded). By the time commissioner Lawrence's carried out census during Maharaja Rambir Singhs rule (Dogra rule) the number had increased to 60,316, of whom 28,695 lived in Srinagar and the rest were scattered about in the villages.[7] As a result the earlier system of the classification of the society no longer survived and suited. Hence it underwent many a changes during the Islamic rule and influenced the basic structure of the KSP social order. Under the new religious set up, the KSP were divided on the basis of religious faith that they observed. Those KSP'S who had the fortitude, stamina and faith to with stand the inhuman tortures, orgies and bans, managed to retain their Hindu faith. These few Hindus were exclusively *Saraswat* Brahmans and they grouped themselves into ***Karkuns*** and ***Bashabattas***.

Karkuns were those who were employed in government services. As Sanskrit was the language of the court and administration, till Persian could be perfected, the Sultans were forced to employ the literate KSP Hindus who were learned in Sanskrit and proficient in administrative services, in their courts, to run the government. Later when they achieved excellence in Persian, they became indispensable to the Mughals. Like wise after gaining expertise in English language the Sikhs, the Dogras and the Britishers too utilised their service. This class almost attained exclusivity like the present day bureaucracy. It almost became a hereditary class of feudal aristocracy and was put at the highest rung of the social order. But they were very few in numbers. The majority of Karkun designates for want of options, poverty and deprivation took up a variety of occupations to earn their lively hood in spite of being Brahmans. G.L.Kaul writes "All the Bhattas are Saraswat Brahmans and in spite of restricting themselves to the state jobs alone, they took to a varied number of occupations like business, agriculture, profession of acting and music, and even the other jobs like cooks, bakers, confectioners, and tailors. Briefly it may be said that, a Pandit may follow any trade or occupation except those of the cobbler, potter, corn-fryer, porter, boatman, carpenter, mason, or fruit seller."[8]

The second group the ***Bashabattas*** who were supposed to be the honoured preservers and preachers of Hindu scriptural knowledge were divided and sub divided to such an extent that some sections of this class were placed at the lower wrung of the social order. So much so inter marriage and social alliances was a taboo between Karkuns and the priestly class. These changes were a great loss to the Hindu KSP society, for the number of learned in the religious and scriptural field staggered over the years, due to the lack of interest in this field, both by the preacher and the preached.

Muslim classification too suffered a great many changes, during this era. Initially they were just **Sunnis** or **Shias.** But this simple and classless division did not last long in their social order. Over the time they were classified on the basis of the genetic hereditary of their ancestry. Those who by matrimony were born of the ***Sayyids*** were put right at the top of the social order. Next followed those born of Mughal, Afghan, and Pathan ancestors and last of all were placed the ***Shekhs*** the descendents of the Hindu converts. Gradually the divisions followed, on the basis of the occupation, and the gravity and stature of the chores involved. To sight an example, the Hanji (boat men class) is divided according to the size and shape of the boat he plies. (*For details refer to Chapter the Kashur)* These gradations in the social order, created different economic levels and deprivations to the extent, like what we observe at the present times among the ST's and SC's in the rest of the country.

Going by the records of European travellers and administrators, it was not a water tight division initially. The recent converts continued their practices and traditions for quite some time. Sufi culture considerably influenced the religious and philosophic thought of the Kashmiris and in turn impacted their social order.

EDUCATION

Due to the change of the literary language, complete confusion reigned in the realms of education in the initial hundred odd years. Prior to the arrival of new faith, the KSP were masters of Sanskrit, the language of administration, literature and other literary exercises. All of a sudden they had to switch over to a new language. How so ever capable they might have been, yet it was no ordinary task. The change did take place but at a cost. Ordinary citizens suffered till they could grasp the subtleties of the Persian language.

This scenario is evident from the frequent references made in Jonaraja' and Shri Vara's chronicles, to Brahmans holding high official posts under the early Sultans and Sanskrit continuing to be for a considerable period, the language of official communication and record in Kashmir after the end of Hindu rule. The various forms of official documents and reports etc, which are contained in the *Lokaprakash,* a handbook of Kashmirian administrative routine are drawn up "in a curious Sanskrit jargon, full of Persian and Arabic words which must have become current in Kashmir soon after the introduction of Islam." The use of Sanskrit, even among Musalmáns is borne out by the Sanskrit inscription on a tomb of Sayyid Khan in the cemetery of Hazrat Baha-ud-Din Ganj Baksh at the foot of the Hari-Parbat in Srinagar.

Brief Sanskrit inscriptions without dates have been discovered by Stein on a number of old Muslim tombs at *Mazarisalatin (Maharaj-Ganj)* and at Martand.

With the passage of time and persistent efforts of the KSP the Persian language and literature, first introduced into Kashmir by Zain-ul-Abidin, further enriched the cultural treasures of Kashmir resulting in a synthesis of the Hindu and Muslim civilizations. Kashmiris attained a great proficiency in the new language and literature and produced eminent poets and scholars like Ghani, Sarfi, Fani, etc

"The Kashmiri Pandits of this period though hardened by the recurring attacks on their religious faith did not allow crippling of their minds. In outdoor life they behaved and described themselves as any other citizen would do. Use of words like *Banda, Bandai Khas, Bandai Dargah, Ahqar, Ibn* etc. with their names would show this. They even offered sometimes their prayers in Persian language, and prefixed even their Gods with such epithets as *Hazrat* etc. Thus in 1742 AD we find writings like, "*Banda hai gulamani Hazrati Sharda Devi Bhawani Barai Qadmbos wa Gusul Dar Kurukshetra Raseed* The Hindu KSP had indeed eagerness to have a dip in the holy tank at Kurukshetra, but did not hesitate in using expressions and style which were not strictly of an orthodox type like:

(a) *Bandai Dargah Rupchand Parimoo Sakini Kani Kadal*

(2) Anand Ram Valoo hamrahi Lashkari Zain Khan Bahadur dar Risalai Qassim Khan

(3) Mehar Chand Kaul Sakini Bagdaji Minmahlati Rainawari hamrahi Lashkari Zain Khan Bahadur"[9]'

It is recorded that many a Hindu KSP's compiled historical treatises in Persian language during this period. Pandit Anand Ram Karihalu's mastery of Arabic and Persian was so complete that even amongst the Muslims nobody could compete with him. Besides Pandit Birbal Kachru (1789-1859AD), Pandit Anand Ram Pahalwan, Pandit Narain Kaul (1712-1785AD) proficient in Persian language, were products of this era. In spite of all this, the education of the masses suffered to a great extant due to the dictates of conservative votaries of the Islamic faith.

Dress

The dress of Kashmiris during whole of Islamic era has often been criticized for being effeminate and conducive to lazy habits. There is a story current among the Kashmiris that Emperor Akbar, enraged at the dogged resistance offered by the people of the valley to his general Qasim Khan, forced them to wear the effeminate Pheran in order to degrade them, to demoralize and control the turbulent and warlike Kashmiris after they had repeatedly risen in revolt during the early part of the alien rule. There is definitely some element of truth in this belief, otherwise how could the KSP all of a sudden adopt a shroud like disgraceful dress to cover them selves from top to toe. As per chronicler records we know prior to these times men wore smart tight jackets and trousers and the women wore bright, flashy clothes stitched to define the contours of their figures, and also wore Saris and blouses from the 10th/ 11th AD onwards.

This traditional belief has been affirmed by scholars like Colonel T. Handley who writes, "Kashmir, in a past age was inhabited by brave men, but the Mughal conquerors broke their spirit, and one of the measures by which they effected this end was, it is commonly believed, by compelling the men to wear the over dress of women, the long coat which impedes their movement. And women naturally partook of this degradation. The use of the Kangri aggravated the situation."[10]

Even Lieutenant Newell writes, "rendering the native Kashmiris less warlike and of breaking their old independent spirit, amongst other measures to effect this, I have been informed but have nowhere seen it recorded, as a fact very generally believed in Kashmir, that the emperor Akbar caused a change to be introduced in the dress of the people. In place of the ancient well girded tunic adapted to activity and exercise, the emperor substituted the effeminate long gown of the present day, a change which led to the introduction of the enervating Kangri corresponding with the French *'chauffe-chamice'* or pot of charcoal fire; without which a modern Kashmiri is seldom seen. And it is possible that this measure, one out of a long series of acts of tyranny and spirit-breaking oppression, may have had its effect in changing the character of this once brave and warlike race."[11]

Some others, however, are of the opinion that the loose gown came into fashion when the Kashmiris were involved in internecine civil strife, and had ceased to be ambitious, and were leading an indolent stay-at-home-life, long before the Muslims captured political power. What ever be the truth, the fact remains that pheran made of woollen cloth in winter and of cotton in summer continued to be a source of many weaknesses and vices. It was a long loose gown buttoning at the neck and falling to the ankles. There was very little difference between the Pheran worn by men and women. A pyjama of the loose type was generally worn under the Pheran and this was all the dress of an average villager. The women wore a skull cap surrounded by a fillet of red colour in the case of Muslim and a fillet of white cloth in the case of Hindu women. A shawl or / a white *chaddar* thrown gracefully over the head and shoulders, more as a protection from the sun than to hide the features, completed their headgear. The headdress of the Hindu women was a kind of veil, which fell over the back of the head. Only the women of the wealthy class would veil themselves from the public gaze. Men wore turbans as a sign of respectability and affluence. It was commonly worn by the inhabitants of cities and big towns. Ordinary peasant would use a long pointed skull cap.

Lawrence has given a detailed description of the dress worn by a Kashmiri while on a journey, and he writes "The Kashmiris assert that their national dress is to be found in Kishtwar, and that it resembles the dress of a Kashmiri when he goes on a journey. The gown is tucked up and bound around the waist by a cloth belt or tucked inside the drawers, and the drawers turn into manly knickerbockers, with leggings, which are simple and effective. Bandages of woollen cloth, the well-known puttee of the Indian army, are wound around the calf of the leg and are said to give great support on long journeys. There is great art in binding the bandage and the Kashmiri knows the art."[12] However in the recent times Kashmiri travellers no longer use such a dress.

Towards the beginning of the twentieth century a crusade was launched against the use of the effeminate dress by patriotic Kashmiris that resulted in the change, among certain classes, to the graceful *sari* and *shalwar Kameez*, in the case of women, and coat and trousers in the case of men. The majority KSP being Musalmáns, slightly modified the ungainly length and shape of the Pheran and that change gave it a smart look. Both men and women mostly use this along with a shalwar as every day wear.

At present Hindu KSP women are increasingly adopting the new look and only old women or those who live in the country side are seen in Pheran and taranga. The reform produced its repercussions in the Muslims too and the younger generation of the community especially educated and upper class girls, who no longer wear pheran, have taken to shilwar and kurta and a few more fashionable are dressed in sari too.

Ornaments

Women continued to wear ornaments as in earlier eras but the shape and size of the ear rings and the necklace was modified and mostly the ornaments were made of silver instead of gold, since the once effluent society was reduced to penury.

Srivara while describing Ratnamala the court dancer, of the fourteenth century, (till then mostly Hindu) gives us an idea of the ornaments worn by the ladies. He records, "her person was decorated with jewels. The beauty of her face was nectar and a drop of nectar hung from her nose in the form of a pearl pendant. The pearls were interwoven in the locks of her hair and fell on her cheeks and looked as drops of nectar melting away from her moonlike face."[13]

Food

The Islamic era was responsible for introducing the Iranian, Afghan and central Asian variety of non-vegetarian dishes in the KSP cuisine. A common terminology used to define this menu is *waazwan.* It differs greatly from the Hindu version of KSP cuisine both in variety, number, flavour and manner of cooking. It is supposed to be a combo of 36 courses, though the normal practice restricts it to 20 course meal. It is a ceremonial feast, and usually cooked by professionals. Some dishes that are a must for waazwan are a*ab-gosht* (mutton cooked in milk). *gushtaba* (painstaking effort for fine succulent delicacy of mince mutton balls simmered in curd),*methimaaz* (mutton and fenugreek green (combo), *kabaab, tabak-maaz,* (baked chunks of ribs marinated in spice ghee and milk), *rista* (spicy chilly format of gushtaba), *martswaangan-korma* (,mince mutton balls cooked in the juicy extract of the red cockscomb flower) r*ogan josh* and some variety of vegetables. Except for the *roganjosh* (red and spicy mutton dish) all other dishes are imported and adopted mainly by the Musalman. The Bhatta prefers their variety of succulent curd meat *(yekhni*), *mutch (keema), kelia* (yellow meat) and k*abargah* (fatty rib sections boiled and cooked in milk and spice till tender and then dipped in curd marinate and fried in pure ghee). Though now a days frying is replaced by baking and grilling. The vegetarian variants of these dishes are *damaloo, chaaman kaliya* (yellow coloured cheese), *nadur yekhni* (lotous stem cooked in curds). Besides these two specially Kashmiri variety of dishes are *choek charvan* (small pieces of liver boiled and then deep fried and cooked with tamarind juice) and s*hupta* (cheese cubes cooked along with dry fruits like almonds, coconut chips, sugar cubes *(mishri)* and cardamom). Vegetables as used in the previous eras continue to be part of the cuisine. KSP usually avoids any form of wheat breads for the main course. Plain boiled rice or occasionally saffron flavoured *pliauf* (both salty and sweet) or k*icheddi* a mix of whole moong and rice are served. *Kheer or phiriny* (rice pudding) is the common sweet dish. *Chai* (tea) is the most common hot drink. It has three varieties, a) k*hewa* sweet black tea, *dhude chai* (tea with milk) and *sheer chai* (salty milk tea). *Lass*i and *gurus* (both prepared with unflavoured yoghurt) are the two common soft drinks. This does not imply that the rest of the dishes from any part of the country or continent are a no go. For that matter of the fact a KSP is past master in the art of adaptability

Modes of entertainment:

After the early phase of proselytizing, and bans on entertainments, the emergence of the Sufi thought-attainment of sublime unity with the Supreme Being, through the medium of dance and singing praises in the name of god, revived the culture of singing and dancing to some extant.

Though dancing and singing was permitted as a source of entertainment in the courts, it was literally prohibited for the common folks, especially during the Afghan rule. Women, who if at all took these professions belonged to the lower strata of the social ladder and were labelled as women of ill-repute. The stigma and impact of this thought process was prevalent almost up to the middle of the twentieth century in the KSP society. So much so that it was a profession not thought fit even for men of higher class and status. Bazaz writes, "The arts of music and dancing were considered as quite unfit for respectable girls, and were thus practiced only by low-caste women and prostitutes."[14]

Arts and crafts

The society attained many an excellences in the arts and crafts during the Islamic era. People practiced and almost reinvented the arts of painting and architecture. Hari Parbat fort and the bastion wall that surrounds the hill, Jamma Masjid and Pa'thar Masjid, Pari Mahal and world-famous Moghul Gardens are living testimonies to the outstanding contribution to architecture by the Kashmiris of this era. The art of weaving shawls and carpets thrived and world renown was accomplished by the crafts men of Kashmir in the art of papier-mâché, wood carving, leather tanning, metal work, polishing and filigree work in silver. The influences of Islamic art from the directions of north and south were responsible for the development of many industries for which Kashmir is famous, e.g. shawl, carpet, papier-mâché, woodcarving, etc.

Though Zain-ul-Abidin is credited to have been responsible for the introduction of these arts from Samarqand and Bukhara yet the information gathered from N.P. that qualifies KSP as experts in these arts and crafts in the Puranic era itself defies the concept.

Learning

Irrespective of the initial contradiction and confusion, on account of the language of learning and administration, in the earlier part of the Islamic era, the culture of learning advanced and continued to flourish over all, under the patronage of some of the benevolent and learned men like Zain Ul Abdin, Hasan Shah, and Dara Shiko. We find, efforts were carried on very earnestly for the spread of Persian language. Many a schools, Madrassa and universities with proper facilities of learned scholars and teachers and proper libraries were established in different parts of the state for the people

Prince Dara Shikoh established the residential 'School of Sufism' on a spur of the Zebarwan Mountain (now known as Pari Mahal) at the instance of his spiritual tutor *Akhund Mulla Muhammad Shah Badakhshan*,

Kashmir received its most powerful impact from the beneficent forces of Islam and came in almost direct contact with the stage of culture Islam had then achieved. And the genius of the people of the Happy Valley was awakened to a degree that excited the admiration of the world when Zain-ul-Abidin ruled the land. Unfortunately the later Islamic zealots especially the Afghans instead of preserving encouraging and enhancing the literary excellence; destroyed and annihilated the very literary spirit of the masses and of the people of calibre, especially the female segment of the society. As per the rulers of that era; a ladies sole meaning and purpose in life was to keep the homes, to gratify the desires of their men and to procreate children.

Status of women and marriage norms

It is an undisputed fact, that a woman by virtue of its numbers in a society has a measure impact on the grooming of its social order as said earlier. She is not only a partner in the process of procreation of a society, but also the architect of the mental, physical and ethical health of its members. The intellectual genre of a society stands directly in proportion to, the mental calibre of the mother figure. We practically visualise this state in the social order of the KSP.

As detailed in the previous chapter, women in the pre and post Puranic era, were soaring high in the social horizon of their community, in spite of the pernicious custom of Sati introduced in the KSP society by the Syctho Tartars and the degeneration of the ancient sacred *Devdasi* cult; they not only excelled in their domestic domain but also in the political arena as queens, and queen consorts. They even participated in the military exercises as generals leading the armies, acted as envoys and even stratigicians. Chroniclers have repeatedly documented their expertise in the field of learning, languages, philosophy, and aesthetic arts like singing and dancing. They were masters of their own life and enjoyed a place of respect in the society. Unfortunately with the advent of fanatic Islam they suffered the most.

The death of queen Kota not only ended the Hindu rule it also sounded a death knell to the special status enjoyed by queens and to the freedom of women in general. Women were gradually and increasingly deprived of the privileges that they had acquired and enjoyed over thousands of years. "Almost throughout the long course of their history until the middle of the fourteenth century, they took no inconspicuous part in the civil administration. In days of need and emergency, they joined the forces of the land; they functioned as leaders of religious thought and as diplomats and, politicians; they achieved reputation as builders and artistes/Undoubtedly, the happy period for / women as for the people in general was that when the country came under the sway of Buddhism, but the privileges earned under the impact of the libertarian creed could not be taken away by the reactionary regimes which were set up on the revival of the Brahmanical reaction. With the downfall of the Hindu rule and capture of power by Shah Mir, however, the social fabric underwent a complete change."[15] Women lost their old rights and prerogatives, education was barred; they ceased to dabble in politics, took no part in public affairs.

Gone were the days when women of cultured wealthy class, as a matter of fact of all classes enjoyed complete freedom to move along with their men folk in the palaces, at market places, on battle fields, in vents, at public thoroughfares and in religious and social gatherings. Now the dignity and safety of a lady lay in being secluded, veiled and unseen by men other than the nearest kin. The process of humiliation reached the farthest limits under the Afghans. It is the unanimous verdict of all Kashmir chroniclers that under these barbarian rulers (1752-1819AD) the valley witnessed the darkest period of national depression. Though men and women were, without distinction, subjected to hardship by the Afghan tyrant, women became special targets of his licentious behaviour. No handsome or youthful maiden was safe from the grasping clutches of an Afghan governor or his lawless underlings, if he desired to have her for the satisfaction of his carnal desires. Nothing could prevent the ruffian from taking possession of her body; and his word was the law of the land. Notwithstanding her heart-rending cries and the pathetic wailings of the parents and neighbours, good-looking virgins and handsome married women were forcibly captured and kidnapped and despatched to Kabul as presents to friends and compatriots. In such distressing and agonising conditions, to talk of freedom would be mockery. Its last shreds disappeared when the practice of

Purdah was more rigorously enforced by the terrified people. No wonder that within a score of years of the Afghan rule, Kashmiri women were physically and spiritually shattered; their presence in every sphere of social activity totally eclipsed.

Kalhana makes no mention of the pernicious custom of *Purdah* anywhere in his Chronicle. Bazaz writes "It baffled the imagination of the civilised Kashmiri that women could be kept in seclusion or girls segregated from boys. It is true there were inner apartments *(antahpura)* in the royal palaces as well as in the homes of courtiers, nobles and other well-to-do families in Kashmir too where women lived in privacy and which were held sacred; but a suggestion to the ladies to move about veiled or to remain aloof from men would have sounded humiliating and offensive in the ears of the men no less than in those of the women."[16]

The soul killing practice of *Purdah*, unknown to the Kashmiris, was introduced at the behests of mullahs and priests. The Muslim women of wealthier classes and high pedigree were first to suffer. They were relegated behind the veil. In imitation of the ruling classes or under threat of molestation, the Hindu ladies of equal status followed.

As a whole this class of royalty was reduced to the state of mere procreators relegated to, "the domestic sphere and confined to the harem. They rarely appeared in public and seldom contacted officers to keep them selves informed of the currents and cross-currents in state politics. They were expected to be devoted wives, giving comfort to their husbands and procreating children for the perpetuation of the royal dynasty; the administration and governance of the country were none of their concern."[17] How ever, due to inherent ingenuity and, intellectual calibre women of general class, in spite of the deprivation of education and strangulated social atmosphere, were able to produce some gems of the KSP womanhood like /Lall Ded, Arnimal, Habba khatoon and Farzi to name only a few, who stand above the rest in stature and who achieved immortal fame though they were the progeny of poor, toiling parents. Lall Ded who composed *vaaks* pregnant with the *Upanishadic* teachings and mysticism of *Shaiva* Philosophy practically acted as a bridge amidst the chaos and confusion of the struggle between two religious streams. Habba Khatoon and Arnimaal made invaluable contribution to the creation of (*lole* songs) romantic, love songs of Kashmiri.

Though the women of class and pedigree were forced to succumb and loose all their rights, so much so as to dress or groom their own person according to their choice and established routine was denied to them, they were deprived of the right to education, illiteracy and unkempt domineer was their virtue and silence was their saviour, yet there can be no doubt the women of the middle and the lower classes, of peasantry labouring multitude, who formed the preponderant majority put up a bold front, resisted to the last and refused to yield. Even when such heroic souls voluntarily embraced Islam or were converted through coercion to the new faith, they courageously stood by their ancient right to move about openly and freely, throughout the past six centuries, and indeed to this day; these brave women have continued their epic struggle and held aloft the banner of freedom with phenomenal success. No woman of the working class be she toiling in the fields, assisting in a shop, or functioning in any other capacity, has recognised the institution of *Purdah.* [18] G.T.Vigne who travelled extensively over India in the first half of the 19th century and had the opportunity to see Kashmiri women in 1835 AD confirms, "In Kashmir there is no *Purdah*, or concealment of the features, excepting among the higher classes." [19]

Even though the Kashmiris would have been aware of the prevalence of the *Purdah* system in the neighbouring regions they were always opposed to it. They held very rational views about the observance of it that have been clearly detailed by Somadeva (11th century AD), in his prodigious composition *Kathasaritsagara* (Ocean of Story). Leela Rey in her book (*Women of India,* page11) reflects the public opinion of that time through the feelings of the princess Ratna Prabha and writes, "I consider that the strict seclusion of women is a mere custom, or rather a folly, produced by jealousy. It is of no use whatever. Women of good family are guarded by their own virtue as by their only chamberlain. Even God himself can scarcely guard the unchaste."

Having detailed the restrictions and deprivations imposed by Islam on the women, one needs to record the genuine efforts made by Islam towards abolishing the pernicious practice of Sati that was prevalent in the Hindu society, especially in the royalty and nobility. In this effort Islam saved the women from the horrors of this inhuman practice upheld by the Hindu society. It took nearly two and a half century to be completely abolished from the society. Till then even Muslim women-those who had recently converted would self immolate on their husbands death. Mughal ruler Akbar had forbidden the performance of sati in India, but even he was not successful to eradicate the practice in Kashmir, after having annexed the valley to his empire in 1586 AD This heinous act was finally abolished during Jahangir's rule. G.M. Suffi while recording an episode in this connection writes, "A shiver passed through the Emperor's spine when he heard, while on his way to Kashmir through the often trodden route of Pir Panjal, that Muslim widows in Rajouri were consigned to the flames with the remains of their husbands.

Royal commands were immediately issued prohibiting the noxious practice. Jahangir was particular to see that his orders were actually carried out and subsequently made enquires about it. Dr. Sufi states that the number of Muslim girls cremated at one time was no fewer than 4,000 in Rajauri and Bhimber."[20]

Islam sanctioned re-marriage of widows and the right of separation and divorce, though hedged by various restrictions. Hindu women however, continued to be governed by their personal laws. Since the majority of the population was converted to Islam they benefited by the liberal Muslim Law.

Status of Women in the later eras

In the long and unrelieved period of slavery, Kashmiris forgot all about the past and the heights that women had scaled in some periods of their history. A time had come when, through force of habit, the people began to believe that the grade status which hard days had forced upon the women was natural to them; a religious sanctity was attached to the disabilities and disqualifications, which the foreign rule had imposed on them. "An ideal woman was depicted as one whose ambition never soared beyond devoted ministration to the wants of her lord, the husband, and maintenance of the home for his children's comfort. In grandiloquent language selfish men-philosophers portrayed her as the queen of the home where man had hardly any say and had to submit meekly to her dictates. But such clumsy attempts at rationalising failed to conceal the hideous truth that woman had become a drudge and all her gifts and talents were rusting unused within her, partly due to the political and social conditions created by foreign rule but partly also as a result of the ignorance heartlessness of the self-centred and conceited men."[21]

Women, who were praised for beauty, dress and fashion, besides their intellectual genius, during the earlier eras, were looked down upon if they dressed in clean garments or adorned them selves. The more dirty and ugly their demeanour was, the more virtuous they were considered. Bazaz records, "During the times of which we are speaking now, all innocent enjoyment was taboo. Gone were the days when women used cosmetics and beauty aids to enhance the natural attractive ness of their bodies. In rare cases would a lady enjoy the luxury of a soap-wash and that without the knowledge of elders? Fragrant powders or scented oils formed no part of their toilette; such indulgences were looked down upon and forbidden. It would have scandalised the society in the nineteenth century to find a lady gratifying her desire of appearing lovely or graceful. To entertain any such unbecoming wish was inexcusable; only prostitutes and harlots would be bold enough to dress themselves in shining clothes or have an elegant style of hair. A gentle woman desirous of wearing fashionable dresses was unhesitatingly declared to be on way to whoredom. Even cleanliness among women unless it is for religious purposes, was, by and large, discouraged and never rewarded or highly spoken of. Sluttish appearance had been fostered first in the days of Afghans; then it had a justification; to protect young and innocent girls from being assaulted or ravished they had to look ugly and untidy. Subsequently, under the Sikhs, it acquired sanctity of a national habit."[22]

Under such circumstances women lost all their accomplishments and arts. They could not sing and dance as it was thought below dignity to be associated in such arts for the women of respectable class of the society. The singers and dancers belonged to the out cast community of 'Watal' (sweeper class) who did the dirtiest work; of removing and skinning the carcases and curing leather. Frederic Drew (1875) writes, "From among them are provided musicians and the dancers; the dancing girls whom one sees at the durbars and festivals which the Maharaja holds are of that race."[23]

The valley had been denuded of its precious wealth, the cream of womanhood, by the Mughals and the Afghans. Those whom good luck or some favourable circumstances saved from falling into the clutches of the grasping foreigner were subject to the observance of *Purdah* and harsh treatment from the moment of birth. Hard labour, colossal ignorance and fresh air together with indifference on the part of men combined to undermine health, ruin physique and the spirit of Kashmiri women. It was not surprising, therefore that beautiful faces or attractive features were rarely to be witnessed in them for generations.

Sir Walter Lawrence writes, "The bodily form of Kashmiri woman had been vastly affected; she was no more her old self but a weakling. Thousands of young females died prematurely and many more eked out diseased existence. The death rate was appalling and the ratio of the population of women to that of men was gradually decreasing. Among all classes there was lesser number of females than that of males."[24]

Polygamy which in ancient times was restricted to royal families, or was, at the most, prevalent among the nobles and well- to-do classes had now spread to a certain extent, to the middle classes. Though Muslims were greater victims of this evil, there were cases among the Hindus also, where men had violated the equitable law of monogamy. As compensation, no doubt, Muslim women enjoyed the rights of divorce and remarriage after the death of husband, but the Hindu women continued to be deprived of both. But in theory and I stress in theory alone, the Kashmiri Hindus still held sacrosanct the scriptural injunctions recognising woman as incarnation of Shakti the left-half of *Ardananishwara (Shiva)* She was to be present at every religious ceremony and sit side by side with her husband on the occasion of the performance of important rituals; otherwise the celebration would be incomplete and would bear no merit to the performer.

Divorce and remarriage of widows were detested by selfish Hindus who attached moral and religious stigma to these essential liberties and thus the unfortunate women remained subservient to the male authority for whole of their lives. The magnitude of cruelty in enforced widow hood can be estimated by the fact that, in 1920 AD during Pratap Singh's days, there were thirteen percent of the girls who had been victims of child marriage and had lost husbands in early childhood, when they were totally ignorant of the significance of marriage ceremony or consequences of widow-hood. Equally distressing was the case of the hundreds of deserted young Hindu wives whom society refused the elementary human rights of divorce and remarriage despite that they were known to be innocent and had been cast aside by the caprice of heartless husbands.

Conclusion

Looking back over the past 1000 years of social, political and religious history of Kashmir, the coming of Islam and its impact on the social order of the KSP can be compared very reasonably to the impact on the society in Mecca and Medina. All three places have undergone almost an identical metamorphosis in religious and social order. The sole breed of KSP was Hindu by faith, when Islam knocked at the gates of the so called secured mountain walls of their land? Neither their mountain barriers could prevent the onslaught of the sly invaders, nor could the people of the valley fight the assault. They failed to judge the intent of the white robed Darveshes.Thus Islam succeeded in causing conversion, destruction, mass migration, loot and annihilation of a highly developed intellectual society. The new faith led them from the era of light and knowledge to an era of darkness, illiteracy, ignorance; retrograde silence and meek surrender to the fanatic codes and laws for almost one whole century, till they withered the initial storm and staggered back on firm fresh foot holds.

In the initial stages, the educational excellence that was the forte of the KSP suffered a huge set back due to the conservative tenets of Islam, change of basic beliefs and above all the language of learning and expression. Women folk bore the brunt of this change.

During Zain-Ul-Abidin's reign many a handicrafts and arts that were imported from Islamic cultures and civilisations and introduced into the Muslim Kashmir's work culture brought them world renown, fame and name. This intermingling of lifestyles brought them closer to the prime Islamic world and such interaction has been of a great advantage to the Muslim KSP. Besides handicrafts the KSP society was introduced to Islamic architecture and the art of calligraphy. Both arts flourished with the diligence of KSP masters and resulted in building of a number of reputed mosques and prayer halls for the faithful.

Turkish and Iranian zealots that followed looked down upon the Kashmiri Muslim as a second grade convert. His Islam was considered as one not recognised by the Caliphs of Islam. The barbarian hordes of Afghans and Mongols treated them on the same footing as they treated the Hindu KSP. For in their eyes they were both preys to be looted, vandalised and disgraced. To be taken prisoners or allowed to perish in the snowy no man lands. In the high tradition of Kashmiri hospitality, the *Kashur* gave asylum to the Shias from Iran who were being haunted out of their land by the Sunnis, but as the fate would have it; these very asylum seekers took revenge on the Sunni Muslim of Kashmir.

Society Twentieth Century Onwards a Short Resume

Over the last hundred odd years of the reign of Sikhs and Dogras, the sceptre of conversion had completely lost its hold on the social behaviour of the society and the Hindu KSP had regained some of their earlier confidence and was slightly better off as compared to their Muslim brethren. So much so that in the middle of the nineteenth century a large number of them was anxious or willing to reconvert en-block to Hinduism. Realizing the situation, the ruler of the state sent a deputation to the *pundits* of Banaras enquiring about the feasibility of the appeal. The *pundits* refuted to countenance any such change of faith and with that ended the initiative.[25] However, atmosphere of bonhomie and brother hood started growing day by day among the two diverse branches of the society. Trust, love and respect for each others norms and faiths grew replacing the sense of animosity and distrust. After the independence of the country the KSP was justifiably aspiring and hoping for a peaceful, liberated and prosperous political climate to live in as the citizens of a free state.

With the end of the monarchical rule and the British residency the reign of governance had been handed over to the elected leaders of the state by its electorate. Process of reform and development was duly initiated with the abolition of landlordism, money lending trade and introduction of the policy of land to the tillers. By such measures the majority benefited, even though complete deprivation of land holdings without any compensation reduced some of the privileged minority members to a penury state. Many an educational institutions were started in nooks and corners of the valley for the general literary progress of the society and the peace and harmony had returned over shadowing the communal and political upheaval of the 1931 riots.

When externally the air of calm prevailed, the inexplicable curse of the KSP raised its head like an apparition with the partition of the country. Pakistan was not ready to accept the combined decision, opted by the people of the state, the sovereign ruler of the state and the elected leaders of the ruling council to be a part and parcel of the republic of India on the premise that the state of Kashmir was a Muslim majority state. Hence the seed for unrest, strife, and violence was once again implanted in the KSP society. Pakistan not only initiated and activated military incursions but also infiltrated the Sufi Islamic culture of the KSP slowly and steadily and replaced it with the fanatic *Wahabi* culture, resulting in senseless violence and chaos in the society. Even now with the fresh fanatic influx and under the influence of the *Wahabi* Islam the liberal Muslim suffers. The blood bath of the co-religionists, vandalizing the KSP social order once again continues despite the fact that KSP population, in the home land, now is literally hundred percent Muslim.

The Hindu KSP was forced to yet another sentence of exile (seventh in a row). Numbering barely six to seven lacs and forced to settle where ever they could seek refuge and shelter; loosing their very roots, homes and hearths. Their social and traditional identities got marginalised to a great extent. Their ethnic exclusiveness suffered a great blow. Yes! They seem to have, for good, lost the class divisions and the matrimonial bans on account of *Gotras* have become irrelevant. Over the last few decades and especially after the last measure exodus in the nineties of the twentieth century, all the divisions and restrictions followed by the *Bhata* have almost completely vanished. Now a *Bhata* is one community. So much so, even the difference of following the lunar and solar calendar is merged in to one that is followed by the whole Hindu community in the country. There are no restrictions followed in marriage alliances. All earlier fanatic considerations are slowly and steadily loosing their impact and validity. The society seems to be converging in to one homogeneous whole giving an impression of the Hindu Kashmiri shifting back to the original root.

People are adopting surnames and *Krám* names at free will; hence the root identity is of no significance. Now the *Bhata Brahman* is the only identity, who takes up any or every profession to earn his or her living, be it medicine, education, music, singing, dancing and above all business that used to be a taboo for the Brahman in earlier times. As the word *Karkun* suggests they would only take up government jobs during the latter Islamic era. Now there are no inhibitions any more. Education as usual is the top priority and equally available to both sexes of the society. No wonder the *Bhata* KSP as a community is cent percent literate. Arts, crafts, dancing, singing and other aesthetic practices and modes of entertainment are highly applauded and encouraged. A *Bhatta,* on the whole, is liberated both in thoughts and deeds. Widow Remarriage and divorce is now an accepted norm. Prevalent modes of dress, ornaments and embellishments are the same, as in the rest of the Hindu society in the country. At a glance it is difficult to pick one from the other a complete merger of our society has taken place with the rest of the Hindu fold. I should say barring the pointed noses and fair complexioned faces, or a few typically Kashmiri dishes of the cuisine like the cup of *Kehwa,* or the festival of *Shivaratri*, or the typical Head gear of a Hindu bride called the '*taranga*' there is now little to differentiate.

The traditional rites, rituals, customs and festivals have considerably reduced in numbers and also lost the venerability of the society, due to the attempts towards logical analysis of the same and indifference and disbelief in the ancient modes of our social order. The traditions and festivals that had survived centuries of bans, taboos, violence and proselytising frenzy have now become irrelevant. They have lost the fragrance of gaiety and merriment. People used to await the on coming seasonal, social and religious festivals, for the rich fares and the fun and frolic associated with them. Unfortunately that culture of the past, due to inexplicable assumptions, seems to be irrelevant now, as though it is devoid of any value. What matters is the present and the future, yet one wonders how can there be any present or future without the roots of past. The present and future can not hang in nothingness like a *trishanku.* It is well said "Historical data, facts and figures in human or natural evolution, socio-cultural technical or entertainment areas define how society's emulsion in every epoch generates incredible invention." Hence the disregard of past as irrelevant and the concept not to get bogged down in the past is a wrong approach, what we need is curiosity and willingness to learn and document the past perspective.

The Musalmáns unlike the Hindu KSP are mostly confined within the beautiful environs of the valley. Only a few have moved out into the rest of the country and the globe, in search of business, education or any other professional options. With the economic affluence and educational standards, their society too has lost to a great extent the codification and division of class and trade and the enforced matrimonial bans imposed by the high breeding of the purest Islamic brands of central Asian missionaries and preachers. Yet we do not see an alliance of a *Sayyed* and a *Galwan (*two extremities in the hierarchy of the Muslim society*)*

Modern technology has greatly enhanced the values and virtues of the hereditary professions, of agriculture, trade, arts and crafts pursued by this society. The international appreciation and demand for the products has given it power and confidence to stand tall. Unfortunately the last three decades have marred their social order with misery, mayhem and violence. The fanatic *Wahabi* Islam supported and perpetrated by the Pakistani terrorists, who have gained a strong foot hold in the valley, has been the undoing of the KSP. Tolerance and love has been replaced by vengeance, anger and hatred. The Sufi traditions are being questioned and are replaced by conservative norms. The *Burkha* and *Hizab* like covering of face for the women is introduced and forced on the unwilling fold. Education is deprived to women especially in the rural society. All sort of inhuman treatment is meted out to non cooperative men and women. Thousands are loosing their young lives for the cause of saving Islam. Ignorance of faith and belief, reigns supreme in the society. The ongoing terrorist culture of protest, loot, destruction of government and private property, ambushes, and random attacks on and by the security forces leading to retaliation of the ruling side, is the order of the day. Mistrust and disaffection is reigning supreme in the society. The prospect of peace and order is dying day by day. Youth is adopting violence as a routine: guns and unwanted martyrdom is eulogised. The descendents of KSP, who would adopt the means of sit in styagrahas in the temples and in royal secretariats, or fasts unto death, to express their anguish and protest, are taking recourse to stone sledging; achieving nothing but death of innocence. Such is the lot of the Muslim majority KSP society, the inheritors of the paradise on the earth. It is a strange paradox that a combined society (Hindu and Muslim KSP), can claim its place among the top five states on the scale of progress in the country, on the parameters of its literary status, per capita income and the numbers below the poverty line and yet suffers from unrest, violence and distrust

The moot question is, if no dictator; foreign invader or instigator is responsible for his scenario, then why this unrest in the rule of democracy, which guarantees the freedom of action and expression in our political and social system. One wonders if it is the throw back of affluence, abundance and inactive boredom pervading in the society that does not allow it to rest in peace and enjoy the bounties of its environment. Only other logical explanation can be the inexplicable curse, referred earlier, that visits the KSP, off and on, to break the momentum of its progress and peace.

CHAPTER-8

K.S.P. CULTURAL HERITAGE AND PROWESS

The scale of progress, perfection and prowess of a society reflects the cultural heritage of its members. Enumerating the term 'culture' we can state, it encompasses in its fold, the accomplishments, achievements, draw backs and misgivings of the members of a particular group of people. It includes the set of values and institutions that enable a society to develop and maintain its identity. It is the barometer to evaluate the strength and depth of the personality of an individual, a clan, a tribe or a community as a whole. It almost serves as a databank, which records and preserves every detail, and makes it available to the seeker at the click of a button, just like the super computers of modern age. Culture has been likened to an aroma or 'the fragrance of a flower'; we may smother the petals, the aroma will persist and probably get very intense. It is the very essence on which, a human beings scale of values and behaviour patterns are moulded. The fragrance of culture can not get rubbed off even in adverse and provocative circumstances. It has the tenacity to survive against all odds. Aristotle wrote that culture remains in a person, when 's'/he forgets all 's'/he has learned at the college, for while bookish knowledge may wither away, the transformed personality and the value system will remain. It is this value system that lays the foundation of civilisations. It is the very base of all the human endeavours and resultant achievements. Prof. Miller has rightly observed "human culture is always evolving and reinventing its own past and present. There is no cultural vacuum from which anything truly new under the sun could arise."

Culture being what it is, it would not be far from the truth to say, that the cultural heritage of the KSP is ancient and unique; it is a *Maha-Kumb.*

It is ancient because its foundation was laid at times when the, 'westerners were just barbarians.' According to the *Sapt Rishi Samvat* or *laukika* calendar (native almanac that reads 5087BP), KSP culture is said to be almost five -millennia old. "The authenticity and antiquity of this calendar is affirmed by the great oriental scholar, Prof. Buhler, who was the first to prove from the extant traditions of the Kashmiri Brahmans and other evidences that this era commences from *Caitra Sudhi* 1 of *Kali Samvat* 25(expired) or the year 3076-75 BC."[1]

Again according to the recent study of the Vedic cosmology, the present *Kali-Yuga* is said to have begun on Friday, February 18th, 3102BC.[2] This correlation supports the antiquity of the KSP calendar that has been used by the local chroniclers like Kalhana, Jonaraja, and Srivara and so on, as a base of their historical chronology of events in their manuscripts. The significance of this calendar can also be ascertained by the fact that, it is still in vogue, to this day, in the Hindu KSP community. They abide by the same almanac to determine the dates of their socio-religious dispensation, like religious rites, rituals, social traditions, and festivals, and even to predict the dates of solar and lunar eclipses annually.

As per a legend "*Sapt Rishis* descended from the Trion's down to the earth to introduce the *Sapt Rishi Samvat.* Without reflections to its credibility; we can safely assume that several of the top-ranking Rishis (probably seven in number) from the valley and elsewhere pondered into the outer space for collecting the requisite astronomical data. They successfully computed and constructed the world's first and the most perfect calendar. This is perhaps why it is called the *Sapt Rishi Samvat.* This calendar is the backbone of the infrastructure of the Kashmiri culture. It is a luno-solar calendar and its new year falls on the first bright moon day *(tithi)* of *Chaitra* called '*Navreh.*"[3]

The antiquity of KSP culture can be proved by the study of *Puranic* literature, for their ancestors, like all ancient people, have left the record of their progress, achievements and evolution for the future generations, in the shape of legends, myths and mythologies. In the process of evolution these treasures got preserved in the Puranic literature and one such is the Nilamat Purana that serves as a reference point for us to figure out what our past has been like. This Purana, as in other aspects of KSP history, enlightens us about our heritage. According to it the region of Kashmir occupied an important place in the country, and Janamejaya was curious to know, that in spite of such prominence, why the king of Kasmira did not participate in the Bharata war, even though his fore fathers participated earlier. Vaisampayana to whom the question was addressed answers that the king had been killed by Vasudeva in the dual and his queen was coronated by Vasudeva /Krishna so that her posthumous child may be allowed to inherit the throne. He was an infant and hence incapable of participating in the Mahabharata war fought between *Kauravas* and *Pandavas.*This dialogue ascertains that KSP culture at least belongs to the Mahabharata era, which is presently accepted as six to seven thousand years BP, and thus in turn establishes the antiquity of the Kashmiri culture.

The KSP cultural heritage is unique, because it is a culmination of the cultures of people belonging to varied hues and environments. It is unique because it is a by product of the churning of different religions and their philosophies. It is an outcrop of the amalgamation of the Vedic thought, Buddhist enlightenment, *Shivite Trika* philosophy and the Sufi cult of oneness- a *Maha-Kumb* indeed

During the course of the KSP's long history, the Jews, Greeks, Huns, Turks, Chinese, Muslims and Sikhs impressed and stamped the cultural ethos of these people. T. N Dhar writes, "Renowned as the Happy Valley, Kashmir has been, for centuries the fountainhead of art and culture in the East. At the cross-roads of the ancient caravan routes in Central Asia, Kashmir has been the meeting point of various cultures. In her spacious valleys, she has harmoniously blended their myriad trends to produce a civilisation distinctive of her people and her heritage."[4] The intellectual contribution of Kashmiri writers, poets, musicians and scientists to the rest of India was comparable to that of ancient Greece to European civilisation.

Various parameters

Learning

While detailing the individual aspects of KSP culture, learning tops the list. For a KSP it includes knowledge and proficiency in all the branches of the prescribed Hindu curriculum, i.e. language, literature, alchemy, astronomy, astrology, mathematics, Arthshastra, Natyashastra, music and *Vastu Kala*. Kashmiri's were well versed in all these branches of learning right from the days of Kashyapa onwards and it is due to this flourishing intellectual ethos of learning and knowledge that Kashmir is labelled as the 'Repository of knowledge'. A store house that is filled with the intellectual exercises of the indigenous Kashmiri scholars and luminaries, born and brought up in the valley, and even groomed and educated within the boundary walls of this 'school of learning' from the earliest times.

C.L. Nagri writes, "Centuries before Christ, the intellectual and spiritual greatness of India, in general, and that of Kashmir in particular, were renowned beyond its own eastern world. The famous university of ancient Kashmir was a fountainhead of knowledge from which went forth varied thought and currents to other parts of Asia. Here flourished various literary and cultural movements, which in time became dynamic forces, influencing the culture and civilizations far away . . . . A convocation of this university used to be held every year on *Gavri Tritya* falling on the 3rd *tithi* (date) of

Magh Shakula paksha (solar fortnight) when certificates of merit were awarded to successful students of the university."[5]

KSP scholars have been ever famous for their piety and scholarship. When the Chinese traveller Hiuen Tsang came to study in Kashmir (631-633 AD), he was so impressed by the attainments of Kashmiris that he paid glowing tribute to their achievements. He was accorded a royal reception by the reigning King, with the invention of a new alphabet. Such was the ingenuity of the *Kashur.* He writes, "This country from remote times was distinguished for learning, and their priests were all of high religious merit and conspicuous virtue as well as marked talent and power of clear exposition of doctrine; and though the other priests, (i.e., of other nations), were in their own way distinguished, yet they could not be compared with these, so different were they from the ordinary class." In another context he further wrote, "the people of Kashmir love learning and are well cultured. For centuries learning has been held in great respect in Kashmir."[6]

Kashmir excelled even Kashi; the learned scholars of Kashi had to come to Kashmir to complete their education. Even today, "the people of Kashi walk seven paces towards Kashmir during the performance of the ceremony of their investiture with the sacred thread as a token of their having gone to and returned from Kashmir after completing their education."[7]

Royal Patronage of learning

The standard and depth of learning and scholarship in the earlier eras was subject to the patronage of the rulers, who were the masters of their subject's lives. It thrived only with their appreciation and encouragement. For this a proper environment was a must and that could be provided only by a king who was learned himself. Kalhana has repeatedly written about the kings who were learned and well-versed in the Sanskrit language. He ridicules kings who did not come up to the established standards of learning. In his chronicle he records the different norms and methods adopted by the rulers to encourage the spread and improve the standard of learning among their subjects. He records how competent expositors were brought from other lands to study and restore the study of *Mahabhāsha* of Patanjali (a Kashmiri). Kings like Jayapida patronized several famous scholars like Bhatta Udbhata who was his chief Pandit *(sabhapati)*; Damodaragupta, the author of the *Kuttani matam*, was his chief councillor *(-dhuryadhisaciva)*; Manoratha, Sankhadanta, Cataka and Sandhimat were his poets and, Vamana and others his ministers.

Not only were the scholars honoured, facilities were provided for students, hospices (matha) for the residence of students from India *(Aryadesa)* who came to Kashmir for education were established, *agraharas* were bestowed on learned Brahmins, men of learning were adorned with jewels and given the privilege of using litters, horses, parasols, etc. under the orders of the kings during early and medieval eras

During the Islamic rule also we have had patrons of learning like Zain-ul-Abidin, Sultan Qutb-ud-Din, Hasan Shah and Dara Shiko who established *Madrasas* for teaching of the Quran and *Hadis*, in all important villages.[8](For details refer notes)

Maximum encouragement and contribution to learning and art was carried out during the reign of the glorious period of Zain -ul-Abidin (1422-74 AD.). "His *Dar-ul-Ulum* or the university at Naushehra was a grand monument of his love of learning. The revenues of several villages were assigned to meet the expenses of the University. A Translation Bureau was established under the auspices of the University. It was here that books were translated from Arabic and Sanskrit into Persian and Kashmiri. The *Mahabharata* was ordered to be translated, *Rajatarangini* was brought up to date by Jonaraja and a history of Kashmir was compiled in Persian. The Sultan's patronage of learning was not confined to Mohammedans alone. Hindu scholars' were also generously rewarded for their eminence in letters and science. Soma held a high place in the Bureau and was the head of what may be called the department of education and he wrote on the life of the Sultan entitled *Zaina Charit.* Bodi Bat had mastered the whole of *Shah Nama* which he recited to the delight of the Sultan. According to Hargopal Koul, the Sultan was called not only Bud Shah but *But Shah* on account of his patronage of the Pandits"[9]

Zain-ul-Abidin spent huge sums on the collection of a library for his university. He sent out agents to different parts of the world to secure books and manuscripts for his library which is said to have vied with the leading libraries of the time in Central Asia and Persia and existed for about a century till the days of Sultan Fateh Shah. In Zainagir the Sultan established a college between his palace and the royal garden. This also served as a centre for the diffusion of learning in the valley. A big Madrassa was also established at Seer, in Dachhanpura, near Islamabad. Mulla Ghazi Khan was the head of the Madrassa.[10]

All this goes to prove that the rulers, who were themselves highly, accomplished and learned bestowed awards and favours to the scholars, for elevation of the standard of learning. It was due to this patronage of the rulers that even in those early eras interchange and exchange programmes of scholars became a part of KSP culture.

Torch Bearers

Kashmir became foremost seat of learning in the first century as reported by the foreign travellers to the valley and attracted students and scholars from abroad. "Between 6th and 12th centuries, scholars from all parts of India flocked to this land of learning". The main centre of excellence was at *Sharda Peeth*-an ancient seat of learning on the banks of Kishenganga in the valley of Mount Harmukh. It provided instruction to the scholars from different parts of the country. "The appellation '*Bhatta*' is a remnant reminder of the honorific that went with the degree *Bhatta* awarded to the graduates coming out of the portals of this prestigious institution."[11]

It was at *Sharda Peeth*-the name is still current—in Kashmir, that Shri Shankara started his meteoric career of preaching, after he paid obeisance to the goddess Sharda, enshrined in the temple. Custom among South Indian Brahmans of prostrating in the direction of *Sharda Peeth*, in Kashmir, prior to initiation to formal education is still prevalent.

Right from the very ancient times Kashmir had become a vibrant clearing house of spiritual knowledge, a laboratory to nourish and to give shape to new thoughts and a place where scholars concourced, conversed and concurred to lay ground rules for thinking processes, language, logic, aesthetics, religious philosophies, music, dance and science. Scholars and spiritual seekers moved regularly from Kashmir to various other parts of the country and Central Asia, and from Central Asia to Kashmir. Some distinguished scholars from Kashmir travelled through out Bharata and also to foreign lands to learn and to disperse Knowledge. Vimalamitra travelled through length and breadth of the country to learn the mysteries of heterodox scriptures.

According to Professor Thattacheriar, head of the Sanskrit department of the Madras University, "the contribution of the Kashniri scholars to South Indian philosophy, aesthetics, dance and music has been very significant. For instance, it is known that Thiramalur, one of the earliest teachers of *Saivism* (1st to 9th century AD) came from Kashmir. Vairochana went to Khotan and introduced the *Mahayana* there. Kumarajiva went to China and succeeded in converting the king and the people to Buddhism. He passed away in 413 AD in China. Gunarvarmalla travelled to Java and succeeded in uprooting Hinduism there. Shama-batta, known as Thumi-Sambhota in the Tibetan annals, was responsible for introducing Buddhism in Tibet. Che-mong is perhaps the first scholar, who stayed in Kashmir for a few years, before his return to China in 424 AD Fa-yong also visited Kashmir for the study of the Sanskrit language. Consequently, the advent of foreign students and scholars influenced the art and culture of the Kashmiris. Kashmir also became instrumental in carrying the torch of learning and spiritual guidance to countries and colonies "beyond the seven seas", known as Further India in the olden days." Famous Kashmiri Sanskrit scholars and Buddhist preachers like Shakyashri Bhadra, Raatnaujers, Suraj Gupta, Sham Bhat and Thumi Sambhatato,-who wrote books in Sanskrit and translated Tibetan books into Sanskrit,- went to places like China, Tibet, Korea and Japan preaching and teaching in their universities as early as 405 AD. Despite many hardships and catastrophes in the face of foreign invasions our culture bears testimony to courage and perseverance of our ancestors. The valley of Kashmir has even been believed by some scholars to be the originating centre of civilisation. Prof. Dharmendra Nath Pal upheld the view as early as 1904 that, "the particular area in Asia which covers Kashmir and the Tibet table lands was the cradle of civilization, ADELUNG, the Father of comparative Philology, placed the cradle of mankind in the valley of Kashmir."[12]

Languages

Kashmiri scholars are renowned to have made considerable contribution towards the evolution and development of different languages that they used during various eras of their history. Sanskrit happens to be the first among these languages.

Sanskrit Language

The state of perfection, acclaim and position achieved by the *Kashur* in the Sanskrit language can be gauged by the fact that no scholar of Sanskrit would deem to have got the degree unless and until cleared by Kashmiri Sanskrit authority.

N.S. Shukla writes, "In the vast field of Sanskrit literature the contribution of *Kasmira,* the ancient seat of learning, has been unique. The country has given us eminent writers in all the forms of literature. Beginning with Matrgupta but more continuously from the reign of Jayapida and his-two courtiers, Udbhata and Vamana, there was a galaxy of eminent Kashmirian writers namely Rudrata, Lollata, Sankuka, Anandavardhana, Candrikakara, Bhatta Nayaka, Bhatta Tota, Bhattenduraja, Abhinavagupta, Kuntaka, Mahima Bhatta, Ksemraja, Mammata, Rajasekhara, Allata, Tilaka, Ruyyaka, Kalhana, Sobhakara, Jayaratha, Bhatta Narayal, Utpaladeva, Srikal) and many others. To this galaxy belongs Ksemendra."[13]

Ksemendra was one of the most versatile figures of this period. He was a great poet, humorist, rhetorician and historian all in one, and is known to have left at least 34 books on various subjects, including descriptions of current affairs, satire and philosophical and poetic works. "Almost every important branch of Sanskrit literature has been enriched by the facile pen of this versatile genius. Some of his famous works are *Dash Avtar, Charit Kaveya, Desh Updesha, Narmala, Loka Prakasha and Samaya Matrica.* poetical epitomes of the two epics-the *Ramayana* and the *Mahabharata*, Guinadhya's *Brhatkatha, Bana's Kadambari, the Buddhist Avadanas*, a chronicle of kings of *Kasmira* and a lexicon to name a few of his compositions in the Sanskrit language. This man was the student of scholars and teachers like Gangaka, Abhinava Gupta - the famous *Achareiya-* and Somapada."[14]

Dr. Surya Kant, in his '*Ksemendra Studies*' writes, "This fairy land of Kasmira has a rich cultural and literary heritage and has for centuries contributed . . . . . . to the development of Indian thought and literature. Most of the classical and philosophical Sanskrit literature, which flourished during the early Buddhist and Hindu periods, belongs to *Kasmira.* Bilhana, the famous writer of the historical *Mahakavya Vikramankadeva Carita* could justly boast of the greatness of this land of his birth, where even women could as felicitously express themselves in Sanskrit and Prakrit, as much as in their mother tongue. The last few decades of the 10th century AD show a landmark in the cultural history of *Kasmira.* The great Kasmiri Saiva philosopher and literary critic Abhinavagupta, author of s *Abhinavabharati-*(a commentary on *Bharata's Natyashastra*) lived during this period. This great scholar of *Saiva* philosophy who was a writer of unquestionable merit, inspired with his genius and wisdom, a love of learning, amongst many students who pursued their studies with such industry and enthusiasm that in many respects they may be: said to have outshone their master. Such a one was Ksemendra,-the polyhistor. It was the middle of the 11th century when the polymath Ksemendra learned rhetoric at the feet of Abhinavagupta-padacarya."[15]

Ksemendra has criticised and praised the skill of a number of earlier writers. The vast list of authors that he mentions and criticises in his *Aucitya-vicāracarcā, Kavikanthabharana and Surttatilaka,*[16] is an insight into his critical mind. His compositions like *Samayamatrika* and *Kalavilasa* reveal his thorough mastery of the science of erotica. Besides he has also given us the summaries of the Epics, and a number of works on all the aspects of society with bitter satire on its evils.

One can asses the magnitude of the contribution of Kashmiris towards the Sanskrit language by what some of the chroniclers like Al-Beruni, Kalhana, Haider Malik Chadurah, and K.M.Panikar and so on have recorded and observed regarding this aspect of the *Kashur.*

Kalhana infers, "Candragomin the founder of *Candra* school of Sanskrit grammar was from Kashmir. He revived the study of Mahabhasya and composed his own grammar. He recast the work of Panini, rearranged and simplified the Master's works." According to some Tibetan records he is even believed to have censured Patanjali's work.

Al-Beruni, comments that the Brahmins do not allow the Vedas to be committed to writing because it is recited according to a certain moderations. They therefore avoid the use of pen as it is liable to cause error in this process. And then he adds, "Not long before, Vaskura a native of Kashmir and a famous Brahmin, and Vedic scholar, undertook the task of explaining the Vedas and committing them to writing down for the first time in Sanskrit Language. He has taken upon himself a task from which all shrunk, because he was afraid that the Vedas might be forgotten."[17] This is yet another achievement credited to Kashmiri Brahmans and especially to Vaskura who wrote the Vedas in about 1000 A.D in Sanskrit.

Haider Malik Chadurah records, "Since ancient times the valley of Kashmir has had the privilege of being the cradle of knowledge, religious philosophy, science and arts with Sanskrit as the literary language and the main vehicle of expression of thought. When the Muslim scientist Abu Rayhan Alberuni visited India in the 11th century, Kashmir and Varanasi, according to him, were the only two centres of learning in India where 'all knowledge of the ancient savants and sages had been preserved."[18]

K.M.Panikar observes, "So far as Sanskrit literature is concerned, apart from Alamkara Sastra in which *Kashmirians* seemed to have excelled, the names of Somadeva, Kshemendra, Damodaragupta, Bilhana and Kalhana, stand out a brilliant galaxy of genius adding lustre to the history of Sanskrit literature. *Katha Sarit Sagara* claimed to be an epic of middle classes is one of the undisputed masterpieces of the world that was compiled two thousand years ago by Somadeva." This epic has, "since gone all over the world, from China to Sweden, from Arabia to Russia and from Greece to France."[19] Such were the giant Sanskrit scholars of *Kashur* breed; of whom we know nothing but their names.

There are no written proofs left for us to confirm the authenticity. Yet we have to accept that Sanskrit flourished in every field of literature and in every other branch of social, political, religious and administrative arena of the Kashmiris life. So much so the native dialect *Kashur* was relegated to second place in order of preference even by commoners. Yes the present state of Sanskrit proficiency in no way helps us to imagine such an accomplished state in this language 'of Gods,' as it is presumed to be for the simple reason that during the Islamic rule, Sanskrit receded to the background and lost its place in the literary milieu of the *Kashur*. Later during the Dogra rule, Maharaja Ranbir Singh tried his best to revive its study. He founded Sanskrit *Pathshalas* and employed proficient Pandits to teach Sanskrit. He set up a translation bureau where Sanskrit texts were edited and some times translated into Persian, Hindi and Dogri. Sahib Ram, a noted Sanskrit scholar wrote his *Tirtha Sangraha* about the legends and geographical description of the famous places of pilgrimage in Kashmir.

George Buhler, on visit to Kashmir in 1875 in search of Sanskrit manuscripts, found the language popular with the Brahmans of Kashmir. Sanskrit learning, however, was not then as flourishing as during the earlier periods, but still there were some remnants of former glory. He met several Sanskrit scholars of the day like Pandit Daya Ram about whom Buhler says, "I obtained at once a great deal of valuable information." He also came in contact with Pandit Damodar, 'the Chief Pandit of the Maharaja's Madrassa. Of this Pandit, Buhler says that he would be able to hold up his head anywhere. "His poetical compositions", says Buhler, "continuation of the RajaTarangni, and a letter-entitled *Praudalekha* which he was good enough to read and to explain to me for hours—certainly surpass Sri Harsha and Bana, and can be compared to Subandbu's *Vasavadatta*." Buhler came in contact with other Pandits deeply learned in Sanskrit, notable among them being Govind Kaul and Damodar Jotshi. He found twenty-two libraries of Sanskrit manuscripts still extant in Srinagar.[20]

Since Sanskrit literature produced in Kashmir during ancient times attracted the attention of several Indian and European scholars, the State Government established a Research Department, where many Sanskrit texts were edited, collated and published. Dr. Buhler discovered some of the valuable series of Sanskrit works like: *Vyasastaka, Bharatamanjari, Ramayanmanjari, Desopadesa, Narmamala, Sevyasevakopadesa,Kalavilasa,Darpadalana, Cirucarya, Caturvargasangraha, Samayamatrkii,Avadanakalpalata,Kavikathabharanaa, Aucityavicracarcii, SuvrttatiIaka,Dasavataracarita,* and other miscellaneous works and got them published, though quite a few have since been lost to posterity.

Scholars who laboured on these classics included *Mahamahopadyaya* Mukund Ram Sastri, Pandit Hara Bhat *Sastri,* Pandit Jagadhur Zadu and Pandit Madhusudan Kaul. The latter, a great research scholar, edited with critical annotations and comments Abhinavagupta's *Tantralok* and other texts, which won him\ recognition and fame among Sanskrit scholars of the world. In spite of these efforts Sanskrit failed to regain its eminence among the masses

Persian Language

Amalgamation of two identities after 13th century

The cultural and political history of Kashmir entered a new phase, when Islam spread over the land. As was natural, classical Sanskrit tradition suffered a set-back and its place was taken by Persian, which was then the official court language. But this era, curiously enough, did not bring about any sudden or radical changes; much less did it mark the beginning of separatist tendencies. Instead, it brought about a harmonious blending or amalgamation of the new and the old, giving birth to new cultural traditions in Kashmir's Renaissance. This phase of popular Kashmiri literature, combining in it Persian and Sanskrit traditions and Islamic and Hindu philosophies, showed a wonderful capacity for development in the later period and left a rich legacy of cultural synthesis.

Towards the beginning of 15th century the KSP not only learnt Persian, the language of invaders, but also achieved such excellence in it that Kashmir came to be known as '*Little Iran*.'

The scholarship of the Pandits in Persian reached its high water mark during this period. They wrote exquisite poetry in Persian and were master writers in prose. Munshi Bhawani Das stands prominent amongst the prose writers of the day. So also Lachhi Ram Saroor who rose very high at the Court of Nawabs of Oudh mainly because of his high poetical merit. Rai Rayyan, Anand Ram Karihalu was a great favourite of Shah Alam and a great poet. He was a great Persian and Arabic scholar. So also Pandits Taba Ram Turki, (1776-1847AD), Sat Ram Baqaya, Pandit Daya Ram Kachru (1743- 1811 AD) Aftab Bhan, Gobind Kaul, Kailas Dar, Lasa Kaul, Deva Kaul, Thakur Das, Gopal Dar (1735-1798 AD), Raja Kak Dar, Rugh Nath Kaul (1735-1807 AD) and many others.

The contributions made by them to Persian literature have elicited the significant remarks from competent critics that in the mastery of the Persian language the Kashmiri Pandits were second only to the Persians. About Pandit Anand Ram Karihalu it is remarked that his mastery of Arabic and Persian was so complete that even amongst the Muslims nobody could compete with him.

Pandit Birbal Kachru (1789-1859AD) to whom reference has been made in these pages has written a voluminous history of Kashmir in Persian language. He has dealt with social and economic conditions of the people in a very detailed and lucid manner. Besides being a historian, he wrote poetry as well.

Persian continued to be the court language for over a century more and we find several Persian scholars and poets in Kashmir attaining distinction.

One of the earliest poets in Persian was Mulla Baha-ud-din Baha (1766-1832AD) who produced a *Khamsa* comprising *Rishi-nama, Sultani, Ghausiya, Naqasbandi'a* and *Chistiya.* Baha's contemporary, Mulla Hamidullah, has given us a fascinatingly humorous poem, the *Chai-nama*

Name of Sir Mohammed Iqbal stands pre-eminent amongst the poets of Kashmiri origin who wrote in Persian language in India. His poetry is too well known, to require any comments or introduction here. Among the Kashmiri Hindus who acquired fame as poets in Persian' during this period may be mentioned Raj Kaul Arzbegi Dairi, Shankar Ju-Akhun Girami, Tabah Ram Turki who flourished in the time of Maharaja Ranbir Singh. Iranians coming to Kashmir were delighted to meet him and to listen to his poems and other Persian compositions. Pandit Raja Kak Dhar Farukh was also a poet of note of the same period. [21]

G. Lal writes, "Kashmir shared fame as an important seat of learning and culture with Nalanda and Taxila. Kashmiri literature combines in itself Persian and Sanskrit traditions and Islamic and Hindu philosophies. A Sanskrit inscription on a tomb in the Cemetery of Baha-ud-Din put up during the reign of Sultan Mohammad Shah in 1484 indicates that both Sanskrit and Persian were in use. A birch bark document in Sharda and Persian characters pertaining to Sheikh Makhdom Hamza, a Muslim saint of Kashmir, about 500 years old, reflects the Kashmiri's Catholicism of outlook."[22]

English Language

The KSP's did not only achieve mastery over the languages of the east, they showed the same calibre when English the language of the west was imposed on them. It is authentically stated that after the Bengali, *Kashur* was the next to learn, practise and master the English language. "Kashmiri Pandits were among the first north Indians to obtain higher education. In Lucknow, for example between 1870 and 1888 maximum Bengali Students obtained B.A. degrees and among the rest there were six Kashmiri degree holders."[23]

Bernier in his book *(Travels in the Mogul Empire)* writing about the Kashmiris who were well versed in English language says, "The British rulers would employ them in the courts to converse with the Nawabs and to translate Persian documents when ever needed. Kashmiris are accounted a gay and lively people, much more intelligent than the natives of Hindustan generally and as much disposed to the cultivation of literature and poetry as the Persians; the common people are remarkably industrious and ingenious."[24]

Education

Kashmir, since ancient times, occupied a unique place in the field of education. It was designated as Shardhapeeth. The varied fields of learning in which the writers like Ksemendra, Bilhana, Kalhana, Mankha and Abhinavagupta attained proficiency, bear testimony to a very high standard prescribed for the students during those eras in Kashmir. We do not have any records of formal institutions like schools and colleges like that of the present times. P.N. Bamzai writes, "The system of education followed was entirely the Vedic system of *Guru-Sheieshu Parampara.* According to this, the children of a house holder lived with *Acharyas* (teachers) in the latter's home. There they used to serve their teacher by gathering fuel for *homa* and offered morning and evening prayers. The recitation of Vedic Hymns with proper accent, preceded by the syllable *OM* took place at day break. Early morning was the time set apart for studies. Consequently *Upanayan Sanskara* (thread ceremony) was the most important event of a child's life. It was the occasion when a child was initiated into three R's on an auspicious day in a festive atmosphere. Gods were propitiated, feasts were arranged and presents were offered, when the initiate was entrusted in to the custody of a teacher. A much disciplined life was laid down by the medieval digest for students receiving Brahmanical education. By the time the student attained the age of sixteen, he was supposed to be the master of all sciences and arts. The educational courses differed according to the needs of the students. The subjects studied were, the four Vedas, the six *Angas,* the various scripts, *Mimasa, Smritis*, Puranas, *Karmakanda Jyotish, Ganita,* music, sciences, Philosophy, art, literature and history. The Kashmiri teachers not only imparted education to the natives but also instructed numerous scholars from distant lands. During Ksemendra's time (8th century A.D), Kashmir attracted students from different parts of India. Admission to this seat of learning was not easy. Local as well as foreign students had to take a difficult test in order to be qualified for a particular branch of learning. Those remaining unsuccessful either returned to their homes or wasted their time loitering in the streets of Kasmira and indulged in activities unbecoming of a student The subjects for study included *Patanjala, Mahabhasaya, Tarka and Mimansha* besides so many others."[25]

Though the tenth and eleventh centuries brought forth a large body of literature in the field of *Saivite* religion and philosophy, it was not the only sphere in which the Kashmirian attained great heights. Side by side with the highest literature on the abstruse *Saivite* philosophy, we have the development of language and literature in grammar, poetics, history (*itihāsa)* and rhetoric. The chief of Bilhanas family, Muktikalasa was learned in the four Vedas. One of his ancestors, Jyeshthakalasa composed an exposition of the *Mahābhasya*. Bilhana reportedly received his early education in Kashmir and obtained proficiency in the Vedas with their *Añgas,* grammar and poetics. Likewise Ksemendra wrote in every branch of language and literature, conforming to the ideals of the branches of learning a scholar was supposed to know of, and touching all the varied fields and aspects of the society of his day. His works also point to the greatness of the teachers of those days, who did not-believe only in textbook theories, but tried to encourage originality. [26]

It was the high standard of KSPs academic and intellectual calibre that was responsible for the respect and position they were given, when ever, due to the political upheavals, at different eras of their history, they were forced to migrate. Their diplomatic and administrative acumen enabled them to gain the posts of Governors, Diwans, Revenue collectors, Ministers and also Rajas of some places during the Mughal, Sikh and British rule in the country. Even in the post independence era KSP's only a few million in number have given two Prime Ministers to a country of more than one billion people; besides many a smaller personages like the Chiefs of Army and Air force, Ambassadors and many a litterateurs and scholars etc are all the products of the rich educational and cultural heritage of the *Kashur*.[27]

Contribution in the Field of Philosophy, Mysticism and Religion

KSP are designated as the originators, creators and modifiers of world's three most renowned religious philosophies, namely *Mahayana Buddhism*, the *Shiva Tantra* and *Sufism*. The world renowned *Shiva Tantric* philosophy owes its origin and fame to the Shiva philosophers of Kashmir. Kashmiris are solely responsible for the *Trika philosophy of Shaivism*; a philosophy, which helped it to become a practical philosophy, meant not only for ascetics and sages but also for a commoner. It received a new dimension in the folklore and enabled its followers to perceive Shakti as a quest for Knowledge. It was in Kashmir only that the essence and the power of Shakti was impressed upon the Shaiva philosophers, as by the 9th century AD, Manu's dictums had most probably superseded the philosophy of *Shakti Agammas*. Pandit Anand Kaul writes, "Kashmiri Pandit's were custodians of one of the greatest heritages of mankind-Rig-Veda, Sanskrit grammar and Shavism. Vasugupta,(8th century) the founder of Kashmir Shavism or the Trika philosophy was a native of Kashmir. He was followed by a succession of scholars like Bhatta Kallata, Utpala Bhatta, Ramakantha and the greatest of them all was Abhinavagupta born in the 10th century, whose monumental work "*Tantriloka*" is even today regarded as a profound encyclopaedia on the subject."

The first book on Shavism, a philosophical treatise, supporting the doctrines of the *Trika* by critical argument and reasoning, *vicara and manana*, was written by Siddha Somananda; probably a disciple of the sage Vasugupta and this came to be known as Pratyabhijna

Buddhism was carried to distant lands by the Kashmiri missionaries by the dint of their persuasion and hard work, after Majjhantika introduced it in the valley. *Milindapanaha* that traces the history of Buddhism was originally compiled in Kashmiri prior to it being translated in to Pali. It was through the efforts of the great Kashmiri scholars that Buddhist culture was introduced in central Asia. According to Kalhana, Ashvoghosha, a Buddhist scholar and a well-known poet, musician and author of *'Buddha Charita'* lived in Kashmir. Kalhana writes, "And a Bodhisattva lived in this country as a sole lord of the land, namely the glorious Nagarjuna, who resided at Sadarhad Vana"[28]According to H.H.Wilson the great Indologist, "he (Nagarjuna), denominated the *Saka* era now in vogue in India".*(For details refer to chapter IV 'Religion.)*

The Culture of sages and *Darveshes*

Kashmir, from ancient times, is often designated as '*Rishi Bhumi*'; the reason being that it is the land of many a Sages and Savants-*Rishis* and *Yoginis*-who have had a major impact on the cultural ethos of the *Kashur*. They have acted as their guides and path finders. Set their every day routine and dharma of life. Their beliefs and philosophy of life has had an embalming effect on the *Kashur*, when ever political circumstances ruffled their social order.

After the violent zeal of fanatic Islamic invaders, the founder of this order, Hindu saint Lalleshwari and Sheikh Noorud-Din, came to the rescue of the *Kashur*. They were the initiators of this humane and serene cult of Islam that thrived in Kashmir for centuries, and enabled to create an amalgamated peace loving social order, among the KSP. Lalleshveri was a saint, philosopher, reformer and poetess all in one. She made a mark on Kashmiri ethos in those chaotic and confused times of religious distortions. She not only calmed the confused masses by giving them the ultimate significance of the reality of God, but also elevated the *Prakrit* /Kashmiri dialect- to the status of a medium of instruction for literary and spiritual thoughts, to enable the common masses to share the gains of her experiences in their own language, as the great king Ashoka and Sant Tulsidas did in their own times. The period of Lal Ded and Nund Rishi was no doubt, a period of spiritual renaissance for all Kashmiris put together. Besides these two towering personalities many a prominent Kashmiri sages, saints and Darveshes helped in this process of cultivation and survival of the Sufi Culture.

With this culture Islam in Kashmir acquired its own distinct colour and hue. A Musalman believed that the true meaning of Jihad was to wage a war against the evils inside man and true victory can be attained by curbing desires. This philosophy of compassion and contemplation was the contribution of a *Kashur* to this great religion. The tremendous impact of this order on the social and cultural life of Muslims and Hindus together can be assessed by the given quote of a seventeenth century poet who wrote, "The candle of religion is lit by the Rishis. This Vale of Kashmir that you call a paradise owes a lot of its charm to the traditions set by them."[29]

Thus the founders of the Sufi cult helped to stabilise the society of Kashmir during the 18th and the 19th century. Their philosophy acted as a healing potion on the injured psyche of the Kashmiris. Despite being poverty stricken and controlled by a feudal aristocracy, Kashmiri masses, both Hindus and Muslims, learnt to live in amity, harmony and peace. Learning and education was, by and large, shelved and replaced by many crafts and creative arts for which Kashmir has attained world fame.

Fine Arts and Crafts

The *Kashur*, as in other fields of culture, inherited a very rich heritage of arts and crafts starting from the ancient times. The antiquity of this tradition in the life of K.S.P's is proved by the reference to the worship of Viswakarma (Originator of all crafts) by the Kashmiris in the N.P. They were proficient in the art of painting, sculpture and idol making, using the medium of clay and metal and also stones. The number of stone idols strewn all over the valley, the paintings that are preserved in the London museum, the paintings that are routinely preserved as ritual arts of the Hindu KSP, are proof enough of their expertise. Sculpture was known, and perfection had been achieved in the art of idol making. Sculptors made idols of mud and various other metals. They even carved figures out of stones. The Brahmans were experts in idol making in those eras. During the ancient period artists were employed for painting and decorating the shrines. Beautiful portraits were painted. Kalhana writes, "When Harsha saw the portrait of a lady named Candala, the queen of Karnata he fell in love with her." So authentic, live and exquisite, was the art of painting in the Valley. Artists were also imported from outside Kashmir. Some of the kings were patrons of fine art and even some of them were artist themselves

The art was so prolific and profound that it indicates the existence of a well-developed system. The old Sanskrit and Sharda manuscripts are full of beautiful paintings and pictures of gods and goddesses. Picturesque flowers and petals are drawn in the margin of the pages and the text is written in a beautiful hand in the centre. The colours used in painting made indigenously from leaves and herbs are so well prepared and mixed that even the passage of time has neither damaged nor faded them. The portraits and figures are exquisite and amazing. Even today one can see samples of these paintings on the margins of the old horoscopes and on the margin of the manuscripts written on hand-made paper. The high quality of the Kashmiri hand made paper and ink can be well assessed by the given incident recorded by Stein himself, when he returned to England in the year 1890 after completing his collation of the RajaTarangni manuscript. One of the Flemish porters carelessly threw overboard the box that contained the codex of the R.T. and it was retrieved from the sea with great difficulty. Stein writes "Happily too the soaking with sea water left no perceptible trace in the codex. Kashmir paper of the old make stands immersion of this kind remarkably well, and the ink used to this day by Kashmirian Pandits for their Sanskrit MSS is in no way affected by water."[30]

Alberuni writes, "The people of Kashmir mark the single leaves of their books with figures which are like drawings or like the Chinese characters, the meaning of which can be learned only after very long practice."

The art of painting did not die with the advent of Islamic culture, yet, it must be stated at the outset that on account of the religious objection to the delineation of natural forms, Mohammedans did not produce the type of paintings or achieve the excellence their genius could rise to in other fields of art. There is, however, a remarkable set of twenty-four large paintings on cotton preserved in the Indian Section of the Victoria and Albert Museum, South Kensington that was produced in Kashmir about the middle of the sixteenth century before Akbar took measures to encourage painting after the Persian manner. These cotton paintings are said to have been illustrations of a manuscript book of stories which has not been preserved or identified. The subjects comprise many battles and scenes of bloodshed. The most pleasing and best preserved composition represents a central garden plot with banyan trees."[31] Trees painted most likely are the chinar trees and not banyan as the latter does not grow in the valley.

In the modern times as well, Kashmiris have attained fame for their accomplishment in the field of art and craft. It is generally believed that these arts and crafts were imported from Iran during the reign of Zain-Ul-Abidin. Actually, most of the arts and crafts like metal sculpture, art of spinning, weaving, dyeing and washing, smithery, pottery, wood work, leather work etc were prevalent in Kashmir even before 6th century AD as per references quoted earlier in the book from the MSS of Nilamat Purana. How ever for some centuries these crafts had gone into oblivion. Zain-Ul-Abidin during his rule revived and patronised the culture of manual arts and crafts. Some of the crafts of Kashmiri artisans' unsurpassed and unrivalled in quality are the art of shawl weaving, the papier-mâché craft, wood-carving, silverware, copper work, silk weaving, manufacture of embroidered *gabbas* and *namdas*, rugs and carpets. The variety and design in all the crafts is mind-blowing and the delicacy of texture is so intricate and fine, that even a three and a half metre shawl can effortlessly pass through the ring worn on the fore-fingre. Bernier has recorded, "They make a variety of beautiful articles of luxury and ornament, which are exported into all parts of India. They are acquainted with the art of lacquering, gilding etc. They fabricate the best writing paper of the East. But what eminently distinguishes them and contributes to the wealth and fame of their country is the abundance of shawls; which are so super fine and soft,"

The world renowned Kashmiri Pashmina shawls that have adorned the delicate shoulders of queens and commoners are witnesses to the nimble finesse of the *Kashur* craftsmen. In this exercise of shawl making the Kashmiri women equally participate. If men weave and embroider these garments of excellence, it is the women who pick and clean the *Pashmina* wool of minutest impurities, and even of the tiniest hair with their nimble fingers and finally spin the slender threads to be woven by men folk.

The artistic calibre and degree of craftsmanship of the Hindu KSP women folk can be gauged by the embellishments added on the dull drab looking tunic (*Pheran*) type dress. The Hindu women with their aesthetic and artistic sense converted this dull drab dress in to a fashion statement. The dress was manoeuvred in such a manner that it not only emphasised the contours of her body but also draped her person from top to toe. It reflected the individual identity of the social status as well as the martial status of the wearer. The head gear specially was embellished with such ornamentation, embroidery and grace that it not only occupied a pride of place in the bride's trousseau but also caused the creation of a small scale cottage industry thus creating job options for a large number of artisans. Even in the twentieth century when this dress is almost obsolete, Kashmiri Hindu brides continue to proudly don the head piece of artistic creation like a crown on their head at the wedding ceremony.

Triloki Nath Dhar, describes this dress in detail and writes, "The *Pheran*' with a snow-white 'Patch' inside is laced with a red border called *dur* on the neckline and the bottom-line. It has a printed attachment on both the sleeves known as '*Narevar*'. There is a woollen muffler like belt tied round the waist called *Loongy*' a corruption from Hindi 'Loongi'. The headgear is a complex item. It comprises a cap on the head known as '*Kalpush*' round which is tied a white folded cloth in four or five layers, called 'Taranga', which is thereafter covered by a plastic strip-either milky white, when it is called '*Doda-Iath*' or transparent like glass, when it is called *Sheesh-Iath*'. Damsels, young in age would sometimes use a shining sheet with sparkles. This was known as '*Zitni-Iath*' - all the three names were true to their type and quality. On the back of this headgear there is a beautifully decorated covering of muslin called '*Zoojyo*' about one foot long tugged inside the cloth-folds decorated with floral motifs using golden thread known as tilla. On the top of it is another white covering with a long twisted tail dangling down the back almost touching the heels? This is called '*Pootch*' (supposed to represent the Naga emblem, reminiscent of our Naga ancestors). When she (the lady) goes out she puts on a cotton cloth, '*Dupatta*' or a woollen cloth, '*Voda Pallav*', depending on the weather, tastefully placed over the head and firmly held in front below the chin with the help of a black-headed pin called '*Kaladar-Tsatchen*'. Incidentally the Malay women in Southeast Asia wear a similar headgear, which they call '*Tudung*' not very different from Kashmiri '*Tarango*'." [32]

Artisans of Kashmir have made a name in embroidery, paper mache and the patterns woven on-carpets, however, in the modern times, where commercialism and competition rules the roost, quantity and not quality takes the upper hand and we do not always get to see the best of the craftsman's craft. Kashmir's arts and crafts have evolved both in design and colour, as well as in theme with times; nothing has stagnated. "To all their spheres of art and activity—indigenous or foreign inspired—Kashmiris have imparted a peculiar freshness and charm. There is colour, imagination and vigour, in every kind and variety of handicraft." [33]

Quoting Wakefield "Kashmiris are also very expert in the manufacture of wooden articles, such as toys and turnery; ornamental carving, inlaid work in wood, ivory, mother of pearl, papier-mâché, jewellery, leather, paper, and attar of roses. The Kashmiris are very ingenious workers in metal, manufacturing good weapons, such as guns and swords and other such articles. But their jewellery specially demands attention, the gold and silver-smiths of Srinagar being very clever at their trade, producing admirable work, great quantities of which are now exported to."

Dancing and Music

Men and women of such artistic and aesthetic excellence would but, naturally be proficient in the art of dancing and music, as the mode of everyday entertainment. The earliest definite corroboration regarding the popularity of music and dancing in Kashmir has been confirmed with the discovery of tiles from Harwan, which cannot be later than 4th century AD as detailed earlier.

Bilhana testifies to the high skill of the ladies of Kashmira in dancing. In his *Vikrammman- Kadevacarita,* xviii, 23, 29, he extols the ladies of his native land for the excellent dramatic performances, which excelled the acting of the heavenly damsels Rambha, Citralekha and Urvasi.

Jonaraja and Srivara while writing about the patronage of dancers by Zain-ul-Abidin and Hassan Shah give a detailed account of the accomplished dancers and musicians who thrived during the Hindu period, and I quote, "They were learned and dignified and displayed their taste and intelligence on the stage. The renowned Tara and the actors sang various songs . . . . . the songstress Utsava who was even like Cupid's arrow, charming to the eye and proficient in dance, both swift and slow, entranced everybody. The dancers, who described the forty-nine different emotions, seemed even like ascending and descending notes of music. As they danced and sang, the eye and the ear of the audience seemed to contend for the keenest enjoyment."

According to Narayana Menon, "The most important work on music in the medieval era is that on Karnataka music, *Sangia Ratnakara*. This was written by Sarangadeva who was a Kashmiri. His father had immigrated to south in the 12th century and worked at Devagiri. Menon says that Sarangadeva's book formulates the basic Karnataka music and there are a few West Asian and European works to compare with Sangita *Ratnakara* when it comes to detailed accounts of theory and practice by scholarly musicians."[34] Captain C. B. Day corroborates the same fact in his book,' Music and Musical Instruments of Southern India and the Deccan.'

The traditions in dance did not, die with the advent of Islam. But as in other branches of learning, the classical dance forms were materially altered with the absorption of influences from the dance technique of Persia and Central Asia. This however, took considerable time to develop. Zain-ul-abidin was a great patron of dance, drama and music. During his reign there was a great influx into Kashmir of expert dancers both male and female. He paid all dancers liberally and employed the best ones in his service. He was so great a lover of music and so enamoured of this art that whenever he was pleased with musicians he used to order that their musical instruments, e.g., *Bin, Rabab,* etc. to be decorated and inlaid with gold.

Srivara was an accomplished musician himself and raised one music department during Hassan Shah's reign. We learn from him that the dancers and musicians of his time were well versed in the art and understood its modes and intricacies.

G.M. Sufi writes, "The Kashmiris have long adapted and assimilated the best types of Persian music. It is to the credit of the musicians of Kashmir that they have assimilated some of the best *ragas* and *ragainis* of Indian music. The Indian *raganis* which are generally sung by Kashmiris are: *Kalyan, Nat Kalyan, Kbamach, Bihhag, Jhajuti, Balawal, Husaini Todi, Asawari, Tilang, Udasi, Purabi, Sohni, Surath, Kaligri, Dhanasri, Bahagra, Aimin* Kalyan. The Kashmiri musicians are also familiar with some of the *talas* (timings) of Indian music, which are *Yakka or duggan, doravi or tintal and mimdaur or chanchala*".[35]

Currently *Sufiana* music-sung in the praise of lord and *Chakri and Roff* -a vibrant form associated with social gatherings and celebrations like weddings-are more prevalent forms of Kashmiri music.

Astrology, astronomy and rhetoric

Kashmiri Brahmans made a special study in astronomy and astrology and in earlier days in every village there used to be an astrologer who was consulted by the people. Bhaskaracharaya, Aryabhatta and Ratna Kantha are some of the famous astronomers whose works are considered authentic even today. The KSPs knew the calculation of time starting from a "Kalpa & Manvantra to 32nd smallest unit of time" and were considered the protectors of astronomy. "In Nilamat Purana the divisions of the time are also mentioned as objects of worship."[36]

Medicine

The KSPs have made note-worthy contribution to the science of Physiology and medicine. Charaka one of the reputed sons of Kashmir, was the court physician of Kanishka. His book on medicine-*Charita Samhita-* is a marvel to the modern medical and surgical world. Beside him, some other illustrious names in the science of medicine and surgery were Narahari, Shriyabhata, Pupahbhatta (990 to 1065AD) and Dridhabala, one of the ancient physicians of Kashmir who revised the great work of Charaka in his book is known as *Agnivesa Sanihita.*

Nagarjuna (1st century AD) the Buddhist philosopher was a renowned chemist and is regarded as the father of the Indian chemistry. The authenticity of his Kashmiri origin is proved by Kalhana who writes, "And a Bodhisattva lived in this country, as a sole lord of the land, namely the glorious Nagarjuna, who resided at Sadarhad Vana".

G.M.Sufi writes,"Kashmir seems to have enjoyed a great reputation as the home of Ayurvedic medicine. Two Ayurvedic physicians who flourished during Muslim rule, were, Narhari Pandit and Sri Madananga Suri (There is a difference of opinion about the exact identity of Narhari Pandit- as he' is claimed as a *Dekhani* Brahmin by some scholars). The Pandit is said to have flourished during the reigns of Simha Deva and Shah Mir. He is also known as Narasimhu or Narsimba who was the son of Iskara a Brahmin of Kashmir. He authored Nirghanturaja which is a dictionary of Materia medica. Madananga Suri the other Hindu physician was a Jain priest who flourished in 1387 AD His work *Rasayana Parkana* treats pharmaceutical preparations and uses of mineral and metallic substances.[37]

Shri Bhat, an eminent physician of Kashmir- about whom a Kashmiri needs no introduction- was known for his expertise as a physician. Firishta writes that for the encouragement of the study of medicine Zain-ul-Abidin had employed him as the court physician and he enjoyed the special favour of the Sultan.

History and Architecture:

The acumen and accomplishments of the KSP, in the field of History and Architecture is so important and impressive that it deserves a detailed study and has been done so exclusively in chapter no. 9 and 10, under the title: The Foot prints of KSP's Architectural Excellence and Prominent Kashmiri Chroniclers.

Conclusion

The composite cultural mosaic of the *Kashur* is a perfect specimen of the culmination of their traits of adaptability; assimilation and amalgamation. We witness the origin, acceptance and adaptation of various religious philosophies, and their enrichment by the labours of the *Kashur*. Be it the religious isms, creeds or taboos, be it the variety of languages, or the variety of arts and crafts, cultures and civilisations from different centres and geo-corners, the *Kashur* adapted, enriched and nurtured them and finally amalgamated these in their every day life like the waters flowing from various directions into their sea of life. Having assimilated and absorbed they disseminated their own version the final product, beyond the borders of their country. The most appreciable part of it is that this connection is a living reality even after so many eras. Time factor has not effaced the calibre, the standard and the expanse of this relationship, in-spite of the tyrannies inflicted on them by hordes of invaders and marauders from the foreign lands.

CHAPTER-9

THE PROMINENT KASHMIRI CHRONICLERS AND THEIR CHRONICLES

Amongst a number of firsts' credited to the KSP, historiography -recording history in a chronological order- has been one of their essential traits; a trait that is recognized and acclaimed universally. From the available sources and records, we can say that the KSP chroniclers have tried to preserve and pass on, the history of their home land and its people, down the ages, through traditions and legends, very much like the Greek chronologists of those eras. What a Greek like Homer tried to convey through 'Iliad', the chronology minded learned men of Kashmir, have tried through Vrehat Kathas, Mahatamyas and the typically Kashmiri variety of Purana: the Nilamat Purana. Besides, they have compiled historical chronicles, at a time, when the art of writing chronological history, as per experts, was not an accepted norm in rest of the country.

Among the chronological records, Nilmata Puran and Kalhana's Rajatarangini merits a detailed introspection, since these two books serve as the foundation and the store house of historical facts of the earlier eras of Kashmir and it's people, and thus have been consulted over and over again by the scholars, researchers and historians of every hue, in the past, as well as in the present. Besides a concise account of the names and works of those illustrious Kashmiris, who made important contributions towards the composition of the History of Kashmir and its people is also given.

KALHANA PANDIT

The author of the Raja Tarangani-The River of Kings- compiled over a period of two years:1148 to 1150AD in the reign of King Harsha, well nigh deserves the honour of recording the history of Kashmir, in a proper chronological order and with proper references to the sources consulted. H.H.Wilson writes, "Kalhana's use of earlier authorities and sources is a remarkable proof of the attention bestowed by the Kashmiri writers on the history of their native country, and attention the more extra ordinary from the contrast it affords to the total want of historical inquiry in any other part of the extensive countries peopled by the Hindus."[1]

Kalhana, son of the illustrious Lord Canpaka, a minister in Harsha's government, was a very gifted man with scientific and critical temperament. His approach was unbiased and he had the courage and honesty to report truth, however, unpalatable. He himself considers only those historians worthy of praise, "Whose word, like that of the judge, keeps free from the love or hatred in relating the facts of the past."[2] This statement, in itself, proves how scrupulously Kalhana must have studied and assessed, the original sources, including the inscriptions recording the consecration of temples and grants by former kings, and laudatory inscriptions of various kinds and written works, before he started writing the Raja Tarangani. In the introduction to his book, he has himself acknowledged that the subject matter of his work had been treated by others before him.[3] Thus we are authentically informed about the existence of chronicles written prior to him. How many and who wrote them we do not know for certain, except what Kalhana states. He mentions that he had inspected "eleven works of former scholars containing the chronicles of the kings," besides the Nilmata Purana. Even in his times, none of these manuscripts existed in complete state. He attributes their partial loss to a composition of Suvrata, who had condensed them in to a small handbook, thus inadvertently leading to neglect and loss of the originals.

Only two of these manuscripts: The Nilamat Purana and the Vrehat Kathas, have been retrieved by tireless and persistent efforts of various European travellers in the 19th century. Rest have been lost to the vandalism and destructive tendencies of the foreign invaders of this land as confirmed by the observations of two avid researchers of the history of Kashmir quoted below.

Moorcroft writes, "The literature of any description is almost unknown in Kashmir, and it is not easy to discover any relics of those celebrated Sanskrit compositions that originated in the patronage of the Princes of the country whilst it was a Hindu principality. Only two copies of the chronicles of Kashmir the Raja Tarangani, and a local legend called Nilmata Purana and a collection of tales entitled Vrehat Kathas, all written on birch bark, was found."[4]

M.A. Stein to justify as to why he put such a humongous effort to preserve the history of old Kashmir writes, "Great are the changes which the last few decennia have brought over Kashmir, greater, perhaps than any which the country has experienced since the close of the Hindu period. It is easy to foresee that much of what is of value to the historical student will before long be destroyed or obliterated. If such were the apprehensions in the onset of the twentieth century, one can imagine the state in the twelfth century AD as by then Kashmir had already been the victim of Greek, Turk and Hun invasions. The favours with which Nature has so lavishly endowed, "the land in the womb of Himalaya," are not likely to fade or vanish. But those manifold remains of antiquity which the isolation of the country has preserved, and which help us to resuscitate the life and conditions of earlier times, are bound to disappear more and more with the rapid advance of Western influences. It is time to collect as carefully as possible the materials still left for the study of old Kashmir and its earliest records. I have spared no efforts to serve this end, in the result of my labours."[5]

Prior to a detailed study of Kalhana's R.T. as a source, attention needs to be paid to the earliest extant source of the cultural history of Kashmir available to us, and that is the Nilamata Purana.

The Nilamata Purana (N.P)

Nilamata Purana is a monument to the habit of a KSP to record facts, for the posterity, almost six centuries prior to the times, Kalhana Pandit compiled his treatise. It is the earliest compiled extant record that we have in the manuscript format. If R.T. records the history of kings, queens and nobles, N.P. is the record of the social, cultural and religious history of the common *Kashur*. There are eight different manuscripts preserved but the authorship of the original one as per the legend has been ascribed to Nila-Naga.

As in case of other Sanskrit literature of Kashmir, this work was also lost in oblivion. It was Dr. Buhler who gave a description of this text in his, Report on tour in search of Sanskrit manuscripts in Kashmir' in 1877. He described it as a real mine of information regarding the sacred places of Kashmir and their legends.

Doctor Jagder Zadoo and Kani Lal were the first to publish it in Sanskrit in the year 1924. Later. L. Vreese edited and transliterated it in 1935. But the credit for a detailed research of all the eight manuscripts and the final presentation of Nilamata Purana in English language goes to Dr. Ved Kumari Gai.(1988)

On the basis of correlative evidence it has been established that the Purana was compiled in late 6th century A.D. In its present form it appears to be the work of the 8th century A.D., for the mention of Buddha as an avatar of Vishnu in this Puran reflects the assimilation of Buddhism into Hinduism that took place in the 7th century. Krishna Mohan writes, "it is possible that the work might have been written, at the time the valley was drained out of water- and these interpolations might have been done in the later periods."[6] Professor Buhler while agreeing, states, "The internal evidence proves that Nilamata Purana must not be more than 6th or 7th century AD."[7] Winternitz thinks this Purana is several centuries earlier than Kalhana's work.[8] The date of compilation of N.P is a point of contention till date.

Nilamat-Purana is basically a legendary source of information about the origin of Kashmir. It isn't strictly speaking a Purana; it is a book of rites and ceremonies for the Hindus of Kashmir and gives us detailed information regarding the legends and sacred places of Kashmir so well recorded later in Kalhana's Raja Tarangani. It contains the 'doctrines of Nila Naga'- the tutelary deity of Kashmir-which were imparted to the Brahmin Chandredeva.[9]

Earlier N.P. was mainly accepted as a detailed record of religious and social ceremonies ; the rites and rituals and Tirthas of Kashmir, till the time Dr.Gai carried out detailed studies, translation and interpretation on research basis of all the eight available manuscripts of this Purana. Her research followed almost the similar pattern as earlier adopted by M.A. Stein while researching and translating the great historical chronicle Rajatarangini of Kalhana Pandita.

Of the eight MSS, of N.P. three MSS are preserved in Shri Ragunath Temple MSS. Library of Dharmarth Council at Jammu, and the rest at the Research Library of Jammu &Kashmir Government at Srinagar.

It is after Gai's stupendous research that the scholars have started accepting N.P as a reference book on the history of Kashmir. Teng writes, "The publication of this book by Ved Kumari proved an event of sorts for the researchers determined to make forays in the hazy and hazardous past of Kashmir. It provided fresh insight to them and became a common thread for their variegated studies."[10]

It is a treasure trove of detail, about the variety of ethnic and tribal people of ancient Kashmir; their social, economic and religious life. It shows the Kashmiris as devout people, worshiping their Gods, firmly believing in the sacredness of their land, celebrating numerous festivals and leading a happy life. It has very scant information about the Kings of Kashmir.

Dr. Gai while summing up her observations writes, "The picture of ancient Kasmira presented by the study of the Nilamata is not complete in itself; never the less it is significant for its value which is supplementary to that of the R.T. While the R.T. acquaints us with kings and queens and ministers of Kasmira, the Nilamata generally speaks of lay men in their homes, streets, gardens and temples. The life of the common people, the food and drink they took, the amusements they resorted to, currents of religious thoughts they followed and rites and ceremonies they performed through out the year."[11]

The significance and value of this chronicle can be evaluated by the fund of information we gather from this Purana. It provides us with rich geographical data of Kashmir, its mountains and its rivers and evidences the familiarity of the people of Kashmir with other parts of India. Highly valuable information about the origin of the valley and its original inhabitants is presented in a systematic order in this Purana. It gives us a classic description of Satisar Lake whose banks constituted the emergent hills, peopled mainly by the Naga community besides other tribes like Dars, Bhutas, Khasis, Damars and Nishads. And round which is beautifully woven the story of the creation of the land known as Kashmir. The fantastically large and enclosed water body of Satisar is known to have also hosted colonies of Lake Monsters like the ones we are told in tales about the mysterious Lope Notch Monster. Jalodbev is the respectable name chosen for the chief water monster living in Satisar Lake. N.P. also provides information about the fourteen tribes who later on settled in the land known as Satidesha primarily and later as Kashmir.

N.P. gives detailed information about the classification of the divisions of the society and the social norms followed by the inhabitants of the valley. It is a source of information regarding their agricultural produce, crops and fruits that were the main items of their every day consumption.

We learn that four Varanas and various subdivisions of the society did exist in the N.P. era, though not in the strict Varna Ashram format and yet the Brahmanas, especially those, who were learned in their scriptures and other subjects like history, astronomy, astrology and Puranas, were highly honoured. The treatment meted out to the servant class was very humane

N.P. details the position and status of the women in the society, the respect and freedom accorded to the women unlike the women of rest of the country during those eras. It records in great detail about the religious life of the KSP and the various cults of Vishnu, Brahma, Siva, Surya, Durga, Nagas, and Buddha etc that flourished side by side during this era. It confers that followers of different cults were free to worship their respective deities, and at the same time honoured one another's faith. We also learn about the various religious codes and rituals enjoined up on the people, the fasts and feasts observed by the people, the significance of some traditional festivals like that the *Yeksh Amavasya* and so on.

There is even information available regarding the arts and crafts pursued by the people, their various pursuits of life and ways of living, their ethics and philosophy of life.

In short Nilamata gives us abundant information about the people, the inhabitants of the valley of Kashmir, rather than the kings who ruled them. And above all, it records the legend of the creation of the valley in such a detailed format and accuracy that it stands the test of the twentieth century scientific analysis of the Earth sciences.

Kalhana's—Rajatarangini

Rajatarangini, a chronicle of 7,830 verses in Sanskrit language, is compiled in eight Tarangas /books and is composed in a poetic format as was the tradition in those days. Kalhana records the history of Kashmir from the Yuga of its creation and brings it up to 1149 A.D. He concludes the poem with a verse comparing to the swift current of the Godavari - the river of the *Dekhan*,- to his own River of Kings-the title of his chronicle.

His chronicle rightly entitles him to be designated as the Herodotus of Kashmir, indeed of India. He himself describes his work as, "an endeavour to give a connected account where the narrative of past events has become fragmentary in many respects."[12]

Rajatarangini, as the title suggests, is a saga of the kings who ruled Kashmir up to 1149 century A.D. It is the record of the lineages and dynasties of the kings, their administration, their foreign policy, their contribution to the cultural, religious, architectural and literary excellences, besides a detailed account of their follies, weaknesses and extravagances. In R.S. Pandit's words, "He shows us what we want to know, namely what his contemporary men and women looked like, what they ate and wore, what they believed and what was their solution to the eternal problem of the relation between the sexes."[13] No history of Kashmir is complete without a thorough study of R.T. as a background.

As per Kalhana, barring the authentic and exhaustive eye witness accounts of his own times, all the data has been collected by him from eleven works of the earlier scholars and from inscriptions recording the consecration of temples and grants by the kings. Some of the sources consulted by him are:1) Nil Naga's Nilamata Purana, 2) Suvrata's poem composition, which is supposed to be the condensed form of the earliest extensive royal chronicles of Kashmir; 3) Ksemendra's Nrapavali, 4) Helaraja's Parthivavali, which was a composition of twelve thousand salokas,5) Chavillakara's composition, and finally 6) the Mahatamyas of various important temples and places of pilgrimages.[14]

Kalhana's consultation, reference, research and critical analysis of the earlier sources undoubtedly place R.T. very close to the set standards of modern chronicles. Stein writes, "We must give credit to our author for the just observation of the historical geography, many characteristic features in the climate, ethnography, economical condition of Kashmir and the neighbouring regions. If the advantages thus accorded to us are duly weighed, there seems every reason to congratulate ourselves on the fact that the earliest and fullest record of Kashmir history that has come down to us, was written by a scholar of Kalhana's type. Whatever the shortcomings of his work may be from the critical historian's point of view, we must accord it the merit of supplying a safe and ample basis for the study of the historical geography of Kashmir."[15]

In-spite of initial disparities in chronology, the Chronicle provides us with proper dates both in A.D. and Laukika eras for the later portion of its narration.

Experts and researchers are of the opinion that the contents of Kalhana's work from the point of view of the critical tests, which we are able to apply to them, divide themselves into two great portions, marked also by a corresponding difference in their intrinsic historical value. From the narrative of Books 4 to 7 which extends from the beginning of the Karakota dynasty to Kalhana's own time, we are able to check on many important points by independent evidence from other sources, such as coins, inscriptions and the notices of Indian and foreign writers. Our position is very different in regard to the first three Books containing the narrative of the earlier epoch. The record here found of the successive Gonandiya dynasties, whose rule is supposed by Kalhana to have filled an aggregate period of nearly 3050 years, consists mainly of bare dynasties lists interspersed with more or less legendary traditions and anecdotes. The persons and events which figure in them, can but rarely be traced in our other sources, and then, too, only with considerable variations as to date and character.[16]

Stein writes, "He gives a short account of the legends, concerning the creation of Kashmir and its sacred river, the Vitasta, and enumerates besides the most famous of the many Tirthas of which Kashmir has ever boasted in abundance. He begins with the legends which represent the popular traditions of the country regarding the earliest history. These he follows up by a narrative of subsequent reigns taken from older written records and arranged in a strictly chronological order. The final portion of the work, considerable both in extent and historical interest is devoted to an account of events which the author knew by personal experience or from the relation of living witnesses. We are able to realise the political and social conditions in which Kalhana lived, with a degree of accuracy rarely attainable in the case of any old Indian author."[17] R.T is full of accurate data regarding the topography of Kashmir. "The accuracy with which he usually specifies the localities of the events he relates, enable us often to elucidate the latter themselves by an examination of the actual topographical facts."[18]

His observations and details given are so accurate that one can plot them on a map with slightest deviation or variation even after centuries. Striking evidence for this is furnished by his description of the great operations which were carried out under Avantivarman with a view to regulating the course of the Vitasta and draining the Valley.

Kalhana describes the environs of his country, its important landmarks like the Sarikaparvat (Hariparbat); the Gopa Hill (Gupkar) the Jyaishta Rudra (Shankaracharya) and host of temples, shrines and Viharas, the numerous architectural marvels and antiquarian treasures of his land of glory.

As per experts and scholars, Kalhana's local names, on the whole, can be safely accepted as representing the genuine designations of the localities, i.e. as those originally given to them. The names must from the beginning have been given in Sanskrit language and hence the modern Kashmiri derivatives of the same are the result of the process of phonetic evolutions

To sum up, "The Kashmir Chronicle stands quite alone among extant works of Sanskrit literature in respect of the exact dates it furnishes. They seemed to offer the means for determining the dates of events and persons in other parts of India, the history of which in the absence of similar chronicles presented itself to the inquirers of the early part of this century as shrouded in hopeless obscurity. It is, therefore, only natural that all those scholars who had occasion to occupy themselves with the Rajatarangini, have devoted a good deal of attention to the determination of these dates."[19]

It is befitting to observe, that RT is a repository of information regarding the topography of ancient Kashmir, social, political and cultural evolution of the history of Kashmiri speaking people; the rulers who controlled and moulded their destinies, their religious evolution right from the Sanatana Naga faith to Buddhism to Shaivism to the era of religious interpolation and evidences of respect and tolerance of faiths; record of architectural marvels and engineering feats, description of natural disasters like famines and floods, the deceits of low born usurpers and their exploitation of the people of the valley. All this un biased observation would have been lost to us but for the selfless inquisitive research of three men, an Indologist, a traveller and a bureaucrat historian.

How the original Manuscript was traced?

Prior to going in detail about the efforts of these three gentlemen; it would be, in fairness, to name some of those Indologists who by their initial efforts and piecemeal discoveries laid the foundation of this monumental research project right in the seventeenth century and onwards. Dr. Bernier (1664), Mr Gladwin, Dr. Hultzsch,Horace Hyman Wilson, Mr.A.Troyer(1840), General Cunningham, Professor Larsen, Mr Yogesh Chunder Dutt(1879-87) are the prominent ones among the list.[20]

Professor Buhler, during his stay in Srinagar for the first time got a Devanagri transcript of Rajatarangini prepared for the Asiatic Society of Bengal. He had obtained it from the learned Kashmiri Brahman Pt. Sivaram, whose family always preserved a copy of this Royal Chronicle. This Calcutta edition was found to be full of discrepancies, and hence a search was taken up by Professor Buhler, once more, in 1857 for the original text. The end result of this search was that the manuscripts written in Sarda, which were available in Kashmir, were derived from a single manuscript and that was the one which Moorcroft had got transcribed. The Sarda manuscripts were superior to the ones in Devnagri script. Professor Buhler failed to get even the glimpse of this ancient manuscript as the owner had died and his grand son Pandit Kesavram guarded his heirloom jealously. M.A.Stein on his first visit to Kashmir in the year 1888 tried to locate the afore said manuscript but failed to secure it as the owner Pt.Kesavram had since expired and his three sons had divided and distributed the manuscript among themselves. In spite of his persistent efforts he was not even allowed to have a glimpse of the same for one whole year. It was finally with the help of Pandit Suraj Kaul and his son Pandit Harikrishan Kaul that he got possession of the Royal Manuscript. This proved to be the complete volume of eight books which Kalhana had composed. It was transcribed by the great Kashmiri scholar Rajanaka Ratnakantha some where between 1648 A.D. to 1685-86A.D. on Kashmiri paper from the original birch bark manuscript. Since Rajanaka Ratnakantha was a prolific writer, his cursive hand writing at times was illegible (a fact often depicted in the native vocabulary in the form of a phrase Reth Razdanen acher) and a contemporary scholar Takde Bhatta Haraka had annotated this manuscript -Takde most probably in modern Kram will be Trakru. In addition to this manuscript, Stein also traced yet another manuscript-referred as Lahore Manuscript-in the year 1895 from Pandit Jaganmohan Handu's residence at Lahore. This was written in Sanskrit on brownish Kashmiri paper. Having located these rare manuscripts, Stein followed it with dedicated research of twenty years with the assistance of Pt. Gundjoo Razdaan, in the analysis, verification and the final translation into English to be accessible to scholars, historians and the laymen.

It is on the bedrock of this solid foundation of a scientific and systematic chronology of Kashmir that the later chroniclers continued to compose the history of the on going times to the best of their capabilities. Though for some time in between the 12th and 14th centuries the learned men of Kashmir were shackled by the founders and perpetrators of Islam in the valley and thus they had to record their history within the permitted norms in a garbled format.

Stein writes, "There was a gradual decline in the content and character of these later chronicles. Hindu learning in Kashmir suffered considerably during the period of troubles and oppression which lasted with short interruptions for two and a half centuries previous to Akbar's conquest. Later Sanskrit Chronicles were composed with the distinct object of continuing Kalhana's work. It is curious to note this gradual decline also in the character and contents of these later Chronicles".

Chronicles referred to are: Rajatarangini of Jonaraja who continued the narrative down to the reign of Sultan Zain-Ul-Abidin,A.D.1459; followed by Jaina-Rajatarangini composed by Jonaraja's pupil Srivara, covering the period A.D. 1459-86; and finally Rajavalipataka initiated by Prajyabhatta and completed by his pupil S'uka, few years after the annexation of Kashmir by Akbar in A.D.1586. "The total extent of these three distinct works does not amount to more than about one half of Kalhana's text." [21]

JONARAJA—*RAJAVALI*

Jonaraja was a learned Brahman and one of the judicial advisers of Sultan Zain-Ul-Abdin (1420-70). He compiled the chronicle: Rajavali at the express orders of the Sultan. It is a continuation of Kalhana's R.T. and extends historical documentation up to the year 1459 A.D. He has frankly confessed that his work is, "only an outline of the history of Kings," and he does not tell us much about the life and the condition of the people from Kalhana's era to the beginning of the Muslim rule in 1320 AD. He does, however, give an account of his own time.

The 'Rajavali' gives a record of twenty three kings out of which, thirteen are Hindu kings, from Jai Simha to queen Kota, one Buddhist and nine Muslim rulers up to the reign of Zain-Ul-Abidin. He has been a contemporary of Sikander and Zain-ul-abidin and hence one can credit his account of these rulers with a great measure of authenticity. Regarding the Hindu rulers his description is 'cursory and brief', where as he has described the Muslim rule in great detail.

Jonaraja gives a graphic description of the plight of the Brahmans during the reign of Ali Shah. He writes about the heart rending description of the invasions of Dulcha and Rinchan. Writing about Rinchan, he states, "As a kite swoops on the bird-ling having dropped from the perch, in the same manner the invincible army of Rinchan dispossessed of all belongings the Kashmiri folk.Jonaraja has not referred to the episode of Bulbul shah, who according to Persian Chroniclers is supposed to have converted Rinchin to Islam. He, however, does refer to one Devaswami who refused to admit Rinchan into the Hindu fold (Verse 193). Further more, he asserts that it was the manoeuvring of Shahmeer who got Rinchin initiated in to Islam."[22]

In this chronicle we find a record of the earlier years of the reign of Zain-Ul -Abidin. A detailed description of the episode of the poisonous boil of the king and its cure by Shri Bhat the famous Kashmiri Hindu physician, and how this incident influenced the great King and how Shri Bhatta used this opportunity to rehabilitate the Hindus and gain well deserved favours from the ruler for a dignified living without any fears of conversion and torture, as had been the practice for nearly two centuries.

Dhar writes, "Kashmiris owe a debt to Jonaraja for erecting the contours of a light house of accurate historicity which reduces to nullity thankless past time of groping in the dark."[23]

Srivara Pandit—*Shri Jaina Raja Tarangani'*

Srivara lived through the reign of Haider Shah (1470-72) as well as Hasan Shah (1472-84). He carried forward the tradition of historical writing in his exhaustive book 'Sri Jaina Raja Tarangani'. He details the last eleven years of Zain-ul-Abidin's rule. Being a contemporary historian of the times when there was extreme civil strife and struggle between the local Kashmiri Musalman and the foreign Muslims like Sayyids, and in this strife the Bhatta being in such a minority, hardly mattered or dared to have an opinion of their own. They merely existed as mere victims of the high-handedness of the groups in power. As such even their historians were cautious. Srivara writes, "I have abstained from giving even a brief account of . . . . . in consideration of the present unsuitable times."[24]

Stein commenting on Srivara's method of writing and vocabulary observes, "Srivara is a slavish imitator of Kalhana, not above reproducing whole verses of his predecessor. His text looks in a great, portion more like a cento from the Rajatarangini, than an original composition. He is probably ignorant of the ancient names of the well-known localities. He more than once betrays his ignorance of the old names for well-known, Kashmiri localities. Thus we have the name of the *Maha sarit* stream transformed in to Mari, an evident adaptation of the modern Mar."[25] Dr.Parimoo believes, this must have been so because Srivara composed the narrative for the learned masses of Kashmir who included both Muslims and Hindus. Further the Sanskrit names must have got distorted with the disuse of the Sanskrit as the official language, and the author preferred to use more prevalent names.

PRJAGYABHATTA AND S'UKA—*'RAJA VALI PATACCA'*

The authors updated history of Kashmir from 1446 to1586 AD, i.e. till after its annexation by the Mogul King Akbar. Raja Vali Pataka/Patacca was started by Prjagyabhatta and later continued by Suka. It lacks continuity and has many gaps. Were these due to the careless attitude of the authors or for fear of apprehension because those were the times of torture, tyranny and anarchy? They have not mentioned how Mirza Haider Dughlat became ruler of Kashmir in 1540? Yet again Stein writes, Prjagyabhatta and Sukas' work is inferior even to S'rivara's Chronicle, as we find the authors are unfamiliar with the original Sanskrit names and hence have given distorted versions like,"the ancient Krtyasrama, the scene of Kalhana's Buddhist legend, figures repeatedly in their, narrative as Kicasrama, i.e. by its modern name Kits'hom; even the well-known Rajapuri is metamorphosed into Rajavira (!), a queer reproduction of the modern Rajauri; the old castle of Lohara reappears as Luha'la."[26]

We can justify these distortions once again by acknowledging that as Sanskrit ceased to be the language used for official purposes, the knowledge of the ancient names of localities and of the traditions connected with the latter must have become gradually more and more restricted hence the distorted versions came in to use and the chroniclers tend to use the Prakrit (language in every day use).

MAHATAMYAS

In addition to the chronicles mentioned above, Mahatamyas of various tirthas, important rivers and famous pilgrim centres were compiled by the KSPs during the medieval era to record historical facts. Mostly anonymous, these works are, however, valuable sources of information about the location, topography, and the rites and rituals followed by the pilgrims in the course of the pilgrimage tours. Stein remarks, "Though we have more than fifty Mahatmyas in number but most of them are recent compositions or redactions as not a single ancient manuscript written on *bhoj patra* has been recovered."[27]

With the end of Hindu period and establishment of Islamic rule slowly and steadily Persian language took over. In this period of transition not many worthy historical treatises were composed. What ever was written was a concise translation of earlier works, especially that of Kalhana's R.T. and most of them, that includes even Haider Malik Chadurah, have avoided to give any detailed account of the Hindu period of the History of Kashmir.

MULLAH SHAH MOHAMMED SHAHABADI—*(BAHR-UL-ASMAR'/ TARIKHI-I-KASHMIR)*

Mulla Shah Mohammed Shahabadi, belonging to Shahabad, (modern Dur) in Anantnag district, on the orders of the Emperor Akbar, translated Kalhana's R.T. in Persian under the name 'Bahr-Ul-Asmar'/Tarikhi-I-Kashmir',1594AD. This book "records the activities of Mir Sayyid Ali and his disciples, and the iconoclastic activities of Sultan Sikander and Mir Mohammad Hamadanis' influence on the religious thought of the Sultan. It also records, Zain- ul- Abidin's enlightened religious policies and patronage of arts and crafts . . . and some biographical notices of Sufis and Rishis."[28]

BAHARISTAN-I-SHAHI' (ANONYMOUS)

It is a very valuable history of Kashmir that gives us a comprehensive account of the periods from 1468 to1615. It narrates in detail the events leading to the Moghul conquest of Kashmir, and mentions the events that caused the death, in Bihar, of the exiled Yusuf Shah Chak and his son Yaqub Chak. This book also deals, in detail, the activities of Shams-ud-din Iraqi. Dr. Parimoo while commenting on this book writes, that there is mention of both Hijra and *Laukika dates*, side by side, in it, although the latter (*Laukika* era) has been referred by the name of *Sana-I-Kashmir.*

HAIDER MALIK CHADURAH—*TARIKH-I-KASHMIR*

Haider Malik Chadurah carried on the tradition of writing the history of Kashmir. Malik belonged to Chodur in Naugam Parganas, the same village where Kalhana was born. It is believed that his ancestors were Rajputs belonging to the Chand sect of the Raina family. Originally they had come to Kashmir from Trigarto (modern Kangra) in the closing years of the reign of Jayasimha, (1128-55). Emperor Jahangir had appointed him as Rais-ul-Malik and later in 1627 Shahjahan appointed him as the superintendent of buildings to be erected around the Verinag spring. He has given us a valuable documentation of the period 1586 to 1627AD, in his book 'Tarikh-I-Kashmir'. He gives a graphic description of the places like Shahabuddinpur, Divsar, Lar, Tolamula, Amarnath cave, Ichber and Hokursar etc.

NARAIN KAUL AZIZ—*TARIKH-I- KASHMIRI'*

Narain Kaul Aziz compiled 'Tarikh-I- Kashmiri' in 1710, giving an account of Sultans and Moguls who ruled the valley. He describes the defection of Yusuf Shah Chak and his struggle against the Mogul rule. It is a very comprehensive and chronologically composed account based on Sanskrit chronicles and Haider Malik's Tarikh up to 1586. This book is the first available Persian chronicle, on the history of Kashmir, compiled by a Kashmiri Brahmin.

KHWAJA MOHAMED AZAM KAUL—*'WAQIAT-I-KASHMIR*

Khwaja Mohamed Azam Kaul, from Diddamar, a locality in Srinagar, has covered the period 1738 to 1747 AD in his book 'Waqiat-I-Kashmir'. In addition to political history, he describes the growth of religious consciousness, sociological trends and literary activities of the Kashmiri Muslim. It throws light on the life and achievements of various Sayyids, Sufies, Ulemas and poets. There are references to the prevalence of Beggar (forced labour) in Kashmir [29]

PT. BIRBAL KACHROO—*MUKHTASAR TARIKH-I-KASHMIR* 1835

Pt. Birbal Kachroo, a learned Kashmiri Brahman from Rainawari Srinagar, has given description of the traditions, social customs and political life of the Hindus under the Sikh rule in this book. He also gives a fearless account of the long period of tyranny and tribulation that befell on the lot of KSP after the peace and prosperity under the Mughal rulers.

HASSAN KHUHAMI (PIR)—*TARIKH-I-HASSAN*

Hassan Khuhami (Pir) was a great scholar of Arabic and Persian in the 19th century. He provides a comprehensive record of the State of J&K. in four volumes of his book, 'Tarikh-I-Hassan':: Vol.1.Geographic description; Vol. 2 Political history up to 1885 AD; Vol. 3, Tuzkir-Ayliya-Kashmir a detailed account of Muslim saints and mystics of Kashmir and Vol. 4, an account of the Persian poets of Kashmir from Chack period to 1891 AD.

PIR HASSAN SHAH—*HISTORY OF KASHMIR*

Pir Hassan Shah, a reputed Kashmiri chronicler and a scholar of Muslim theology, was born in 1832 at Gamru village, near Bandipur. It is said that Moulvi Gulam Hassan, during his research, is supposed to have laid hands on the manuscript of one Mullah Ahmed's translation of an ancient book on history of Kashmir under the name of, 'Ratnakar Purana' referred earlier. This book contained the account of the rule of the 35 kings that are missing in Kalhana's, Rajatarangini because, apparently Kalhana either failed to collect any information about them or he considered them to be Mlechhas and hence ignored them. This information was later used by Badi-Ud-Din in his book. Hassan Shah gives us an unbiased account of a Hindu uprising against the tortures and tyrannies inflicted on them and the punishments meted out by the rulers after Zain Ul- Abdin. He writes "The patience of the Pandits having reached the breaking point they rose in a body and set fire to some mosques which were built with the material of the Hindu temples once demolished by Sikander. The rising was quelled by the sword, many more were drowned in the rivers, and loot and plunder was practiced with unbridled licence." [30]

DEWAN KRIPA RAM—*GULZAR-I-KASHMIR' AND 'GULAB NAMA*

Dewan Kripa Ram (1857-85) in his books 'Gulzar-I-Kashmir' and 'Gulab Nama' writes about the exploits of Maharaja Gulab Singh. It is a summary of the history of Kashmir as told by its own historians.

HAJI MOHI-UD-DIN—*TARIKH-I-KABIR-I-KASHMIR*

Haji Mohi-ud-din, (1892), a Kashmiri who lived at Zaribal in Srinagar has given a racy summary of political, religious and literary history of Kashmir in one handy volume 'Tarikh-I-Kabir-I-Kashmir'.

PANDIT ANAND KAUL BAMZAI—*THE KASHMIRI PANDIT*

Pt.Anand Kaul besides writing the book 'Kashmiri Pandit' wrote a series of papers in 1910, in the Journal of The Asiatic Society, giving a detailed account of the geography and the archaeological remains of Kashmir. He even wrote about various aspects of the *Kashur* culture, like their social customs and traditions; their casts and race distinctions; and their language that is Kashmiri.

PANDIT HARGOPAL KAUL—*GULDASTA-I-KASHMIR*

Pandit Hargopal Kaul in his book, 'Guldasta-I-Kashmir' enlightens the reader about the geography and important historical events of Kashmir from the earliest times.

Shri P.N.Bamzai—*History of Kashmir 1962*

P.N.Bamzai, like his illustrious father Anand Kaul, compiled and published a very exhaustive history of Kashmir right from ancient times to the present century modern Kashmir. He has covered political, social and cultural aspects of Kashmir valley under three sub-heads namely: i) Early history of the Buddhist and Hindu period; ii) Medieval Kashmir- foundation of the Sultanate to the end of Afghan rule and (iii) Modern history up to 1960.

Semi Historical works of Kashmiri poets

Not only have the history minded men and women of Kashmir recorded the history of their land, even its poets in their poetic compositions have preserved information of distinct value about themselves about the people, their culture and the topography of the valley. "It is a fortunate circumstance that several of the older Kasmiri poets, whose works have been preserved for us, have had the good sense to let us know something about their own persons and homes".

1.**Damodara Gupta** the Prime Minister of the king Jayapida (755-86 AD) wrote,Kuttanimatan, which is a didactic poem written in the form of an advice given by a Kuttani (Procuress) to a prince. She tells him how to escape the wiles of a corrupt woman. Apparently sexual vices must have degraded the society at that time, and Damodara Gupta attempted to root out the evil not by legislation but by educating the public opinion. The impact it had can be judged by the fact that even to this day her exploits survive in the degraded popular expression, '*pha pha Kuttan.*'

2.**Ksemendra** In the middle of the eleventh century in his books- *Desopadesa, Narmala* and *Lokaprakasa*-gives a detailed study of the sociological trends before the establishment of Islam.

(i) Desopadesa illuminate the social and administrative life of the people of Kashmir under Hindu rule. In this Ksemendra depicts the life and character of various characters like, *Khala* (villain), *Kadarya (*miser), prostitute, *Kuttani* (procuress),an old man marrying a young girl and foreign students receiving instructions in the math's etc.

(ii) Narmala may be treated as an addendum to Desopadesa. It describes the character of *Kayasthas* or the official community. In fact the *Kayasthas* by their unsociable activities, vicious conduct and unspeakable cruelties had become a disgraceful element of the society. Pandit Madhusudhan Kaul Shastri has ably edited both Desopadesa, and Narmala.[31]

(iii) Lokaprakasa a monumental work, is an encyclopaedia, a dictionary and a practical handbook, all in one, dealing mainly with sociological, economic and administrative subjects. The author (Ksemendra) mentions the names of the administrative units (Parganas) of his time and also enumerates specification of bonds, hundis and social contracts in vogue in his time. Originally composed in eleventh century, many additions and alterations seem to have been made to it up to the end of the reign of Emperor Shahjahan. [32]

In addition to these mammoth works of chronological history by the local historians, and poets there are many more small, but perfect, publications by the students of history about specific topics like language, culture, Archaeology and ancient monuments, to name a few subjects.

After independence of the country and in recent years after the trauma of the nineties, a large number of books on different aspects of the history of Kashmir have flooded the bookstalls. Most of these are based on the earlier sources and references that have been given in detail above, except for the portions dealing with last fifty years or so. This period of fifty years is the most documented one by the people of this land, be they expatriate Kashmiris, diplomats, journalists, literates, fundamentalists or commoners. Books written during these tumultuous years of strife and mayhem, and due to the religious and political inferences, are at times biased and also tinted in various hues. Majority of them fail to rise up to Kalhana Pandits maxim about a historian's work, "Whose word, like that of the judge, keeps free from the love or hatred in relating the facts of the past." It is simply impossible to write about all these works of the present era for they are so many in numbers.

It would be fair enough to write, that not only have the local historians chronicled the history of Kashmir and its people, the notices, travelogues and researches of the scholars, Indologists and historians both from east and west, be they Greeks, Arabs, Persian, Chinese or Europeans have preserved the history of Kashmir and it's people and they serve as very essential sources of our information about our homeland. Yet they do not in any way lessen the importance of the local sources of the history of Kashmiri speaking people about whom the great researcher M.A. Stein writes, "Having learned what little the outer world knew or recorded of the secluded alpine land, we shall appreciate all the more the imposing array of Kashmirian authorities which offer themselves as our guides in and about the valley."[33]

Shalimar Garden-Mughal Architecture

CHAPTER-10

THE FOOT PRINTS OF KSP ARCHITECTURAL EXCELLENCE - A RESUME

Dr.Arthur Neve's quotation, "Ancient India has nothing more worthy of its early civilization than the grand ruins of Kashmir, which are the pride of the Kashmiris and admiration of the travellers. The massive, the grotesque, the elegant in architecture may be admirable in parts of India, but nowhere is to be found the counterpart of the classically graceful, yet symmetrically massive edifices except in Kashmir", aptly sums up the standard of KSP's architectural monuments, and their acumen and proficiency in the art of architecture. Alas! Most of these precious relics of the past have been destroyed, devastated, demolished and burnt by fanatic zealots and vandals, who ruled Kashmir at different periods of its history. Besides at times even the natural agents also must have played a role in destroying these unprotected and neglected monuments. What ever is left for us to observe are bare foot prints.

While writing about the ancient monuments of Kashmir one is of and on, apprehended, with the thought of disbelief that might arise in the readers mind. For what, at present, are either oft visited tourist spots or neglected and dilapidated villages, institutions, buildings or mounds, were once very famous monuments built, under the patronage of prestigious rulers of Kashmir, by Kashmiri artisans and architects. The designers and the builders of these ruins have been those acclaimed Kashmiris, who were known as, '*shestrashilpiras*,' (great architects) as early as the 5th-6th century AD. Their handiworks and architectural monuments are a mute testimony in stone, bricks or wood of their excellence in the field of architecture over thousands of years. Progress and evolution of their architectural acumen, can be traced from the varied designs, motifs and artistic imagery that they have carved on these monuments, and the varied type of material they have used for the construction of these structures. These monuments, not only reflect the rich cultural life of the Kashmiris, but also show their high technical skill in engineering and profound knowledge in the selection of sites, besides the judgement of foundation conditions.

THE FOOT PRINTS OF KSP ARCHITECTURAL EXCELLENCE - A RESUME

Like every other aspect natural or otherwise, the history of the land, has left deep impress on the architecture of Kashmir. The oldest edifices that exist in fragments are markedly reminiscent of Naga culture, which was later taken over by Buddhist and Gandhar influences, followed by Greek and then the Persian or Mughal architecture. In the present era what ever is constructed has a stamp of modernity-a 20th century stamp.

The Kashmirian architecture of the Hindu era has been found by scholars to resemble various Grecian Orders. Cunningham writes, "The architectural remains of Kashmir are perhaps the most remarkable of the existing monuments of India as they exhibit undoubted traces of the influence of the Grecian art."[1] Remnants of which are still visible, though as disintegrated shambles, in almost every nook and corner of the valley. Lawrence writes, "I have rarely been in any village, which cannot show some relics of antiquity. Curious stone monuments of the old Kashmiri Temples. Huge stone seats of Mahadev (*Badri pith*), phallic emblems, innumerable carved images heaped in grotesque confusion by some clear spring have met me at every turn. They were the works of the Buddhists or the Pandus. When one comes to the most recent period of the Mughals, tradition becomes more definite. And I have seen many mosques built in style unlike the present, of wooden beams with stones between, mostly raised by Aurangzeb." [2]

Kashmiris, going by the references in the Nilamat Purana, knew about the various types of architecture in the early eras of the present millennia. Terms like *bhavana, grha, nivesana, alaya, vesma, aytana and attalaka* have been used in the N. P. to describe individual sections of a dwelling. Archaeologists have found that the chambers of Buddhist *caityas* and dwelling places of monks called *sakyavasa* were surrounded by circumbulatory passages. Kalhana, as a mark of appreciation, addresses these architects and sculptors, as, "*Shastra Shilpina*" (proficient architects).

Superiority of the Kashmirian architecture would appear to have been known to the Hindus themselves, for using the term *'shestrashilpiras'* could only have been applied to them, on account of their well known skill in building Lawrence writes, "Kashmiris who are the most expert handicraftsmen of the East and excel as weavers, gun-smiths and as calligraphers, must once have been the most eminent of the Indian architects."[3]

The remains of the monuments that we find, are remarkable for their almost 'Egyptian solidity, simplicity, and durability'. One wonders in awe to imagine, how grand a sight it would have been to behold them in their full glory, and to witness the graceful elegance of their outlines, the massive boldness of their parts, and happy propriety of their outlines. "The ancient Kashmirian architecture, with its noble fluted pillars, its vast colonnades, its lofty pediments, and its elegant trefoil arches, (that is) entitled to be classed as a distinct style".[4] On account of these characteristics, Cunningham has classed the Kashmirian architecture as of the "Arian order". The reasons forwarded by him are that this label rightly depicts what is the style of the Aryas or the Arians of Kashmir and secondly, because its intercolumniations are always of four diameters, an interval which Greeks called Araiostyle.[5]

R.C. Kak, reputed Kashmiri archaeologist, writes that the mediaeval architecture of Kashmir depends for its effect upon:"(I) the simplicity and unity of its design, (2) the massiveness of blocks of lime stone and granite that were used, (3) the finish of drawing and last but not the least, (4) the natural beauty of the site chosen for erection of the temple and its main feature is a happy combination of the column and the arch".[6]

There are about 50 ancient monuments of different size and stature, which have been recorded by the Archaeological Survey. Some of these monuments have been disfigured beyond recognition so far as their representative significance is concerned. Most of these monuments were once temples dedicated to various Hindu gods and goddesses, or Buddhist Stupas and monasteries but have, since, either been converted to Ziarats or mosques or lie scattered as sheer structures of grandeur in ruins that have survived the ravages of man and nature.

Most important archaeological remains of the Hindu era are: the ruined Martand temple at Mattan, temples at Avantipura; Narasthan; Pandrethan; Pattan and the ruined temple at Payech. Besides these, a few remnants of the earliest architectural specimens like the caves at Bhumju, an apsidal temple with a court yard surrounded by a pebble walls discovered at Uskur (2nd to 5th century A.D) and Harwan (3rd to 6th century AD) [7]

In addition to these model representations, hundreds of monuments, mostly in ruins and a few in composite shapes be they temples, Buddhist Stupas or forts and cave temples are found every where in the valley. All represent antiquity and are famous for their diversity. These are mostly built of stones of very large dimensions that have helped them to survive to some extent the devastation and destruction caused by the bigoted rulers and the climatic conditions of the valley. They stand as evidence of the advanced civilization that existed in Kashmir.

With the end of the Hindu rule the art of massive and grand monuments was almost forgotten. "Muslims in Kashmir were at the beginning too few to initiate an architecture of their own." [8] However revivals did take place slowly, primarily with imported labour and then the converted Hindu architects created a Muslim style of architecture that made use of wood for construction instead of stone blocks.

THE FOOT PRINTS OF KSP ARCHITECTURAL EXCELLENCE - A RESUME

G.M. Sufi writes, "Mohammadan architecture in Kashmir must be pronounced as rather disappointing in comparison with the grand edifices of Hindu rule like the temples at Martand, Avantipura and else where. Even for an ordinary hill fort on Hariparbat, Akbar had to import a large number of masons from India as one can see from the inscription on the *Kathi Darwaza* of the fort. The art of masonry seems to have died long before the death of Hindu rule in the valley but the wooden architecture of Kashmir that commands our admiration to this day originated with the Mohammedans, and it appears that the Kashmiri Hindu mason of old had his re-birth in the Muslim carpenter of the latter-day rule."[9] For it were these Muslim carpenters who created a very distinctive style of the wooden architecture of Kashmir.

Cunningham and Cole in their accounts of the antiquities of Kashmir dealt almost exclusively with Hindu and Buddhist monuments and left the wooden style, practically unnoticed. It was Fergusson, the historian of Indian Architecture, who unravelled the beauty of this architecture of the Mohammadan era. W.H. Nicholls writes, "Mohammadan architecture in Kashmir, broadly speaking, falls under three heads,

(i) the pre-Mughal masonry style

(ii) the wooden style, and the

(iii) pure Mughal style

and out of the three the wooden style is a very distinctive style of this group of architecture". The Mosque (tomb) of Madani, and the tomb of Zain-ul-Abidin's mother are the earliest genuine example of the wooden style in Srinagar

This style existed in the days of Zain-ul-Abidin and his palace was made of wood. Mirza Haider describes the construction of it thus, "Sultan Zain-ul-Abidin erected a palace in the middle of the Wular Lake. First of all he emptied a quantity of stones into the lake and on those constructed a foundation or floor of closely-fitting stones measuring two hundred square *gaz (yard)* in extent and ten *gaz* in height. Here upon he built a charming palace and planted pleasant groves of trees, so that there can be but few mere agreeable places in the world. He then built for himself a palace (named after him *Zaina Dab*) in his town of Naushahr, which in the dialect of Kashmir is called *Rajdan.* It has twelve stories some of which contain fifty rooms, halls and corridors. The whole of this lofty structure is built of wood." [10]

A few monuments representative of different architectural styles have been described here to exhibit the expertise of the KSP architects.

Harwan Temple

Recent excavations carried out at Harwan have revealed the existence of one of the oldest monuments in Kashmir, where the Saint Philosopher Nagarjuna is reported to have held a Buddhist congregation. A temple and some tablets belonging to Kushan period have been unearthed here. This apsidal temple is the representation of the diaper pebble style (pebbles and mud- mortar combination) of construction adopted by the KSP architects during the earliest eras. Where as the Stupas and a set of rooms close to it are constructed using the method of diaper-rubble style (insertion of irregular blocks of stone at intervals). These styles of construction were replaced by massive stone blocks, by the architects of Kashmir later on for saving their structures from the climatic hazards Little did they imagine that human hand would be more destructive and powerful and damaging for their works of art?

The Martand Temple

Martand temple is the most impressive and representative monument of Kashmiri architecture and at present we can say the grandest of all the ruins in Kashmir. It is situated nine kilometres east-north-east of Anantnag. The word 'Martand' means Sun, so it is believed that the temple was dedicated to the Sun god. Historians and the archaeologists have varying opinions regarding its date of erection; compromising date accepted is between 370 AD and 500 AD. The Sun temple of Martand stands in the middle of a large courtyard and as per the archaeological reports, "This temple was about 200 feet (60m) long and about 150feet (45m) broad. There were about 84 carved pillars, most of them now lying prostrate on the ground. Remains of the three gateways are still standing. They are rectangular in shape and built of enormous blocks of limestone, six to eight feet (1.8m to 2.4m) in length-one of them is nine feet (2.7m)-of proportionate solidity cemented with mortar. Central building is 63feet (19m) in length and 36 feet (10.8m) in width." The temple proper contained *garbhagraha, antarala* and closed *mandapa,* approached by a grand flight of steps. The pliant supporting the central shrine had two tiers, both with niches having 37 divine figures. It is worth studying how such huge stones were piled, one upon another, to such a great height with such exactitude. Mutilated carvings and decorations that are still visible, here and there, on the stones are an ample proof that the temple had been covered with ornamental carvings of high class. It is because of its beauty that a poet has said Martand is, "a dream in stones designed by Titans and finished by jewellers."

It is believed that when the iconoclast rulers of the valley tried to demolish this temple by organising a huge blazing fire within the complex, the latter raged for nearly two full years, and still the temple could not be raised to the base; such was its strength and solidity.

Cunningham, while praising the architectural grade of the Martand Temple writes, "We are not looking upon the monuments of the dead. We step not aside to inspect a tomb, or pause to be saddened by an elegy. The noble pile in the foreground is rather an emblem of age than of mortality and the interest with which we perambulate its ruins is not less pleasurable because we do not know much that is certain of its antiquity, its founders or its original use."[11]

Sir Frances Young Husband while eulogising the architectural status of the Martand and specifically its location observes, "of all the ruins in Kashmir the Martand ruins are most remarkable and the most characteristic. No temple has ever been built at a finer site. Not only is the Martand the finest, and as it is not only typical of Kashmiri architecture at its best, but is built on the most sublime site occupied by any building in the world,—finer far than the site of the Parthenon, or of the Taj, or of the St. Peters, or of the Estuarial,—we may take it as the representative, or rather the culmination of all the rest, and by it we must judge the people of Kashmir at their best. Though Hindu it defers from the usual Hindu types; and is known distinctively as Kashmirian and owes much to the influence of Gandhara."

Temple at Avantipura

Temple at Avantipura that lies on the right bank of Vitasta is yet another specimen of the massive magnanimity of Hindu architecture. Situated around twenty-nine kilometres from Srinagar; this locality was originally called *Vishwaika Sara*. It is believed that the King Avantivarman, who ruled Kashmir from 855-883 AD and had his capital at this place, embellished the town of Avantipura by constructing two temples dedicated to Lord Shiva and lord Vishnu.

The Shiva temple, now in a dilapidated condition, is located in a 70x60m courtyard; with the central building and the main shrine enclosed by a massive stonewall. The gateway, which still possesses two pillars supporting the entablature, is located in the middle of the western wall. Beautiful carvings and graceful figure sculptures showing (statues of Avantivarman and his queen) have been obtained from the excavated ruins of this temple.

The Vishnu temple is located a kilometre off the Shiva temple by the side of the National Highway linking Srinagar to Jammu. Main shrine is in the centre of a spacious oblong courtyard and four subsidiary shrines at the corners. The temple is of rectangular shape (52x 45 m) with the central building of 11m square. It is surrounded by an array of 69 cells around the periphery of a paved courtyard and has an imposing gateway in the middle part of the western side. The sanctum is a tirtha on plain and the parapets on either side of the staircase, leading to this sanctum, are engraved with figures of Kamdev, king Avantivarman, his queen' and entourage.

The elegant forms, proportionate layout, exuberant carvings and graceful sculpture of the temple are a masterly composition of architect and art prevalent in Kashmir during that period. The temples are made of large, dressed rectangular blocks, slabs and columns of limestone-masonry stone, which in native tongue *Kashur* is called *'Diwer ken'.* Builders used big stone slabs for ensuring more stability. Locally available calcareous material of Karewas, which has a good binding property, has been used as mortar. Construction site obviously was selected close to the river, as transportation of the stone blocks was easier, for the quarry site is also close to the river Vitasta.[12]

Ruins at Pattan

Two Shiva temples reportedly built during the reign of Sankarvarman—833 to 900 AD are situated 28 km North West of Srinagar at Tapar, Pattan. Both these temples have square platforms with a flight of stairs from the four sides and a framework of masonry towers and contain numerous carvings above the platform. The individual masonry blocks have huge dimensions ranging up to 5.5m in length as seen in the lentils. There shaping is so precise and angles so exact as if made by mechanical means and not by hand. In the complex construction of the cornice meeting the roof at different angles, instead of using a number of stones, the entire combination was made monolithic by skilfully cutting out one huge block-an architectural ingenuity indeed. [13]

For the construction of these temples, blocks of limestone bonded by lime mortar have been used. Limestone of this type occurs at many localities in the valley and in the case of these temples the same may have been obtained from Manasbal area about 40km from the temple site. Destruction and the damage of the Pattan temple, like many other temples of Kashmir, have been primarily caused by iconoclastic rulers, and later, to some extent, lack of maintenance has reduced these monuments to skeletal remains.

Shankaracharya Temple

It is a temple that stands unique for its location and antiquity. It is situated on top of an extinct volcanic cone, named the Shankaracharya hill by the Hindus and, often referred as *Takht-I-Sulaiman* in the recent times by the Muslims. The hillock according to "Tarikh-i-Hassan", (pp 394-496, Vol.11) and "*Waquiat Kashmir*" of Mulla Ahmed was known originally as "*Anjana*" and later as "*Jeth Ludrak*", and the temple was built by King Sandhiman of the Gonanda Dynasty of Kashmir. He gave the name "*Jeshteshwara*" to the temple and the hillock came to be known as, "*Sandhiman Parbat*" after the name of the King.

THE FOOT PRINTS OF KSP ARCHITECTURAL EXCELLENCE - A RESUME

According to Dr.Stein, King Gopaditya (369-309 B.C.) repaired the temple and donated two villages (the present Gupkar and Buchhwara-*Bhaksira Vatika*) for the maintenance of the temple and changed the name to "*Gopadari*" or *Gopa Hill*. This name of the hillock and "*Jeshteshwara*", for the temple continued till it was dedicated to Adi Shankaracharya, who visited Kashmir and stayed at the temple complex. This is also confirmed in "*Tarikh-i-Hassan*" (pp.80-82, Vol.1), since then both the hillock and the temple came to be known as Shankaracharya.

This Shiva temple commands a fascinating bird's eye view of the city and the celestial valley. It is a massive stone structure built on a high octagonal plinth strictly in accordance with Hindu tradition. The temple has 84 recesses on its exterior and is surrounded by a parapet wall enabling devotees to have the *Parikrama*/circumbulation of the temple safely. The stairs leading to the sanctum sanctorum number 36; first flight of 18 steps followed by 12 steps and again followed by six steps on either side of the landing terminating the second flight. This total of 36 steps is also in accordance with Hindu tradition, denoting as many elements of which cosmos is made. Recently an alternative track of about 599 chiselled stone-steps with side walls and landings has also been built.

It is said that the original Shiva Lingam in the temple, along with over 300 precious idols of Gods and Goddesses there in and other structures and residential quarters around the temple, were destroyed by Sultan Sikandar during his rule (1389 - 1413 AD)

This temple was originally connected with Vitasta (Jhelum) by a finely sculptured stone stairs overlooking the present Badami Bagh cantonment off Sonawar, near the temple of Goddess *Tripursundari* on the right bank of the river, now known as *Shurahyaar (Shudash Dashyar*). This stone stair way was dismantled during the rule of King Jahangir and the stones were used to build a huge mosque, known now as 'Pathar Masjid midway between Fatehkadal and Zaina Kadal in Srinagar.

Mrs Walter Tibbits describes the physical aspect and the spiritual significance of this temple in her book *The Cities seen in East and West*' in the chapter titled 'City *of the Sun*' and she writes, "The hill is rough and jagged as the path of yoga (the Path of Union with God). The elements have stained its every shade of ochre, the colour sacred to the lord of Universe. Sharp rocks break the path as the trails of the way out and wound the feet of the aspirant of knowledge. On its summit stands in simple, solemn dignity a small fane of grey stone. Its columns are fluted; its dome is round, rounded by a trident. Inside is one thing only, an upright black stone. The Lingam is the oldest religious symbol in the world. It is also the simplest. But to the

Shavites, no gorgeous imagery of the Mass, no elaborate ceremonial of Mecca, can compare with the solemnity of that black stone . . . Guardian of the austere glories of Maheshwara, crowning of the fort-like hill, high, serene, ascetic, bearing no ornament save that of the quiet spirit of Shiva himself, the Jeshtrudra shall command the Happy Valley long after we and those that come shall have passed away".[14]

Hazratbal Shrine

Hazratbal shrine is the representative of an amalgam of Mughal and Kashmirian architecture. While Martand is built on one of the most picturesque sights on high plane, Hazratbal is built along one of the most beautiful sights on the banks of the Dal Lake within the amphitheatre of chinar trees.

The mosque at Hazratbal (*'Hazrat'* stands for the prophet and '*bal*' means the hair) on the western bank of the Dal Lake has acquired special sanctity for it is the repository of the holy relic of the prophet and hence highly venerated. It was originally built by Emperor Shah Jahan and depicts curious blend of the Mughal and Kashmirian architectures. The walls and the portico of the mosque were built in brick masonry, resting on a plinth of dressed stone. The roof in three tiers follows the traditional style of Islamic architecture of Kashmir. The carvings on the walls and the latticed windows of the mosque are specimens of exquisite art. In recent years it has been completely renovated and redone in white marble.

As to how the sacred relic came to Kashmir is an interesting story. It is recorded that, "the relic initially remained with the descendants of the Prophet and then it was handed over to Sayyid Abdullah, the *Mutwali* of the Prophet's shrine in Medina. In the year 1634 the Sayyid along with his family came to India and lived in Bijapur (Deccan), where the ruler granted him a jagir and he stayed permanently there. Prior to his death he handed over the sacred relic to his son, Sayyid Hamid. Latter continued to live in Bijapur till the kingdom was conquered by Aurangzeb in 1692 AD Sayyid Hamid went to Jahanabad to get his jagir returned, where he met a prosperous Kashmiri trader by the name of Khwaja Nur-ud-din Ashwari and sought his help. The Khwaja readily gave him the money and requested for the sacred relic in exchange. Emperor Aurangzeb wanted to keep the sacred relic at Ajmer, thus Khwaja Nur-ud-din Ashwari was detained and deprived of the relic. Nur-ud-Din was so shocked that he could not bare the loss and he died at Lahore. Prior to his death he expressed his last wish to a friend Khwaja Medanish that he should try to get the relic back and take it to Kashmir and keep it there at a suitable place. Aurangzeb handed over the relic to Khwaja Medanish, who carried it to Kashmir, where, in the words of Khwaja Azam, an eyewitness, "There was great enthusiasm among the people who rushed like a stream in flood to pay their homage to the holy relic. After being kept for sometime in the Khanqah of Naqshband it was finally lodged in the mosque at Hazratbal. The body of Khwaja Nurud-din is also buried near the Ziarat."

Madin Saheb

This mosque is a typical distinctive symbol of Muslim wooden architecture. It is the earliest important mosque and tomb in this style. This prominent mosque was raised in the 15th century and was built on the plinth of a Hindu temple. Some carved temple columns are in the porch of this mosque, and two similar columns have been used in the inner chamber of the tomb raised in memory of the saint. The base is square and is built entirely of materials belonging to the plinth of a mediaeval temple. The super structure of four walls, adorned externally with trefoil brick niches represents Islamic influence. Its entire wall surface was decorated with glazed tiles, particularly in the spandrels. These glazed tiles were multi-coloured and as such presented a brilliant spectacle. Most of these have unfortunately been removed, stolen and sold out of Srinagar. A few fragments have been preserved in the museum at Srinagar. What is noticeable is that the tile work in its style, design and execution has every appearance of Persian influence. Its wooden doorway is elaborately carved. A pyramid of earth and birch bark roof, overgrown with flowers, covers the chamber. On the apex of the roof was the spire. To the north of the mosque is the saint's tomb. The principal features of the first tomb are the glazed and moulded blue bricks, which are studded at intervals in the exterior walls, the semi-circular brick projections on the drum of the main dome, and the moulded brick string courses and sunk panels on the drums of the cupolas.[15]

Nicholls in his archaeological report writes, "Though the tomb of Madni is a small building quite neglected and very dilapidated, yet it possesses a feature of extraordinary value and interest in its coloured tile work, fragments of which are still adhering to its walls. The tile work is made in squares with various brilliant colours in contrast with each other on the same piece of tile. But its great interest lies in subject which is represented in the southern half of the spandrel of the great archway in the east facade. The representation is that of a strange beast. Besides this spandrel, there is more tile work in the building, thus showing that tile work was used on masonry buildings in Kashmir before Mughal days. The tomb is supposed to have been built about 1444 AD in the reign of Zain-ul-Abidin. Jahangir bears testimony to the remains of the other buildings which were still to be seen in Kashmir during the gay Emperor's visits."[16]

Shah-e-Hamdan Mosque

It is reported that Kutub-ud-Din built the present Shah-e-Hamdan mosque by dismantling the existing temple dedicated to Goddess Kali. Roof of this mosque, a conical pyramid, unlike domed Muslim architecture, apparently retains the original Hindu temple design.

This mosque was built in honour of Sayyed Ali Hamadani, who came to Kashmir from Hamdan in Persia. The mosque, primarily made of timber got burnt and was rebuilt in 1479 and once again in 1731 AD A spring exists within the premises of the main structure, it is reported that recently, while the paramilitary forces were scanning the spring for the hidden weapons, reportedly dumped by the militants into the spring, a large number of damaged and broken idols were retrieved.

Pather Masjid

Pathar masjid meaning- a stone mosque-built entirely of large and massive stone blocks-is one of the largest mosques built by Mughals-Empress Nur Jahan in 1632 AD in Srinagar. It comprises nine arches with the large central arched portico. The arched openings are enclosed in shallow, decorative, cusped arches, in turn enclosed in rectangular frames. Having been built by a woman, locals do not use this mosque for offering prayers.

A word about residential architecture

A *Kashur* did not invest his architectural talent only in building monuments of repute. Residences and buildings of common usage that reflect the architectural expertise of their builders were also built with as much thought and care. Utilitarian and convenient sections of a home like the trellised windows, the chequered and interwoven (*Khutumband)* ceilings and the mural painted (*Gach*) walls of these habitats are in it self representative of the KSP's architectural sense. It is about such constructions that, Mirza Hyder writes, "The beauty of their exterior defies description, the buildings of Srinagar are high and extensive, each floor containing apartments, halls galleries and towers, and their beauty is such that all who behold them for the first time bite the finger of astonishment with the teeth of admiration."[17]

Such were the creations of the KSP architects and builders of the valley and yet we have been responsible, in the past, during some unusual times and circumstances for the destruction of these edifices. Time shall prevail and undo the harm that has been done, and shall repair and preserve what is left as foot prints, and from these foot prints once again new monuments shall arise and stand tall in their glory.

Shesh Nag

CHAPTER 11

KASHUR THE LANGUAGE-SINGLE BINDING LINK

Tenacious grip of a binding link is always reflected by the longevity and the social standard of the group it binds. To identify, and label a group or a community as a single unit, we have to consider specific characteristics associated with the group or the community at large. The significant binding links that act as the assessing medium or say the barometer of the specific group are in the order of importance: spoken language-mother tongue, geographic environment, social and religious traditions, rites and rituals, ceremonies and festivals, physical features, attire and food habits. Out of the given list, environment, physical features, attire and religious traditions are all variables, dependent on the location and time scale that they belong to. What we, in *Kashur*, refer as *samay-aachar* (time bound) and *desh-aachar* (place bound).

Ii is, however, the language spoken by the people that is the single fool proof medium of binding or identifying any community or clan. "One's *pehchan* (identity) as a member of the *beradari* (community) begins with the knowledge of the mother tongue—the first link to ones identity."[1] Pococke, however, states otherwise and believes, "The similarity of religious manners, affords stronger proof of original identity than languages."[2] Language he believes under goes change.

In the case of the KSP identity, this fact stands to be interpreted differently. Their religious stream has undergone greater metamorphic changes, than their language. Though, it is an established fact that Kashmiri language has definitely changed in the process of its evolution, like every other language system, yet it has retained, down the ages, its individual accent, intonation, pronunciation and phonetics. These factors in turn, have left a stark, audible and pronounced imprint on the speaker's speech. So much so, when a Kashmiri speaks in any other Indian or European language, he or she can easily be identified. This character of the *Kashur* language acts as a perfect binding link, for all the KSP's, be they Hindu, Muslim or Sikh or any other Kashmiri speaking group.

KASHUR THE LANGUAGE-SINGLE BINDING LINK

An effort has been made to trace the history of '*Kashur*'-the language spoken by the Kashmiris-from the very initiation and it's evolution to the present times. It is a study from a lay person's perspective, no doubt substantiated by the observations of experts, for I do not claim to tread in to the domain of the specialised linguistic studies.

Kashmiri language-*Kashur*- as the natives of the land call it, is full of many a paradoxes. It is the language spoken by less than five million people, a miniscule group in the world of languages; yet it is the most researched language. It has been the enigma of scholars now for nearly last two centuries. It is a language that has no alphabet of its own. Yet it is recognised and incorporated in the 8th schedule of the Indian constitution. A language that is supposed to be more than '8000 years old', but does not have a single written literature extant, till up to the 13th century AD. Either because the literature in olden times was compiled in Sanskrit, or what ever was compiled in Kashmiri was destroyed and vandalised by the invaders; like the rest of the literary treasures of Kashmir. One is forced to assume that Kashmiri is a language with mysterious origin; yet it is one of the most scientific languages phonetically.

LOCATION

The northern most state of India is divided into three geographic divisions, i.e. Ladakh, Kashmir and Jammu. *Koshur (*Kashmiri) is the language spoken by the inhabitants of the valley. It would be, however, wrong to state that its domain is restricted to the valley alone. It is, in fact, also spoken in some pockets of Jammu where Kashmiris have migrated or were forced to move, under historic pressures, at different times of their long journey, from antiquity to 21st century space age. It was in this process of movement of Kashmiri's that this language moved out of the valley to Doda, Kishtwar and Baderwah, south of valley and parts of Punch district in the south west of the valley. Today, thanks to post Independence migration, it is also spoken in each and every state of India, in every continent (that includes even Antarctica), i.e. wherever a Kashmiri has gone or settled in, *Kashur* can be heard or even written. According to the 1971 census of India, Kashmiri language and its dialects are spoken in an area of approximately 16,000sqkm and total number of Kashmiri speaking people is around 24, 38,360 with the main concentration in the Kashmir valley. I am sure by now the number of the Kashmiri speakers would have increased considerably i.e. in proportion to the increase in the population of the KSPs'.

Dialect

Kashmiri is mostly referred as a dialect and to justify this assumption, Prof J.L.Koul asks, "Do we have a Kashmiri alphabet? Has there been ever, in our history, Kashmiri in use as a subject for study, either as a language or as a literature? I think not. Had this been so we should have had an alphabet of our own, no matter what the script would have been? We should, that is to say, have had a set of letters to indicate all the sounds of our language, the sounds of which are common to other neighbouring Indian languages, as well as those which are peculiar to it." [No3]Thus he prefers to call it a dialect and so do most of the Kashmiris.

Inspite of the given perception that it is a dialect, a lot of research on the Kashmiri language has been carried out to establish its origin, language grouping and philology by a perceptible number of Indologists, linguists, philologist, grammarians, historians, travellers and common folks. Why so? Is it because Kashmir has a unique place in the history of Bharata that is India? Is it because this abode of Gods, the Sati Desha was the Shrada Peeth of yester years? Or is it, the Kashmiri speaking people in spite of not having any alphabet of their own have borrowed three scripts i.e. Sharda, Devanagri and Persio-Arabic to write their Kashmiri. It may be noted that KSP's have not adapted these scripts after modifying or introducing any new signs or letters to indicate sounds peculiar to Kashmiri, such as Roman alphabet was adapted to Turkish, Indonesian and Malay and Persio-Arabic to Pashto and Sindhi.

O.N.Koul and Peter Edwin Hook say, "Kashmiri is assumed to be about '8,000 year's' old dialect. It has initiated a lot of interest amongst linguists and scholars. Since at least the time of Patanjali, as is evident from the given verse: *abhijanasi, devadatta, Kashmiran gamisyamah* (excerpt from his discussions of Varttika 22 ad1.1.44)."[4]

We have to accept that Kashmiri is one of the oldest ethnic dialects. Its origin is embedded some where in the pre-historic era, when Neolithic humans felt the need to a vocal mode of communication to convey and share their feelings. It is very difficult to pinpoint that time period. The Kashmiri dialect has travelled a long way to evolve upto the stage when it had a specialised script-the Sharda script-an *upper- Brahmasha* of Sanskrit and, finally arrived at the present status of a language recognised under the 8thschedule of the Constitution of India. It has mostly been a spoken dialect, which like many other dialects has been liable to continual mutations and alterations.

Kashmiri, both ancient and modern, is a language whose philological importance is well known to scholars. Dr Grierson reputed for his linguistic research of Indian languages writes, "Besides those who wish to study Kashmiri for its own sake, it is also of considerable interest to comparative philologists. I know of no Indo Aryan language, which in her grammatical construction is so naked and unashamed. With, but the thinnest veil of mystery, she freely displays to the ardent eye of the student, not only the general contour of her graceful form but each joint, each articulation. Devoid of every feeling of false modesty she discloses many a secret, which is jealously hidden by her more prudish sisters of the south. It is sufficient to point out that, a study of Kashmiri is an essential preliminary to any enquiry which deals comparatively with the mutual relations of the modern Aryan vernaculars of India."[5]

Research Works

In the early twentieth century quite a few research works were published on the linguistic content of *Kashur*. Topping the list is the monumental work of George A Grierson *The Linguistic Survey of India* and Pandit Ishwar Kaul's-four volumes of Kashmiri English dictionary and Grammar. Grierson also published some articles on *Kashur* language in the Journals of the Asiatic Society of Bengal and in his massive publication *The Linguistic Survey of India.*

Braj Kachru writes, "Grierson and C.Temple have put every admirer of Kashmiri literature in their permanent debt by their meticulous scholarly work on Kashmiri language and Literature. N. C. Cook and others have since added to the legacy."[6] These efforts were followed by Pandit Kaula's work on Paninian description of the language in Sanskrit.

In the later part of the 20th century, we have a large number of research works published; some detailed and some on specific aspects like: grammar, phonetics, literature etc. like T Grahame Bailey's work on *Kashmiri phonetics,* followed by the works of Fredric Drew, Dr. Buhler, Morgenstierne, Block Turner, Suniti Siddheshar Verma, Prof. Shrikanth Toshkhani, Suniti K. Chaterji, Braj B. Kachru, Prof. J.L.Kaul, Dr, Shashi Shekhar Toshkhani and. O.N.Kaul etc. To make a language so research worthy, definitely forces us to assume that there is something unique about it. "It is one such language which has amalgamated many a language systems and yet retains individuality. Its basic stock is Sanskrit, phonetic inventory and phonology is Altaic North, and maximum vocabulary and writing system (at present) are of Islamic heritage." [7]

KASHUR THE KASHMIRI SPEAKING PEOPLE

No two scholars agree to same point of view on any aspect of this language, like its grouping, classification, linguistics and even the script of the language. Different theories have been put forward, particularly regarding its origin and linguistic grouping. Yet we can not deny, that Inspite of variances, there is a dominant strain of connectivity running through the basic perceptions of most of the linguists and researchers of *Kashur* language, as we shall perceive from the versions quoted below.

ORIGIN OF THE *KASHUR* LANGUAGE

A number of research workers ascribe its origin to Dardic group of Aryan or Indo Iranian, while some others, especially the locals, ascribe it to the Sanskrit group of the Indo-Aryan Vedic languages. Prior to going in to the details about the reasons given for such categorization, it might be prudent to go to the very source of the language. For every chrysalis has an embryo and it is that embryo we have to locate. For that we have to go beyond the period of recorded history-the Prehistoric era- of which we may not have written words, but abundant proof, like the discovery of the stone implements at Burzahoma, as witness to the fact that humans were living in Kashmir in the Neolithic age. It is during those times a mode of communication or articulation would have come in to existence. Languages are always born out of compulsive instincts of communication. It is these early dwellers of Kashmir who would have created a mode of conversation or say a dialect that we call *Koshur* today. Just, as the earliest humans discovered the conch shell as a tool or means of signalling to the distant members of its clan: a signalling system, which, in course of time, evolved into modern communication system. Similarly all dialects initially must have developed in the form of preliminary and crude form of speech, to finally evolve into literary excellence. *Koshur,* when it must have originated millennia ago, would neither have belonged to a Dardic group nor to a Sanskrit one. Gradually over the centuries it must have evolved, concretised, polished and systematized according to the geographic environment, social needs, cultural identities and intellectual progress. We do not have any records to prove whether it was written in any form and what was the script but surely it was there when Kashyapa an explorer, traveller, and a discoverer landed in the valley of Kashmir. Nilamat Purana compiled in Sharda is an evidence enough to prove the point. Nila, the king of Kashmir, at that time, apparently had such a command on the language that he could lay down a set of laws and rules to be followed by the inhabitants of the valley.

We have evidences to prove that Kashmir valley had a very developed agricultural society 6,000 to 7,000 years ago. It is but logical to presume that such a society would have had proper means of conversation, which obviously must have been the off shoots of the primitive words (two letter words in local dialect) like *ath'* (hand), *nus*,(nose), *be'*(me), *che'* (you), *n'a* (no), *k'er* (do*), n'er* (arm), *m'as* (hair), *kh'as* (climb) and *v'ath* (way), etc.

It is this elementary language system, which has evolved over thousands of years and attained the status of a perfect, scientific language. Every language changes according to the habitat and according to the degree of social and cultural status of the particular people. A.M.Ghatage records, "Besides these factors, languages develop in a spontaneous fashion due to the inner forces which manifest as so many tendencies peculiar to each language. All languages are perpetually growing and have their special evaluative tendencies, which depend upon the earlier history of the language and are realised in successive stages."[8]

Hasnain seems to be supportive of the same argument when he writes, "The aboriginal tribe of the valley evolved their own language, which can be termed as *Kashmiri.* But with the advent of the Aryans, the Kashmiri underwent a change and was replaced by the language of the outsiders. Though it was completely sanskritised in succeeding centuries, yet, the Kashmiri continued to adhere to their vowel intonation as well as their own way of pronunciation. They also did not forsake their own method of forming sentences. Research into the Kashmiri linguistics would surely reveal that original Kashmiri-words, idioms and proverbs can still be traced in the present day Kashmiri language, which is but a mixture of many languages, such as Aramaic, Sanskrit and Persian."[9]

To mention, as an example, a few Kashmiri words used as invectives, abuses and gentle remonstrations, like: *pra'h ga'chi'nay (*be haunted); *thr'ath pe'yn'ey* (be struck by lightening); *Tche' za'ha'rbaad* (be inflicted by anthrax) and *Ad'chot* (Life is cut short) etc bespeak of their aboriginal origin. These words are crude both in sound and genre, and lack the delicacy of a highly developed language like Sanskrit and, to be honest, have almost got extinct from the vocabulary of the modern KSP's.

G.R.Gierson localising the place of origin and grouping of *Kashur* writes, "Kashmiri belongs to the Dard group of the Dardic languages. It is most nearly related to Shina. It has, however, for many centuries been subject to Indian influence, and its vocabulary includes a large number of words derived from India,- implication of the term 'Indian' if it refers to language, is not clear since India has a different language in every state- its speakers hence maintain that it is of Sanskrit origin, but a close examination reveals that illustrious as was the literary history of Kashmir, and learned as have been its Sanskrit Pandits, this claim of Sanskrit origin can not be sustained for the vernacular of the later Kashmiri is a very old language. Three words in it are quoted by Kalhana (circa 1150AD) in his *RajaTarangni* and these are not very different from the language of the present day. The words are "*Ranga'ss He'lu din'na*", which in modern Kashmiri would be *Ra'nga's Helu dyun*. The village of Helu is to be given to Ranga". We have in these words probably the earliest extant specimen of Kashmiri. Those who may desire to study old Kashmiri literature will find that, Hindu writers have been more extensive and valuable than that the Muslims. Besides these two differences of dialect, Kashmiri has numerous local variations, which is to be expected of a language spoken in such a mountainous country where inter-communication must have been restricted at the time of the origin of the language and even later".[10]

Grierson while defending his argument adds, "That the commonly held perception of the natives about its Sanskrit origin is because, it would be most unnatural if the bulk of the Kashmiri vocabulary were not closely connected with the vocabularies of the neighbouring Sanskrit languages, since Sanskrit flourished in the valley for nearly a period of 2,000 years and many a masterpieces of Sanskrit, besides at least one of the great Indian religions-Shaivism-was founded in Kashmir, and some of its most eloquent teachers flourished on the banks of Vitasta (Jhelum), some of the greatest Sanskrit poets were born in the valley, and even issued in Sanskrit language a world famous collection of folklore. Hence it is but natural for the Kashmiri to believe in the Sanskrit origin of *Kashur*."[11] In reality, "It's phonetic system, its accidence, its syntax, its prosody is Dardic, and it must be classed as such and not as Sanskrit form of speech."[12]

Sir Herbert Risley supporting the Dardic theory writes, "When we find small tribes clinging to a dying form of speech, surrounded by the dominant languages, which have superseded the neighbouring tongues, and which are beginning to supersede this form of speech also, we are fairly entitled to assume that the dying language used is the original tribal one, and that it gives a clue to the racial affinities of the tribes who speak it. This is the case with the Dardic languages." [13]The whole of Daradistan, prior to the arrival of Pisachas, was once inhabited by the ancestors of the present owners of Hunza and Nagar (now under the control of Pakistan). H.Risley writes, "It is not impossible that they were identical with Nagas after whom every spring in Kashmir is named, and who, according to Kashmiri mythology, were the aboriginal inhabitants of the happy valley before the arrival of the Pisachas. Be that as it may, at the bottom of all the Dardic languages, there is a small and quite unimportant element of Burushaski-the unclasped non-Aryan Burushaski of Hunza and Nagar."[14]

KASHUR THE LANGUAGE-SINGLE BINDING LINK

According to J.C.Chaterji, "The vocabulary of the Kashmiri language has some Sanskrit words, but the language itself is not basically Sanskrit. It belongs to the Dardic group, which branched off from the parent Aryan group and had a parallel development with Indo-Aryan. In some respects, it shares the characteristics of both the Indo-Aryan and the Iranian. The Indian grammarians dubbed this Dardic language Paisaci. The Dardic-speaking people appear to have lived originally in the Pamirs whence they migrated to Kashmir through Chitral and Gilgit. The language of Kashmir contains a sprinkling of Burushaski, the language of the non-Aryan race of the same name." [15]

Fredric Drew while supporting the Sanskrit connection writes, "Kashmiri language is of great interest for its elaborate inflexions and for the relation, both in vocabulary and grammar, which it bears to Sanskrit. Kashmiri has hitherto been spoken of as a language quite by itself, unlike any other spoken tongue, and not allied, except in the distant way in which all the Aryan tongues of India are allied to one another with any neighbouring speech. Some of the most notable characters of Kashmiri are the position of the sound 'z' and the use of it where Hindi dialect would have 'j' and of the sound 'ts' where in Hindi there would be 'ch'."[16]

Dr. S. S.Toshkhani, on the basis of some letters prevalent in the present *Kashur* vernacular states, that *Kashur* belongs to the earliest era of Indian languages, for these letters are found only in the early Vedic language and are not in use in the modern Sanskrit. Such as:

Kashmiri *(Yudh-vi)* Sanskrit and Indian version, *(yadhi)* Vedic Aryan version *(yaduvi)*

Kashmiri *(adh)* Sanskrit and Indian language *(ab, tb,t'oo, Atah)* Rig Vedic *(adha)*

Kashmiri *(achu-n)* . . . *(aana,gusna, prevesh)* Vedic *(ateyeti derivate of achati)* This letter is not found in any Indian language.

Kashmiri (*tashun*) (*khurakna)* Vedic *(taksh)*

Kashmiri *(baste)* . . . *(.Dhokni*) Vedic *(vaste)* etc[17]

Dr. Sedeshar Verma is also of the same opinion as that of Dr. Toshkhani about the antiquity of the *Kashur* and in support of the argument provides a list of Kashmiri letters as off shoots of the Vedic language: like *'Kulal'* for Kashmiri *'kraal'* and states that the Sanskrit letter *'kumbkaar'* from which the Devanagri '*kumhaar* derives, belongs to a much latter stage.[18]

Suniti Chaterji writes, "The Dardic branch forms a sort of half way house between its sister branches of Indo-Aryan and Indo-Iranian, partaking some of the special characteristics of both. The more important Dardic speeches are Kashmiri dialects, which have come very largely under the influence of the Sanskrit."[19]

Dr. Buhler remarks, "Kashmiri has the greatest importance for the comparative grammar of the Indian vernaculars, because, for instance, it so clearly reveals the manner in which the new cases of the declension have been formed from the old bases, a point which in other languages is exceedingly difficult".[20]

I believe that the dialect *Kashur* was the innovation of the aboriginal *Kashur* (the people) irrespective of whether he or she belonged to the higher reaches of Daradistan and Chillas or the valley of Kashmir. The foundation of *Kashur* was laid by them, and the first language to overlay and influence it, was the Sanskrit spoken by the Kashyapa's clan who were proficient enough in the Vedic language. It was this interaction that, in time, enhanced and supper imposed the basic tongue. Later, other influences followed. One can use a simple anomaly. If a substance as delicate as a drop of water falls, non-stop, on a particular spot of a rock, it is bound to leave it's impress on it permanently. What to say of a language, which by character is always supposed to be influenced, and also to influence mutually other languages. The aboriginal Kashmiri being a part of the Indo-Vedic Aryan civilisation, his or her language / dialect was bound to be influenced by the same and, like every other language; *Kashur* improved itself to attain the status of a complete language system.

Various Dialects of *Kashur*

Even though the valley is a small geographic unit, still there are two to three dialects in use, and there is a great difference between the urban *Kashur* that is spoken in Srinagar and the rural *Kashur* that is spoken in the villages. The language of the urban areas is more influenced by the historical events, which resulted in intrusions of many a foreign dynasties, and their languages. For example in the city of Srinagar we come across a Persian synonym for nearly every *Kashur* word that is spoken by its inhabitants. Where as the *Kashur* spoken in the villages is more akin to the aboriginal dialect. Their vocabulary is rich and the phrases are direct, unambiguous and are full of poetic thoughts

Dr. Buhler has tried to divide the Kashmiri dialect in to three geographic divisions. He writes, 'The dialect of *Kamraj*, the northern portion of Kashmir, differs from the dialect of *Maraj,* the southern portion, and both differ from that of *Yamraj*, that is Srinagar.'[21]

Dr. Grierson, however, is of the opinion that, in spite of minor differences in the standard Kashmiri of the valley it does not entitle us to divide it in to further dialects. He agrees that the *Kashur* spoken by the Muslim KSP differs from that of the Hindu KSP's; both in vocabulary as well as pronunciation. "The Muslim Kashmiri has pronounced effect of the Persian language where as the Hindu still sticks to Sanskrit origins. The Hindu dialect is purer Kashmiri than that of the Muslim, because the Hindus have a bond with the original language that is the only language they have inherited and learned from their ancestors, where as Muslims who are later converts towards a religion, which prevailed in Persia and was brought both by missionaries and invaders from those lands, they are more akin to the Persians and adopt it to spread its influence in their life style and speech form."[22]

The Muslims have a tendency to shorten the final vowels, like Muslims say, '*kya*' and Hindu will say, '*ky'ah*'. Muslims often tend to avoid pronouncing the alphabet 'r' in a word. As for example, a Hindu says '*bronth*' (before); a Muslim pronounces it as '*bonth*', a Hindu says, '*grangal*'; a Muslim pronounces it as '*gangal*,' (distraction). We can not deny that there is a pronounced distinction between the language spoken by the village folk and that of the urban areas. The rustic Kashmiri has preserved the original forms, inflections and pronunciation of the *Kashur*, which is missing in the refined *Kashur* of the towns and cities; something universally common to all other language systems.

O.N Kaul renames these two dialect divisions, as the social dialect and the regional dialect. Braj B. Kachru further divides the social dialect as Sanskritised and Persianised Kashmiri. These dialects vary in phonology, morphology and vocabulary

The regional dialect again is subdivided as: (a) one spoken in the valley and (b) spoken outside the valley. Dialects spoken in the valley are categorised *(i) Maraz, (ii) Kamraz and (iii) Yamraj* (Srinagar,) as given by Dr. Buhler. The last variety is used by the mass media. However, these divisions are interchangeable. Besides these dialects there are many a minor spoken dialects like that of *Siraji, Rambani, Pongli, Pahari, Kishtawari* and so on.[23]

We can conclude that in local parlance the Kashmiri dialect is divided into two groups: the rustic Kashmiri and the urban Kashmiri.

The rustic Kashmiri can be further subdivided into Pahari and village dialect. Pahari dialect has the influence of Dogri and Lahandi languages where as the rustic dialect spoken in the villages have the traces of the aboriginal *Kashur.*

In the urban areas it, can be further sub-grouped into: a) Kashmiri spoken by the Hindus and b) Kashmiri spoken by the Muslims.

SCRIPT

Written *Kashur,* the language of the Kashmiris, is said to be a '*Prakrit*' of the pure and original Sanskrit, and some say, that it was in former times a written language in Sharda characters; latter being a brother form of the Devanagri. Most of the learned Kashmiris state, the *Kashur* vocabulary in the present times is a polyglot and that out of every hundred words 25 will be Sanskrit, 40 Persian, 15 Hindustani, and 10 Arabic. The remaining 10 will be Tibetan, Turki, Dogri, and Punjabi.

Dr. Buhler writes, "*Kashur* has a grammar of its own, which distinctly recalls one's faint efforts in Sanskrit grammar. It is highly inflectional, and offers not only forms of reduplication, but also makes changes within the root . . . . . . I feel therefore not certain that the Sharada alphabet is not one of the Ancient literary alphabets, dating perhaps from the times of the Guptas, or earlier. Kashmiri is a Prakrit, one of the languages descended from the Sanskrit, or rather from one of the dialects out of which the classical Sanskrit was formed. It differs, however, very considerably from all its Indian sister-tongues. Nearest to it comes Sindhi."[24] While C.L.Nagri writes, Sharda is a modified script akin to Sanskrit.

Prof J.L. Kaul does not agree that Sharda was, "the script used to write *Kashur* that expressed more or less adequately, all the sounds of Kashmiri alphabet. Nor was the Perso Arabic script ever adapted to Kashmiri so as to enable it to express more or less adequately the sounds peculiar to our language." [25] He does, however, accept the existence of a few manuscripts of Kashmiri written in these scripts

Whether or not *Kashur* the language is a *Prakrit* or a modified Sanskrit script, it is considered a very developed, profound and phonetically perfect language, which is capable of expressing any inflection, mood or situation. It is said to posses, almost a scientific grammar, which is rich enough to express high philosophy and mundane situations with equal ease, and has expressions and proverbs for every stage and incident of life. A language that is capable of having a literature of its own. A literature, which constitutes all the branches of literary expression like-prose, poetry, dramatics, essays, encompassing humour, tragedy, mysticism, love, satire, folk lore, philosophy and so on.

Yet! Why does not Kashmiri/ *Koshur*, like that of the other Indian languages, have a proper standard script of its own, is a profound question.

It is my belief that Kashmiri was still a spoken language and the Kashmiri speaking people most likely had not developed the art of writing when Kashyapa, who belonged to the later Indo-Vedic-Aryans reportedly, came to Kashmir, around 3000 BC ? Sanskrit happened to be the language of early Vedic people, which had, by then, attained some eminence in the world of languages, especially in the Bharata and Kashyapa's clan was able to introduce a ready-made Sharda script of Sanskrit into the valley. The native Kashmiri speaking people in majority had been over powered and they either perished or were pushed high up into the mountainous terrain of Dard and Chillas regions. Those few who continued to stay in the valley were able to continue the colloquial language, but were not capable enough to prepare a Kashmiri script. One cannot positively ascertain that the Kashmiri of those days of antiquity would have been as rich in its vocabulary and phraseology as it is in the present form. The latter Indo-Vedic *Saraswats,* who settled in the valley, in course of time, adopted Kashmiri as their everyday spoken dialect, and with their superior intellect were able to shape, trim, enhance and enrich the language almost to the same standard as that of the Vedic Sanskrit that they used for writing. Since they possessed a script that they could use for writing Kashmiri, they probably did not feel the need of creating a separate script for Kashmiri. Instead they derived and used its Sharda and Devanagri character for writing the *Kashur*. As long as the KSP belonged to Hindu and Buddhist stream this script worked fine. It was the period of change over in the 13th/14th century, which was so drastic that there was complete chaos in every aspect of the KSP life as recorded earlier. This resulted in neglect and metamorphosis of the, 'written word' and later the Muslim Kashmiris incorporated Persio-Arabic script for writing Kashmiri language as that was akin to their adopted Islamic culture.

Regarding the scripts adopted for writing Kashmiri, Grierson, in his essays on *Kashmiri grammar* writes, "Nearly all the old written literature of the country is Hindu. Hindus use Sharda and Devanagri characters. There is no fixed system of spelling Kashmiri and hence every writer is a law unto himself. The true alphabet of Kashmiri is Sharda. Anyone who is not familiar with the pronunciation of the language from practical experience, it would be impossible to gain merely a faint idea of the correct pronunciation of the words. The Sharda system is based upon the actual facts of the language. Kashmiri differs from other Indian languages in using vowels at the end of the words, which are either silent or nearly so." [26]

Religious differences are evident in vocabulary and choice of alphabet. Muslims employ Persian and Arabic words freely; they also use the Persian form of the alphabet (Persio-Arabic), to write Kashmiri, although it is not truly suited to the task as it lacks symbols for the many Kashmiri vowel sounds. The majority of the educated Kashmiri Hindus favour words derived from Sanskrit and write Kashmiri in the Sharada alphabet or Devanagari, a script of Indian origin. In printed books written by Hindus mainly Devanagari character is used.

Persio-Arabic script is also used by those KSPs, who are well versed in Urdu language. Rest use the modified computer friendly Devanagri script. A group of computer experts under the guidance of Dr. Roop Krishan Bhat have made a serious attempt to create a new set of modifiers for making the Devanagari script computer friendly, and thus easily type-written, and composed for printing without any difficulty. It has been ensured that the phonetic nuances and pronunciation of *Kashur* is duly taken care of in the given script. On account of this effort we have Kashmiri soft ware like *Arnimall, Yemberzal* and so on.

It wouldn't be factually wrong to say that there is no individual script for writing Kashmiri, till date, in spite of all the efforts of the linguists. It is still written in Devanagri by the Hindu and in Perso-Arabic by the Muslim KSP. Latter script, in recent years, has no doubt gained recognition and is being used in various forms of media, both audio as well as visual, on the stage and publications in almost all forms and expressions in literature that are being written in Kashmiri. Even news papers are published in this language, mainly dominated by the Perso- Arabic influence since the majority is familiar with that script.

PROGRESS OF *KASHUR* FROM A DIALECT TO A RECOGNIZED MEDIUM OF *KASHUR* LITERATURE- A SHORT CHRONOLOGY

A language has to conform to a certain set standards to gain its rightful place in the domain of any literature. It has to attain an exhaustive vocabulary and have the fluency of both vernacular and written form, to enable it to compose in all the branches of literature. Kachru writes, "The development of *Kashur* literature is related to the socio-cultural, historical and linguistic context of the Kashmir valley. Its literature is distinct from other literatures of India due to the linguistic characteristics of Kashmiri and an essentially bicultural context in which Kashmiri language and literature have developed". No27

When exactly did the process of writing in Kashmiri start is very difficult to establish for want of proper-recorded material. Bilhana, in the 8th century AD, writes about the proficiency of women in Sanskrit besides their mother tongue albeit *Kashur*.

KASHUR THE LANGUAGE-SINGLE BINDING LINK

Dr. Shashi Shekhar Toshkhani records that for the first time a few words of Kashmiri are traceable in Jayant Bhat's *Aagmdamar* written in the 9th century AD.

Following it, in the 10th century AD some words that resemble Kashmiri language have been traced in *'TANTRASAR'* composed by the great philosopher Abhinav Gupt.

Alberuni refers to the existence of local language of the Kashmiris In the 10th and the 11th century.

There are many a fragmentary evidences of the written Kashmiri words and sentences in *Mahayana Prakash* by Shitikanth, where in the author writes the language used is (*sarve gocher desh bhasha*) there by meaning the language spoken by the masses.

We find Kashmiri words in *Banasur Kaatha* and in Rajatarangini of Kalhana and also in the *Chumb* manuscripts.[28]

It seems in the Hindu and the Buddhist period of our history, Kashmiri was mainly used as a spoken language. For nearly 2000 years, the Sanskrit culture, after the early Vedic times, dominated the state and hence left a visible mark on the Kashmiri language. As mentioned earlier, may be it was due to the primitive nature of the language, or the social and elitist tendencies, that the need of adopting the Sanskrit script primarily and later the Persio-Arabic character was considered essential for the purpose of writing, and there by leading to the neglect of Kashmiri as a written medium, thus forcing it to remain only a spoken language.

Kelkar writes, "Since Sanskrit was the literary medium of the KSP, there was no steady unified Kashmiri literary tradition as such, till about early 14th century, though works of undoubted importance have been produced from that time onwards."[28]

In spite of the intrusions and dominances of the Indo-Aryan and Indo-Iranian languages, Kashmiri, in the written form, did not die in the unknown realms of past. There was a revival in the early fourteenth century. A revival, most compulsive and indomitable brought through the poetry of a mystic woman-Lal Ded. It is not known with certainty whether she dictated or wrote herself the *Vaakhs*-her couplets, or these were carried forward and spread by word to mouth. But for sure her poetry poured out from the depths of her heart spoke of high philosophy and spiritual ecstasy, through the language of the common masses. Yes the *Kashur* of those times would have been vastly different to what we know today. It would have had more of Sanskrit words of which modern KSP are ignorant. Her poetic compositions, four line stanzas known as *Lal Vaakhs*, spread like wild fire and the people through out the countryside awoke and accepted the beauty of their language. Kashmiri language owes its revival to this great poetess-Lalleshwari; to her poetic expressions, energy of idiom, homely imagery and her capability of expressing the most complex and eclectic sayings in flawless and simple vernacular. Kashmiri dialect was almost born as a language with her works and has since never looked back.

According to Sir George Grierson, the oldest author is Lalla or Lal Ded (born in the reign of Sultan Ala-ud-Din) hundreds of whose verses are quoted all over the valley and are in every one's mouth, MS. collections of which have, from time to time, been made under the Sanskrit title of *Lalavakyani.* Lal Ded's verses were translated by Sir Richard Temple Cambridge University Press, in 1924

Grierson further records names of some highly poetical works written in pure Kashmiri in Hindu dialect that can be dated. The names are Banasurvadha on music—anonymous - written in the reign of Sultan Zain-ul-Abidin, "*Satpar* by Munuji on medicine and astrology, *Lengparan by* Paruthji on the Hindu law of inheritance, *Ramaratteracharita*' a history of Rama, with a sequel entitled the *Lava kusa charjta*, *Krishnavataralila* the history of Krishna, *Sivaparinaya* history of the circumstances connected with Siva's marriage with Parvati." In 1923 these books were printed in the Persian character.

D.N.Raina writes the Shaiva Sufi mystic synthesis of the earliest period is represented by *Lalla Vakayani*, and Sheikh Noor-Ud- Din Noorani. Lala Ded who lived in the 14th century AD expressed herself as a link between the classical Sanskrit traditions of the past and the Persian poetic patterns of later period. While Lal Ded composed *Vaakh* a four line stanza, Noor-Ud-Din the patron saint of Kashmir composed *Shrukh* in which he used the language of the common folk to express his pithy sayings and instructions to the masses, there by excelling in the usage of Kashmiri, for over fifty years (1377-1438 AD), in a simple vernacular. The theme, form and tone, was essentially as that used by Lal-Ded in her Vaakhs.[29]

Kashmiri literature in 15th and 16th century was hugely dominated and enriched by the poetic innovation of the *Vaakh* and *Shrukh.* In 1625 Rupa Bhawani followed in the same vein. She only lengthened the stanzas and there by the *Vatchun* was introduced. The next followed the mystic and lyric strain of *lole* (love and romance) by Haba Khatoon and Arnimall. These were composed as short poems expressing the emotion, mood, longing, anguish and elation of a lover's heart in simple language, what we can term as the language of the heart, the definition of a true poem.

KASHUR THE LANGUAGE-SINGLE BINDING LINK

Next category is the Pandit tradition and it is represented by long narrative poems labelled as *leelas* on Hindu mythological themes, poems written in praise of God, creation and its joys. These compositions were written in highly Sanskritised Kashmiri. This tradition was mainly contributed by Parmanand from 1791-1885. His *Sudamacarit* (the story of Sudama), *Radha svayamvar* (the choice of Radha's spouse), and *Siva Lagan* (the marriage of Siva) are very significant besides other allegorical poems which he wrote.

Prof. J.L. Kaul writes Parmanand's, "Diction was not strained, never stilted, not drawn from book learning but racy of the soil and rich in metaphor. His poetry is written in words obviously drawn from the speech of his day, and even his symbols are figures from the epics which have become a part and parcel."[30]

Finally with the beginning of the 20th century a new era dawned on the literary scene of the Kashmiri language. Its writers achieved the proficiency to compose narrative themes on social ills and reforms, through various mediums of the language. They were no longer restricted only to the poetic format. Writers like Shamsud_din_Hairat and Daya Ram Ganju wrote on social and political themes in the language of the masses, which was 'sweet, rich and expressive'.

Master Zinda Kaul (1884-1965) further enriched his mother tongue. He introduced new rhyme patterns and stanzas in his native language, which were both regular and irregular. A rhyme pattern most modern known as free verse and this style is prevalent to this day. He conveyed the theme of Upanishads in simple and sweet lyrics like *Sumran*

Ghulam Ahmad Mehjoor, poet laureate of Kashmir, dominated the scene from 1925 to 1948. He was known as the 'representative poet of the new literary urges of the time'. He recovered much of the sweetness and music of his native tongue and retrieved it from the straight jacket discipline of the Persian language. He introduced new and modern themes. He expressed the yearning and the hope of the new times to come in his poems like *Vanda chali Shien gale, Bey i bahaar (*winter will loose its sting and spring shall take over) etc. In the same tradition followed poets like Fazil and Ambardar.

Once the poetic tradition of Kashmiri language was well established and the functional role of the language had developed fully, the Kashmiri writers who mainly used either Sanskrit or Persian for the prestigious out pouring of their feelings and intellect, switched over to Kashmiri.

Till early 1940s, formal prose in Kashmiri was practically non existent except for a few stray texts written in restricted type of formal prose by the Christian missionaries in the year 1821 when they presented a translation of the New Testament in the Sharda script, and then the *Pentateuch of Joshua and kings* in 1827 and 1832 respectively. These translation were literal translation and somewhat artificial.

In 1879 Ishwar Kaul also attempted formal prose in his treatise on Kashmiri grammar.

Prof. J.L.Koul believes Pandit Mahadev Gigoo's rendering of the first part of Euclid was the first book printed in Kashmiri. It was printed on hand made paper in 1876.

Srikant Toshkhani made a distinct contribution by writing various textbooks in Kashmiri based on Devanagri script

First literary drama based on Indian mythological theme of *Harischandra- Satech kahvet*-touchstone of truth-was written in 1929. This tradition was continued by the dramatist like Nilkanth Sharma, Tarachand Bismil and Ghulam Nabi Dilsoz.

First realistic social drama-*Gris Sund Gare*-house of a peasant-written in colloquial Kashmiri is by Mohi-ud-din Hajini.

The post '47 literary renaissance had a very positive effect on other literary forms like that of drama, prose, short stories, novel, literary journalism, essays and translations. It was only after the Independence that, as with the rest of the country, the Kashmiris also realised and awoke to the social and economic needs of the times. Many cultural clubs came into existence and plays were written to project the social evils like dowry system, widow marriage. Writers like Prem Nath Pardesi came into limelight. The Sudar Samiti drama clubs and the cultural fronts produced plays like '*Zamin Grees Senz' (*the land belongs to the peasant), *tchuri bazaar* (black market) and *tre bata tchor* (Three over four).

While the literary drama stabilised in Kashmiri eyes, Dina Nath Nadim made a bold attempt in presenting a Kashmiri opera: *Bomber Te Yamberzal* (Bumble bee and the narcissus) in 1953. It was acclaimed all over and later translated into many languages. It was followed by plays as well as operas by Nadim, Prem Nath Dhar, and Mohamed Amin Kamil etc. They were accepted in the literary circles as pioneers of a new format of *Kashur* that had the revolutionary instinct awakened in the society.

The cultural academies and the Kashmir Radio station encouraged the writers to further the cause of Kashmiri plays. Plays were written on all kinds of themes and experiments were made in various styles and techniques. Ali Mohamed Lone's *Vuze chi tsone;* Som Nath Zutshi's *Veth Hind Bathe* ze- two banks of Vitasta and Pushkar Bhan's *Tan ta dak* and *Hero macham* to name a few were landmarks in new techniques. Even the old *Band pather* was revived and adjusted to the needs of the contemporary theatre by Moti Lal Kemu an actor, playwright and a promoter all in one.

Radio plays and TV serials did a yeomen service to the Kashmiri language by popularising it in their literary circles and raising it to the medium of scholarly and artistic expressions, as the language of these plays was closer to the spoken language of the people colloquially and contextually appropriate.

Since the writers in Kashmiri had started experimenting and creating different technical nuances it was but natural to use story writing as one of the forms of expression in order to enrich the language further. Story writing experiments have been going on now for almost four decades and there have been some very successful attempts within the available linguistic resources. Somnath Zutshi's *Yeli phol gash (*when it was dawn) in 1950; Mohamed Amin Kamil's *kathimanz katha(a* tale within a tale); Akhtar Mohi-ud-din's *Sath sangar(*seven hill tops)were landmarks on the path of this new adventure. Writers like Ali Mohamed Lone, Sufi Ghulam Mohamed, Autar Krishen Rahbar, Deepak Kaul Kashmiri, Hari Kishen Kaul and Farooq Masudi carried the torch further.

In recent years, authors like Mohamed Amin Kamil, Ali Mohamed Lone and a few more have tried their skills in writing novels too. There are, in all, about half a dozen novels in the language, which certainly does not count much in any language form. Yet the first step has been taken. One wonders whether this art form will flower and flourish in Kashmiri language as its greatest handicap is the limited readership and inadequate publication facilities.

Though Urdu language, at present, dominates the Kashur script, in spite of that, we have had successful experiments in *Kashmiri* prose as well as translation of works from different languages. Publications of full fledged journals like *Siraaj* and *Son Adab* and essay forms like Autar Kishen Rahbar's *'Kasri Adbich Tvarikh'* (history of Kashmiri literature) are proof enough of the steady progress and evolution of Kashur dialect to the stage of a literary language. Hopefully one day the disparity of the script will be resolved for the benefit of this ancient and aboriginal dialect. [31]

I am confident that in-spite of these limitations, *Kashur,* once freed from the dominance of other languages like Sanskrit, Persian, Urdu and Hindi, will, in times to come, develop into a full fledged language on its own and be capable of composing in every form and pattern of literary exercise, and will produce compositions of great merit, worthy of its ancient heritage.

CHAPTER-12

POLITICAL CHRONOLOGY

{This chapter deals albeit briefly with kings and their representatives who governed the KSP from the earliest eras up to the end of monarchy in 1947 and there after, for I wanted to restrict to the basic theme of the book, i.e. to delineate the evolutionary history of 'Kashur the people'}.

The political chronology of a place and its people emerges during that stage of human evolution, when in the modern sense; the term civilisation applies to that society. That is, when the society has reached the stage of community living, in habitable units, under the supervision of the head of the society, elected or otherwise. Question that confronts us is when that stage came in the life of the Kashmiri Speaking people. There are no valid and dependable records about this period of their existence, as it is true in the case of most primitive and aboriginal ethnic groups.

Fixing the chronology for the earliest eras of the political history of the KSP's is not a simple exercise. Yes! from the extant material available to us we may be able to obtain quite interesting information about the kings who ruled them. But, a list of kings does not represent the history of a country or its people, however accurate and detailed that list might be. It is in this context that Earnest Neve in his book, *Beyond the Pir Panjal.* (1915) writes "The history of Kashmir is wrapped up in mystery . . . Nothing is known of the early ages when the aboriginal tribes dwelt on the shores of the great Kashmir Lake or in the recesses of dense forests. The earliest legends are Hindu. But when or how that cult was introduced we know not- for certain."[1]

Our major source of information about the rulers and the ruling dynasties of Kashmir till eleventh century is Kalhana's Rajatarangini, compiled on the basis of earlier records of chronicles consulted by him. His records have been in some cases, substantiated by some foreign travellers like Hiuen Tsang, Oukang, and Alberuni to name a few. In addition there are some numismatic, archaeological and geographic evidences and folk traditions that further add and support the authenticity of Kalhana's records. There is a major discrepancy however, in the names of the rulers, their eras and period of the reign ascribed by Kalhana to each ruler of Kashmir, up to the 7th century AD. That is when, in the modern sense, the well documented historic period of Kashmir begins, and this historic period is labelled as the Karakota period.

Prior to the Karakotas, Raja Tarangani mentions the names of some well known rulers of Kashmir as in Indian history, like Ashoka, Kanishka and Mihirkhula, and there is a complete resemblance in their reigns, administration and numismatic proof of their presence in the valley. All of them are, however, placed in eras much earlier than given in the Indian historic traditions. One wonders how could two kings of the same name exist in two different eras and yet be so similar to each other.

Some historians believe them to be different entities while most feel that Kalhana must have placed them wrongly. Stein writes it is impossible for us to trace the cause of this remarkable chronological confusion.

Jogesh Chander Dutt comments, "Kalhana is perhaps the only author in Sanskrit now known, who attempted to write a sober history. If he did not write quite in the spirit and style that would be approved in the modern times, it was more the fault of the spirit of the national literature than his own. To him belongs the credit of discovering as it were a new department in literature which it was the duty of his successors to improve."[2]

The political chronology of Kashmiri speaking people can be classified as follows:

i. **Hindu period: from antiquity to 14th century.**

ii. **Muslim period: 14thcentury to1819**AD**-The crusaders, Sultans, Chaks, Mughals and the Pathans**

iii. **Sikh period 1819 -1846** AD

iv. **Hindu Dogra rule 1846 to 1947** AD

v. **Democratically elected government- mainly Muslim majority rule 1947** AD **onwards.**

Maximum space in terms of eras and years is occupied by the Hindu rule, that begins almost simultaneously with the arrival of human civilisation in the valley and it lasted till the end of 13th century AD

As per the available sources, up to the 14th century A.D, Kashmir was principally ruled by the followers of what can broadly be termed as the Hindu faith (Sanatan Dharma) and its subsidiary cults, irrespective of their origin as Indians, Huns, Kushans or Turks. In between there was a shot aberration when Greek suzerainty extended over the valley of Kashmir.

A lot of controversy exists regarding the initial period of the Hindu rule. As mentioned earlier our main source of information about this period is Kalhana's *Raja Tarangani* (The River of kings) and the facts recorded by him in this chronicle. Kalhana states that he had consulted 11 sources prior to writing the history of Kashmir, how far and in what state the material available to him was, is at times questionable. I do not mean to cast any doubt on Kalhana, but he himself acknowledges in the R.T. that, "the narrative of past events has become fragmentary in many respects".[3] He has expressed his doubt regarding the list of kings and their reign as recorded by Chavillakara, and he writes, "This narrative of mine which is properly arranged and which resembles a medicine is useful where the accounts regarding the place and time of kings are fluctuating."[4] He begins the chronology of kings of the valley with Gonanda first and his successors during the year 2268 in the Kali Yuga.[5]

Commenting on the same, Tyndale Biscoe writes, "As per traditions ancient Kashmir has long been under the sway of various bona fide rajas. The first raja that appears is Adgonand, who ascended the throne in 4249 B.C., at a time when Egypt was ruled by demigods." [6] There are no doubt different versions regarding the name and the era of the first ruler of Kashmir.

As per local tradition the culture of kingship in the valley is supposed to have begun with the era of Ramayana. It is believed that Ram Chandra the hero of the epic is supposed to have ruled the valley after the arrival of Kashyapa and his followers from the plains of Bharata. Once these people permanently settled in the valley and started flourishing, the land was divided into several Kuttirajas or kingdoms and each one of these Kuttirajas started dominating the other. This resulted in small and big feuds among the heads of these kingdoms. Since they were all Brahmins, they lacked the merits of kingship. So they invited a Rajput named Dayakaran, son of Purankaran and grandson of Jambu Lochan-the founder of the Jammu town - to restore order, and rule the valley.[7]

Some historians connect him with the line of rajas of Mathura. How ever Dayakaran is taken as the first king of Kashmir as per native tradition and after him 55 Rajah's of *Suraj Bansi* dynasty ruled Kashmir.

Next came the Pandava dynasty and the first King of this dynasty was Gonanda I. Both N.P. and Kalhana begin the political chronology with this ruler. His reign is supposed to have started 20 years before the Mahabharata war.

The premise that political chronology of Kashmir begins at the time of the Kuru war is supported by various researchers and scholars on the basis of various lines of astronomical and chronological arguments. The date that is assigned to the event is supposed to be around 12th to 14th century before the birth of Christ. As per J.C.Dutt scholars like Colebrook, Major Wilford, Dr.Hamilton, and H.H.Wilson, also place the event roughly around the same time.[8]

Yet we can not ignore that there is a general consensus among the historians that the political chronology up to the Mauryan era, especially till the reign of Ashoka is fragmentary, laced with myths and legends, lacking in historical authenticity so for as the dates and time of the ruling dynasties is concerned. It is only with the advent of the mighty Mauryan monarch Ashoka that Kalhana is, to some measure, on historical grounds. And thus it is quite natural the Mauryan rule over Kashmir cannot be doubted.

Starting from the times of Gonanda1, a brief account of most of the rulers, who have influenced very effectively the history of the land till the Karakotas, is given here. As per Kalhana fifty two kings, beginning with Gonanda1, ruled for a period of1266 years

Chronology of Kings

Gonerda or **Gonanda1** is the first sovereign of Kashmir as per Kalhana. He was the contemporary of Jarasanda the king of Magadha, and was involved in a fierce battle with Krishna; in the course of which he was slain by Balrama, Krishna's elder brother.

Damodara1 who succeeded Gonerda was, like wise, killed in a battle with Krishna's friends while returning from a marriage in Gandhar.

Yeshowati wife of Damodara1 was reportedly pregnant at that time and Krishna sent Brahmins to appease her anxiety and established her in the kingdom, a decision not liked by the local populace. Krishna is reported to have silenced the remonstrations of the people with this quotation from the Puranas, "*Kashmirah Parvati tatra raja jneyoHaramsajah /navajneyah sa dushto' pi vidusha bhutimichchhata*" "Kashmir is as Parvati and the king is a portion of the Hara, if even victorious. Therefore he is not to be disrespected by the same who hopes for heaven."[9] As Yeshovati's son Gonanda 11, was a mere infant at the time of Mahabharata war he could not participate in that war. He, however, ascended the throne later.

Following Gonanda 11, the details about the 35 Hindu kings who ruled the country are missing in Kalhana's Rajatarangini. However, an old manuscript titled *Ratnakar Purana* and written on birch bark contained the record of these kings. King Zain-ul-Abidin had a Persian translation of this manuscript made (neither the original nor its translation are extant), a copy of which is said to have been obtained by Hassan, who wrote the history of Kashmir in Persian. Muslim historians of the later era have included the names of these missing kings with a Muslim garb[10], as 1.Isaun-Solomon's cousin, 2.Cassal khan, 3 Meharkaz, 4. Pandu Khan, 5.Ladi Khan, 6.Lidder Khan, 7.Sunder Khan, 8.Cunder Khan, 9 Sunder Khan-II,10Tudu Khan, 1.1Beddu Khan, 12. Mohand Khan, 13 Durbinash Khan, 14 Deosir Khan, 5. Tahub Khan16 Culju Khan, 17 Sukhab Khan, 18. Shermbaram Khan, 9 Naurang Khan 20, Bairag Khan, 21. Gawasheh Khan, 22 Pandu Khan 23 Haris Khan, 24 Sarzil Khan, 25 Akbar Khan, 26. Jabbar Khan, 27 Navder Khan 28. Sanker Khan, the last king named was attacked and slain by Bacar Raj, a neighbouring chief who headed the Kashmiri Nobles driven into the rebellion by the tyranny of the king Sanker Khan.

Sanker Khan's six sons succeeded in due order their father's sovereignty and reportedly met the same fate as their father. Their accession and death were the work of a few hours.

Authenticity of the personages and their names are doubtful. Are these real names of kings who ruled the valley or sheer distortions? Names sound Hindu but the appellation Khan is Muslim and the era in reference is centuries prior to induction of Islam.

Wilson Hymen in an article published in the Journal Asiatic Society, while analysing the list writes, "The list above inserted, although of an obviously fabulous construction still contains matter to excite the curiosity and awaken some speculation to the possibility of any part of it being true; it seems very probable that it originates with tradition and is not altogether unfounded, although no doubt much disfigured and most probably misplaced. The title of Khan attached to the names, few of which appear to be Hindu, indicates a race of Tartar princes . . . . . ."[11] who might have ruled Kashmir at some time. These princes are supposed to have ruled the valley for nearly 13 centuries according to the sources mentioned above. Their certainty is doubtful though.

Further on we have once again to trust Kalhana's chronology. The authenticity of his successors can be verified only by the names of the cities, villages or temples, or Agraharas and Viharas that are still surviving in the nomenclature of places in one form or the other writers Stein.

POLITICAL CHRONOLOGY

Bacar Raja took over the possession of Kashmir after defeating Sankar Khan, the last of the kings' mentioned in the list above, and bequeathed his throne to his descendants.

- **Lava / Lodoo** is supposed to have been a very brave and mighty ruler. He founded the city of Lolara that had 84 lakh stone buildings.[12] Stein writes the only village nearest to this is the Lolab valley, which is even mentioned in Ain-I-Akbari. He bestowed the Agrahara of the *Levara* on the *Ledari* to the Brahmin community and then ascended to heavens.
- **Kusa**-son of Lava followed his father and like wise conferred land upon the Brahmans.
- **Khagendra**-son of Kusa is supposed to have built the town of Khagi and *Ehanmusha-* modern *Khunmoo* and is believed to be the destroyer of the 'hostile Naga dynasty'.
- **Surendra-** Khagendra's son was a philanthropic king and he founded a vihara in the Dard country. He died issue less and was succeeded by a prince named Godhara of another family.
- **Godhara** was follower of Brahmanism. He bestowed many Agraharas to the Brahmans. He was a noble minded king.
- **Suvarna-** who succeeded his father Godhara is reputed for having brought the canal (*kulya*) called Suvarnmani near present Zainapor for irrigating the Karewas. This canal was also known as *Sun-man-kul.*
- **Janaka**—Suvarna's son Janaka established a Vihara and Agrahara near Jalore present Zolur in the district of Vihi. According to Bedia-Ud-Din, Janaka sent one of his princes to invade Persia where Dorab, Brahman's son, defeated him.
- **Sacinara-** ascended his father's throne and is remembered for having founded Agraharas in Sumangasa and Sanara. Stein writes that these two places where seats of iron industry. (Haider Malik also proves the authenticity of these places.) Sacinara died issueless. With the end of this line of rulers' we enter the chronologically recorded era of the rulers of Kashmir termed as the Mauryan Rule

Mauryan Rule

Kashmir's contact with plains of India dates back to hoary antiquity. We have it on Kalhana's authority that the Mauryan Emperor Ashoka founded the city of Srinagara, and set up some religious establishments.[13] It is likely that, during Ashoka's time, there was a brisk social and cultural intercourse between Kashmir and the Indian plains. As a result, quite a number of people from the plains must have settled there, an assumption confirmed by the following references that shows how monks and Theras were going to different countries to preach and spread Buddhist faith after the third Buddhist council.[14] "Ashoka gave up all Kashmir for the benefit of the Buddhist church."[15] These references confirm the social, religious and cultural intercourse between the people of the valley and that of the plains.

Ashoka happens to be the first and the most important Mauryan ruler of the valley. There is, however, a stark discrepancy between the date of Kalhana's Ashoka and Mauryan Ashoka. As per Kalhana, Ashoka the great ascended the throne of Kashmir in 1400BC, while the Mauryan Emperor Ashoka, at best, can be put around 3rd century BC post Alexander's invasion.

Stein writes, this erroneous pedigree to Ashoka, has given rise to certain doubts in the minds of a section of scholars, as to whether the king, referred to by Kalhana, is the same as Ashoka the Great- Mauryan king.[16]

It may be noted that while the discrepancy in the dates concerning the rule of Ashoka are at variance there are, however, a number of similarities that overwhelmingly are in favour of the two being one and the same. Kalhana records:

a) Ashoka adopted Buddhism in Kashmir. Viharas were built in different places like Suskaletra (present Haklitri) and Vitastatra a village near Verinag.

b) The king is referred to as having accepted the doctrine of Jena, alluding to his acceptance of the Buddhist faith and is credited with the construction of several Stupas and caityas in Kashmir,

c) He is also credited to have built the town of Srinagar, a town that was endowed with the 96 lakh of houses, resplendent with wealth. This town was located at the present site of Pandrethan, though the number of houses given raises doubt about the authenticity of the statement,

JALAUKA

As per Kalhana Ashoka's son Jalauka is credited to have freed the country from the invasion of Mlechhas-foreigners- who had over run the country. The term Mlechhas was most probably used to refer to the Bactarian

Greeks.(pre Alexandria Greek colony on the northwest as referred by Bhandarkar).

Jalauka encouraged and welcomed righteous people from other parts of the country, particularly those well acquainted with legal procedures, as righteousness and values of the people under the foreign occupation had gone down. He improved the administrative system of his state.

Kalhana writes, "Kashmir, till then, had only seven main state officials, the Judge, the Revenue Superintendent, the Treasurer, and the Commander of the Army, the Envoy, the Purohita and the Astrologer. Jalauka for the first time established 18 offices in accordance with the traditions of Yudishtara."[17] Apparently Jalauka seems to have introduced the Mauryan principles of administration, which were based on Arthshastra.

Jalauka a staunch follower of Brahmanism, introduced its four fold divisions as till then, the basis of Karma (work), the original Varna-ashram divisions of Brahmanism were not prevalent in Kashmir. Brahmanism was re-established in the valley and its' social order came to be guided on its precepts. Jalauka is celebrated in the history of Kashmir as a great propagator of Savisim and had temples of Shiva made at Buthsher and Vangath. He had the great stone temple *Nandkeshwara* made in honour of Shiva.

Damodara-II: Jalauka was succeeded by Damodara-II, who was also a devote Saiva like Jalauka. He undertook constructions of irrigation facilities for his subjects and in this connection had a dam called *Guddasetu* built near the present Damodar Wuddar with the help of *Guhyakas*-most probably the aboriginal Kashmiri speaking people. These dams were built to provide water to the newly founded city *Damodar Suda* by the king, an act indicative of the fact that the kings were considerate and tried to protect their subjects from the natural disasters like frequent floods and famines

Greek rule

After the fall of the Mauryan Empire, India as a country was practically fragmented into a number of petty states and became an easy prey for foreign invaders. Kashmir, on the north western and northern frontiers of the country, was also victim to such invasions. Tarn suggests that for a few years Demetrius was the lord of a realm, which included southern Kashmir. This fact is further corroborated by Ptolemy who gives the names of two provinces in Menander's home kingdom east of the Jhelum of which *Kasperia* the upper valley of Jhelum, Chenab and Ravi would correspond to southern Kashmir. [18]

Besides Cunningham also records to have found a large number of silver coins of Azes and Azilises on the bank of the Jhelum River in the hills between Baramulla and Jhelum.[19] Yet Dr. Ray writes, "In spite of occasional influence of the Indo-Greek or Indo-Scythe rulers, there can be little doubt that valley in the period following the extinction of Mauryan rule was mostly ruled by local rulers. No authentic account about the names and activities of such rulers, however, can be traced."[20]

Kushans

Kushans, who were supposed to be of Turkish origin, occupied the valley after the Greeks. Kalhana mentions the names of three Kushan rulers: Hushka *(Huvishka)*, Jushka (*Vaheshka)* and.Kanishka. All the three kings were followers of Buddhist faith and during their rule quite a few Stupas and Viharas were constructed. Each one of them had a city built in his name, which exist even to this day under changed nomenclature. Huvishka built the city of *Huvishkpur* now known as Usker; Jushka founded the city *Jushkapur* modern Zukur and Kanishka built the city of *Kanishkapura* modern Kanispur.

It is during the reign of Kushans the illustrious Buddhist scholar Nagarjuna is supposed to have visited the valley to study the Mahayana Buddhism under some learned monks. He resided at Sadarhadvana-modern Harwan. During the Kushan rule the Naga practices and customs were almost given up.

Local Rulers

Abhimmanyu. He was a local ruler of Kashmir who over threw the Kushans by the end of the 3rd century A D. He was a great follower and supporter of Saivism and founded the city of Abhimanyupur- modern Bemina It is during his reign that Sanskrit learning was revived and popularised in the valley, which had suffered and gone into oblivion during the Greek rule. '*Bauddhas*' (Buddhists) lost the control and the Brahmins once again occupied the land. Kalhana records that to escape excessive cold during the winter season caused by incessant heavy snow fall the people along with the rulers were forced to move to Daaruabhisara (an area close to Rajouri and Bhimbar) till a Brahmin named Chandradeva-11, who was descendant of Kashyapa helped to remove the affliction of excessive snowfall- it is a repetition of the legend -given in the Nilamat Purana -ascribed to the settlement of the people from the plains in the valley; [21] where in Chandredeva 1 got rid of the Pisachas.

One wonders is this repetition a mere reshuffle of the ancient legend as suggested by Stein or did a natural calamity, similar to the earlier one, occur in the valley that would have once again disturbed the ecology. One thing, however, is certain that Buddhism lost its hold in the valley after this event.

GONANDIYA DYNASTY

GONANDA-111

He succeeded Abhimmanyu and established the Gonandiya dynasty. He was also follower of Shavism. His rule lasted for 35 years

VIBHISANA -1

He was son and successor to Gonanda and ruled for 66 years. Subsequently Indrajit, Ravana, Vibishana2, Nara Siddha, Utpalaksha Hiranyaksa and Vasakula followed in the given order. Of all these rulers Nara deserves some mention. He followed the customs of the land and founded a town on the sandy banks of the Vitasta named Kimnarapura or Narapura. Kalhana states this town was abundantly provided with splendour, with abundance of flower gardens and orchards, and as per him would even surpass *Kuberas* town. (*Kuber* is purported to have been the richest man in the Hindu mythology.)

In context of this town there is mention of a 'Nag'-a pool of sweet clear water- called Susrvas by the side of which resided the *Susravas Naga* and his family, who, as per the Naga customs, used to worship Taksaka Naga on *Jyaistha Purnima.* A pilgrimage mentioned even in Ain-I-Akbari (p 358). It is believed that the cultivation of saffron in the valley has originated from the Taksak Naga.[22]

During Vibhisana reign a queer law was prevailing in the land that was a binding only for the Nagas. And under this law, Nagas were not supposed to partake of the food crops cultivated by them unless and until it was eaten by the Brahmin guard on duty, and he often avoided to do the needful, forcing Nagas to eat *Kacchaguccha* (grass) to survive. An ascetic Brahmin helped the Nagas to change this law. As per Kalhana's description it appears there was a revolt by the Nagas and a fight ensued between the Brahmins and the Nagas and thousands of terrified people fled to the temple of *Cakradar,* which was burnt by the Nagas and so was the town of Narapura. The clash ended once the Nagas moved to the upper reaches of the valley beyond the Susram Nag also known as *Jamatrsaras* (Zamtir Naag- the son in law's Lake) en-route to Amarnath cave.[23]

Hun Rule

Mihirkhula (528AD)

Rule of the valley, once again, passed in to the hands of foreigners, and we come across the name of Mihirkhula, a well-recognised name of a Huna king in the historical tradition of India. Who he really was is a debatable preposition? Kalhana states, "Vasukula's son Mihirkhula ruled the valley, which was over run by hordes of Mlechhas. This kings parentage, as given by Kalhana, is at variance to what is generally accepted in the Indian historical tradition, where in Mihirkhula is referred as a Huna king who was defeated by Narasimha Gupta Baladitya and forced to flee to the northern boarders to seek asylum with the ruler of the valley.

Sung-Yun the Chinese Ambassador -writes about Mihirkula's war with the country of Ki-pin, (Kashmir)and Hiuen -tsang in his book Si-Yu-Ki writes about Mihirkhula the son of Toramana a white Huna who ruled in Kashmir.

Mihirkhula was one of the most powerful kings of the age and his name was a terror for the people. He has been represented as a blood thirsty tyrant, who took immense pleasure in the murder of human beings and even did not spare the old or the women. Kalhana writes that he was a personification of *Kala* [death] himself. Where ever he went vultures preceded him. He is believed to have massacred millions of people in his kingdom. He was a staunch antagonist of Buddhist faith and destroyed a large number of Viharas and Stupas in the valley. The reason, given for his anti-Buddhist activities as recorded is quoted here, "Some centuries ago there was a king called Mo-hi lo-kiu- lo (Mahirakula) who established his authority in this town and ruled over India. He was of quick talent, and naturally brave. He subdued all the neighbouring provinces without exception. In his intervals of leisure he desired to examine the law of Buddha, and he commanded that one among the priests of superior talent or eminent virtue should wait on him. Now it happened that none of the priests dared to attend to his command. Those who had few desires and were content did not care about distinction; those of superior learning and high renown despised the royal bounty (glitter). At this time there was an old servant in the king's household who had long worn the religions garments. He was of distinguished ability and able to enter on discussion, and was very eloquent. The priests designated him to enlighten the King about the Buddhist philosophy and answer his queries about the same. The king felt insulted by this reaction and said, I have a respect for the law of Buddha, and I invited from far any renowned priest to come and instruct me and now the congregation have put forward this servant to discuss with me. I always thought that amongst the priests there were men of illustrious ability, after what has happened to-day what further respect can I have for the priesthood here". [24]

It is then that he issued an edict to destroy all the priests through the Indies, to over throw the law of Buddha, and leave nothing remaining. He was a follower of Siva faith and had the temple of *Mihireshvera* built at Srinagri and the town of Mihirapura at Holada. Stein identifies Holada as the modern Wular. [25]

He bestowed granaries to Brahmins imported from Gandhar who were looked down upon by the Brahmins of the valley. Kalhana writes that after ruling the land for seventy years this terror of the earth became afflicted in his body with many diseases and immolated himself in the flames.

Baka

Mihirkhula was succeeded by his son Baka, who was quite a contrast to his father. He was very sympathetic to his people and executed many a projects for the welfare of the tortured masses. Kalhana writes, "He was a reliever of humanity as the burst of rain which follows an excessive hot day."[27] Law and order; and security returned to the valley. His reign lasted for 63 years. The white Huns were sun-worshipers, who built many a sun temples in the valley. Baka was followed by a string of faceless kings: Ksitinanda, Vasunanada, Nara II, Aksa till we come to the reign of Gopadatiya.

Gopadatiya

He was a just king who treated people of all casts equally. He is said to have prohibited killing of animals except for the sacrificial purposes. He bestowed agraharas on the Brahmins. The shrine of Jyesthesvara on the hill of Gopadari bestowed to the Brahmins of *Aryadesha* was built through his orders. This location is the same as the present *Jeethyar* at *Gupkar* and the original temple at the Shankaracharya hill, though the present structure was built much later.[28] His sons Gokarna, Narendra Ditya and Yudishter I and later Pratapditya and Jalaukas succeeded him in the given order.

Tungina and Vakpusta

They succeeded Jalaukas and both ruled the land justly. They allowed people of every Varna to prosper. They built a Shiva temple named Tungesvara in the town called Katika. During their reign a very severe famine struck the valley. Kalhana narrates an interesting story describing this event and how the king and the queen, in spite of all their efforts, failed to save their subjects from starvation. The king, in desperation, decided to emulate himself than to witness the sufferings of his subjects. It was, as if by a miracle, caused by the queen's prayers, that dead pigeons dropped from the skies and people were spared from starvation. The queen, as a thanks giving, established the agrahara of Katimusa for the Brahmins. Katimusa, as per Stein, is a place very close to Shupian. Several old sculptures have been discovered from this site confirming the existence of an earlier structure. Tungina died issue less and his wife performed sati. This is the first reference to the existence of the custom of sati in the valley.

Vijaya

He was a descendant of a different family and succeeded after Tungina's death and ruled for eight years. He is supposed to have built the town of Vijayesvara around the shrine dedicated to Vijayesa.

Jayindra

He succeeded his father and ruled well but he was all along scared of being over thrown by his minister Samdhimat whom he finally imprisoned and even tried to kill. In spite of all his efforts Samdhimat managed to ascend the throne

Samdhimat

He was a very religious and spiritual person, and during his rule, Kalhana states, no calamity descended on his subjects either from God or men. He was a great Siva worshiper and had many lingas, temples, images of Siva's Bull and *Trisul* (trident) made. He had the shrine of Vardhamanesa built. This shrine, as per the local tradition, is supposed to have stood on the right bank of Vitasta within the precincts of present *Ganpatyar* and *Malayar.* Sandhimat was so enraptured by the beauty of the land and its spirituality that most of his time was spent in worshipping the Shiva lingas and enjoying and appreciating the various varieties and hues of flowers and fruits, natural landscapes and gardens, thus resulting in neglect in the affairs of his state. People of Kashmir were forced to bring Meghavahana from Gandhar to replace Sandhimat.

Restoration of Gonandiya Dynasty

Meghavahana

He was the son of Gopadatiya, who according to Kalhana had fled earlier from his homeland to Gandhar. Meghavahana was a kind hearted ruler who banned slaughter of the animals and compensated and rehabilitated the butchers by giving them financial help. He was himself a follower of Buddhist faith and yet very lenient towards Brahmins. He had many a Viharas and temples built. In honour of his teacher, he had a magnificent Vihara built at Leh known as *Tson-pa.* He married the Assamese princes named Amrit Prabha who was also a follower of Buddha. She had the great vihara of *Amrit Bawana* built for foreign travellers. Meghavahana's rule saw the revival of the Buddhism in the valley

Sresthasena better known as **Praversena I or Tungina II** succeeded Meghavahana. He built holy shrines at Purandeshthana (present Pandrethan). Cunningham and Vigne have reported a number of remains of ancient buildings, carved stones and a Linga of colossal dimension at this site. [29]

Hiranya and Toramana Pravarsena's two sons succeeded their father after his death. Kalhana states Toramana the younger brother put into circulation coins called Dinara struck in his name. At this daring act his elder brother Hiranya imprisoned him.

Pravarsena II, Toramana's son was born and brought up at a potter's home in hiding. Yet he was named Pravarsena II after his grandfather. He grew up into a brave lad and rebelled against his uncle Hiranaya and secured the release of his father who died soon after. Hiranaya died issueless and there was no ruler in the valley for some time as Pravarsena 11 refused to ascend the throne after Hiranay's death.

Matrigupta: Kalhana records that it was at this juncture, Vikramditya Harsha the ruler of Ujjayini sent one of his court poets Matrigupta, a very learned and virtuous and accomplished person to take over the vacant throne of Kashmir. Matrigupta ruled well for a period of five years. He prohibited slaughter of animals for sacrifice and instead *Kheer* and images made of fruits and flowers were offered for the sacrifice. He abdicated the throne as soon as Vikramdatiya his benefactor died and soon left for Varanasi to live an ascetic's life.

Pravarsena II ascended the throne after Matrigupta. He is reported to have conquered many a territories in Bharata and also brought back the throne of his family that had been carried away to Ujjayini by Vikramaditya.

He founded the town of Pravarapura which by location and the description of different features like streams, *Parvats*, and shrines as for example *Mar, Mahasarit, Tchunthkul,Sarikaparvat* and the *Jayasvamin* shrine (*Ziarat of Baha-uddin-Saheb* near Jama masjid) match the current Srinagar city.

While describing this town Kalhana writes, "Pravarsena built a city which provided with regularly arranged markets, at first only on the right bank of the Vitasta River. There are mansions that reach to the clouds, and ascending which one sees the earth, glistening in the rain, at the close of summer and covered with flowers in the month of *Caitra*. Apart from that city, where else can one find easily streams meeting pure and lovely, at pleasure residences and near market streets? Nowhere else is seen in the centre of a city pleasure hill from which the splendour of all the houses is visible as if from the sky. Where else do the inhabitants on a hot summer day find before their houses water like that of Vitasta (cooled) by large lumps of snow. In that city the kings have provided for each temple such riches that with them the earth up to the encircling ocean could be bought a thousand times over".[30]

References to this town are also found in the writings of Kshemendra, Bilhana, Chinese annals and other later chronicles.

Pravarsena was a great Shiva disciple and built the temple of Pravarasa

Pravarsena II was succeeded by his sons namely Yudishtara II, Lakhana/ Narendraditya and Ranaditya.

Ranaditya was a brave, ambitious and caring king. He married Ratisena daughter of the king of the Colas. This royal couple built the temples of *Ranarambhasvamin* and *Rana Rambhadevi* and a *Math* for Pasupata on the hill of *Pradumana*. Stein writes Pradumana is the present Hariparbat slope. This slope is covered by a number of buildings and sarais connected with the famous Mohammadan shrine of Muqaddam Sahib and Akhun Mullah Shah. [31]

Ranaditya took great care of his subjects and Kalhana writes, "Among the numerous royal families there have been two families and in them only two kings who showed to perfection utmost care for (their) subjects. These are Ranadatiya of the Gonanda family and Rama of the Raghu race who even had their happiness in another world shared by their subjects". [32]

Kalhana assigns a rule of three hundred years to Ranaditya; definitely there is some mistake about the number of years assigned. Stein has tried to explain this fallacy thus; he writes "possibly either there was a period of peoples rule or a group of very unimportant rulers ruled during this period and Kalhana did not take the trouble of recording them".

Vikramaditya son of Ranaditya was the next ruler and was followed by his elder brother Baladitya. They were Shiva followers and built temples and Jan-sarais for the Kashmiri Brahmins. Baladitya had only one child, a daughter named -Anangalekha-whom he married to Durlabavardhana one of the capable officers of his court, who later on ascended the throne bringing an end to the Gonanda Dynasty

Karakota Dynasty-625-753AD

Durlabavardhana being a Naga Karakota by birth did not, as such, have a royal lineage.Nagas being the original inhabitants of the valley, we can say that Durlabavardhana was the son of the soil. He was a man of high intellect, a capable ruler and a sagacious king. The date of his accession, on the basis of various references from Chinese Annals, has been placed round about 625 A.D; almost the same era as and when Harshvardhana ruled Kanauj. Durlabavardhana revived the worship of Vishnu faith and built the temple of Vishnu Durlabhsvamin at Srinagar. He ruled for 36 years and after his death was succeeded by his son.

Durlabhaka/ Pratapaditya II adopted the later part of his name from his grandfather's family. He encouraged trade and traders from different places and founded the city of Pratapapur and the illustrious shrine of Narendreshvara. He had three sons Candrapida, Tarapida and Mukhtapida, better known by the names as Vajraditya, Udayaditya and Lalitaditya respectively in the history of Kashmir.

Candrapida/ Vajraditya was the eldest and ascended the throne after his father. He was a very righteous and law abiding king and believed that the law was equally applicable to an exalted and the meanest of the mean. He believed, "If we, who are to look after right or wrong, do unlawful acts, who should proceed by the right path?"[33] He consecrated the shrine of *Vishnu Trimbhuvanaswamin*. Kalhana describes him as the "Crest jewel among the kings." He was a man of noble character and possessed high administrative skill. It is mentioned that when the Arabs were marching towards the southern borders of Kashmir, he tried to seek help from the Chinese emperor in order to avert the attack.[34]

Tarapida /Udayaditya succeeded Chandrapida. Unlike his elder brother he was very oppressive, ruled ruthlessly and derived pleasure in inhuman acts. He punished those Brahmins who practised sorcery/ *Khaarkhodavidya*. It seems sorcery was being practised in Kashmir from early times. As quoted by Buhler, Marco Polo writes 'The people of Kashmir' have an astonishing acquaintance with the devilries of enchantment; in so much that they make their idols speak. They can also by their sorceries bring on changes in the weather and produce darkness and do a number of things so extraordinary that no one without seeing them would believe them"[35] It may be unbelievable, yet it is true that some kind of *jodhmantra* under the *Tantrik* cult is even now days practised in the valley. Tarapida's reign lasted only for four years and like his brother Chandrapida, he is reported to have met with a mysterious death attributed to witch craft.

Lalitaditya Muktapida the youngest brother turned out to be one of the most illustrious sovereigns (699-736A.D) of Kashmir. He is referred as the very crown jewel of the Karakota dynasty. K.S.Saxena writing very eloquently about this king states, "In the galaxy of heroes, empire builders and monarchs of the 8th century AD all over the world, the name of Lalitaditya Muktapida has lustre of its own. While Europe could be proud of Charlemagne, west Asia of a just Harun-al-rashid and China of the mighty Hu-suan of the Tang dynasty, India can justly be proud of Lalitaditya . . . . who not only held sway over a large area in the northern region of India but also extended his suzerainty over a considerable portion of the sub continent and large tracts of the Central Asian regions probably second time in the annals of the Indian history, a millennium after imperial Mauryas. This mighty conqueror is not only remembered in the annals of India for his wars and conquests but also for his qualities as a champion of justice, promoter of literary and creative activities, and for his patronage of art and architecture. Under his benevolent rule the valley rose to the heights of unprecedented glory and prosperity." [36]

Al-Beruni mentions Lalitaditiya as a great king who subjugated Punjab, Kanauj, Tibet, Badakshan and Peking. Some sceptics do not believe in these claims but there does exist a proof to substantiate the claim. About this time Kashmir had embassies in China. In a letter written in 712 AD addressed by Babar to Mohamad Kasim occurs the following passage: "If I had sent against you, the King of Kashmir on whose Royal threshold the Kother rulers of Hind had placed their heads, who sways the whole of Hind, even the countries of Makran and Turan, whose chains a great many noblemen and grandees have willingly placed on their knees and against whom no human being can stand." [37] This basic claim is strengthened by the fact that, the second of Chaitra is a great festival day In Kashmir in honour of victory of its king over the Turks.[38]

Kalhana has recorded a unique habit of Lalitaditiya. The king would make the people of the subjugated territories to adopt various characteristic traits as an indicator to their defeat at the hands of this ruler: Turuskas were to carry their arms at their back and shave half of their head; Dakhanis and

Bengalis were to tuck their dhotis like a tail of an animal. Stein writes these habits still prevail in these people.[39]

Lalitaditiya enjoyed great fame as a builder. It was during the reign of this king that the famous Martand temple of Kashmir, an architectural marvel, was built, in honour of Vishnu Surya, at the edge of the alluvial plateau *Wuddar* of Mattan. The temple, though in ruins now, is one of the most extensively studied and visited places in Kashmir. Kalhana writes, "The shrine had massive walls of stone within a lofty enclosure and its town swelling with grapes". All that is in ruins now. Jonaraja records, "The temple was among those which Sikander the idol breaker destroyed."[40]

This group of temples is the most striking representation of ancient Hindu architecture in the valley. Even in their present state of decay they command admiration both by their imposing dimensions and by the beauty of their architectural design and decoration. In addition to Martand many a shrines, Viharas and towns of equal grandeur and architectural magnificence were built during the reign of Lalitaditya. Kalhana records, "there is no town, no village, no river, no sea and no island where he did not consecrate a shrine."[41] Images and idols were made of gold, silver and copper. There was affluence in his empire. The famous town of Parihasapura was built during his rule. Kalhana writes about its grandeur thus, "It mocked the residence of Indira"

It was during his reign a system of irrigation by water wheels to carry water from Vitasta to various villages was built at Chakrdar modern Tsakdar below Vijbrore (Bijbihara).

Yet in spite of his grandeur and greatness he seems to have been suffering from the fear of the Dammar assertion. He practiced and proclaimed such laws that would keep them weak and dependent. Kalhana records when the king proceeded on an expedition he ordered, "Action should be taken repeatedly so that the people in the villages should not possess grain for consumption and bullocks for the area of the fields in excess of annual requirements . . . . . For, if they were, to have excessive wealth, they might become very terrible Damars:" [42]

Lalitaditiya lost his life in one of his distant expeditions in the north and according to one version perished through excessive snow while proceeding towards Iran. To the Kashmiris of later periods, Lalitaditya was a hero and his glorious reign has served as a beacon light to them in many a depressing days. He is ranked among the greatest sons of Kashmir.

After him a string of weak and face less rulers like Kuvalapidiya, Vajraditiya, Prathivyapida and Sangram pida ruled for short durations and did not play any significant role.

Jayapida was yet another powerful ruler (764-795AD) like Lalitaditiya and is also depicted as an ambitious king and keen to conquer the world. He is supposed to have defeated Jayanta the king of Bengal and married his daughter Kalyanadevi, and on his return is said to have defeated the king of Kanauj. While no authentic details are available about his exploits, yet references to scholars and poets like, Ksira, Bhatta Udbhatta etc. who were famous in his court have been authenticated from various other sources. A conqueror, he was also lover of learning and reportedly Katayayana's commentary on Panini was recompiled under his patronage. Vasugupta the great Shiva philosopher belonged to this era.

Jayapida built his capital Jayapura in the marshy ground near the Wular/Volur, his name is remembered in the local tradition in the context of the famous Wular Lake. Towards the end of his rule as per Kalhana, he became avaricious and taxed his subjects, particularly the Brahmans. Numerous Brahmans of the tirtha of *Tulamuliya* went on a protest fast unto death against his avarice and a malicious act, till it is said that he met with an accident and passed away.[43]

For nearly eighty years following his rule, the valley witnessed nothing but installation and dethronement of puppet kings, and intrigues among the rising chieftains, till the beginning of the Utpala dynasty.

During the Karakota rule, Kashmir not only achieved many a glorious heights in the field of learning and language but enjoyed great power politically, as it was the over lord of most of northern India. The origin of the Sarda character of the Kashmiri language is assigned to this era. Gwasha Lal Kaul writes, "that Sarda descended from a western variety of Guptas first in about 800AD in Kashmir and the North east Punjab and has maintained itself in Kashmir since."[44] The kings were mainly followers of Shiva and Vishnu and the Brahmins as a class were ministers of religion and government officials. The Kshatriyas were mostly in the government service and also occupied in literary and academic profession.

The Utpalas- AD 855

Avantivarman: Beginning with Avantivarman's rule (855-884AD), Kalhana's work attains a historical record. Avantivarma was the head of the Utpala dynasty and his reign is supposed to have consolidated the country after the internal strife' that was prevalent towards the end of the Karakota rule. Avantivarman was a very sagacious and considerate ruler and thought full of the problems his subjects faced. He effected improvements in his administration in order to ameliorate the people's troubles. Some new appointments were made and one among them was Suyya, his Chief Minister. His reign brought an era of peace and prosperity to the valley. Religious activities, pertaining to Hinduism were resumed and shrines, temples and maths were built both by him and his ministers. *Vaishnavism* and *Shakti* worship also attained prominence in Kashmir during his reign. [45]

He also patronised Shaivism, which was propounded by Vasugupta the author of Shiva sutras. Great Shiva philosophers like Kayyat Acharya, Somananda, Muktakantha-Swamin Shiva-Swamin and Kallata flourished during his reign and consequently Buddhism lost its importance as a prominent religion of the valley. This led to indifference towards the literature on Buddhism.[46]

He was a great patron of art and letters and during his reign learned men and scholars came to Kashmir from abroad and were placed on important posts. Kalhana credits him with having built many monasteries for the benefit of ascetics. The Towns of Avantipur, Surapur and Suyapur were founded by him.[47]

Avantivarman did not go for territorial gains but his humanitarian achievements shine with a rare brilliance. Dr. Goyal in his book *Kashmir,* writes, "His reign is renowned for the victories of peace. The town which still stands by the side of the Srinagar was founded by him. A literary scholar, Anandavardhan, propounded the theory of *dhavani /a* suggestion in literary criticism in his rule."[48]

The most outstanding figure of Avantivarman's reign was Suyya- the civil engineer whose skill and achievement were curiously modern in character. With rare ingenuity, he diverted the waters of the Jhelum and altered the place of its confluence with Sind. He also conducted de-silting operations in the river, thus saving the people from the havoc of frequent floods. The story of this operation as narrated by Kalhana, (*see notes*[49]) purports that when no labourer was ready to plunge into the gushing waters of the river at Sopore, he requested the king to let him have a few Jars of gold coins, and surprisingly the request was granted with a feeling of distrust in the minds of the spectators. Suya threw the gold coins in the river. The labourers on seeing the treasure in the river rushed to every part of the river to get the coins and in that process removed boulders and any other impediments to get the gold. This enabled the water to rush in smooth flow and then it was channelled and distributed all over the farms and fields of the valley. He joined the waters of the lake Mahapadma with those of the Vitasta, and built many populous villages after having rescued the land from the waters . . . He examined several places and irrigated many villages (the produce of which did not depend on rain) by means of artificial canals. The town of Sopore near Wular Lake named after him (Suyapur) is a memorial to this great figure of Avantivarman's reign.

Sankarvarman who ruled Kashmir from 883/4-902AD like Lalitaditiya went on warring expeditions and is believed to have occupied Darvibhisara and some hill tracts extending towards the plains of Punjab that had been lost during the later part of the Karakota rule. Significant victory attributed to him is that of defeating Alakhana-the ruler of Gurjara (present Gujarat). He is believed to have died in course of his expeditions through Urasa (Hazara).

Kalhana has dealt in detail, his manner of administration and various means of taxation for raising the revenue of the state, and also the impact of heavy taxation on the cultivators of the land.[50] Even the practice of *Beggaar* existed in his time, as per Kalhana's records.

After Sankarvarman's death till the year 950 AD a string of insignificant rulers ascended the throne of Kashmir. Their reign varied from a period of a year or two and in some cases even less. His successors plunged the land into hopeless confusion and anarchy. Power fell into the hands of perfidious ministers and they during the next sixty years deprived sixteen kings of their glory, lives and treasure. During this period the dreaded Damars and the Tantrines gained supremacy and caused many an intrigues and supported some of the profligate rulers.

Cakravarman (923-933), was one such ruler who took to his seraglio a Domba women and raised, in status, all the members of the *Domba* cast. One of the singers of the group was named Ranga and, it is in connection with the reward given to him that Kalhana uses a Prakrit Kashmiri sentence: *Rangas Helu dina-a* village was to be given to Ranga, in his chronicle. [51] The last among the list was Parvagupta, who descended from a humble family.

Ksemagupta succeeded his father in 950AD He was sensual and vicious by nature and became more wicked when he came to the throne. A habitual drunkard, he absorbed himself with his parasites in wine and women. According to Kalhana the royal court became an assembly of whores, villains, idiots and corruptors of boys! The king himself was a shameless brute and spent his spare time in jackal hunts and plundered and sat on fire the famous Buddhist vihara of Jayendra. Previous relics as well as golden statues of

Buddha and other deities were got melted, under his orders, reportedly by the minority community living at *Mleechimar* in the capital.[52]

Queen Didda wife of Ksemagupta was the daughter of the king of Lahorin. It was a political marriage, which not only brought Kashmir closer to Daradistan, but also finally under the Lohara family. She was a Shahi princess, who became the ruler of Kashmir in the tenth century. Didda though very young at the time of marriage, combined in her character all the qualities needed for a sovereign. She was kind and generous but at the same time cruel and crooked. Didda dominated the Kashmir scene for about 50 years, initially as the queen, later as the regent for her son and the grandsons, and finally as the ruler of the state.

Her sway over the King Ksemagupta was so strong, that the courtiers had started calling him Didda Kshema. After the death of her husband, she became a regent for her minor son, King Abhimmanyu II and consolidated her rule progressively. She took on her adversaries one by one and defeated all of them and at the end of it was firmly' in the saddle.

Her character and modus operands have been verily described. It is recorded, "In spite of her limp, Didda attracted everyone with her beauty and exploited it by conferring favours, including physical, to the senior functionaries of the kingdom, who mattered. After using them to achieve her objective she got them killed or removed them. It is believed that she even got her three grandsons eliminated by death . . . . . . Didda was one of those enigmatic characters of history whom one condemns as well as admires. She survived the politics of intrigue, murder and debauchery for about 50 years and held the troubled kingdom together through sheer competency and courage. But she also caused incalculable harm by being sinister and sinful and by spreading moral pollution all around."[53]

Didda was unscrupulous in some ways, partially for the fact of being the wife of Ksemagupta, an absolute debauch, who was strong neither for evil nor for good. This being the situation, Didda took over the responsibility of restoring order and royal authority. She controlled the destiny of her people for a long period. She was unconventional in her ways, but that was the need of the hour. It was due to her undaunted courage, authoritative and strict handling that she was able to suppress rebellion after rebellion and curb and defeat the cunning and crafty courtiers of the Karakota house. She did not believe in the custom of Sati and consequently did not perform Sati on the death of her husband and, instead, gave preference to the task of looking after the subjects of her state. She was held in high esteem by the common people who had no complaint against her rule. A living proof of her popularity and high esteem is that to this day the Kashmiris of all classes and communities use the epithet 'Ded' for mother or a lady whom they hold in high regard and respect. Queen Didda was able to manipulate the crown for Sangramaraja, a member of her family from Lohara-the principality to which she herself belonged before her marriage.

First Lohara dynasty-1003-1101A.D

Sangramaraja 1003-1028 and his Chief minister Tunga

It was during the reign of Didda that the country had again attained order out of chaos. Intrigues and conspiracies had been checkmated; rebellions and dissentions suppressed and the minds of people turned towards national glory. She had succeeded in creating a strong government.

The Kashmiris, after many years of turmoil, misery and revolutions, had resumed their peaceful walks of life. Such was the conditions in the valley when the new king Sangramraja came to the throne with Tunga as the chief minister. Tunga being ambitious, capable and diplomatic took all powers of administration in his own hands and the king, who was weak, occupied himself in the pleasures of the world. The Brahmans, who believed in their caste superiority felt dissatisfied with this arrangement, since Tunga belonged to low caste and the Brahmins would not tolerate a Shudra to occupy the highest post in the kingdom. Moreover, Tunga who was clever, cunning' and powerful did not give them undue attention. The Brahmans in-order to denigrate him resorted to religious coercion and started a hunger strike to seek some concessions that went on multiplying as soon as an old demand was acceded. Kalhana writes that the Brahmins finally thought of a strategy; displaying a few dead bodies and declaring that some Brahmans had been murdered by Tunga. A big turmoil followed in which the Brahmans, under the leadership of Kalasa, fought against the forces of the king. The rebellion was suppressed and its leaders were imprisoned. Most of rebels were killed and some fled to foreign lands. Having succeeded in crushing his opponents, Tunga became proud and powerful and the king out of suspicion began to fear him. He now thought of killing Tunga through intrigue but his scheme got exposed.

During this period the frontiers of Kashmir seemed to be in the state of turmoil because of the impending attack of 'Sultan Mahmud of Gaznah'/ Gaznavi, who after capturing some parts of Northern India decided to capture Kashmir. His repeated attacks were successfully repelled by Sangramarajas' forces convincing him about the impregnable strength of the Kashmiri kingdom. Al-Beruni writes about this and remarks "the Kashmiris are particularly anxious about the natural strength of their country and, therefore, take always much care to keep a strong hold upon the entrances and roads leading into it."[54]

After Sangramraja there was a short negligible rule of his son Hariraja for a few days and even his mother Srilekha tried to occupy the reign, but the royal guards did not allow her to succeed, instead her younger son Ananta was crowned the king.

Ananta succeeded Sangramaraja and ruled from 1028 to 1063 AD During his reign Mohammadan tribes men (referred as *Mlechhas* by Kalhana) tried to attack but were defeated by his soldiers under his personal leadership as has been recorded both by Kalhana and the poet Bilhana, who were contemporaries of those times.

The reign of Didda, Sangramaraja and Ananta in the Kashmir history can be termed as the glorious period for the Kashmir Shaivism. Ksemaraja a reputed Shaiva scholar belonged to their times and is well known for his contribution to the Kashmir Shaivism. Like his guru, Abhinavagupta, he was a prolific writer and is said to have written two dozens books on the tantra poetics and philosophy. Among his famous works can be enumerated his *Siva-sutra-vali, Siva-sutra-vimarshini,* and *Spanda-airraya.* In these works, he' discusses the means of attaining salvation, the impurities that engulf the individual and the power which infuse life into the' physical senses.

The Administrative System

Ksemendra has given a detailed account of the administrative system followed in Kashmir during Ananta's rule, i.e. in the 11th century AD It definitely shows that the system was well organised and efficient, but the top officials were to a great extent dishonest and insincere in their execution. Though King Ananta tried to improve and reform the existing administrative system yet he could not rid it of the vice of dishonesty.

He records, "During king Ananta's reign the whole kingdom of Kasmira was divided into several *'Mandalas'* or divisions for Administrative convenience, the *'Mandalas'* were divided into several *'Visayas'* and the *'Visayas'* into *'Gramas'*/villages". The kingdom was inhabited by, amongst others, a considerable proportion of intellectuals and in the opinion of Ksemendra even

Indira envied this paradise of the earth. The prime officer of the State was the *Sarvadhikarin* or the Chief Minister. [55]

Ksemendra has not identified the person who held this office during the reign of King Ananta. Kalhana, however, states that this office was held by Haldhara[56]who was succeeded by Jayananda during the reign of Kalasa.

Prior to King Ananta rule, most of the administrative offices were held by the Kayasthas', who were in the habit of extracting money by illegal means from the populace. Ananta, on ascending the throne did not abolish the various offices which were meant for the smooth running of the administration but dismissed the corrupt Kayastha officers.

Ksemendra in his delineation of how the administration was run has named various offices and officials and the corrupt practices followed by them.

Officer in charge of each '*Visayas*' was known as, *Margapati* or *Vyaparika or Niyog.* His functions Included the supervision of the roads, the 'Visayas' and the villages under it, and the checking of the accounts. He was also the executive officer with magisterial powers to decide the civil and criminal cases.[57]

The contempt, with which Ksemendra portrays this officer, shows how even in trivial affairs such officers employed their high' handedness and punished the public with severe penalties.

Ksemendra mentions the village: administrator (*'Gramadivira')* had the same powers as that of a modem *Patavari,* of keeping records of land holdings and the revenue paid by the villagers. [58]

There remained jealousy between *Gramadiviras* who used to be appointed and dismissed by *the Margapati.* Their energies were mostly concentrated to pinpoint the faults of the *Muladivira* and they were successful in ousting him perhaps by bribing the *Margapati.* Ksemendra also points out that they could tamper with the records and torture the villagers.

The department of revenue was controlled by the officer known as *Grhakrtyadhipati* or *Grhakrtyadhikari.* Every revenue officer desired to obtain this office because he would be empowered to manage the Home affairs, expenses like grants to temples, Brahmans, the poor and the strangers, the fodder grants for animals and the salaries of the royal servants. Officers in charge of such an important office could make money through sources more than one. He had several officers to assist him and they were appointed by his consent. These included *Paripalaka, Lekhopadhyaya, Ganijadivira, Saulkika,*

Gramadivira and Asthanadivira, who most of the time adopted corrupt practices.

The revenue officer-*Paripalaka, was* next to *Grhakrtyiidhipati*, and had the charge of collecting taxes from the villagers. Ksemendra depicts him as pilferer of the temple properties. It seems that the people were religious minded and used to donate their movable and immovable property to the temples. The priests used to live with their families in the apartments attached to the temples.[59]

Lekhopadhyaya who worked as the clerk-in-chief to *Paripalaka w*as the custodian of the confidential official records. To please his superior officers he would indulge in extortion and resort to any illegal means.

Ganjadivira supervised the finances and acted as treasurer. His duty was to present a budget of income and expenses, for every six months, to the *Paripalaka* for sanction. He had control of the temples, their property and the granaries of the villages, which, If dishonest, he would sell and make profits for himself and his superiors. [60]

Another officer designated as *Saulkika* was in charge of the octroi on the commodities that would come in or go out of the villages.

In the military department the highest officer was The *Senapati* or the commander -in- chief. There were spies to keep track of any unlawful activity and report the same to the *Grhakrtyadhipati.* [61]

Ananta came under the influence of the Sahi princes of Punjab, who had taken refuge in Kashmir after Mahmud of Ghazni on capturing their principalities, forced them out. These princes with their influence brought about the marriage of the King with Suryamati, the daughter of the ruler of Jalandhar; Suryamati after becoming the queen entrenched herself well and helped the Shahi princess to increase their influence considerably.

Ananta, by nature, was a good ruler but could not control his wife which resulted in frequent turmoils. He could not bear the taunts of Suryamati and, in desperation, committed suicide. This chastened the queen and struck by remorse she performed sati and burnt herself on the funeral pyre of her husband.

Ananta's successors Kalsa and Harsa were indifferent and proved to be inadequate. During their rule A.D1063 to1089 many a calamities, like floods, famine and epidemics struck the valley.[62]

Harsa-King Harsha (1089-1101AD) who ascended the throne in 1089 AD was a typical specimen of a duel personality, who in the initial stage is pictured as a young energetic and learned person well versed in various sciences, lover of music and arts, and very generous towards men of learning, even forgiving those who plotted against him. It was due to his patronage of the poets that Bilhana-the court poet of Calukya king Parmadi-regretted having left his native land during the reign of Kalasa. Though known for his patronage of arts and learning, yet due to the spendthrift nature he was involved in debt. So to collect the revenue, high taxes were imposed on the people. An impost was levied even on night soil, but still, needs could not be met. He had images of gods with precious stones stolen. "There was not one temple in a village, town or in the city which was not despoiled of its images," says Kalhana. He appointed Udayaray a prefect, for seizing the divine images. In order to defile the statues of gods, he had excrement and urine poured over their faces by naked mendicants whose noses, feet and hands had rotted away. Ropes round their ankles dragged along divine images with spit instead of flowers.[63]

SECOND LOHARA DYNASTY- 1101-1150 A.D

After Harsha', only two Kings deserve a mention, Uccala (1101 to 1111 AD) and Sushala. Uccala was from the same dynasty as Harsa and with him began the rule of the second Lohara dynasty.

Uccala (1101-1111A.D)-had a tough time controlling the Dammars and his younger brother Sussala, with whose help he had ascended the throne. Uccala during his reign introduced many an administrative reforms to improve the working of the state; removed corrupt officials and brought justice to his subjects. He rebuilt and renovated some of the temples destroyed by Harsha and to a large extent was able to repair the damage done by his predecessor Harsa. His strict actions led some conspirators, especially those Tantrines, whom he had dismissed for their inefficiencies, to revolt against him and plan his assissnation.[64] He was cremated along with his two queens Jayamatti and Bijjala, who consigned themselves to the flames along with their husband.

Following his death, half a dozen descendents and usurpers occupied the throne within a period of four months till Sussala ascended the throne in 1112AD and ruled till 1128 AD.

Sussala (1112-1128 A.D) set up efficient administrative system and worked for the welfare of his subjects. The country attained all-round progress, industry and agriculture flourished. New projects for the growth of the economy were introduced. Luckily no natural calamities like floods, famine and earthquake struck the valley. Kalhana has highly praised the qualities and capabilities of Sussala. [65] In spite of his good administration; he did not enjoy a peaceful and stable reign. There were regular revolts and trickeries to be dealt with. The Dammars were very active and supported the revolts and plots against the king. Sussala like his elder brother was assassinated, even more ruthlessly than his brother.[66]

Jayasimha (1128-1150A.D) son of Sussala ascended the throne in the year 1128 AD The process of intrigues, revolts and efforts of usurpation of territories by the feudal lords continued through his reign also, even after he had established himself with the help of some Dammar leaders. The king consolidated his authority by diplomacy though he lacked firmness and decision, which led to the rise in power of quite a few favourites of the king. After defeating most of his enemies and establishing peace in the kingdom, his final years were very peaceful and the country was well provided. Most of the temples and ruined Mathas and establishments which were neglected due to the unstable conditions and civil wars were repaired and some new ones built. Attempts were made to establish and further strengthen relations with kings of other states like Kanyakubaj /Kanauj and Konkan.

Several administrative reforms were introduced and a person by name Dhanya was appointed the prefect (*Nagaradhikrita)* of the city. He discouraged the use of barter system in large scale transactions and encouraged people to use cash in all commercial transactions. He also took measures to raise the standard of morality in the valley and fined and punished those who were guilty. He, by being himself honest and economical, tried to infuse in the masses these values. And all this was possible after peace and amity was established. [67] As per Jonaraja, Jayasimha ruled up to the year 1155A.D, i.e, six years more than assigned by Kalhana in R.T. It may be mentioned here that the chronicle R.T. concludes in the year 1149AD

Parmanuka (1155-1164 A.D), who is variedly named as Parmandi/ Parmandeva or Paradeva ascended the throne on the death his father Jayasimha. His rule lasted for a period of one decade. Jonaraja characterises him as a weakling, who ascended the throne because of popular choice. He was least interested in administrative affairs; his chief occupation seems to have been accumulation of wealth. However he was deprived of his riches by his cunning ministers, especially Prayagya and Janaka. As per Muslim chroniclers, his lack of political acumen and control led to independence of many a small chieftains like those of Kishtwar, Jammu, Rajori and the ruler on the Kashmir Tibet border.[68]

Vantideva (1164-1171AD), son of Parmanuka was the last king of the Lohara Dynasty. These were the times, when the feudal lords, Damars and

Lavanyas were the real power and the kingmakers, resulting in selection of such people to ascend the throne, who were mere pawns in their hands?

Gopadeva (1171-1181 AD) was one such pawn. Varied names of this king and his relation ship to the previous royal family are given, but there is no definite information on this point." Jonaraja and Hassan agree on one point that this king was mentally deficient, as is evident from his chief hobby of collecting stones and pebbles of any size and value.[69]

Jassaka-(1181-1199 AD) younger brother of Gopadeva was selected by the Damars to follow his brother, in spite of his reluctance to ascend the throne. Even though he ruled for nearly two decades Jonraja does not mention about any important historical event in his times.

Jagadeva (1199-1213AD) was next to follow in line of the Hindu kings; once again selected by the Lavanyas.

It is pertinent to note that the 'office of king ship', was elective all through in the era so far written about, and people played a very important role in the choice of the coronation of the Kings and also in their dethronement, in case the king did not rise up to the expectations of the people. In the earlier days of their history the Brahmans and Purohitas played a leading role; where as down the ages the ministers and feudal lords took over the selection of the successors of the kings. It was seldom taken for granted that the son would succeed his father. Selection of Baka, Samdhimat, Yasaskara etc are pointers to the fact mentioned above.[70] Of course this system did not always guarantee the selection of the best, as we find in the present democratic election process too, wherein criminals and mafia leaders even get elected in the name of democracy.

Another feature worth noting is that though as a rule the kings belonged to Kshatriyas caste, yet persons from other castes were not debarred. There are many instances, when persons of other casts were called upon to ascend the throne. For example, Matrigupta was an outsider; the Utpalas were no descendents of a noble clan and so on. Hence one can say that caste regulations were never followed scrupulously in the valley during the early and medieval eras of its history as recoded else where.[71]

R S. Pandit supports the argument in his comments in this connection and records, "Kalhana's history shows the kingship in Kashmir to be elective in the early stages. At the end of the fifth Taranga, there is an interesting account of the election of the king as a result of which Yasaskara (939-948A.D) ascended the throne. The history of hereditary, monarchy is the history of mediocrity; the Kasmiri kings were controlled and exhibited by powerful individuals or cliques "as are snakes by snake-charmers."[72]

Towards the end of the thirteenth century AD, due to the internecine struggles of the native nobles and the decline of the war like powers, the rulers became so weak that the surrounding states began to send armies to invade the country or to intrigue for the over throw of its' government. The political environment and the feeble kneed and weak hearted Hindu rule acted as an invite for the neighbouring crusaders and usurpers to try their luck

Raja Simha Deva (1295-1325 AD), occupied the throne of Kashmir for a period of 30 years, which, in the history of Kashmiris, was a very significant period; not for achievements of any kind, but for transition from one era, one religion, and one way of life to an absolutely new unknown phase in every respect. Simha Deva's rule was characterised by general decay all round and the absence of justice and proper administration. He lost the affection and respect of his people due to his incapacity and indifference to the welfare of his subjects, and the neighbouring chiefs did not fail to grab the opportunity.

In the beginning of 14th century AD Zul Qadar Khan and Dalcuh or Zulju/ Caan- believed to be the descendants of Halaku Khan- as per Jonaraja;- came down from Turkistan with an army of about seventy thousand strong and entered Kashmir via Baramulla. Simha Deva a weakling had not the strength to meet Zulju and give him a battle and instead took flight and left Zulju as the master of his land.

"Intoxicated by his success Zulju's followers oppressed and plundered to their hearts content cities, towns and villages suffered unspeakable horrors of vandalism, while the inhabitants, irrespective of either age or sex were ruthlessly done to death. In short Zulju's advent in Kashmir revived the bloody orgies of Changez and Halaku. Some historians have also recorded that in addition to blood shed and massacre, Zulju also captured no less than fifty thousand inhabitants most of whom were women and were sold as slaves, while a small number of them had their afflictions curtailed by the merciful hand of death." [73]

Jonaraja has described the event, "Then this son found not his father, not the father his son, not did brothers meet their brothers. Kashmir became almost a region after creation, a vast field with few men without food and full of grass." [74]

A great famine struck Kashmir around this time, as if due to the hand of providence, for it turned out to be a boon for its inhabitants, as it forced

Zulju to leave Kashmir for other parts of the country. Not being acquainted with the hill tracks, he sought the help of his captives, who, however, led him to his destruction. Zulju along with his soldiers and captives reportedly perished in a snowstorm in the Devasar pass. Pt. Birbal Kachru sums up his eight months in these words "He came, plundered, killed and seized and departed."

Raja Simha Deva who did not resist Zulju, nor made any effort to save his subjects, had fled to Kishtwar leaving the country in disarray, with people unhappy with him for his cowardice and neglect.

In spite of his in- capabilities he is said to have been a great host and it was this tradition of hospitality that cost him his throne and reshaped the destiny of Kashmir. Three persons, from different parts of the world came to seek asylum in his court, and all of them were not only granted asylum, but were also granted small estates. These three thankless seekers, who changed the destiny of Kashmir and KSPs, have been assigned varied origin by the chroniclers:

- Rinchin Shah a Tibetan prince who had been defeated by his uncle and had run away from his homeland.
- Shahmir a runaway from Swat.
- Lankar Chak ruler of Daradistan had been defeated by his enemy.

D.J. F. Newall writes, "Shahmir, was son of King Wuffoor Shah of Sawadgere; Lunkar/(Sunkar) Chak (the ancestor of the Chaks) was a chief of Darads and Rainchen Shah was Prince Rawjpoee son of Yuftun of Tibet."[75]

Though there are some misgivings regarding his parentage, common perception, however, is that Rinchin was a member of a Tibetan ruling dynasty. Historians even differ regarding what his real name was. Some call him "Ratanju" or "Ranju Shah" while others Rinchan or Ralanchan Shah. G.M. Sufi writes "One would accept Ratnju because there is no controversy about his Tibetan origin, and Tibetan names generally end in "*Ju*" it is very likely that Ratanju was the name by which he was generally known. This possibility is admissible on the ground that the city 'Ratan Charipura' which was founded by him in the earlier part of his reign and it still bears this name. Besides we have definite historical evidence on Khwaja Muhammad Azam's work in which there is a reference to a mosque named after the King as Ratanju's Mosque, and this mosque existed when the book was compiled and printed at Muhammadi Press."[76]

Rinchin took the advantage of the assassination of Ramchand the Prime Minister and ascended the throne of Kashmir. He married Kota Rani Ramchand's daughter, and being a Buddhist even decided to convert to Hindu fold in order to be accepted by his subjects. But alas! The conservative and short-sighted Brahmin orthodoxy headed by one Deva Swami did not accept him in the fold on the excuse of being unsure of his heritage. Jonaraja writes, "Deva Swami turned down the royal petition because, being a Bhotta, even though a king, Rinchin was unworthy of such initiation."

Refusal and rejection at the hands of the Hindu Pandits upset and humiliated the king. According to some narrators, he then decided that he would adopt the religion of the person whose face he will like and to do so he decided to go regularly down the river Jhelum, early morning, in a boat. As the destiny had to intervene and shape itself, Rinchina liked the face of an elderly person, dressed in white and with a flowing white beard, whom he witnessed offering prayers along the bank of the river. Rinchin took the decision of accepting the faith of the old man. Latter was a Muslim preacher by the name Bul Bul Shah, who had come to the valley to convert people to his faith. Nothing would please Bul Bul Shah more than to have the king as the follower of his faith. Rinchan after accepting the Muslim faith adopted the new name Sadar-ud-Din-/Sharifudin, from that day onwards. Incidentally the river bank, immediately downstream of Alikadal, where Bull-Bull Shah was offering his morning prayers, has since been known as Bul-Bul Lankar. Thus Rinchin's conversion to Islam heralded the Islamic rule in the valley.

The Islamic Era

Malik Sadar-ud-Din /Sharifudin (1323-1326AD) ruled for two years and seven months only and tried to restore peace and tranquillity in the valley, and in this task of regeneration he was helped by his consort Kota Rani.

Kota Rani: Turks under the leadership of Urdil attacked the valley around 1326 AD, immediately after his death, but were repulsed and brought to terms by the brave strategy of the Queen Kota. She is supposed to have made a deal with them, under which it was arranged that the Turks would be allowed to leave unharmed if they withdrew immediately. Shahmir helped to execute her strategy against Urdil. After getting rid of the Turks the queen withdrew herself to Inderkote to establish her court there and appointed Shahmir as a minister in-charge of the affairs of the Kashmir state as a reward for his help, which unfortunately cost her both life and the crown.

No sooner did Shahmir get an opportunity to intrigue against her, he invaded Inderkote, with the intension of forcing the queen to marry him, which she rejected. The heroic queen is reported to have made every effort to defend herself, and finally when she discovered that there was no alternative she gave her consent. There are varied opinions and descriptions of this episode. D.J.F. Newall writes, "Thus the hostilities ceased and preparations for the marriage commenced; but the devoted princess, indignant and despairing, rode slowly forth, surrounded by her train of maidens, from the beleaguered fortress, advanced in to the presence of the usurper and upbraiding him for his ingratitude and treachery stabbed herself before him. Thus perished by her own hand Queen Kotereen or (Kotadevi as she is often called) the last Hindu Sovereign of Cashmere and thus prince Shahmir ascended the throne under the name Sultan Shums-o-Deen Kashmir."[77] Hassnain writes that the stories regarding her suicide are fictitious interpolations made by the Persian historians of the later period. Quoting the available authority for the period, Jonaraja's RajaTarangni, he records that Kota Rani passed her life as a prisoner along with her two sons. [78]

SULTAN'S 1339-1554A.D

Sultan Shams-Ud-Din (1343-1346 AD) Shahmir ascended the throne, assuming the title of Sultan-Shams-Ud-Din. He was the real founder of the Islamic period in Kashmir. During his reign Islam was introduced as the court religion and Islamic *Hijri* calendar was brought in to practice. The system of paying one fifth of the agricultural produce as land tax was introduced besides law and order was strictly established. Roads were made safe for travelling. The usage of the Sanskrit language continued in the administration as only Brahmans were available for the job and they were not conversant with Persian or Arabic.

To keep the feudal chiefs under control he raised the status of two families: Chaks, who had migrated from Daradistan and the Magres of indigenous origin and drew from them his generals and soldiers as they had converted to his faith and were of ferocious nature.

Sultan Jamshed succeeded his father Shams-Ud-din and ruled only for three months, as he was slain by his younger brother Ali Sher.

Sultan Ala-Ud-Din (1346-1358 AD) Ali Sher took the title of Sultan Ala-Ud-Din and ruled for twelve years. His rule is reported as peaceful. He attempted to ameliorate the sufferings of his subjects during his reign. A great land mark of his time was the birth of a great Kashmiri hermit, saint poetess and philosopher Lala of Padmanpura, known more famously as Lal Ded. She elevated the Kashmiri dialect to the status of a language by her renditions in *Kashur.*

Sultan Shahab UD-Din (1358-1373 AD) ascended the throne after Ala-Ud-Din. His reign among the rule of the Sultans of Kashmir is considered a glorious period for the military prowess shown by the Kashmiri's for after conquering Jammu and Kishtwar, he proceeded to Punjab where he was opposed by the ruler of Sind whom he defeated. The Sultan subdued and took the possession of Multan and also fought against the armies of Ferozshah Tughlaq, with whom he later signed a peace treaty on the intercession of Mir Syed Ali Hamadani, who had arrived in Kashmir in 1372 AD. He is also accorded to have conquered Tibet, Kashghar, Badakshan and Kabul.[79] How far these victories are genuine is a matter of conjecture? Sufi writes, "Almost all the statements of these victories are based on the authorities of all the known Persian historians of Kashmir". [80] Newall and Rodgers however write, "There is no mention of these conquests in the Indian or provincial histories and these were mere conquests and did not lead to any long well established occupation."

He encouraged learning and proclaimed an equal administration of laws. It is said that during his time a regulation was imposed on the boat men of Kashmir and under that law they were supposed to serve him without any remuneration. A kind of tax called *baj* was levied upon the people to collect revenue.

Sultan Qutab-Ud-Din (1373-1389 AD) Shahab-ud-din's younger brother Hindal ruled under the assumed title of Sultan-Qutab-Ud-Din. He ruled for fifteen years. Firishta says that this Sultan was remarkable for his extreme attention to public business, which he transacted personally with justice and modernization. He was an efficient ruler and patron of the learned. He made great efforts to assuage the sufferings of his subjects. During the early part of his reign, there were very few Muslims and the society was still following Hindu customs in the manners of dress and behaviour. People visited temples and performed *Yagnyas* to seek blessings irrespective of their faith.

The king had two wives, who were sisters by relation; an act not permitted under Islam. Syed Ali Hamadani the scholar of Muslim Theology, who had arrived in Kashmir a year before, to escape from Timur, intervened and made the king divorce one of his wives. Thus began Hamadani's mission of preaching and spreading his faith (Islam) during this era.[81]

Famous Kashmiri saint and the founder of 'Rishi order', Nand Rishi, who later after converting to Islam assumed the title of Sheikh Noor Din, was born during this period in the year 1377 AD. He carried forward and popularised the Lal Ded cult of mysticism and one ness of the Supreme.

Sultan Sikander-(1389-1413 AD) succeeded his father in 1389 AD. His rule is considered as a landmark in the propagation of Islam in its conservative and fanatic format in the valley of Kashmir. It is because of this nature of proselytising that Sultan Sikandar has been called "*Butshikan* or the iconoclast." During his rule the Hindu KSP was subjected to inhuman indignities and they were forced to leave their native land or suffer the shame of conversion.

In AD 1395, Syid Muhammad Hamdani son of Ali Hamdani, and commonly known in Kashmir as Shah Hamdan arrived in Kashmir accompanied by hundreds of his followers'. Mohammed Hamadani like his father had fled from Hamdan, a town in Persia, to save himself from the hands of the Emperor Timurlang. The story of their flight is recorded thus, "Tamer lane, like many Oriental monarchs, was in the habit of going round his capital cities at night, in disguise, in order to find out for himself the condition of his subjects and their opinion about him. One night he stood outside the house of a very poor man. His children were weeping for want of food and his wife was in a very miserable condition. In her plight she implored her husband to go out and beg food for the children, but the man, being a respectable person, he was unwilling to beg. Tamer lane, hearing their conversation, was sorry for them, and quietly threw a few gold mohurs into the house. In the morning the woman of the house was overjoyed to find the pieces of gold lying on the floor. Her husband bought some food and fed his children, his wife and himself. His neighbours seeing them eating good food, guessed that they might have stolen the money. They brought a charge of theft against this poor man and being Syids—i.e., the descendants of Ali, the son-in-law of the Prophet—they would have very easily succeeded in getting him punished and tortured. But happily the King came to know about this so-called theft; so he summoned both the parties before him. The accused told him the whole truth, which of course the King knew himself. The Syids contradicted his statement, and declared on oath that they had really been robbed of the money. The King was furious, and he ordered a horse of seven metals to be made. He made it red-hot and ordered all the Syids to ride it in order to prove that they were truly Syids, because according to Mohammadan tradition fire cannot harm the Syids. In this way those Syids who obeyed the order of the King were burnt to death, and those who disobeyed him were killed by his soldiers. Sayyid Ali Hamdani managed to escape this ordeal, and he fled to Kashmir".[82]

If this story is correctly recorded, it exposes the vulnerability of the protagonist's moral and ethical standards and no wonder that it was through the efforts and influence of this father /son duo that the Hindus of Kashmir were ruthlessly persecuted by Qutb-ud Din and his successor Sikander the Idol Breaker. Many a sacred places of Hindu's and monuments of historical importance were demolished and the material was used to build mosques and Ziarats. Many an ancient temples and architectural wonders were damaged beyond any repair.[83] Inspite of such demolition drives, "to destroy all would be impossible".[84] as is observed by Bernier and Tyndale-Biscoe

Lieutenant Newall trying to analyze Sikandar's title 'Butshikan' writes, partly by the influence of Timur and partly no doubt urged by the fanatic Muslims who had lately entered his country, Sikander was about this period instigated to religious persecution and he began to force his subjects to abjure idolatry and thereby acquired the surname Butshikan or Iconoclast . . .

According to Newall Sikander probably acquired gun powder from Timoor he writes, "As early as 1397 he had perhaps acquired a supply of gun powder from Timoor Lang (Tamerlane), who invaded India at that time as it is recorded of him that he threw down the idols and temples 'by fire' and this may be regarded as one of the earliest allusions to the use of that explosive in Indian History."[85]

Sultan Sikander, as stated earlier, was greatly influenced in his process of persecution of Hindus by Shah Hamdan, considered as a great saint by the Sunni Mohammedans of Kashmir, a ziarat-Shah Hamdan mosque- built in his honour by Qutb-ud- and located below the 3rd Bridge in the city, is highly revered by the locals.

Sultan Ali Shah Sikander was succeeded by his son, Ali Shah who ruled for a very short period and was followed by his brother Shahi Khan.

Sultan Zain-Ul-Abidin (1422-1472AD): Sikandar's grand son Zain-ul-Abidin, who had spent some of his growing years in Persia, acceded in the year 1422 AD His reign is identified as the golden period in the history of the Muslim rule in Kashmir and he is known in Kashmiri as *Bad shah the Path shah*, (the most benevolent king). The Sultan adopted certain laws relating to the Hindu KSPs, which granted them a just administration and a trial of their cases according to their own laws. The odious persecution measures instituted during Sikandar's rule were revoked and a general toleration of all religions proclaimed.

The Brahmins and the Hindus who had migrated out of the valley during Sikandar's reign were recalled; complete religious independence was granted and some of the temples which had been demolished were rebuilt and permission was accorded to erect new ones.

The sultan remitted the *Jazia*/ Poll-Tax, banned the killing of cows and granted Jagirs to Hindus. He was very tolerant towards the Hindus and took into his service such men from among them as deserved his patronage and recognition of merit. He celebrated Hindu festivals and visited their *Tirthas* with great reverence.

Like Ashoka he also had laws for administration engraved on copper plates. He abolished death penalty and even released all prisoners of the former ruler. Historians compare his rule with that of Akbar.

Zain-ul-Abidin was a passionate admirer of art and architecture. Many important buildings and townships like Zaina Kot, Zaina Marg, Zaina Gir, and many a palaces and caravan sarais were built during his reign. The mausoleum on his mother's grave at Zaina Kadal was one of the majestic tombs built in his times. On the foundation of an inundated temple in the Wular Lake, he had a palace and a mosque built which still exists. The king named the island Zaina lank. Besides towns and palaces he had the canals of Zainngiri, Lachman Kul, Kakapura and Chakradara dug out for the improvement of irrigation system.

Zain-ul-Abidin during his eight years of stay in Samarqand had picked up many an aesthetic tastes and he tried to adopt them in his state. He invited craftsman and artisans like Chunnu, the expert fire work artist and Jab a man who made gun powder from Iran, and other accomplished men from Turan, Turkistan and other parts of the country (Hindustan) and offered them high prospects and concessions to settle down in Kashmir.

He was a learned king well versed in Persian, Sanskrit and Tibetan languages and also devoted his attention to the art of medical sciences, and letters. He reintroduced from other parts of India some of the classics written in Sanskrit that had been destroyed by his predecessors and even got some translated into Persian.[86] He encouraged scholars from other lands to settle in Kashmir, and some of the reputed scholars of his time were, Kashmiri Maulana Kabir, Mulla Ahmad Kashmiri, Mullah Parsa, Mulla Qazi Jumal-UD- Din, Soma a Kashmiri scholar, Bodhi, Jonaraja and so on. He forbade the killing of fish in certain tanks and also banned cow slaughter.[87]

Zain-Ul-Abidin died in the year 1472 AD after a reign of fifty two years and his death was a great loss to the people. It meant an end of the golden era of peace and prosperity during Muslim rule.

POLITICAL CHRONOLOGY

Sultan Haidar Shah son of Zain-Ul-Abidin was a drunkard and undid all that was achieved by his father. Srivara writes that a barber (Riktetara/,Purni or/ Luli)was king's favourite for his notoriety and, "The relentless and sinful barber cut off the Thakuras and the courtiers of the king's father by a saw and then left them on the roadside for days shrieking till death relieved them." During Haider Shahs' reign once again the Hindus/ Bhatta suffered a lot. Measures were adopted against them, but having been emboldened to some extent by the sympathies of Zain-ul-Abidin, Hindus rose in revolt and reportedly set fire to some mosques which had been built with the material obtained from demolished Hindu temples. This act cost the Hindus/Bhattas greatly and they were punished and disgraced by barbarous methods. Srivara writes, "Nonadeva, Shikhajada and others . . . had their tongues, noses, and hands cut off. Jaya the son of an Acharya, as also a Brahman named Bhima was maimed, and they struggled and threw themselves into the Vitasta."[88] Torture was so intense and unbearable to the extent that quoting Srivara, "They gave up their cast and dress and exclaimed *Bhatta na ham (I am not a Bhatta*/ I am not a Bhatta." [89]

Haider Shah's sons Sultan Hassan Shah and Fateh Shah followed him. They ruled for a period of twelve years and this period is labelled as an era of 'revolutions and constant changes of ministers' and is supposed to have sapped away the very foundation of authority and administration in Kashmir.
Hassan Shah as a person was a great patron of learning, art and music. He had the palaces at Didamar and Sopore built. The burnt down mosques of Jama masjids and Khanakah Maula were rebuilt in his time. During his reign, 'The country was divided into four parts and governed by Jahangir Padr, Kaji Chek, Sunkur Reina and Fateh Shah.'

Muhammad Shah During his reign Kashmir became a favourite soil for all unmanly qualities, like jealousy, dissensions and rivalry, and blood thirstiness. Factions grew and found strength, resulting in constant feuds among the nobles. Kazi Chak who was his powerful *Wazir* deposed the king and installed his son Ibrahim shah on the throne. It was during this time that Babar-Mughal emperor- sent his army to attack Kashmir. Kazi chak fought him well and forced Babar's forces to retire.

Ibrahim Shah The state of affairs continued to be the same like the previous incompetent rulers and ambitious nobles who were always engaged in conspiracy and combat.

Shams-Ud-Din, son of Ibrahim Shah was just a name sake ruler who was actually dominated by his astute minister Kazi chak. Latter established a matrimonial alliance with the ruling family and, by virtue of it, acceded the throne of Kashmir

Sultan Habib Shah was deposed by Ghazi Chak in the year 1553, and thus heralded the Chak dynasty rule in the valley. Sufi writes, "There appears to be no cause of lamentations over the displacement of the old dynasty in Kashmir. Its rulers had become quite effete and sadly lacked those essential qualities of initiation and capacity to command which are, and should always be, possessed by a king. Moreover, they had been displaying their weakness of character, and could not; therefore hold their place any longer. It was only a divine mercy or it might be said with equal justification, diffidence of the Chaks that they were allowed to play the role of supernumerary kings under the Chak domination. As a matter of fact they should have long been displaced to make room for stronger kings of fresh blood and virility."[90]

CHAKS (1554-1586 AD)

Chaks supposedly had originated from the Dard country-around Gilgat. As per folklore "The first Chak is said to have been born of a Kashmiri woman and an amorous demon. The lively pools of Trigam were their frequent haunts. There are other stories equally fantastic current about them in folklore." In all seven rulers of this clan sat upon the throne of Kashmir and ruled for a brief period of thirty three years.

Ghazi Khan-1554-1563AD descendent of Lunker Chak was the first ruler of this dynasty. Being a Shia Muslim by faith, he converted a large number of Hindu KSPs to Shia faith. He imposed on the state Shiite doctrine that was promulgated earlier by Mir Shams-UD-Din Iraqi, and also offered a code of law for all the subjects. He affected the forcible conversion of many Hindus and Sunni Muslims to the Shia faith.[91]

Hassan Shah Chak-1563-1570AD was the best ruler amongst the Chaks and his reign is often compared to that of Naushirvan-i-Adil, the great Emperor of Persia. During his reign Babar's forces attacked Kashmir thrice but were unable to defeat him. Humayun then sent his Governor Kamran to invade Kashmir which was repulsed by Qazi Chak. Humayun did not stop at that and ordered Mirza Haidar, Babar's first cousin, to invade Kashmir shortly after. Haidar's forces of around 4000 troops went on a rampage in the valley. S'uka writes, "Hundreds of houses were burnt and the city that had been populous before now became like the ground for burning the dead. No regard was paid either to age or sex, nor was any distinction made between the Hindus and the Non Hindus." [92] Kashmiris, however, continued to give him a tough fight, under the leadership of Kazi Chak, forcing Haider to leave the valley after signing a peace treaty. Haider, to fulfil his master's command, attacked the valley second time when he succeeded in his mission.

Mirza Haidar's regency lasted for ten years. Writing in his 'Akbar Nama' Haider states he found the country in a state of ruin and desolation and raised it into a land abounding in cultivation and flourishing towns. He extended its frontiers and also ruled with moderation and justice.'

Abul Fazal writes, "The country being in a distracted state, he took possession of it without any blood shed. He ruled for ten years and afterwards ordered the *Kutbah* to be read and the coins to be struck in Humayun's name."[93]

Hassan writes, "Though he was an accomplished man, a lover of art, culture and literature, but these qualities of his were offset by his excessive religious fanaticism. In his enthusiasm to preserve Islamic orthodoxy he banned Shafi'te school. He also persecuted Nurbakshiyas and put to death many of their leaders. Other Sufi orders were also banned. While in Kashmir he thought he was in exile and never identified himself with the people and treated them with arrogance". [94]

Mirza Haidar was a Sunni Musalman and, since he did not like the ways of Shias, he resolved to crush the very existence of this faith, that in turn led to rebellion and retaliation in which his nobles were sacrificed and he himself was killed. After his death Abdi Reina became the *Wazir.* Salim Shah Suri son of Sher Shah Suri sent Haibat khan to attack Kashmir but was defeated by Daulat Chak, which resulted in latter's ascendancy in prestige.

Daulat Chak again reviewed Shiite tenets in the country forcefully. He compelled the Imams of mosques, on pain of death to recite the names of twelve Imams in Friday sermons. However his reign did not last long.

Yusuf Shah Chak-1579 was dethroned within a year of his ascendancy. He had to take the help of Mughal Emperor Akbar to regain his kingdom; in return placing his son Yakoob as a hostage with the emperor. Yakoob, with the help of some of the nobles of Kashmir, managed to escape and return to the valley.Infuriated by this move, Emperor Akbar sent an army under the command of Bhugwan Dass to enforce compliance with his demand. Yusuf Khan Chak was forced to surrender and delivered himself to the Emperor's general and was never heard of after that, though it is believed that he died of grief in Bengal in 1587 AD With the capture of SultanYusuf shah Chak, Kashmir finally became the part of Akbar's empire.

Yusuf Chak still survives in the folk lore, not for his capabilities as a ruler but for his talented Queen Habba-Khatoon, the eminent founder and par excellence representative of *lol (*romantic) tradition of Kashmiri poetry in the Islamic era.

Mughal period

The rule of Shamirs and Chaks was a period of local unrest and civil strife. There was no peace and people suffered from lack of education and opportunities. "Homage to ones' religion was paid by reviling that of others". People were divided into groups and cliques. Thus circumstances connived for the Mughals to take over the valley under their governance. Mughal emperors -Akbar, Jahangir, Shah Jahan and to some extent Aurangzeb too-were so enamoured by the beauty of this land that they adopted all means-by hook or by crook-to make this jewel part of their empire, yet they hardly spent any time to take care of its subjects, whom they had acquired after repeated pains taking invasions as trophies for their Empire. Mughal rule was mostly represented by their Governors and other equivalent representatives whose only aim was to please their rulers by contributing hefty sums to the royal exchequer, irrespective of the sufferings caused to the people. The rulers in person adopted the valley as their summer residence and had many a gardens, caravan *Sarais* and pleasure spots built to beautify the valley.

Mughals did not favour giving any political or military power to the Muslim *Kashur,* as they associated mischief as part of his nature and hence tried to curb them in every manner. Hindu *Kashur,* by then, had been reduced to a negligent number; the Mughals' took advantage of their intellectual calibre and used them where ever profitable intellectually. This policy was followed by every foreign ruler who followed the Mughals, be they the Pathans, Sikhs, Dogras or even the British residents as we shall see later on. This tactical device planted the seed of distrust and divide in the future generations of the *Kashur.* A few posts held by some prominent noble *Bhattas* created a psyche in the majority *Musalman.* They felt, they were deprived and subjugated by *the Bhatta Tehsildar, Patwari* and the *Okhun* (teacher) while in reality the culprits were the rulers.

The Mughals arbitrarily deprived the Kashmiris of the ownership of their land and the emperor was declared as sole proprietor of all cultivable land in the valley and the Kashmiri landlords where entered in the revenue registers as tenants (right up to 1932 when, after a mass uprising, during Dogra rule, Hari Singh restored the ownership to the people). Mughal rule was based on political principals rather than religious aims.

Akbar (1586) was the most humane and secular face of Mughals, by and large, followed in the foot steps of Zain-ul-Abidin so far as his administrative and religious policies were concerned. He proclaimed religious tolerance and abolished Jazia and *Begaar*. S'uka records, "He repealed the practice of levying fines on them . . . He announced that he would without delay reward those who would respect the Brahmans in Kashmir".[95] The revenue system was reorganised and whole country was divided into fourteen divisions for convenience of revenue collection. There are many instances to show how just and tolerant Akbar was towards other faiths. He respected the Brahmans for their knowledge and capabilities. Yet at the same time some of the acts and legislations imposed by him do not fully substantiate the general belief. For all important administrative posts people were deputed from Delhi and if at all any local help or guide was essential then the services of *Bhattas* /Pandits were acquired. Like in case of Land assessment Pt.Tota Ram was appointed to help Qazi Noorullah and QaziAli.

Having been repulsed twice by the Kashmiri forces, in his attempts to conquer the valley, Akbar after annexation of the valley on his third attempt, in order to break the marshal spirit of the conquered people and to subdue them for ever, forbade recruitment of the Kashmiris in the armed forces. This, not withstanding the fact, as stated by Abu Fazal in 'Ain-I-Akbari', that, "the valley furnished 6,420 cavalry and 50,533 infantry to the Imperial Mogul army". This nefarious practice of disarming of Kashmiris was later followed by the Pathans, Sikhs as well as the Dogras. Dress of the people-well girdled tunic adapted to action and exercise-was forcibly changed and replaced by the effeminate long gown-*pheran* on his orders-.- This simply changed the very character of the people; the vigorous war like Kashmiri went in to oblivion. Subjugated people forgot the glorious traditions of living like self respecting human beings and of heroically defending their home land and standing against injustice.

Several famines and floods struck the valley during the Akbar's reign and majority of the people were reduced to extreme poverty. Akbar who visited the valley thrice during his reign, in order to bring succour to suffering people, provided work to them by undertaking the construction of a fort-great wall (*kalai*) around the Hariparbat hill and also established a township by the name of Nagar Nagar in the vicinity. This fort (wall) is a majestic construction with numerous huge bastions and should not be confused with the one built on top of the hill by Atta Mohomad Khan the Pathan Governor. An inscription on one of the gates of the fort (wall) reads "its builders have been duly paid by the emperor from the royal treasury and no beggaar (free labour) was forced." This fort thus stands witness to his humane and honest persona.

Jahangir was an avid admirer of the natural beauty of the valley. He was a regular visitor along with his Queen Noor Jahan during summer season and he took a lot of interest in enhancing the beauty of the valley. He was responsible for plantation of the magnificent Chinar-*Buen* (supposed to be the derivation of the word *Bhavani's* tree- tree belonging to goddess) through out the valley. Lawrence writes that during the Mughal times, "It is said there were 777 gardens around the Dal Lake. The roses and bed musk brought revenue of one lakh rupees".[96] The famous Mughal gardens: Shalimar, Nishat and Naseem and the palaces and baths at Manasbal, Achibal, and Verinag were built by the orders of Noor Jahan during his reign. The system of '*Mirabs*' was introduced by him for improving the irrigation facilities of the villages.

He visited the valley for the last time in 1627. It is said that on his death bed, he was asked whether he wanted anything and his reply was, 'Only Kashmir'.

Shah Jahan (1628-1658AD)-succeeded Jahangir and visited Kashmir accompanied by poets and savants immediately after ascending the throne. Like his father he added immensely to the grandeur and beauty of the valley. He was generally kind to his subjects and was responsible for bringing in some changes in the behaviour pattern of the recently converted KSPs. The Rishi and dervish cult of the valley receded and was superimposed by the cult of musicians and entertainers. He changed the Hindu names of places into Islamic and destroyed some Hindu shrines. When he learnt that the Muslims gave their own daughters in marriage to the Hindus and also took wives from them he had the practice stopped. "There was an understanding that Hindu women married by Muslims were to be buried and Muslim girls married by Hindus to be burnt according to Hindu custom after death. The Emperor as the protector of the Faith ordered that the Hindus who married Muslims women must be compelled either to renounce infidelity or to part with their Muslim wives". He took interest in the welfare of the people and with this view tried to select good and efficient governors to represent the crown and function loyally.

Itiqad Khan (1630-1640AD) the first governor to be posted by Shah Jahan was, unfortunately, the reverse of what the king desired. He was one of the most oppressive in this era. He levied high taxes and made life miserable for the Kashmiris, yet he was allowed to continue for a long period of ten years.

Zaffar Khan (1640-1642AD) who followed was comparatively better in governance, and abolished many taxes, like tax on saffron, on wood and poll-tax on sheep and boatmen.

Ali Mardhan Khan (1650-1657AD) during his time an expedition was mounted to proceed from Kashmir to Tibet to subdue a rebel, Mirza Jam, and to capture fort Skardu.[97]

Shah Jahan's reign came to an end when he was deposed by his son Aurangzeb

Aurangzeb (1658-1707AD) was a staunch follower of Islamic faith and undid what his father had done. He visited Kashmir only once in 1665 for reasons of his health. During his reign 14 Governors were deputed to Kashmir. Most of these governors were indifferent to the plight of their subjects. On top of their indifferent attitude natural calamities like the great fire in the year 1673 in which nearly ten thousand houses were gutted in the capital Srinagar, and again a severe famine struck in 1683. As if that was not enough, it was followed by a devastating earthquake and to top it a conflict erupted between the Shias and Sunnis.

With the decline of the Mughal Empire the Subhas in Kashmir became independent and established their own rule. The Subha leaders fought among each other and there was disorder in the state of Kashmir.[98]

When Abdoola Khan became the governor of Kashmir in the year 1752 it is said that during his tenure of six months he plundered and exhorted a crore of rupees from the people of the valley who were already exhausted by pestilence and famine, in order to gift the same to his master Ahmad shah Abdali. These governors perpetrated worst kind of religious fanaticism against the Hindu and Shia KSP. Many Kashmiris left their homeland to settle in the plains. It was at this juncture two Kashmiri gentle men 'Mir Muquim and Zahir Dadamari approached Ahmad Shah Abdali of Afghanistan to conquer Kashmir and annex it to his empire. This act later proved a Himalayan blunder. For Abdali easily conquered the valley and laid foundation of one the worst tyrannical rule of Durani's primarily, followed by other Pathans.

Pathan period AD 1751-1819

Kashmir, which had become hereditary and practically independent of Delhi by 1751AD unfortunately became subject to one of the cruellest and worst rule of the Pathans (1751-1819AD). Afghans/Pathan rule was a period of anarchy, savagery and inhumanity.

When Nadir Shah was assassinated, his successor Ahmad Shah Abdali assumed the title of *Doordowran* (pearl of the age) corrupted into Dooranee, and thus became the first Durani Governor of the valley.

In all 28 governors were deputed to Kashmir during the Pathan rule. Most of these were ruthless and barbaric. They made their own coffers as rich as they could in the shortest possible time. They sucked the very life blood of the wretched people of the valley and imposed all sorts of indignities on them. It is said Azim Khan made a fortune of two crore rupees in his tenure of six years, where as Ishaq Aqasi compelled people of all communities to surrender all their wealth on the point of death during his tenure of six months.

Raja Sukh Jeevan (1753-AD) who followed Aqasi "was a native of Gujarat and was serving in the army of Ahmad Shah Abdali, when he was deputed to serve under Abdullah Ishak Aqasi in his Kashmir campaign." [99]He was the first Hindu to be in charge of the valley after a gap of four centuries. He tried his best to give some relief to his people and tried to free Kashmir from the Dooranee rule. He began to form a confederacy amongst the surrounding hill tribes and managed a large force of 40,000 soldiers. With this force he attacked Ahmad Shah, but, as a result of the desertion of some nobles, was defeated and captured by Nooroodeen Khan. As per records, he was blinded and brought in chains in front of the emperor Ahmad Shah and trampled to death under the emperor's and his courtier's horses. His tenure in the valley is considered as peaceful and is remembered in the local phrase *"Sukh joon raaj"* /a reign of happiness.

Nooroodeen Khan was the Governor of Kashmir for eight years and was followed by a long train of governors one after the other from 1754 onwards. Most of them were tyrannical and least interested in the welfare of their subjects.

Among the Pathans the best ruler was Amir Khan Jawan who is remembered for having had the Amirakadal and the Shergarhi palace built, yet at the same time, he destroyed the Mughal gardens on the Dal.

The other Pathan governors are remembered only for their brutality and cruelty. It is said of them that they' thought no more of cutting of heads than of plucking a flower. The victims were Pandits, Shias and Bombas of the Jhelum valley.

The worst among them was Asad Khan under whose orders Bhattas/ Pandit were subjected to the worst form of inhuman tortures and dictums.

Madad Khan followed Asad Khan both in word and deed

Alla Muhamad Khan was ferocious. He was a libertine and his agent was an old woman named Koship, and she was the terror of the Brahman parents, who rather than allow the degradation of their daughters destroyed their beauty by shaving their heads or cutting off their noses.

Mir Hazar was even more ruthless. He had the road closed at Baramulla so that no one especially a Hindu could leave the valley. Having suspected some of his Hindu retainers were against him, "he had them bound in large cooking vessels or boilers and threw them into the river Jhelum".

This misrule continued till 1819 when Kashmiris, fed up with the Pathan rule, thought of seeking help from the Sikh ruler Ranjit Singh to relieve them of the miseries, because they themselves were reduced to such a state of in-action, starvation and poverty, that they had no capacity to revolt on their own. William Moorcroft, who travelled the valley extensively and met all shades of people during the Sikh rule, gives a detailed account of this event.[100] (*See notes*)

Sikh Rule

In 1819, Ranjit Singh's general Mir Diwan Chand along with Raja Gulab Singh of Jammu entered the valley via Shupian and defeated the Governor of Kashmir. Thus Kashmir once again passed into the hands of non-Muslims. Ranjit Singh inherited the subjects who by now had become haggard and emaciated in body, indolent and had lost the zest for life. Almost continuous oppression and suppression for centuries had affected every part of their existence. Even though the nature was ever benevolent and environment soothing and peaceful as before but the rulers and their tyrannies had killed the spirit of a *Kashur* and in consequence, "They became absolutely hopeless and sullen, and each man played for his own hand—. This sullen temper is one of the worst points in the Kashmiri character and joined to deep rooted apathy makes it very difficult to improve the condition of the people." So pathetic was their plight that K.F.Knight called a Kashmiri, "A bearded disgrace to human race who would howl, weep and throw himself down merely when a dog ran up to him and barked."

With the Sikh rule there was some relief to the people of Kashmir, especially the peasant class, though it would not be right to say that the Sikh rule was very benign or good rule, as is evident from this extract from Moorcrafts observation, "The village where we stopped was half deserted and a few inhabitants that remained wore the semblance of extreme wretchedness, without some relief or change of system, it seems probable that this part of the country soon be without inhabitants, yet the soil seemed favourable for agriculture and the crop appeared to have been good one. The poor people, however, were likely to reap little advantage from their labours, for a troop of the tax gatherers were in the village, who had sequestered nine tenths of the grain for their employer as the revenue. The number of Kashmiris who were to accompany us over the mountains proved here to be no exaggeration, and their appearance- half naked and miserably emaciated- presented a ghastly picture of poverty and starvation. Yet wretched as they were the relentless Sikhs would have levied a price per head for permission to pass the post, had we not interfered. The Sikhs seem to look upon the Kashmiris as little better than cattle. The murder of the native by a Sikh is punished by a fine to the government of rupees 16 to 20 of which four rupees are paid to the family of the deceased if a Hindu and rupees 2 if he was a Musalman. Some of the people accompanying us were seized by the Sikhs as unpaid porters, and were not only driven along the road by tying together by the arms, but their legs were bound with ropes to prevent their escape"[101].

The Sikhs banned killing of cows and if a Muslim Kashmiri, who is permitted by Islam to eat beef, slaughtered an animal of this species he was hanged or stoned to death. Many a Muslim mosque were seized and converted to go downs.

Moti Ram was the first Sikh Governor of Kashmir and Hari Singh and Birbal Dhar were associated with him. Hari Singh was able to control the Bombas and Kukas, a very brave and trouble some tribe who lived in the Jhelum valley and claimed Turkish origin.

Kripa Ram (1825 AD)was a ve*ry* self indulgent man fond of boating and boat women, and was nick named "*Kripa shroin*" (the sound produced by a boat paddle). During his time a severe earthquake hit the valley in 1827, and nearly destroyed whole of the Srinagar city. It was followed by cholera. (In this year also three Brahmin women were burnt as the Satis' as quoted by Moorcroft.)

There is an interesting saying in Kashmir that Kripa Ram introduced crows in the valley considering that they were necessary to the due performance of funeral rites, as it was the custom in Punjab to feed crows on such occasions.

Sher Singh son of Ranjit Singh became the nominal Governor in 1831. He left everything in the hands of Baisakh Singh. In his time a severe famine struck Kashmir and Jamadar Khushal Singh was sent from Lahore to organize aid for the people and bring succour to the victims, but he mismanaged the things so much so, that life worsened and most of the Kashmiris fled to Punjab.

Colonel Mian Singh reportedly the best Sikh Governor Kashmiris could hope for was sent to the state in 1833. He introduced some reforms to assuage the sufferings of the people and also modified the revenue system by which the farmer would keep half of his produce and pay only half of his produce to the state as revenue. Agricultural advances were made free of interest. He imported grain seeds and eggs from Punjab, as the villagers had lost all the seeds and fowls in the terrible famine. Proper weights were introduced, and fraudulent middlemen were punished. He decided cases justly and quickly. He was murdered by a group of mutinous soldiers and to revenge his murder Raja Gulab Singh came with a large force to attack. After affecting his objective he left Sheikh Ghulam Mohidin in charge as Governor in 1842 AD.

Imam-ud-Din took over the Governorship in 1845. He is remembered for his reform in the shawl weaving industry both in their wages and employment rules. The weavers could not leave their employers as per the existing practice and they were paid very low wages. All that was changed by his orders, besides they were supplied paddy from the state granaries at lower price than normal. He did not stay for long in the valley as a year later on March 10th 1846 a land mark event happened in the history of the valley. Kashmir and all the hilly and mountainous country situated east of river Indus and west of river Ravi, which had been ceded by the Sikhs to the British Government, in lieu of indemnity, was made over to Maharaja Gulab Singh and his male heirs against a sum of Rs. 75 lakhs.

By then the Kashmiri spirit was so demoralised and inert that they were almost lying prostrate at the mercy of any individual who ruled them. With this political change over, at last there was some consideration and mercy shown to the Kashmiri people. Dogras were not Kashmiri speaking people; their land, however, was closely connected to the valley by being the southern section of its plains and the Rajputs of Kishtwar had connection with the valley right from ancient times. With the advent of Dogra rule the era of torture and degradation for the KSP marginally came down.

Dogra Rule

Gulab Singh (1846-1860AD) signed the Treaty of Amritsar with the British government on 10th March 1846, and there by was declared the ruler of the combined state or Jammu and Kashmir, yet he was not in possession of the valley. The Sikh Governor of Kashmir Sheikh Imam-ud-Din refused to surrender the province. "It was only after the intervention of the British, Lahore and Jammu Governments that he surrendered personally to Colonel Lawrence". With his surrender Kashmir and its dependencies passed into the hands of Maharaja Gulab Singh, who entered Srinagar on the 9th November1846.

During his rule, which lasted for almost 15 years, Gulab Singh tried to consolidate most of the hill territories and restore order in every part of the state to provide some relief to the people following the anarchy created towards the fag end of the Sikh rule, especially after the death of Ranjit Singh.

Gulab Singh abolished *beggaar*-forced labour, which was widely prevalent and caused a lot of inconvenience to the Kashmiris. It was decided that only a certain number of men in each village would be liable to do labour for the government when need arose for which they would be paid one *kherwa*r (80kg) of rice per month and other rations during the period of employment.

Another important reform introduced, during his rule, was the rationing of rice-a staple diet in the valley. It was sold at a fixed price to the people thus hording of rice by the grain dealers was prevented. This also ensured proper distribution of the grains at the time of scarcity and famines.

In order to provide proper wages and free the shawl weavers from the bondage of the big proprietors, the shawl trade laws were reorganised. According to the new laws: (a) the tax was regulated by the price of the shawl in the market instead of the number made or stamped in the year; (b) the *Karkhanadar*/(entrepreneur) had to pay only according to the work done in the shop; (c) the *shagirds* (interns) were no longer a serf.

Gulab Singh also abolished some unnecessary taxes and the *Moulut* system by which the accounts were continued to the 14th month. These reforms helped to, some extant, restore prosperity in the valley.

Sir Henry Lawrence writing about Gulab Singh's government says, "His government was mild, conciliatory, and even merciful. He himself personally looked into all affairs, great and small"

In the words of an Englishman present in the country at the time of his reign, "He was always accessible and ready to listen to complaints. He was much given to looking into details so that the smallest thing might be brought before him and has his consideration. With the offering of a rupee as *Nazar* anyone could get his ear even in a crowd by crying out *Maharaj urz hai*/ a plea".

On the whole he was kind and just though with a slight tilt in favour of the Hindu Kashmiri speaking people and the condition of the subjects started limping back to better days. His decision to support the British at the time of the 1st war of independence (Mutiny) in 1857 was un-patriotic act as an Indian, though by then he was unwell and had already installed his son Ranbir Singh as the maharaja of the state in the year 1860.

POLITICAL CHRONOLOGY

Ranbir Singh (1860-1885AD) ruled the state for almost 25 years. He continued the policies of reform that were initiated by his father with an appreciable tilt towards the Hindu Kashmiri speaking people. It was during his reign that an appeal was sent to the religious heads in Kashi for permitting the re-conversion of those Hindus who had been forcefully converted to Islam. Kashi pundits, however, turned down the appeal.

Ranbir Singh was a model Hindu prince devoted to his religion and to Sanskrit learning. He, at the same time, was kind and tolerant to the Muslims to whom he allowed the free exercise of their religion. He started a large number of schools and dispensaries in the state in order to improve the educational and health standards of his subjects. Separate departments for revenue, civil, police and military were set up. Courts of justice were opened and the judicial system was reorganized. A penal code was set up. He was responsible for laying the foundation of the silk factory and its trade, besides the shawl industry was further strengthened to guaranty proper income and employment to his subjects.

Pratap Singh (1885-1925AD) succeeded his father in 1885AD and reigned till 1925. He over hauled the administration and introduced many a reforms especially in the land settlement and revenue assessment. In this exercise he was helped greatly by Sir Walter Lawrence who was the Revenue Commissioner of the state of Jammu & Kashmir then. It was during Pratap Singh's tenure that a college namely Sri Pratap College was inaugurated and commissioned at Srinagar.

Sir **Hari Singh** (1926-1947AD) succeeded his uncle Pratap Singh on his death as the latter had no issue of his own. Hari Singh was a just and secular ruler who believed in modern and progressive laws. He introduced reforms for the relief of the agriculturists, compulsory primary education and prevention of child marriages. Marriages of boys under 18 and girls less than 14 years of age were declared unlawful. He enforced the recruitment of state subjects against all government jobs. Hari Singh's reign that came to an end as a consequence of series of events, detailed latter, also culminated in the end of the Dogra rule and the monarchy in Kashmir. For the political history of the Kashmiri speaking people this event was almost like opening of the Pandora's Box, a box beyond the control of their monarchs. This period because of the impact these years and events have had on the life of the *Kashur* has been widely and variedly written about in the recent years.

This short span of sixty years, a negligible period in the time scale of a community, that is the proud inheritor of a chronology of thousands of years, belongs to democratic era in the political parlance. A very short resume is given about these few years; listing mainly the political parties and their elected leaders who were designated as the Chief Ministers of the state of Jammu and Kashmir over this period.

Partition of India happened on August15, 1947, and it had quite unexpected repercussions on the state of Jammu and Kashmir. In the year 1947 when the British finally decided to quit India; all those treaties under which the rulers of various Indian states were bound ceased. The states were, supposed to retain their independence and would legally be sovereign. However, the geographical and economic considerations would not permit such an arrangement. Hence Lord Mount Batten, the then Viceroy of India urged on the rulers of the states to come to some agreement within the preview of the Indian Independence act of 1935; with the new Indian and Pakistani governments before August the 15th 1947. Majority of the states either joined India or Pakistan. Hari Singh the maharaja of Kashmir opted for stand still agreement, till he would finally decide which country to join as that was the third option given to the rulers of the states. But this situation was not acceptable to some of the non-Kashmiri speaking Muslims of the state, who had been directly or indirectly affected by the disastrous consequences of the carnage and destruction resulting from the partition of the country. There was a large-scale exodus of Muslims from India and Hindus from Pakistan and everyone narrating the harrowing tales of torture. The result was that people close to the borders of Kashmir were aroused and Pakistan took advantage of this situation. Violent tribals of north-western frontier's were encouraged at the behest of the Pakistani government to loot, rape and murder the defenceless people of the state especially along the boarders. Further to grab the state, Pakistani army attacked the territory of J &K state. Thus once again there was an attack on Kashmir almost after a break of 128 years that is after the year 1819 when Maharaja Ranjit Singh had annexed the state. In order to save his subjects and his state, the Maharaja of Kashmir sought accession of his state to the Indian Union, on October 26, 1947, which was accepted by the Government of India. And on the very next day Indian troops and forces landed in Srinagar on October 27 1947. The Maharaja after signing the treaty left from Srinagar, the capital of the valley, to Jammu and by this action also declared that he was no longer in effective control of his state. In the meantime the invaders were thrown out of the valley and the democratic process began taking shape under the able guidance and leadership of some Kashmiri speaking men like, Sheikh Mohamed Abdullah, Shyamlal Saraf and Mirza Afzal Beg and Bakshi Ghulam Mohamed who were the constituents of National conference, a secular party, which was founded in the year 1939 by Sheikh Mohammed Abdullah.

POLITICAL CHRONOLOGY

Sheikh Abdullah a prominent political leader of Kashmir was appointed Head of the Emergency Administration on October 30th 1947. Following that on March 5, 1948, the Maharaja conferred on Sheikh Abdullah the Prime Minister ship of the state by a special Proclamation and he was authorised to get the constitution of the State framed by a Constituent Assembly elected on the basis of adult suffrage. By yet another Proclamation issued on June 20, 1949, functions of the head of the state, hitherto carried out by Hari Singh were passed on to his son Karan Singh.

Interim cabinet constituted mostly of the Muslim Kashmiri speaking people, after centuries of rule by foreign dynasties and tribes. It passed a resolution in 1950 for the formation of a constituent assembly, which would decide the future of the State. So elections for 75 seats in the assembly were proclaimed for September /October 1951. As there was no opposition, all the candidates secured their seats without any contest and the constituent assembly duly came into existence in October 1951. The un-opposed contest in itself was proof enough of the unity and unified process of the working of the mind of Kashmiri speaking people. Thus under such cordial tradition was born and based the democratic form of government in the state of Kashmir. The first task of the new assembly was to pass the Jammu and Kashmir Constitution Act 1951 in which the maharaja was given the role of constitutional head acting on the advice of cabinet. In the following year an amendment to the constitution was made under which the constitutional head of the State would be known as the *Sadar-I-Riyaset* and would be selected every five years.

Thus immediately after Kashmirs' accession to India a democratic form of government was put in place. New government left no stone unturned to set right the situation that had arisen out of the tribal invasion and India-Pakistan conflict of 1947. In order to put the state on the path of democracy, series of reforms and changes were brought in. Land reforms like land to tillers, abolition of feudal Land lords; reforms in the Education and Health policies were initiated by Sheikh M Abdullah in his short tenure of six years. In the year 1953 Abdullah's government was dismissed and he was arrested soon after.

Bakshi Ghulam Mohammed: (1953-1963A.D) was appointed as the new Prime Minister, on Sheikh Abdullah's arrest; a position he continued to hold till 1963 when he resigned under the Kamraj plan. Bakshi was the leader of the common masses, and a man of determination and practical wisdom. He, in some respects, achieved for the state what Sardar Patel did for India. During his Prime Minister Ship constitution of Jammu and Kashmir State,

1957 was adopted confirming the state's accession to the Union of India by J&K Constituent Assembly.

Shams-Ud-Din succeeded Bakshi and remained the Prime Minister of the state till February 1964. His tenure was cut short because of the peoples uprising that followed the theft of the sacred relic of Prophet's hair from Hazratbal mosque.

G.M.Sadiq took over from Shams-Ud-Din on 29th February 1964 and continued to hold the position till his death in December 1971. His very important contribution to the political history of Kashmir was change in the nomenclature of '*Sadr-i-Riyasat*' to Governor of the state and changing the title of the executive head from Prime Minister to Chief Minister.

Mir Qasim was elected the next chief minister. It was his untiring efforts that resulted in an agreement called 'Kashmir Accord of February 1975' between the Prime Minister Indira Gandhi and the Sheikh M. Abdullah after his release from the prison.

Sheikh Abdullah as the head of National Conference once again got elected and took over as the Chief Minister of the state and continued till his death on 8th September 1982. Aged and having lost the aura that he had gained during the struggle for independence, his second tenure was routine.

Dr. Farooq Abdullah, son of Sheikh Abdullah took over as the Chief Minister after his father's death in 1982. A relatively young flamboyant Chief Minister, he believed in enjoying and merrymaking in the land of beauty that he inherited. It was during his tenure that militant terrorist activities raised their head and a bus load of them after being arrested were pardoned and let off. This simple act of leniency by the State government led to all the future troubles and ignominies that were thrust up on its people from that day onwards and has continued till today. Resulting in the exile of almost every Hindu KSP from their ancestral home land within three months at the instigation of fanatic islamists, a catastrophe that Farooq Abdullah's government could not prevent.

Sayyid Mufti Mohamed of the Peoples Democratic Party came to power and became the next chief minister after defeating the National Conference the ruling party in the State legislative assembly elections. As his party was short of absolute majority an alliance was made with the Congress party and under the agreement of the alliance he stayed in power for a period three years according to the arrangement reached at the beginning of the election.

Ghulam Nabi Azad of Congress party took over as the next Chief Minister and soon after M. Sayyid (PDP) withdrew their parties support and Azaad's Govt. lost the majority

Omar Abdullah: Once again elections were held and there was a turn around. National Conference won and the youngest icon of the Sheikh family Omar Abdullah was elected as the chief Minister and he is till today in the chair. For him it has been a tough and demanding assignment due to the terrorist activities instigated by Pakistan and duly supported by fanatic elements in the state under the pretext of achieving *Aazadi* (liberation) from whom? God alone knows! It is a Muslim majority state that has driven out the Hindu minority and is ruled by Muslim leaders'. Yet they seek liberation.

Conclusion

As we look at Kashmir in retrospect, the striking thing is the strong continuity and identity which it has preserved throughout the many changes of its history, its philosophies, its religions, its cultures, and its turns and twists of civilization. Inspite of the Greeks, Huns, Turks, Mongols, and Sikhs and their impositions; the Kashmir of the old chronicles and tales of travel is easily recognizable in the Kashmir of the present age, and very often it is the same things that were noted centuries ago which attract the visitor's attention today. Its philosophy of love and hospitality, its traditions, its customs, its sacred places of pilgrimage, its arts and crafts, are remembered, cherished and transmitted from generation to generation by the Kashmiri.

A million dollar question that haunts me is, as to why did the accession of Kashmir alone have to be controversial, out of the 560 states that acceded to either of the two countries India and Pakistan, at the time of independence of the country? Why did only the KSP, especially Hindu KSP have to suffer the indignation of rootless-ness and uncertainty? Why they were over and over again uprooted from the land of their birth, they lovingly refer as *Maej Kasheer*? A land famous not only for its ethereal beauty and landscape; for its snowy mountain barriers, its rivers, lakes and heavenly meadows, but also for its amalgamated culture of love and peace, for its unity of social and cultural ethos, for its religious and philosophical pragmatism, for its unique principal of hospitality that only believes in giving and not demanding any returns, believes in giving and sharing its treasures with who so ever asks for, without assessing the character of the seeker. Why this paradise can't be left in peace, a lasting peace devoid of blood- sheds and the dark clouds of terror.

Appendix

Appendix-I

Festivals celebrated by the KSP's during the Puranic era - (Source Dr. Ved Kumari's translation of the Nilamata Purana Vol 1 p189 209)

Puranic Era

In the Puranic era, as per Nilamata the, KSP were celebrating as many as sixty five festivals in a year. Nilmata gives detailed instructions about the practices and taboos meant to be followed by the people of the valley during these festivals. These were classified under two heads: Vratas and Utsavas. Former involved fasting and restrictions regarding food and behaviour, and the latter i.e. Utsavas were primarily celebrations and commemorations of events like seasonal festivals and social festivities. Many a similarities, however, existed between the two, like fasting or singing and merry making.

Account of the Vratas and the Utsavas:

Alvayuji Maha or Kaumudi: It is celebrated in commemoration of Nikumbha's return to Kashmira after killing the Pisacas dwelling in the sea of sand and continues for three days. The houses are decorated to welcome Nikumbha and on the first day, all excepting the sick and the children, have to undergo a fast, which is broken at night after the worship, of various deities and Nikumbha, performance of fire-sacrifice and honouring of the Brahmanas. Vigil at night is observed with singing and dancing around the sacred fire. For the second day are prescribed feasts, sports and fire-worship during the day and sleep at night. On the third day, people have to behave licentiously, using even obscene language and throwing mud upon their fellow beings. In the evening they have to take bath, worship the god Kesava, honour the Brahmaas and feast themselves in the company of friends, servants and relatives. Keeping the fire lit for six months of winter and lighting an oil lamp outside the house for the month of Kãrttika are two long-standing features of this festival. Nilamata, vv. 376-97; K.K,N pp. 411-13.

Sukha Suptika: The component parts of this festival are fasting at day time on Kãrttiki Amavasya by all excepting the sick and the children; worship of Karisini (Lakshmi) in the evening; placing lamp-trees in temples, crossings of roads, burning grounds, rivers, hills, houses, shops, pastures etc.; decoration of shops with clothes; dining with friends, relatives, the Brahmanas and the subordinates after wearing new clothes; playing at dice on-the second day; dining again with friends etc.; listening to musical concerts; decoration of the bed rooms with lights, perfumes, clothes, jewels etc; passing the night with beloved women, and honouring of the Brahmans and the friends, the relatives and the servants, next morning, with new clothes.(Nilamata, vv. 398-407; K.K.N., pp 42 1-22.)

The MSS of the longer recension of the Nilmata while describing this festival has also used the name Dipamãlã at the end of the description. The term Sukha Suptika as well as the description of the festival is important for tracing the history of Dipamala. Vãtsyãyana's Yaksaratri and Hemacandra's Jakkharatti is the same as Sukha Suptikã or Dipamãla of the Nilamata and it would be reasonable to suggest that this joyful festival was originally associated with Yaksa worship whose traces are found in Kashmira as well as in other parts of the country.

Devotthana: As per this festival Visnu goes to sleep in the month of Asadha. Then follows the festival of Awakening which occurs after four months of the god's sleep and spreads over five days of the bright half of Karttika. It comprises the following items: Observance of vigil at night; awakening of Visnu with songs, dances, musical concerts, dramatic performances, earth-decorations etc. and worship of Visnu image with various sorts of eatables and cosmetics on the 11th of the bright half of Karttika; bathing of the image on the 12th, in accordance with the procedure of the Pañcaratra, with butter, oil, honey, curds, milk, five products of cow, various sorts of cosmetics, perfumes and clays; making gift of golden pitchers full of leaves and flowers amidst sounds of musical instruments and professional singers; worship of the image with flowers, incense and eatable offerings; worship of the Bhagavatas; performance of fire-sacrifice; worship of the Brahma with clothes, ornaments, cows, horses, elephants and cash-money; honouring of actors, wrestlers and the Bhattas on the 13th; fast on the 14th and the 15th; worship janãrdana, Karttikeya, Khaçlga, Varuna and Hutasana; throwing in water the lamp which was kept burning throughout the month of Kãrttika; and the gift of a fish of sand with pearls substituted for its eyes and of a bull along with clothes and grains for Brâhmanas. Daily bath in the cold water of a river and avoidance of non-vegetarian meals is prescribed for all these five days (Nilamata vv. 4O8-449 K.K.X., pp. 427-31.).

Nava Samvatsara Mahotsava: 1st of Margasirsa is observed as the New Year day on which Kashyapa brought the land of Kashmira out of water. Well anointed and dressed in new clothes, people are 'enjoined to eat, drink and be merry on this day.

Saptamyah: The 7ths of the bright halves of (Mãrgasirsa), Magha and Asadha are dedicated to the worship of the sun.

Margasirsa Purnamasi: On this day, a fast to be broken at night after the worship of the moon with white garlands, grains, eatable offerings etc., and the worship of the Brâhmas is prescribed. The Brahmana lady, the sister, the aunt and the wife of a friend, each is to be honoured with a pair of red clothes.

Navahimapatotsava: Peculiar to Kashmira this festival covers the following components: Worshipping the mountain Himavan, the seasons Hemanta and Sisira, the Naga Nila, the local Naga and the goddess Syãmã; offering Kulmãsa; giving food prepared from Kulmasa and purified butter to the Brahmanas; feasting; listening to musical concerts; seeing the dances performed by courtesans and honouring the ladies. Dressed in heavy woollen cloaks, the people are enjoined upon to sit on snow and drink fresh wine if they are used to drinking.

Astamitraya: Srãddhas with offerings of vegetables, meat and cakes are to be performed respectively on the dark eighth of Pausa, dark eighth of Magha and bright eighth of Phalguna. Srãddhas to the females are to be offered on the 9ths of these very months and fortnights.

Pausa Paurnamaşi: If there is Pusya constellation on full moon of Pausa one is enjoined to apply white mustard-paste to one's body, to bathe oneself firstly in purified butter and thereafter in water mixed with all medicinal herbs, to worship Närãyana, Sakra, Soma, Pusya and Brahspati with eatable offerings, garlands etc., to perform fire sacrifice with mantras dedicated to the worship of the above deities, to honour the Brahmanas with wealth, to give new clothes to the priest, to eat milk of rice mixed with purified butter and to obtain in this way, all round prosperity.

Uttarayana: For this ceremony are prescribed Bath of the image of Visnu or Siva in purified butter; worship of stone image (of Visnu or Siva) with purified butter for three months; and gifts of purified butter, images made of purified butter, fuel arid grass (for the cows) to be given to the twice born.'

Tiladvadsasi: Celebrated on the 12th of dark half of Magha, this festival is marked by six fold rites performed with sesame. Five of these described in the Nilamata are: Bath with sesame, homa with sesame, naivedya of sesame, gifts of water mixed with sesame and gifts of sesame for the Brăhmanas.

Tararatrih: On the 14th of the dark half of Magha, bath in the water of a river or a pool, offerings of seven handfuls of water to each of the seven names of Yama, worship of Dharmarăja with flowers, incense, krasara etc., of the fire with sesame mixed with purified butter and of the Brahmanas with krasara and sacrificial fee are prescribed.

Sravanamavasya: The merit of bath etc. on the 15th of the dark half of Magha joined with sravana constellation is stated to be inexhaustible

Caturthya: Worship of Umă with lamps, eatables and cosmetics is prescribed on the 4th of the bright halves of Magha, Asvayuk and Jyestha. The ladies whose husbands are alive and sisters also are to be worshipped on these days.

Măgha Pürnima: Performance of srăddha with sesame and offerings of food for the crows are the only rites prescribed for this day.

Mahimăna: This festival is celebrated over a period of three days-on the 8th, 9th and 10th of the dark half of Phalguna. On the 8th, Sita the goddess of agriculture is worshipped with caru and cakes; on the 9th the goddess Karisini is worshipped and the Brăhmans are fed; on the 10th, the Brahmans, the friends and the subordinates are feasted and the musical concerts are attended.

Sravana Dvădasi: Fasting and the worship of Visnu are prescribed on the dark 12th of Phalguna conjoined with Sravana constellation.

Sivaratri: Sivalinga, from which the blanket like plaster of purified butter has been removed, is to be worshipped on the dark 14th of Phălguna

Second Mahimăna: Continuing for three days-8th, 9th and 10th of the bright half of Phalguna festival comprises these rites: Fast during the day and placing of oil-lamps on the snow on the evening of the 8th; decoration of the houses and the temples, worship of the goddess Sită, special feasting, singing, dancing and prohibition regarding giving of gifts except the cooked food on the 9th and decoration of the self, drinking of wine and other drinks and sporting of men with the ladies on the 10th.

Phalguni: The ceremonials of this festival begin on the full moon day of Phălguna and continue up to the dark 5th of Caitra. The worship of the sun and the moon, listen to musical concerts, seeing dramatic performances, self-decoration and taking meals consisting of parpatas are the main features. of this festival

Rajnisanapana: The image of Kasmira a personification of land of Kasmira stated to be rajasvala for three days from the 5th of the dark half of Caitra is to be worshipped for 1st three days with unguents, clothes and eatable offerings but not with flowers, incense, ornaments and milk which may be offered to her after her bath on the 8th. The rites to be performed on the 8th of the dark half of Caitra are: bath of Kahmirā's image firstly by women and then by the Brahmanas, worship of fire and the Brahmanas, sending food o the friends houses and listening to the music of *Tantri* instrument. The Brahma Purana explains the name of the festival by stating that the earth is the queen of the sun.

Krsyarambha: It is a festival celebrated at the commencement of cultivation. The Goddess earth and the cattle used for ploughing and various minor gods and goddesses along with sun and the moon and the five elements are worshipped.Singing, dancing and giving gifts to the Brahmanas are part of the celebration.

Chandodevapuja: Only women are supposed to worship Chandodeva on the 11th and 12th of the dark half of the Caitra with flesh of aquatic animals, various edibles, and garlands and fragrant saffron. A peculiar rite of sending Chandodeva out of the house through the door and bringing him in through the ventilator is also to be performed.

Pisācacaturdasi: On the dark 14th of Caitra, both Nikumbha and Sankara are to be worshipped. Offerings of meat etc. for the Pisacas; baptism of children and vigil at night, in the company of courtesans, are other features of this festival.

Caitrāmā: Srāddha is to be performed on this day and the dogs to be fed.

Navsamvatsara: The 1st of the bright half of Caitra is deemed to be the 1st day of creation. The two component parts of this festival are worship of Brahmā and the performance of Mahäsanti. Latter comprises the worship of Brahma, Visnu and Mahesvara, the planets and constellations, the divisions of time, fourteen Devendras, fourteen Manus, the sages, the daughters of Daksa, other goddesses, seven continents, nine divisions of Bhārata, seven worlds, seven nether worlds, five elements, the intelligence, the soul, the Püru the mountains, the rivers, the Vinayakas, the nymphs, the Adityas, the Vasus, the Rudras, the Visvedevas, the Asvins, the Bhrgus, the Angirasas, the Sādhyas, the Maruts etc.; names of the year, the month and the day, and the deities presiding over them; and feasting of the Brahmans and the relatives. (Nilamata, VV. 561 -643.)

Sripanchmi: Worship of Sri is prescribed on 5ths, especially on the bright 5th of Caitra. The worshipper, throughout his life, is endowed with prosperity and obtains Visnuloka after death.

Caitra,sasthi: The 6th of the bright half of Caitra is dedicated to the worship of Skanda and is associated with the health of children.

Caitranavami: Observance of fast and worship of Bhadrakāli with flowers, incense, food etc. are prescribed on this day.

Vastupujā: The worship of Vāstu, the deity of architecture, is prescribed on the bright 11th of Caitra.

Caitradvādasi: This festival is dedicated to the worship of Vāsudeva.

Madanatrayodasi: Celebrated on the 13th of the bright-half of Caitra, this festival has the following features Worship of a cloth- painting of Kāmadeva, self-decoration by men, honouring of the ladies of the house and bathing of the wife by the husband with the water of the pitcher which is to be placed before Kāmadeva on the 12th.

Pisacaprayana: This festival on the bright, 15th of Caitra commemorates Nikumbha's march to the Sea of Sand to fight with the Pisachas dwelling there in. A clay effigy or a grass effigy of the Pisaca is to be made and worshipped in every house at noon and at moon-rise. Then the Pisaca should be given farewell with songs, sounds of musical instruments and pronouncement of svastyayana by the Brahmans Next day, the worshippers should climb a nearby hill for following the Pisaca and observe a great festival with music and the din of people.

Iramañjaripujā: After the festival celebrating Nikumbha's departure there occurs the festival of Ira-flowers. Iramanjari is deemed to be the incarnation of a nymph who, being attached to Visvavasu, was cursed by Indra to become a plant on the Himalaya. The rites prescribed for this festival are visit to Ira-garden (Ira is the flower called 'Yurukam/'Virkin in Kasmiri and is used for the worship of Siva in Shivaratri festival); worship of Irāmañjari with flowers, eatables and lamps; common feast in Ira-garden; honouring the Brāhmanas, the friends, the wife and the relatives with Ira-flowers and garlands of Ira-flowers; taking drinks mixed with Ira-flowers and offering Ira-flowers to Kesva, Rudra, Brahmā, the Sun, the Moon, Laksmi, Durga, the Nagas and the Naga chief NiIa.

Aksayatritiya: River Gañga was brought down on the earth from Brahmaloka on the bright 3rd of Vaisākha, so the worship of Visnu with barley and that of the Gangā, especially on the bank of the Sindhu is prescribed on this day.

APPENDIX

BUDDHAJAJANMAMAHAH

Vaisakha Purnima: Honouring of five or seven Brãhmans with sesame mixed with honey, and worship of Dharmaraja are prescribed on this day.

Yavagrayana: This festival is celebrated when the barley becomes ripe. Offering new barley to the gods and the manes, and eating barley amidst sounds of musical instruments and the Brãhmanas are its main features.

Vinäyakã,Ashtami: All the 8th days are prescribed for the worship of Vinayaka but the dark 8th of Asadha is specially efficacious in giving success if one worships Vinãyaka and his ganas with sweetmeats, music and pleasing of the Brãhmanas on that day.

Svatiyoga: On a day conjoined with Svãti constellation, the worship of Vãyu with scents, garlands and food is prescribed.

Prasvapana: The Devaprasvapana ceremony is to be observed for the last five days of the bright half of Asãdha. The rites are: Performance of Dhanahotra and vigil at night on the 11th and the 14th, worship of the Brãhmanas and the Sãtvatas on the 12th and the 14th and gifts for dramatic performances on the 13th.

Vaisvadevapuja: The worship of all the gods is to be performed when the conjunction of Vaisvadeva constellation takes place in the end of the month of Asadha.

Daksinayana: The southern progress of the sun is to be celebrated with gifts of ground and parched grains, snow, sugar, vegetables, umbrella, shoes etc. made to the Brãhmanas.

Rohinisamyoga: The worship of Kashyapa the founder of Kashmira and of cows with their calves is prescribed on a day of Sravana conjoined with Rohini constellation.

Sravani: The ceremonials of this festival are: Bath at the confluence of the Vitastã and the Ganga, worship of Visnu-pronouncement of benedictory formula by the Brãhmanas chanting of the Sãmaveda; indulging in water-sports in the company of unmarried girls.

Krsnajanmaha: Krisna's birth-day festival is to be celebrated on the 8th of the dark half of Bhãdrapada. The god Krsna, his wife and his mothers Devaki and Yasodã are to be worshipped. Next morning the images of all these are to be carried by women to the bank of a river or a lake, amidst charming sounds of vocal and instrumental music. Barley food along with preparations of sugarcane, pepper and purified butter is to be eaten.

Maghamavasi: The dark 15th of Bhādrapada conjoined with pitr constellation is dedicated to the worship of seven groups of manes.

Bhadrapadasuklakrtya: 'On each day of the bright half' of Bhādrapada, Mahendra is to be worshipped along with his wife Saci, ganas, weapons and mount. The king should worship him in the way suggested by an astrologer. On the bright fifth of this fortnight, Nila and local Naga are to be worshipped.'

Sraddhapaksa: The whole fortnight is for the performance of Sraddhas, but while on other days the performance is optional, on the 13th it is compulsory. The 14th is prescribed for Sraddha of the one who were killed by means of weapons. The worship of the guardians of the quarters is prescribed on the 14th falling in Srāddhapaksa.

Mahanavami: Ved Kumari records, a few verses in the beginning seem to have been lost and whatever remains describes the worship of weapons at night in the temple of Durgā and the performance of Sānti called Nfrājanā on this festival day.

Agastyadarsana: To be performed when the sun is united with Kanyä constellation, this ceremony consists of these rites: Fast during the day, worship of Agastya at night with various eatables, flowers, sandal-wood paste, cow, bull, clothes, jewels, umbrella, shoes, staff and slippers, worship of the fire and the Brihmanas, abstinence from one fruit for one year, worship of an astrologer and seeing of the sage Agastya as shown by that astrologer.

Navaannavidhdna: The ceremony of new grains is to take place when the fresh crops are ready. Listening to vocal and instrumental music, recitation of Vedic texts, worship of gods, manes, Brahma, Ananta and guardians of the quarters, and making of gifts of rice and preparations of other grains to the Brahmans, the servants and the relatives are prescribed on this day.

Varunapancami: This day is dedicated to the worship of Varuna, Uma and Dhanada.

Asokikasatmi: Spread over three days of the bright half of Bhādrapada, this festival is dedicated to the worship of Umā and that of Asokikā_ probably personified Asoka plants. Bathing of virgins, decoration of men, women and children, dance performances and musical concerts are other features of this festival.

Vitastotsava: The 13th (of the bright half of Bhādrapada) is deemed to be the birthday of the river Vitastā. The birthday festival, however, includes three days preceding and three days following this 13th. Bath in the water of the Vitasta, worship of the Vitasta specially at the confluence of the Sindhu and the Vitasta, with scents, garlands, eatable offerings etc., gifts for dramatic performances and worship of actors etc. are prescribed for this festival.

Mahadvddasi: The bright 12th falling in Vitastotsava is called Mahadvādasi and is to be necessarily observed. If that 12th be conjoined with Buddha, the recital of God's names, bath, charity, funeral rites etc. performed on that (12th) become twelve-fold. Conjoined with Buddha and Sravavana, that day is called Atyantamahatidvādasi

Caturthtritaya: On the 4th days of Asvayuk Magha and Jyestha the faithful ladies whose husbands are living and also the sisters etc are to be honoured.

Asvadika: Worship of Uccaihsarvaha is prescribed when the moon is united with Svāti constellation in the bright half of Asvayuk and that of horses in general if that union takes place on the 9th. Pacificator rites are to be performed and threads coloured, in five colours are to be tied round horses' necks. Beating of horses and horse-riding are prohibited.

Hastidiksa: Similar rites for the elephants are to be performed when the moon is united with Sakra constellation.

Bhadrakali pujana: Performed on the 8th of the bright half of Asvayuk this ceremony consists of the worship of Bhadrakāli with incense, garlands, clothes, lamps, jewels, fruits, roots and drinks; the observance of vigil at night with music and dancing, worship of books, tools and weapons in the temple of Durga, eating of food mixed with curd, offering of balls of food to an eagle and feeding of the Brahmanas, friends and the relatives.

Grhadevipūja: In the beginning of the year, i.e. on the 1st of the dark half of Marga the goddess of the house is to be worshipped.

Syamadevipuja: This festival in honour of the goddess Syāma—personified as vine creeper—is to be celebrated when the grapes are ripe. Worship of Syamā, offering of first fruits to the Brāhmanas, eating of grapes, dance-performances and musical concerts are its main features.

Yatrotsava: As the ceremonies of pilgrimages to the temples of different deities are similar, the Nilamata describes them together though prescribing different dates for different pilgrimages. The dates are:4th day for visiting the abodes of Vinayaka, Dhanada and Mahādeva.;5th day for visiting the abodes of Varuna and sri.;6th for visiting the abode of Kumāra; 7th for visiting the abode of the Sun; 8th for visiting the abodes of Mahādeva and Sakra; 15th for visiting the abode of the Moon.; 5th, 12th and 15th for visiting the abode of the Nagas; 15th of the bright half for visiting the abode of all gods.The guest houses may be visited on all days.

Seven days preceding any *Yātrotsava* are prescribed for the worship of *Vinayaka,* the Gandharvas, the Pisachas, the Nagas, the Brāhmanas and the poor. The temple of the deity concerned is to be whitewashed and decorated: The image of the deity is to be bathed with the water brought from a sacred place by the citizens with a procession leading them. The image, thereafter, is to be placed in a nicely decorated conveyance which is to be carried around the city in a procession attended by the king or the president. Arrangements for dramatic performances and for honouring the spectators are also to be made.'"

Only on one day in the bright half of *Phalguna,* giving of gifts is prohibited, but even on that day the prohibition does not extend to the gifts of cooked food. This prohibition seems to be based on some superstitious agricultural sign as the festival, during which it occurs,

A few words may be said about the nature and significance of these vratas, utsavas and other religious practices.

Two festivals commemorate the New Year Day. One of these falls on the dark 1st of *Margasrisa* (Purnimānta month) according to the reckoning prevalent in Kashmira and the other occurs on the bright 1st of *Caitra* (Amānta month) according to the reckoning prevalent in most parts of the rest of India.

Some ceremonies like *Hastidiksā and Vāstupujā*, in which the fire is kept lit for six wintry months, are mere attempts to attach sacredness to objects and customs necessary for the well-being of the society.

Asvayuji festival and the festival of *Pisacaprayana* celebrate a historical event—occupation of Kasmira by the Pisacas. As regards the remaining vratas and utsavas, they are performed in honour of either a holy tithi or a sectarian deity"

Appendix-II

Festivals celebrated by the Hindu KSP during the medieval era

Anand Koul Bamzai the pioneer of modern research on the history and folklore of Kashmir has listed and detailed the festivals celebrated by the Hindu KSP during the medieval era in his book *'Kashir'*. The names of the same have been reproduced here barring any details as most of them are detailed in the book under the Chapter Rites, Rituals and Festivals of KSP.

Shiv Rattri or Herath, Tila Ashtami, Sonth 1st Chetr Sankrant, Navreh Amavasysa, Navreh, Baisakhi, Durga Ashtami, Ram Nawmi, Shraddh of Rishi Pir, Ganesh Choudas, Jeth Ashtami, Nirjalalkadashi, Haara Saptami, Hhara Ashtami, Hhara Nawami, Mela Jwala Bhagawati, Shrawan Punim, Chandan Shashti, Janam Ashtami, Vinayaka Chaturthi, Ganga Ashtami or Radha AshtamiPun, Indar Bah, Vitha Truvah, Anant Choudas, Kanyagat, Nava-Ratra, Durga Ashtami, Maha Nawami, Dasehra, Diwali, Kali's birthday, Khechri Mavas, Shishir Sankrat, Gauri Tritiya, Bhishma Ashtami, Shiv Chaturdashi, Sumri Amavasya.

APPENDIX-III

AMARNATH YATRA

Amongst the various sites of Hindu worship in Kashmir valley, one of the most revered and probably the most ancient and sacred of them all is the abode of Shiva in the Amarnath cave. Pilgrims throng, every year, on the Shravan Purnimashi day, during the month of August, to have the darshan of the ice Lingam, the antiquity of which has been well documented in the ancient literature of Kashmir including the Nilamat Purana.

"The cave which is adorned by the ice lingam, is a large solution cavity developed, probably, during the interglacial periods of the last ice age. It is carved out of dolomite- lime stones of the Triassic age (100 million years). The north western corner of the cave, which is a raised platform, is the seat of the ice lingam which forms at the extreme corner adjacent to the wall of the cave".

"This sacred cave situated at about 3,300 meters above the sea level, forms the western valley wall of the Amravati nala. Latter, a snow fed stream, is a tributary to the Panchtarni nala, which in turn flows into the Sindh River, a major tributary of the Jhelum. The ice lingam, an ice stalagmite, forms when the water, which percolates through the cracks and fissures of the roof, drips on the cave floor and starts to freeze, taking the complete shape of a large lingam by early May. When complete this magnificent structure attains a height of more than three metres. With the advent of summer, it begins to melt gradually, a process accelerated by the offerings of milk and water by the devotees, who start visiting the cave by early July. The melting continues till up to end of August and the lingam is rarely at its full glory at the time of the customary yatra. By the month of September no trace of the lingam remains".

APPENDIX

ROUTE OF PILGRIMAGE

The shrine is located to the south of Kashmir; about 140 Kms from the capital city of Srinagar.The pilgrims can approach this shrine by two routes. One is to drive down from the Srinagar city to Sonamarg and then to Baltal.There after a trek over a narrow mountain track and snow beds till one reaches the cave. After the holy darshan, one can be back to the base camp at Baltal, the same day. This route though a very short one is not open in summer when the ice bridges melt. Where as the conventional route is the picturesque and long march that starts from Pahalgam (2,180masl) the famous tourist resort in the Liddar valley. The pilgrims halt at three places overnight, on way up the shrine. These are Chandanwari (2,878masl), a vast grassy meadow surrounded by tall fir trees), Vavjan and Panchtarni. Between these two camps lie the most enchanting and mesmerising blue water mountain lake, the Sheshnag situated at a height of 3,554masl. It is generally believed that one can visualise the eminence of the supreme, at the sight of reflection of the setting sun on the lake waters. Excitement, among people peaks to behold a view of the Sheshnag /snake around midnight when slight commotion or ripples create in its otherwise still waters. Unauthenticated reports speak of its appearance on the surface of the spring around this time.

From Sheshnag a kilometre further is Vavjan that in local dialect connotes a place where violent cold winds blow. In earlier eras, many a fatal accidents would happen while climbing these ridges. Next stop is Panchtarni (3,857masl), a valley formed by five glacier melt streams and encircled by lofty snow-covered peaks. Amar Katha records,this confluence of five rivers is sacred because it is here that Lord Shiva is believed to have renounced the earth, water, wind, air and fire the five elements, (Panchatatvaha) of which he is the master and custodian.

Finally on the fourth morning the pilgrims reach the cave trekking over the frozen ice for a couple of kilometres to have a darshan of the holy lingam and the two smaller ice formations representing Parvati and Ganesha. The hardships and sufferings, which people undergo during the long and arduous journey, are compensated in this one great moment of celestial bliss.

"The entrance of the cave is some 24-25 metres high; with an inside huge enough to hold 1000 people at one go. So spectacular and splendid is the interior and exterior of the cave that it looks as if the imagination of thousands of architects and toil of an equal number of engineers has gone into the making of this magnificent piece of work. However, though, most amazing remains the sight of ice stalagmite. It defies all logic and earthly wisdom how water, drop by drop, trickles down through a seepage in the middle of the cave only to freeze down below and take the form of a lingam. The process reaches its highest point on the full moon night of the Shravan month. Two smaller formations of the ice on its left and right are taken as those of Goddess Parvati and Lord Ganesha respectively."

It is said that during the mediaeval times and till early part of the Dogra rule, many a pilgrim-mainly sadhus-used to jump down the slopes of the mountain offering their life in sacrifice to Shiva. Be that as it may, what appears to be more probable is that the treacherous nature of that route caused many a fatal accidents.

Pilgrims visiting the holy shrine feel doubly blessed if they get glimpse of a pair of snow pigeons-common in this area-which the devote Hindus believe to be the reincarnation of Shiva and Parvati. Pilgrims, before entering the holy cave prefer to have bath in the cold waters of the Amravati nala and rub their bodies with the vibhuti (rock powder brought down by the glacier ice) in preparation of one of the finest sites of supernatural glory, a site of unmatched serenity when calm and tranquillity descends on the mind and the time stands still.

The legends about the origin of the cave

This cave shrine situated in the Himalaya has, within, an ice lingam that is worshiped as a (svayambhu) Linga and is considered as the representation of the Lord Shiva, known in Kashmiri as Amburnath. Ice stalagmites of similar nature have been reported from other parts of the world to form once and never to repeat at the same place. The magnificent ice lingam of the holy cave of Amarnath has been forming every year for the last two thousand years or so of recorded history, despite the tremendous physiographic changes in the entire Himalayas including the Kashmir valley since last ice age. Indeed a miracle!

There is an interesting legend recorded in the Amarnath Mahatamya that states Lord Shiva, when implored fervently by Parvati to narrate her Tale of Eternity or Amarkatha, set out to look for, a forlorn and desolate place, where no life- human, animal or plant was possible. Because, in the Divine Trinity order, Shiva represents the Lord of Destruction and Amarkatha entwines in itself the secrets of life. Now the dilemma Lord faced was that under his divine jurisdiction, every life had to end in death and mere listening to the Katha would result in immortality of the listener, hence this spot at the altitude of 3300 meters approximately, was selected as it could not sustain any form of life.

Having selected the site, therefore, on his way to the cave, Lord Shiva began abandoning his personal effects and escorts, like son Ganesha, bull Nandi, snake and even the ever flowing Ganges. It is believed that Lord Ganesha was left at Ganeshbal, a placid and small hamlet just before Pahalgam. Traditionally, the purohits from this village perform puja at the shrine. The picturesque resort town of Pahalgam immortalised in many celluloid frames is actually said to be the distortion of *'bailgaon',* where Lord had kept his *bail* or bull. Further up at Chandanwari, he had left his *chender,* (Half Moon) at Sheshnag, the Naag (snake) and just before the cave the Lord placed the celestial river, the Ganges at the foot of the cave. River Amravati is believed to have flown ever since.

The legend says, "And then the Lord struck the mountain with his trident and formed the cave, and after taking a position began narrating the tale of eternity. While through with its day-long narration, Lord was astonished to find Parvati deep in slumber, however, equally astounded to discover two white velvety pigeons perched overhead in a recess of the wall chirping loudly 'yes, yes we heard the story; when Lord ostensibly wanted to know whether Goddess Parvati had heard the story. Thus, divine boon followed soon after-Liberty from the bounds of Time and Space, a perpetual state of eternity. Perhaps that explains their presence in the cave even today. Pilgrims consider their yatra even more successful if the divine creatures are beholden in full view."

Legends about the origin of the Yatra

This shrine and the annual pilgrimage to this place, is continuously recorded from the times of Nilamata Purana 6th century AD onwards in the Kashmiri literature, as well as local oral tradition. The origin of the yatra precedes the recorded history. As per legends, it is believed that Maharishi Bhrigu was the first person to identify the cave where Lord Shiva in absolute seclusion narrated the secret of *Ameretav (*immortality) to his consort Parvati. The Maharishi advised his disciple Takshat to guard the Shiva lingam and propitiate the deity. This happened on a full moon day in the month of Shravan. Subsequently, other Rishis also paid obeisance to the Lord in this cave on Shravan Purnimashi day that is also celebrated as Raksha Bandan day.

Yet, according to another popular myth, King Nara, (1008-1048 B.C.) a great devotee of Lord Shiva would visit the holy shrine on Raksha Bandan every year. This is how the tradition of the annual Yatra originated and in the days of yore it was more of a localised affair due to rigorous hazards of communication and transport. This pilgrimage has now transcended the geographical boundaries and the devotees, from across the country and abroad now makes a regular pilgrimage to the holy cave during the months of July to August culminating on the Raksha Bandhan day /Shravan Purnimashi.

Generations of holy men and pious laymen have paid their homage to this divine cave. In the 9th century AD, the Hindu teacher, Shankara, and in recent times Swami Vivekananda went on a pilgrimage to this holy spot.

It is believed a good part of Vedas was composed here and that the Buddhist Tripitakas were also collected and edited at this very place. As per Jonaraja, the Muslim ruler Zain-Ul-Abidin is said to have performed a holy pilgrimage to this sacred shrine to win the goodwill of his Hindu subjects.

Prescribed period of the Yatra

The Amarnath Yatra, according to Hindu belief, begins on *Ashadha Purnimashi* (day of the Full Moon in the Hindu Month of *Ashadha*) and ends on *Shravan Purnimashi*'(day of the full moon in the' Hindu month of *Shravan*).

Chronology of Amarnath Pilgrimage

Amarnath cave temple is reported to be about 5,000 years old. Exact manner of discovery of the cave is not known. There is ample and conclusive historical evidence to prove that the holy cave and the ice-lingam was known to the people since very ancient times and has been continuously and regularly visited by pilgrims both from Kashmir and other parts of the country. Original name of the tirtha, as given in the ancient texts, is Amareshwara, and the name Amarnath is of much later times.

The earliest reference to Amarnath is in the Nilamata Purana (v.1321). The pilgrimage to the holy cave has been described with full topographical details in the Bhringish Samhita and the Amarnath Mahatamyas, both ancient texts said to have been composed even earlier than the N.P.

Next in order are the references in the RajaTarangni compiled by Kalhana in the years 1148-49.AD and recorded in Rajatarangini, Book I verse. 267. Book v, 138, Book VII v.183 (English Translation by M. A. Stein.)

While recording the legend of the Naga Sushruvas, who in his fury burnt to ashes the kingdom of King Nara when he tried to abduct his daughter already married to. a Brahmin youth, and after the carnage took his abode in the lake now known as Sheshnag (Kashmiri *Sushramnag*), Kalhana writes, "The lake of dazzling whiteness [resembling] a sea of milk (Sheshnag), which he created [for himself as residence} on a far off mountain, is to the present day seen by the people on the Pilgrimage to Amareshwara."(Rajatarangini, Book I v. 267. Translation: M. A. Stein).

At another place in the Rajatarangini Kalhana says that the king Samdhimat Aryaraja (34BCE-17CE) used to spend "the most delightful Kashmir summer in worshipping a Linga formed of snow in the regions above the forest." This too appears to be a reference to the ice Linga at Amarnath.

There is yet another reference to Amareshwara or Amarnath in the Rajatarangini (Book VII v.183 and185) Queen Suryamati, the wife of King. Ananta (1028-1063), "granted under her husband's name agraharas at Amareshwara, and arranged for the consecration of *trishulas, banalingas* and other [sacred emblems]".

In his Chronicle of Kashmir, a sequel to Kalhana's Rajatarangini, Jonaraja relates that that Sultan Zain-Ul-Abidin during the construction of a canal-Shah Kol- along the left bank of the river Lidar (1420 AD) paid a visit to the sacred tirtha of Amarnath.

In the Fourth Chronicle of RT named *Rajavalipataka,* which was begun by Prjagyabhatta and completed by Shuka, there is a detailed reference to the pilgrimage to the sacred site (v. 84I, v 847-849) According to it, in a reply to Akbar's query about Kashmir, Yusuf Khan the Mughal governor of Kashmir at that time, described among other things 'the Amarnath Yatra in full detail. His description shows that not only was' the pilgrimage in vogue in Akbar's time (1586 AD)-but the phenomenon of waxing and waning of the-ice Linga was also well known.

Amareshwara (Amarnath) was a famous pilgrimage place in the time of Mughal Emperor Shah Jahan also. Famous Sanskrit scholar Panditraj Jagannath, in his eulogy of Asif Khan, Shahjahan's father-in-law, titled "Asif Vilas", has mentioned Amareshwara (Amarnath).

Francois Bernier, a French physician who accompanied Emperor Aurangzeb during his visit to Kashmir in 1663AD, while giving an account the places he visited in Kashmir, writes in his book "Travels in Mughal Empire' that, "I was pursuing journey to a grotto full of wonderful congelations, two days journey from Sangsafed, when I received intelligence that my Nawab felt very impatient and uneasy on account of my long absence". The "grotto" he refers to is obviously the Amarnath cave as the editor of the second edition of the English translation of the book; Vincent A. Smith makes clear in his introduction. Smith writes, "The grotto full of wonderful congelations is the Amarnath cave, where blocks of ice' stalagmites formed by dripping water from the roof are worshipped by many Hindus who resort here as images of Shiv a . . . ."

Another traveller, Vigne, in his book 'Travels in Kashmir, Ladakh and Iskardu', writes about the pilgrimage to the sacred spot in detail; clearly mentioning that "the ceremony at the cave of Amarnath takes place on the 15th of the Hindu month of Sawan" and that "Hindu's of every rank and caste can be seen collecting together and travelling up the valley of Liddar towards the celebrated cave . . . ."(1840 AD) Later in 1900 AD Stein records about this pilgrimage "as a popular one which attracts many thousands of pilgrims, not only from Kashmir, but from all parts of India."

Great Sikh Guru Arjan Dev is said to have granted land in Amritsar for the ceremonial departure of Chari Mubarak, the holy mace of Lord Shiva which marks the beginning of the Yatra to the Holy Cave.

Noted Kashmiri naturalist Pandit Samsar Chand Kaul in his booklet titled 'The Mysterious cave of Amarnath' writes, "In 18I9 the year in which the Afghan rule came to an end in Kashmir, Pandit Hardas Tiku "founded the Chhawni Amaranth at Ram Bagh in Srinagar, where the Sadhus from the plains assembled and where he gave them free rations for the journey, both ways from his own private resources".

All these records prove beyond any doubt that this pilgrimage has been going on continuously for millennia's' and is still thriving as one of the most important symbols of Hindu KSPs faith and presence in the land of their origin.

Appendix-IV

Prehistoric finds of Kashmir

The account given here is based on Dr H D Sankalia's book '*Southern Neolithic and other Cultures*', pages 163 . . .167. He writes, "The Karewa terraces at Burzahom and Gurfkral are found strewn with huge stones, which are foreign and were certainly brought by man who had erected megalithic monuments. Not much is known about this man but of his predecessor(s) we have fairly good knowledge. Long after the last flat terraces—the Karewas! Were laid the men who appeared did not live on the shrinking river banks; instead they chose to live on these terraces. The evidence from Burzahom and Martand (not yet published) indicates that instead of building with either mud/clay or stone, the man preferred to scoop out earth from the Karewas and live in the dwellings that are called 'pit-dwellings.'(Page 164)"

Continuing further, Dr. Sankalia writes, "The inhabitants of the Karewas primarily depended upon hunting and fishing and were naturally growing fruits, vegetables and eatable grasses the alley offered then. However, no exact idea of the animals can be had, unless the bones found in the several storage pits and on the floors of houses are studied. But the presence of ibex, wild dog or wolf and deer is suggested by the skeletons of the first two found intentionally buried in pits and of the latter from refuse found in small storage pits. The intentional burial of the first two might also suggest the love and regard these early Kashmiris had for the animals who helped them in hunting. These animals or their selected bones were buried either separately or deposited with the human skeletons. In one instance are found the skeletal remains of five wild dogs"

"So far five human burials of this phase have been noticed. These were found buried in pits which were generally circular or oval on plan and in most of the cases narrow at the top and wide at the base. Their inner sides were often coated with lime. Four of the human skeletons were found buried in a crouched position. It is not clear as to which period they belong. Both the ground or polished stone and bone industries are rich and varied. They give an idea of the comparatively sophisticated or complex life of the inhabitants of these high, elevated places."

The tools discovered are polished broadly and are of two grades '(a) heavy duty tools and (b) light duty tools.'

In each category, there are axes, wedges, chisels, adzes, hoes, perforated pick, harvesters, flake knives, mace-heads and double pointed poker.

Though in the remains of the houses no grains or traces of clothes have been found, one can definitely postulate two things.

First, the high karewa inhabitant was not a nomad, living only on fishing and hunting. Though these arts for eking out a livelihood were practised, as the bones of the animals from the kitchen middens would testify,- different kinds of ground stone tools particularly the large and small hoes, stone querns and the harvesters—show that the man needed these tools for various agricultural practices, such as digging, sowing, planting and cutting the grains (which should be rice and millets. There are indications that the grain was pounded and also mixed with meat, cereals and vegetables. Another very important feature is the presence of large and small bone needles among the stone implements. These they must have used to stitch their clothes. The bigger needles (bodkins) must have been used for stitching the skins and other thick material, since they lived in a cold country. Those of the earliest phase, called Period 1, "were narrow at the top, and wide at the base with a flat floor and side walls occasionally plastered with mud." These pits were provided with landing steps, but as these steps do not take one, to the floor of the pit, it is presumed that for further descent a ladder was used.

Post-holes on the periphery of the mouth of the pit were probably meant for constructing a roof with wooden posts and no other superstructure, while the small-sized storage pits on the ground level probably belong to the dwellings of Phase (or Period) II and not to that of Phase I.

So far 16 dwelling pits have been exposed, of which the largest measured 2.74 metres at the top, 4.57 metres at the bottom and 3.96 metres in depth. That these pits were meant for habitation, including cooking, is indicated by bands of ash and charcoal in the pit walls. For kitchen refuse and storing grain (not yet found) small pits were dug in at ground level, but for storing wood, birch, hay and pots, larger crescent-shaped pits were dug close to the living pits.

Conical shaped, but irregularly dressed leaning stones, 0.91 to 1.51 metres in length and 0.22 to 0.44 metres in width, found in three pits of Phase I as well as in a burial of the megalithic period (II), might have some religious significance . . . As more extensive area was exposed the pits used seem to be bigger and rectangular rather than round or oval. The houses were now prepared by plastering the floor of the filled up pits of the earlier phase with mud, and further covered with a thin coat of red ochre. Since the houses were big, mud platforms with partitions were provided; and as the house plans were repeatedly changed (because of destruction by fire, of which there is plenty of evidence), the floors at several levels are riddled with post holes. In one trench (about 3.96x 1.21 metres ;) at a depth of 2.13 metres below surface, no less than 45 post-holes occur. These houses were provided with hearths and grind stones (Page 165)

So far five human burials of this phase have been noticed. These were found buried in pits which were generally circular or oval on plan and in most of the cases narrow at the top and wide at the base. Their inner sides were often coated with lime.

Four of the human skeletons were found buried in a crouched position. It is not clear whether in these or the Period III burials the interments were both primary and secondary. Since a reference is made to extentended articulated skeletons one may think that it refers to the megalithic or Period III, but the caption of the plate mentions Phase II.

Two noteworthy features of the burials of Phase 11 were the use of red ochre on the bones, and the evidence of trephining- (operation on the skull by removing part of bone to relieve pressure on the brain)—seven finished and four unfinished circular holes on a skull were found. The orientation of the human skeleton or the physical type represented is not mentioned.

Initially in Phase 1 the pottery is not only handmade but the fabric and the surface finish were coarse. Only three shapes—bowl, vase and stem—seem to be represented, but later in Phase11, the types increase and are grey or black, and burnished ware also appears. The repertory pots and pans at Burzahom(page 166)-consists of: (1) hemispherical bowls with a ring base; (2) bowls with outgoing sides, with probably a stand, (3) deep bowls or cups with straight sides or outgoing sides; (4) funnel-mouthed vessels (lower part unknown); (5) small elongated vessels with a bulging belly, cylindrical neck and ring base; (6) large high necked jar in black and red burnished surfaces; (7) small, wide-mouthed vessel with a beaded rim; (8) a small thick-based dish or plate (usually these are used for kneading dough, though here the vessel is comparatively small); and (9) stand with a triangular perforation and parallel grooves on the body.

A few vessels have mat impressions, which suggest that the pit, hut or the place where the potter kept their pots had woven floor mats.

Both the ground or polished stone and bone industries are rich and varied. They give an idea of the comparatively sophisticated or complex life of the inhabitants of these high, elevated places.

Appendix-V

Cast division of India

Arian's detailed description of cast division of India when the Greeks visited the country

Greek historian Arrian writes, "The people of India are divided into seven castes" and describes each cast in detail thus:

(1)The Sophists are not so numerous as the others, but hold the supreme place of dignity and honour, for they are under no necessity of doing any bodily labour at all, or of contributing from the produce of their labour anything to the common stock, nor indeed is any duty absolutely binding on them except to perform the sacrifices offered to the gods on behalf of the state or on behalf of a private person. To this class the knowledge of divination among the Indians is exclusively restricted and none but a sophist is- allowed to practise that art. They predict about such matters as the seasons of the year, and any calamity which may befall the state; but the private fortunes of individuals they do not care to predict. But if anyone fails thrice to predict truly he incurs, it is said no further penalty than being obliged to be silent for the future, and there is no power on earth able to compel that man to speak who has once been condemned to silence.

These sages go naked living during winter in the open air to enjoy the sunshine, and during summer when the heat is too powerful, in meadows and low grounds under large trees. They live upon the fruits which each season produces and on the bark of trees,-the bark being, and no less sweet and nutritious, than the fruit of the date-palm.

(2) the Tillers of the soil, who form the most numerous class of the population. They are neither furnished with arms, nor have any military duties to perform, but they cultivate the soil and pay tribute to the kings and the independent cities. In times of civil war the soldier are not allowed

to molest the husbandmen or ravage their lands; hence, while the former are fighting and killing each other as they can, the latter may be seen dose at hand tranquilly pursuing their work,-perhaps ploughing, or gathering in their crops, pruning the trees; or reaping the harvest.

(3)The Herdsmen consist of the both shepherds and neat herds and these neither live in cities nor in villages, but they are nomadic and live on the hills. They too are subject to tribute, and this they pay in cattle. They scour the country in pursuit of fowl and wild beasts.

(4) Handicraftsmen and retail dealers they have to perform gratuitously certain public services, and pay tribute from the products of their labour. An exception, however, is made in favour of those who fabricate the weapons of war, for which even draw pay from the state. This class also includes shipbuilders and the sailors employed in the navigation of the rivers.

(5)The Warriors are second in point of numbers to the husbandmen, and lead a life of supreme freedom and enjoyment. They have only military duties to perform. Others make their arms, and others supply them with horses, and they have others to attend on them in the camp, which takes care of their horses, clean their arms drive their elephants, prepare their chariots, and act as their charioteers. As long as they are required to fight they fight and when peace returns they abandon themselves to enjoyment, the pay which they receive from the state being so liberal that they can with ease-maintain themselves and others besides.

(6) Superintendents. They spy out what goes on in country and town, and report everything to the king where the people have a king and to the magistrates where the-people are self-governed, and it is against use and wont to give in a false report- but indeed no Indian is accused of lying.

(7) Councillors of the state, advise the king, or the magistrates of self-governed cities, in the management of public affairs. In point of numbers this is a small class, but it is distinguished by superior wisdom and justice, and hence enjoys the prerogative of choosing governors, Chiefs of provinces, deputy-governors, superintendents of the treasury, generals of the army, admirals of the navy, controllers, and commissioners who superintend agriculture.

The custom of the country prohibits inter-marriage between the castes. It is permitted that the sophist only be from any caste: for the life of the sophist is not an easy one but the hardest of all.

Notes and References

Preface

[1] Anthropological studies of the valley have revealed that the aborigines, (ancestors of this linguistic group) were lake dwellers. Geologically, the Kashmir valley was a land of lakes and marshes during the Neolithic era.

Chapter - I - Kasheer Our Homeland

[1] Baron Charles Von Hugel: *Kashmir and Punjab*, preface p., xiii, Pub, Light and Life Jammu 1972

[2] Ramlal Kanji Lal and Pandit Jagadhar Zadoo: *translation Nilamat. Purana*, Introduction p.4-5, 1924

[3] Samuel Beal, Trans. *Life of Hiuen Tsiang* by Shaman Hwuili, 111, p. 10, Pub1973- Hiuen Tsang has recorded the legend of the creation of the valley according to the Buddhist tradition thus, "This country was once a dragon lake, while the Buddha was flying over this lake with his disciple Ananda, he remarked, After my decease, Madhyantika, an arhat or monk will, in - this place, establish a country, settle people and propagate Buddhism." When Madhyantika heard of this he was delighted and repaired to a wood. A dragon was greatly impressed by the various miracles that this monk performed. He came to him and asked him what he wanted, whereupon - the arhat made a simple request for the grant of a dry land in the lake which should be enough for him to sit on cross- legged. The dragon immediately agreed and withdrew some water from the lake to provide space for the monk. But Madhyantika with his superhuman powers enlarged his body so much that the entire lake was almost dried up. Then the dragon appealed to the monk to settle there permanently, which request could not be complied with at that time, for his Parinirvan or salvation was near. In the fifth year after the nirvana he drained the lake, subdued the Naga and peopled the land He, however, left 500 other arhats to live in Kashmir for propagating Buddhism."

[4] Wilson Hymen: *The Hindu History of Kashmir*, p.8, notes 1, pub London, 1841.

[5] Muhammad Azam in his Book; *Wakiat-I-Kashmir* (1747 AD) records the Muslim format of the creation theory thus, "The country was entirely covered with Water,

in the midst of which a demon, Jaldeo, resided; who preyed upon mankind and seized on every thing and person he could meet within the neighbouring regions. It happened at length that Kashef, the son of Marichj, and according to some accounts the grand son of Brahma, visited this country, and having spent some time in pious abstraction on mount Sumeru, turned his attention to the desolated appearance of the earth, and enquired its cause. The people told him of the abode of Jaladeo in Sati Sar, and his predatory incursions upon them. The heart of *Kashef* was moved to compassion and he took up his residence in Noubadan, near Hirapur, for a thousand Years, employing that period in religious austerities. In consequence of which Mahadeo appeared to him, and assented to his prayers for the extirpation of Jaladeo. Mahadeo accordingly sent his servants Vishnu and Brahma to expel the demon. Vishnu was engaged in the conflict for 100 years, when finding that the mud and water afforded a secure retreat to the Deo, he at last made the chasm at Baramulla by which the waters were drained off, the demon exposed, taken and slain, and the country recovered and rendered habitable being thence called *Kashef*-sir, or the mountain of Kashef

6 Wilson Hymen: Op.cit: *The Hindu History of Kashmir* p 8, notes 1. "According to Forster the legends of the country assert that Solomon visited the valley and finding it covered, except one eminence, with noxious water, which had no outlet, he opined a passage in the mountains and gave to Kashmir its beautiful plains."

7 Sir Walter R. Lawrence, in his book *The Valley of Kashmir*, p 184,(1895) has recorded two versions of the legend of creation on the basis of his personal assessment of the same as prevalent among the inhabitants of the valley. He writes "KSP's mostly believed that the valley was once a vast lake, on which the Goddess Parvati sailed in a pleasure boat from her mountain home of Harmukh in the north, to Konsar Nag Lake in the south. In her honour the Lake was known as Sati Sar, the tarn of a chaste woman. But their dwelt in the lake a cruel demon Jal Deo, whose patron was Brahma, and this demon destroyed all life and rendered the country waste. By chance Kashaf, a grandson of Brahma, found his way to the lake, and distressed at the havoc wrought by Jal Dev resolved to overcome the demon. For 1,000 years Kashaf gave himself up to religious exercises and then braced himself up for a struggle with Jal Dev but the demon eluded and hid under the water. Then Vishnu came to the help of Kashaf and struck the mountain at Baramulla with his Trident, and the waters of the lake rushed out. But Jal Dev entrenched himself in the low ground near Hari Parbat, and though the Gods searched for him with the sun in one hand and the moon in the other, the demon baffled them. But at last the Goddess Parvati dropped a mountain on top of him, crushing his life out, and the mountain is now known as Hari Parbat, and on it is a great shrine in honour of the Devi. After this the valley was known as Kashafmar, the home of Kashaf now corrupted to Kashmir.

Yet another legend with a slight twists records: Kashaf was a mighty wrestler, who, becoming suddenly religious, was smitten with a desire to worship at the 1,000 temples, which were hidden under the waters of the lake. He pierced the mountain at Baramulla with a trident and so dried up the valley. When Jaldeo was crushed to death the smaller demons lost heart, and men began to visit the valley in summer. As winter came on they withdrew to the warmer and drier regions of Kishtwar and were leaving Kashmir to the demons. But by chance an old Brahmin, who was unable to walk, spent the winter in the valley and went to Nil Nag and the deity of the mountain gave him the Nilmat Purana. By studying the precepts of the Purana the Brahmins were enabled to rout the demons and Kashmir became permanently inhabited about the 20th century B.C"

8 Dr. Ved K.G: *Trs. N.P.Vol.11*, p.37,{ Verse 131-140(Ed. Leiden v.v. 134-137 }pub., J& K Academy of Art & Culture 1973.

9 V.K Raina (Paper) *Kashmir the Legend* it is, (Scientific analysis of the Legend of Creation of Kashmir,) Panchtarni Annual No, p 36 (1997-98}

10 ibid p37

11 ibid p.38

12 Ibid p 40

13 Bernier François: *Voyage de Kachemir travels in the Mogul Empire Including Kashmir Translat*ed by John Stuarts Calcutta, 1826. pub., 1914 {H.H. Wilson, *Hindu History of Kashmir*, p.9}

14 Fredrick: Drew, Northern *Barrier of India; popular account of Jammu and Kashmir territories*. p. 211-12, London 1971

15 V.K.Raina: 0p.cit, *Critical analysis of The Legend of the Creation of the Valley* Panchtarni Annual Number Vol. 1, p 41,-

16 *Historian's History of the World*, Vol, I1, P. 485

17 Kaumudi: *Kashmir*, p 1

18 Pearce Gervis: *This is Kashmir*, preface p. xv, pub., Cassel & Company London, 1954

19 Sir Francis Young Husband: *Kashmir* p.115, pub., Edinburgh, 1909

20 Lawrence; Op.cit, *the Valley Of Kashmir* p 13

21 M.A. Stein, translation Kalhana: *R.T. Vol. 11* p 386-7

22 V. K.G.: Op.cit *N.P. Vol 1*, P59, verse 226 -227

23 Ibid. N.P. vol. 1 p., 22;

24 IbidR.T.Vol.11 p387

25 Dr V.KG: Op.cit, *Nilamat Purana vol.1*, p 23

26 G.M.Sufi: *Kashir,* pp12-13

27 Ibid: p. 22-23-, Stein R.T.vol.11 p365

28 Hiuen Tsiang: *Siyuki,* AD 629 translated from Chinese by Samuel Beal, I p148; R.T. Vol 11 p 353-.355

29 Thomas Watters M.R.A.S.: *On Yuan Chwang's travels in India* (AD629-645) P 259-260. Oriental Publishers India Delhi

30 M.A.Stein op cit: *R.T.Vol.11,* p 353, 386 -387

31 Ibid. *R.T.* p.351, Ptolemy, I 42, Dionysios Dionosiaka xxvi, 165

32 Ibid Op. cit *vol. 11*, p. 386

33 Ibid *R.T. Vol. 11* p 387

Chapter -2 - Physiographic description

1 M.Griffith: *India's Princes*, P. 1

2 Dr. Ved K.G: Translation. *N.P.Vol.11,* p.45, 48, verse 169,-170, p 48, (v181)

(Ed. Leiden v.v. 134-137 Pub, J& K Academy of Art & Culture 1973

3 Lawrence: *The valley of Kashmir*, pp. 14-15,

4 James P. Ferguson: *Kashmir,* P. 140, pub., 1961.

5 tein: *R.T., Bk IV*, note 593, Moor craft *Travels*, ii pp 153

6 DK Bhat: *Memoirs, GSI. Vol. 122, Lithostratigraphy of Karewa group, Kashmir Valley, India and Critical review of its Fossil Record 1989* (Buin-Chinar-*Platanus orientalis kashmiriana* is probably one of the oldest trees found in the valley, going by the fossil leaf impressions belonging to *Genus Acer* (Maple tree) and Genus Quercus (Oak tree) reported from the Hirpur Formation of the Lower Karewas of the Kashmir valley.

7 Abul Fazal: *Akbar Nama, trs. H.Beveridge Vol iii* Pages 624, & 956, pub Rare Books Delhi 1973

8 Jawaharlal Nehru The essay 'Escape' included in the *Volume Unity of India.*

9 Stein Trs Kalhana, R.T. *Bk 1*, Verse 40-43, Bk. 111, verse 358-363

10 Sir Walter R Lawrence, *the Valley of Kashmir*, p13 . . .17 Oxford University press London, 1895

NOTES AND REFERENCES

[11] François: Bernier *Travels in the Mogul Empire Including Kashmir* Translated By John Stuart Calcutta, 1826. (Earlier editions AD 1656-i668 London, latter editions 1891 1914 Bernier visited Kashmir in 1630)

[12] Stein: Op.cit *R.T.Vol, 11*; p.445

CHAPTER -3 - *KASHUR* THE PEOPLE

[1] Ved K.G.*: N.P vol.11* Page 61 verse 235.

[2] G.A. Grierson, *Z.D.M.G. LXVI.(Zeitchrift der Deutschen Morgenlandischen Gesellschaft* {Ved Kumari, trans., N.P. vol. 1 p.,69}

[3] De Terra and Paterson: *Studies on, Ice Age in India* pp. 230 and 310-113 Gordon, D.H., the *Prehistoric Background of Indian Culture*, p. 113)

[4] G.E.L.Carter, I.C.S: *Memoirs of the Archaeological Survey of Kashmir No. 2, The Stone Age in Kashmir {1924} "Catalogue of remains 1*

[5] P.N.Bamzai: *History of Kashmir*, pp.54-57

[6] Sunil Chandra Ray: *Early History and Culture of Kashmir*: p,2 De Terra and Paterson: *Studies on i, Ice Age in Indi*a pp. 230 and 310-113, Gordon, D.H.: *The Prehistoric Background of Indian Culture*, p. 113

[7] R.C.Kak: *ASI, No. 9*, p.73, 1935

[8] D Terra, H.: '*Excavations at Burzahom*', *Miscellanea of the America Philosophical Society*, 1936, Gordon, D. H.: *the Prehistoric Background of Indian Culture*, p. 3JJT)

[9] DR.H.D.Sankalia: *Prehistory of India Southern Neolithic and other Cultures*, pp 163-167

[10] Dr. Sunil Chander Ray: *Early History and Culture of Kashmir*, pp32-33, A.K.Sharma: *Neolithic Human Burials from Burzahom Kashmir*

[11] P.N.Bamzai, History *of Kashmir, sec. Primitive History*

[12] Dr.Ved Kumari: *The Nilamata Purana Vol 11*, trs.p232-251.1973

[13] Hiuen Tsiang: *Si-Yu-Ki,* Op.cit i, p. 148 compo N.P, pub. AD629, (*ANCIENT GEOGRAPHY OF KAS'MIR Chap. II)*

[14] Ved Kumari: *N.P. trs Vol.1* p46

[15] Hiuen Tsiang: Op.cit Vol I, p., 28-31

[16] Vogel: *Indian Serpent Lore*, pp 22

17 Dr C. F. Oldham: *Serpent Worship in India in* J.R.A.S., p391, pub 1891,

18 Dr Ved Kumari: *N.P Vol.1*, p.58.

19 Prof. G.M. Rabbani; *Ancient Kashmir* p 6 pub 1981

20 Kaumudi: *Kashmir its Cultural Heritage.*

21 C.E. Tyndale Biscoe: *Kashmir in Sunlight and Shade*, p. 60

22 M, Griffith-: *India's Princes and Heritage*, Pub London 1894

23 Bernier: *Travels in the Mogul Empire Including Kashmir* Op.cit, p. 390

24 Pt., Anand Kaul: *Kashmiri Pandit*, p.20

25 V.K.G: Op.cit. *Nilamata manuscript*, vv.62, 335, 458,773{Gai trans., Vol 1 p 117}

26 Wakefield:, Happy *Valley, History of Kashmir, p. 38.*

27 Ibid. Happy *Valley, History of Kashmir*

28 Lawrence: *The Valley of Kashmir*, pp, 276-277

29 Ibid p 272

30 G. M. D. Sufi: *Islamic culture in Kashmir*, p.12-13

31 Dr. Ved Kumari; *N.P . . . T.; Vol. II*, vers.280-281,290,294-296

32 Lawrence: Op.cit, *the Valley Of Kashmir*; p. 9, 6, 272.

33 James P. Ferguson: *Kashmir* p137

34 Ibid; *Kashmir* p. 145

35 Lawrence: *The Valley of Kashmir* p 278

36 History of Aurangzeb, *Ruqat-i-Alamgiri* Vol.V, 1924 edition, page 415,

37 G. L.Kaul: *Kashmir*, Chapter, XIV. p., 247, pub., 1967

38 Note: There are different versions about the time of the origin of this division among the KSP Hindus. Some believe that the original inhabitants of the valley and their descendents are the *Malmasis*, whereas those who migrated from plains into the valley are the *Banamasis.* Some historians, however, state the Malmás Hindus are the descendants of Kashyapa, the saviour of the valley, and that the Banamás Brahmans were foreigners, who came from other countries. Yet another concept is that the people, who continued to stay in the valley in spite of all the hardships of conversion during the 13th century, are the Malmasis and those who ran away and returned from exile during king Zain-ul-Abidin rule are the Banamasis.

NOTES AND REFERENCES

39 Greek Historian Arrian: *Classical Accounts of India 111, Indika,* p 226

40 FM. Husnain: *Hindu Kashmir Twilight* p.13o, 131

41 Dr. Ved Kumari; *N.P. vol., 1*, p.77

42 Stein*; R.T. Bk., 1* 170) 53 (R.T. Bk., 342; Bk. IV 96,645 Bk. Vii, 48, 274, 325 360, bk. Viii, 376, 3031, 3232, 1190

43 S., C, Ray: *Early History and culture of Kashmir* P.100-101

44 Krishna. Mohan: *Early Medieval History of Kashmir,* p211

45 *N.P. vv.,* 385, 431,475,490 {V.K. Trans. N.P. Vol. 1 p 78}

46 *N.P. vv.* 631-632 Ibid Vol. 1 p 79, 82

47 *Nilamata v.*829 Ibid Vol.1 p82

48 *Nilamata vv.* 562, 705, 794, 800, etc Ibid Vol 1 p 84

49 *N.p. v,* 384, 863, N.P.vv.528, 688,813 etc Ibid Vol 1 p 87

50 Stein*: R.T, viii,* 2383

51 Ibid *R.T, vii.*39-41

52 S.C.Ray; *Early History and Culture of Kashmir* p112)

53 R.S.Pandit trans. Kalhana, Bk V. verse 74-78

54 Ibid, Bk V, verse 387

55 Jyoteeshwar Pathik: *Glimpses of History of Jammu & Kashmir*, p 32

56 Abu-l-Fazal: *Ain-i-Akbari (Jarrett's translation), Vol. 11,* p.351,{R.T Rajat Pandit. Invitation}

57 J. F. Hewitt: *The Ruling Races of Prehistoric Times in India, South Western Asia and Southern Europe*, P 145

58 Dr.S.S Toshkhani: *Rites and Rituals of Kashmiri Brahmans*

59 Pandit Anand Koul: *Kashmiri Pandit*, p.20

60 Ibid, *Kashmiri Pandit*, p.20

61 D.D.Raina: *Kashmir Distortions and Reality'* p.39

62 N.N.Mujoo.: *Panchtarni Annual No Vol 11,* p.38

63 Lawrence: *The* Valley Of Kashmir p313

64 Ibid: *The Valley of Kashmir* p.306

65 Ibid, *Valley Of Kashmir* p.306

66 Ibid *Valley of Kashmir* 306-7

67 Lawrence: Races and tribes P.300 -301

68 Lawrence: *The Valley of Kashmir* p.301

Chapter- 4 - Religion

1 Dr. S.S.Toshkhani: *Kashmir sentinel Vol. 14 No. 8* P.17)

2 George Feuerstein, Subhash Kak and David Frawley: *In Search of the cradle of Civilisation*, p. 193 Pub., 1995

3 Dr. Ved K. *N.P. vol.* 1,

4 Op-cit.: N.P.Vol 1, P.193 {vv, 469-71 3 V.471-77}

5 "*Navahimapatotsava* peculiar to Kasmira, this festival consists of the following Component parts: Worshipping the mountain Himavan, the seasons Hemanta and Sisira, the Naga king Nila, the local Naga and the goddess Syama offering Kulmasa as bali; giving food prepared from Kulmasa and purified butter to the Brahmanas; feasting; listening to musical concerts; seeing the dances performed by courtesans and honouring the ladies. Dressed in heavy woollen cloaks, the people are enjoined upon to sit on snow and drink fresh wine if they are used to drinking." Dr. Ved K. N.P. vol., 1, p193-94 Nilamata, vv. 461-68

Iramanjaripujana,:"Nila and the local Nagas receive; worship along with various other gods and goddesses. Nila says '.Ira is dear to the Nagas and to me she is specially so, whosoever pays worship to me in an Ira garden with Ira flowers;, with him I am pleased excessively". Nilamata, vv. 469-71 3 Ibid. vV.471-77

Varunapancami "On the bright fifth of Indra's fortnight the receivers of the offerings are Nila and the local Nagas. Fifth, twelfth and bright fifteenth of a month are prescribed for pilgrimage to the abodes of the Nagas.' Before going on Pilgrimage, one had to worship different gods on different days of a week and of these days; the fifth one is reserved for the-.worship of the local Naga. *Varunapancami is* dedicated to the worship of Nila under the name Dhanada."

6 Stien: trs. Kalhana *R.T. Bk. 1* p 28, v 128)

7 Ibid: R.T. BK.1 P. 201-273;

8 Ibid: R.T, bk. III p 530

9 Ksemendra: *Samayamatrika* p11, 88 ;(R.T. Bk)

NOTES AND REFERENCES

[10] *Mahavamsa,* xii, 3; S.C. Ray Early History of Kashmir p.,156

[11] Boston: *History of Buddhism* Trans, Obermiller, ii, p 90

[12] Abul Fazal: *Ain-I-Akbari Vol, ii,* Trs. Jarret, 2nd edition, p.356

[13] Dr. Ved K: *N.P., vol.* 1p193-94 1,

[14] J.N. Ganhar and P.N. Ganhar: *Buddhism in Kashmir and Ladakh* P.61)

[15] Kalhana: *R.T, vol.1 Bk.1*, p.102

[16] Thomas Walters: *On Yuan Chwang*, Vol, 1 pp.270-271

[17] *Samuel Beal Tran's. Hiuen Tsang*, p.156

[18] Ibid, *RT. Bk.111*, p.463-464

[19] Samuel Beal; Trans *Hiuen Tsang*, p. 157

[20] Ibid p 157

[21] Stein *R.T., IV*, 200-203

[22] *Ibid R.T. IV*, 211

[23] *R.T: Bk IV,* verse-, 213, 259, 262

[24] *R.T.,* iv, verse, 507

[25] R.C Kak.: *Ancient Monuments*, pp, 146-149

[26] N. Dutt: *Gilgit Manuscript (Ed.).* I. Introduction p, 45

[27] Kalhana *R. T., VI.* 174

[28] *R. T., V,* 172-173

[29] *R. T., VI,* 175

[30] R.T.Vol vii 1082-1108

[31] J.N. Ganhar and N. Ganhar: *Buddhism in Kashmir and Ladakh,* P.61

[32] Ibid, P.61)

[33] Dr. S.S.Toshkhani,: *Kashmir sentinel Vol. 14 No. 8* P.17

[34] Dr. Ved, Kumari*: N.P.Vol.1,* p163,

[35] (R.T. bk.1, verse 106

[36] R.T. Eng. trs, by Stein*; R.T.1,* v.107

[37] Ibid:*R.T., IV*, 190

[38] Ibid *R.T., IV*, 45)

[39] Ibid *R.T, iv*, 115

[40] Ibid; *R.T. vol.1*, p 194

[41] R.C.Kak: *Ancient Monuments of Kashmir*, pp. 114,126,127, 154, Kak, *Handbook* pp, 55-56

[42] J.C. Chatterjee: *Kashmir Saivism*, p36

[43] S.Shukla: *Cultural Trends in Kashmir and Ksemendra*; p 193

[44] Kaw R.K.: *Doctrine of Recognition*, p. Sun Rise 63

[45] Kamalakar Mishra:, Kashmir Shaivism. p. 39 pub., 1993

[46] C.L Raina: *Essay, Swami Ram Ji Maharaj, Panchtarni Annual No. vol. 10*, p1

[47] Kamalakar Mishra: *Kashmir Shaivism*, p 32 pub. 1993;

[48] Ibid. Abhinavagupta in his *Tantraloka*, P 172;

[49] Dr, Ved Kumari trs. N.P. vol. 1, p 145

[50] N.P., v 1158-9, 1358

[51] N.P . . . Dr, Ved Kumari vol. 1, p 157

[52] R. T., III, 350-351

[53] R. T., III, 144-158

[54] Srikantha Carita, Bk 111,4,

[55] *Srikantha Carita* ; Bk 111,4,

[56] Kalhana; *R.T. Eng. trs*, by Stein; R. T., IV, 6

[57] Ibid *R. T., IV*, 6

[58] Ibid *R.T.IV*, 196, 201;

[59] Ibid. R. *T., V*, 100

[60] *Annual Rep.: A. S. l.*, 1915-16 p 62; Hand bookpp.48-52, 61-63, *Ancient Monuments*, p.162

[61] Kalhana; R. *T., VI.* 178

[62] ibid R. *T. V1*, 300-302

NOTES AND REFERENCES

[63] R. *T., VIII*, 79

[64] *R. T., VIII*, 2433

[65] Jonaraja :(*Bombay. Ed), verse III*, And page 265

[66] Sunil Chandra Ray: Early *history and Culture of Kashmir, pp., 179-180*

[67] Ksemendra: *Samayamatrika*. ii, p77,

[68] Kalhana:*R.T. Vol., 1*, footnotes on I, 34 p. 7

[69] P.N. Bamzai: essay *Sarada Temple in Kashmir, Vitasta Annual No Vol xxv*, p. 113

[70] Alberuni: *Kitabe- Hind* Trans., Sachau

[71] Abul Fazal: *Ain Akbari* v. ii-p 365

[72] Abul Fazl's: *notice of the site Ain V. ii*-p 365

[73] Kalhana trans. Stein: *R.T. volume I1* pages488-489 (1989)

[74] Dr. V.K. Gai: *Nilamata*, 1 p188, 194

[75] Alberuni: *India, trans. Sachau* pp 99-100

[76] *The Travels of Marco polo: The Venetian* edited by Manuel Komroff, p 64)

[77] Stein: in his introduction to the Kalhana's trs, *RT. vol. 1 p., 130*

[78] Rashid-ud-Din Fazl Ullah Rabbani: *Ancient Kashmir*, pp12-13

[79] Ibid: *Ancient Kashmir* P14

[80] Ibid: *Ancient Kashmir*. p15

[81] Jonaraja: *R.T. Rajavali Pataka*; Trans. Dutt, Jogesh Chander p., 15

[82] Rabbani: Ancient *Kashmir*, pp. 16- 18))

[83] J.L. Kilam: *History of Kashmiri Pandits* P 30)

[84] Pir Hassan Shah: Tarikh-i-Kashmir *Vol. I, pp. 392-94; also see pp. 385-90; Vol. II, pp 178-79. Kelam*, pp30-31

[85] Pir Hassan Shah's: *Vol. I, p. 180, Fauq: History of Kashmir, (Kilam: History of Kashmiri Pandit* p.32

[86] G.M.Sufi, *Kashir*, P, 489

[87] Ibid Op.cit, P, 75.

[88] Ibid.: *Kashir*. Vol, I, p. 89

[89] Pir Hassan Shah: *Tarikh-i-Kashmir*, Vol. I, pp. 392-94;

[90] Pir Hassan Shahs, Fauq, History *of Kashmir Vol.* I, p. 180;

[91] Tyndale Biscoe: *Kashmir in Sun light and shade* p- 71,

[92] Jonaraja: Rajavali Pataka; trans. Dutt, Jogesh Chander pp.65 -66; Pir Hassan Shah: *Tarikhi-Kashmir*Vol.11. p186; Fauq: *History of Kashmir*; J.L. Kilam *History of Kashmiri Pandits* Pp. 33-34.

[93] Lieutenant Newall: Sketch of the *Mohammadan History of Kashmir*, J.A. S.B. No. 5 1854, P 415

[94] Dutt, Jogesh Chander, pp. 65-66; Pir Hassan Shah, Vol. II, p. 186;Fauq, *History of Kashmir.)*

[95] Abul Fazal Allami: *Ain-I- Akbari, Trans., H.Blouchmann,* V0l, 1

[96] Lawrence: *The Valley of Kashmir* p 286

[97] Bamzai P.N: *A History of Kashmir* p 527

[98] Lawrence: the *Valley of Kashmir* p 286)

[99] Pearce Gervis: *This is Kashmir,* p. 259.

[100] Tyndale Biscoe: *Kashmir in Sun light and shade*, P. 100-2

[101] Note- Lawrence in his book, *The Valley of Kashmir* writes about the elaborate procedure followed by the Hindu KSP in their every day religious routine thus. "They would generally rise very early in the morning and before leaving their beds lie on their stomachs and offer a short prayer. Those who are of a religious turn of mind sit square over a clean piece of cloth or a carpet of *kusha* grass or the skin of an antelope and tell their beads, reciting sacred Vedic mantras like the Buddhist; or they practise concentration of mind or regulation of breath some times. This is done in absolute privacy. Then they leave the bedroom and go to the river-side, and some of them perform necessary ablutions, while others sit for some time on the bank and perform daily worship (*sendhia).* Having stripped himself, the Hindu sits on the steps of the bank. First he washes his left foot and then the right. This is because the body is believed by the Hindus to be androgynous and the left side is considered to have feminine characteristics. As woman (*Shakti)* is believed to be superior to man, the left foot is washed first. And every woman always sits on the left of her husband whenever they have to perform a ceremony. No ceremony is complete unless the woman takes part in it. Most Hindus worship God in the form of a woman. (Would that these Hindu men would put into practice some at least of their doctrines with regard to women, for then much of their unnecessary suffering would be lessened.) Having washed his foot, he holds handful of water and invokes through Vedic incantations all the spirits of the sacred rivers, such as Ganges, Jamuna, Gaya, etc. With this water he washes his face, and then his

Brahmanical thread and the tuft of hair on the top of his head with a separate mantra. After this he raises his hands with open palms towards the sun, invoking *Varuna,* the god of the air, to make him clean. Then he sprinkles water three times towards his left. After this he places a piece of clay on the bank, divides it into three parts, sprinkles water over these portions with separate mantras, invoking the sun god to cleanse him. He picks the first part and throws it towards all the four points of the compass; with the second part he: besmears his body, and the third part he throws into the water. Then holding a handful of water he steps into the river and begins to bathe. When standing in the river he sprinkles water three times, in the name of the ancestors, in the name of ancient sages of India, and last of all in the name of the gods. Then he comes out of the water and puts on clothes, and again sits on the bank to regulate his breath and perform the remaining part of the ceremony. First he inhales a long breath through the- left nostril, retains it for a few seconds and then exhales it very, very slowly through the right nostril. It is said that mental calm follows the breathing practice which lasts for some time. This is done three or four times. The ceremony is concluded 'with special movements of the hands, telling of beads and sprinkling of water in a peculiar way too tedious to be described here."

Chapter-5 - Rites and Rituals Note

1 *"The KSP has had a distinct Karma Kanda and it is still held in great esteem by all of us. It relates to our long past. Isolation from the rest of the country necessitated the requirement of a Karma Kanda suitable to the environment, climate and the living habits of the people. The term Karma Kanda owes its origin to the Ramayana era. Maharishi Vasishtha along with other royal dignitaries went to meet Prince Rama in jungles to offer their condolences on the sad demise of King Dashratha. The Rishi advised Rama to perform certain obsequies in accordance with the then prevailing customs. Rama was not made aware earlier of those rites during the Gurukul days. Actually, the practice till then was that Kulpurohit (a family mentor) would give on-spot guidance to his Yajmans on all occasions and on all matters. Lord Rama, realising the necessity of a written code, pleaded with the Maharishi to prepare a suitable code of Karma Kanda for the benefit of the people. Vasishtha on return to Ayodhya prepared a brief code which later on laid the basis for various Karma Kandas in India."

2 Toshkhani, Shashishekhar: Kashmir Sentinel Vol. 14, No. 8 P.17

3 Ibid: p 18

4 Ibid, Panchtarni, Annual No. 2006, Vol, 6 p 9

5 Ibid P.14

6 G.H.Anantnarayanan; Hindu Samskara in a Nutshell, p., 21-22

7 Hindu religious order identifies as many as eight types of marriages; the one inherited by the KSP is the "Brahman Marriage," In this type of marriage parents invite their relatives and friends who believe in the rituals of the community, to participate in the various functions of the wedding of their off springs. Parents impersonate their daughter as Mother Parvati and bridegroom as Lord Shiva. The journey towards the ultimate union for the divine play of creation starts from the Mehandiraat, (a night of gaiety and feasting; an essential part of this day is the Henna ceremony, (application of the herbal paste of Henna in floral designs on the hands and feet of the bride in particular and rest of the female members of the gathering.) Next follows the Devgone ceremony, a ceremony to elevate the concerned boy and the girl to Brahman hood. It is believed that the would be-partners assume the form of Shiva and Parvati after this ceremony and are treated so on the Lagan (main wedding ceremony) during the Posh Puja, the bride and the groom sit together-side by side-under a canopy and amidst the recitation of Vedic mantras flowers are showered on the couple thus granting them the sanctity of representing Shiva and Parvati, which culminates in the ultimate union after performing the rituals of Saptpadi system (A journey of seven steps), when the father bestows his daughter into wedlock by reciting a Mantra denoting union of the groom and bride. As part of the marriage ceremony the groom takes on the religious obligations of his wife (the bride) by symbolically adding three more sacred threads to his Janau. Bride, like wise, on her part takes the responsibility of guarding his wealth by keeping her foot on a stone pestle that symbolically represents the God of Wealth) This is best described by Lord Shiva in his "Ardh Narishwar roop"(half male and half female) posture, representing the equality of the status of both partners after their marriage.

8 Ibid: Hindu Samskara p.50

9 Dr. Ved K.:N.P,. Translation vol.1, p213-14

Chapter -6 - Social Order

1 .Ved K: N.P.vol.1 p. 82 Pub.1988

2 Ibid: N.P. vv p.358-65, 978-979, {Ved K. vol. 1 p 85}

3 Ibid: N.P., Vol 1, p85.,

4 Dr Ved K.: N.P. Vol. 1 p. 87

5 Kahan (.Stein) R.T,. V l., Verse, 192

6 Ved K., N.P., Vol. 1, P. 129; Mahabharata, Sabhaparva, 47, 19-23,

7 Ibid, p 242-243

8 Dr. S.C. Ray: Early History and Culture of Kashmir, pp. 100-101

NOTES AND REFERENCES

[9] Kalhana Trans. M.A.Stein: R.T, V11, Verse, 661-63.Pub.1989

[10] Ibid: R.T.V111, Verse, 2407,.Pub.1989

[11] Ibid: R.T. Bk, verse 440.

[12] Pandit Ranjit Sitaram: trs Kalhana. R.T. Bk.V11 verse 1090-1095

[13] Kalhana: RT. V v,-440, VII 1091-1094

[14] R. T., IV v.469- 496

[15] R. T., VI. v., 168 194.284

[16] R. T.: VII, v., 91.

[17] R.T. Bk. VII, v., 1177

[18] Ibid: R.T.V111, v., 472

[19] R.T. Bk.V1, verse 108-112

[20] R. T., bk., IV, 5,415, 673, V, 16.17, 120, VI, 89, V11, 295-97

[21] R.T bk., I v., 87-88, 96, 341, V, 103, 442 VI 89, VII, 184

[22] R.T., bk., V, v., 168

[23] R.T, Bk., V111, 2383)

[24] R.T. V111, 254; V111, 648,929,1124,1153,2505

[25] Alberuni: India (tr. Sachau, Bk I, and p.206) Stein Notes on Ou-kongs account of Kashmir

[26] R.T. IV, 628.

[27] Kshemendra. Samayamatrika, 49

[28] R.T. IV, 11

[29] R.T., V, 23, V11. 124-36,708

[30] R.T.V11, 207-8

[31] RT., V., 387

[32] Ved K: N.P.-vv 97-98{V.K., N.P.,p.,89}

[33] Ibid: Nilamata, 748, 754, R.T.1, 246, 11, 18)

[34] Nilamata, 696-97; verses 499-505

[35] Dr.Ved. Kumari. Nilamata Purana Vol. 1.p.111

[36] Ibid: N.P. 450-453

[37] Ibid: Nilamata 526-529

[38] Kshemendra; Desopadesa III, 32; R.T. V111, 143

[39] Kalhana: R.T., 1, verse 342

[40] Kshemendra; Narmamala, 126-128

[41] Yule, Marco Polo, I, P.166, The Travels of Marco polo, p.87

[42] Kalhana: R.T.V111, 866-67; bk.V.65

[43] R.T. iv; 427, vii 544, 787, 945, 1067, viii, 1735-37, 1947

[44] R.T., vii 1124

[45] Kak R.C.: Ancient Monuments of Kashmir, P. 1 xxv111, xv11)

[46] Bilhana: Vikramankadevacarita, xv111.23, 29 ;{ V.K. N.P. Page 108}

[47] Nilamata: v.546-547;

[48] Nilamata, v, 714;

[49] Nilamata v, 543,863;

[50] Nilamata, v.v.403-4;

[51] Nilamata, v.21;

[52] Ibid. v.648;

[53] Nilamata v.403-4; {V.K., N.PTrs. 109-112}

[54] Kshemendra: Kuttanimata Kavyaya 75-123)

[55] R.T., 1V, 423,

[56] R.T. VII, 1606

[57] Kshemendra: Kuttanimata Kavya, 728. "S.C.Ray, Early History and Culture of Kashmir p 259}

[58] Alberuni:, Kitab-ul-Hind, Eng.tr.(India)(E.C.Sachau) 1,p.206

[59] Watters, On Yuan Chwang: Huien Tsang, I, p. 262.

[60] R.T. 1V., 423

[61] R. C. Kak: Ancient Monuments of Kashmir, p. 109.

[62] M.A. Stein; R.T., 1, 201-202

NOTES AND REFERENCES

[63] Kalhana: R.T, trs. R.S.Pandit Invitation

[64] Prudman Purana, Lx I.vv.II-40.,{ V.K.; N.P. p90}

[65] Bilhana: Vikramandevcharita, XV 111,6{ N.P., trs. V.K p. 94- 95

[66] N.P.v 524-525 {V, K: N.P., p91}

[67] N. P. V.K.G_.* Note - (Sharika, believed to have been born of the land, and like the Greek mother Goddess Sri, is the founder of the Sharika Hill and the Sri Tantra, thus propagating the aboriginal culture of sacrifice. Raginya, as the legend goes, migrated from the island of Lanka and propagated the culture of offerings. Thus both have initiated the socio- religious base for the dwellers of the land.

[68] Kadambari (purvardha) p.308; Ksemendra's: Kuttanimata Kavyaya, vs.480, 559-61,565.

[69] P.N.Bazaz: Daughters of Vitasta pub 1959

[70] Krishna Mohan: Early History and Culture Of Kashmir, p. 98

[71] (Lila Ray, "Women Writer" in Women of India, p. 179. D.O.V. Bazaz p 6

[72] R.S Pandits: Trans. Kalhana River of Kings, Appendix D p. 733-734

[73] Ksemendra: Deso-upadesa p 16

[74] Ibid: Desopadesa Bk vii

[75] R.S., Pandit: Trans. Of Kalhana's R.T., INVITATION p., xxxix,

[76] Alberuni: Kitabe- Hind Trs. India, vol. 11, p., 155

[77] Altekar, A. S.: Position of Women in Hindu Civilization, 126-27. 'Majumdar, R. C. (ed.) the Age of Imperial Unity, p. 568. 'Altekar, A. S. Position of Women in Hindu Civilization, p. 116.}

Note: Although the custom of Sati was widely known in ancient times, it is not sanctioned by the Dharma or by the Smrtis. Manu and Yajnavalkya is reticent about it, though Vishnu seems to commend it in passages which are regarded by many as later interpolations. Discussing the general prevalence of this custom among the primitive warlike tribes, Altekar is of the opinion that fighting races are very jealous of their women and often prefers to kill them, rather than take the risk of their going astray after their husbands' deaths.

There was also the general belief that the warrior would require in his next life all those things which were near and dear to him in the present existence. The custom started to become popular in Kshatriya circles. From AD 400 to AD 700, fiery advocates began to come forward in increasing numbers to extol the custom of sati. There does not appear to be any attested instance of force being exercised on unwilling widows to mount the funeral pyre. The Padmapurana though it highly extols the custom, expressly prohibits it for the Brahmin women. Later on, the Brahmin community, with its self-denying code of life, began to feel that it should not allow itself to be outdistanced by the Kstriyas. The custom, therefore, began to be followed by a few Brahmin families soon after AD 1000

78 Premnath Bazaz: Daughters of Vitasta, P12 pub. 1959

79 Ibid: Daughters of Vitasta pp. 6, 7, 9

80 V.K. N.P. Vol.1p., 95

81 Nilamata, v. v.62, 335,458,773)

82 Huien Tsang: Siyuki, tr. Beal, p.76

83 R.C.Kak: Ancient Monuments of Kashmir, pl. XX 5; pl., fig. a

84 R.T: VII, 928 31, Bazaz: D. O.V, P, 7

85 Bazaz: D.O.V., P. 8

86 Kalhana R.T. vii, 928-931

87 Ibid: R.T., Bk. Vii, verse. 928-931

88 Prem Nath Bazaz: Daughters of Vitasta p. 6

89 Samay. Mat., 11.5 70, 73; Vf Baja V.257; 356-69; (Source) K.Mohan: Early Medieval History of Kashmir, p.258

90 Ibid; Sam- Mat: 11.70; 111.37; Baja: 111.326; IV.720; V.359, 373. Ibid}

91 Prem Nath Bazaz: Daughters of Vitasta p., 8,

92 Sam- Mat., VIII. 65, K.Mohan: E.M.H. Of Kashmir, p.258

93 Ksemendra: Kuttanimata Kavyaya, p742 Ibid

94 Kalhana. R.T., VII, 876

95 Kalhana: R.T. vii 928-31 Shalokas (.Bazaz D.O.V. p8-9 0

96 Kalhana: R.T. V11, 922

97 Krishna Mohan: Early. Medieval. History Of Kashmir, p.244

98 Beal: S. Op.cit: tr. Si-Yu-Ki, vol. II p. 189; (1958).

99 Alberuni: India, vol. I, p. 126

100 Bilhana: Vikramaṅkadeva Charita, XVIII.1-8

[101] Dr. 'Suryakanta; Kshemendra, Studies, p. I11. 'Supro, p. 178}" (Krishna Mohan Early Medieval History of Kashmir p.245)

[102] Ibid: Ksemendra Studies P11

[103] DR. Suryakanta; Ksemendra Studies, p. 2.fra, Appendix P, 170, 171

Chapter- 7- Social order during and after the Islamic era

[1] Baron Charles Hugel: Kashmir and the Punjab, Preface p. xvi

[2] Jona Rajas: Kings of Kashmira Dutt Jogesh Chander Translation. Vol.111, p.59

[3] Shirivara: Rajavalipataka, p., 188, P., 334, {J.L.Kilam: History of Kashmiri. Pandit, p., 50]

[4] Pir Hassan Shahs: Tarikh-I-Kashmir

[5] Ibid: Vol., 1, p. 180; Fauq: History of Kashmir {J.L.Kelam History of Kashmiri Pandits, pp. 31-32}

[6] Jonaraja :trs., Dutt Jogesh Chander,pp.,65-66;Pir Hassan Shah, Vol.11, p.186; Fauq: History of Kashmir, {Kilam H.K.P.;p.33-34 }

[7] Lawrence: The Valley of Kashmir, p.296

[8] G.L.Kaul: Kashmir, p.131

[9] Walter, R Lawrence: The Valley of Kashmir, p. 252, London 1895

[10] Colonel T. Handley: Antiquary vol., x1v, p226. October 1885

[11] Lieutenant Newall: J.A.S.B., No. 5, p. 433, 1854

[12] Lawrence: The valley of Kashmir

[13] Srivara; Rajavalipataka, p.133

[14] Prem Nath Bazaz: Daughters of Vitasta, p.,197 (1959),

[15] Ibid: D.O.V. p.14;

[16] Ibid p. 10;

[17] Ibid p 15

[18] There are different opinions about the system of *Purdah*/veil, however it is generally believed that there was some sort of seclusion often in the Hindu society. K. M. Panikkar thinks that in Midd1e Ages at least in North India the seclusion of women had become the rule among the higher classes. He is further of the opinion that there is evidence to show that such seclusion, among kings and nobles, was

practised even in the earlier times His views are corroborated by Bhasham who says that Kings at any rate, kept their womenfolk in seclusion. The instructions of the Arthshastra make it quite clear Anthapura, or royal harem, was closely guarded, and females were not allowed to leave it freely.

19 G T. Vigne: Travels in Kashmir, Ladak. Iskardu, Vol. II, p, 143, pub 1842

20 Dr G M D Sufi: Kashir Vol I pp. 262-63, University of the Punjab Lahore, 1949 (Bazaz; B.O.V p18)

21 P.N.Bazaz: D.O.V, p 196. pub., Year 1959

22 Ibid p 16

23 Frederic Drew: The Northern Barrier of India, (Edward Stanford, London 1877) P132.

24 Lawrence: Op.cit: The Valley of Kashmir p318 (Bazaz, D.O.V. p 201

25 Pt. Jawaharlal Nehru: The Discovery of India, p.311

Chapter - 8- Cultural Excellences of KSP

1 Kalhana: R.T., Stein Translation, Vol, 1, bk. IV, p.58

2 A.N.Fotedar:; 'Kashmir the legend and scientific facts', Vitasta Annual No xxxv p 15

3 C.L. Nagri Reminiscence - An Ethnological Synthesise ii, Panchtarni Annual No 2005 p 42

4 T N. Dhar (Kundan),:R.P Raina Memorial Lecture delivered, on December 17, 2000 at New Delhi

5 C.L. Nagri, *Kashur* Samachar

6 On Yuan Ch Wang's Travels in India, Trans, Waters, v.1, p.262

7 Pandit Anand Kaul: Kashmir. 1924 (D.N. Raina- Kashmir Distortions and Reality)

8 "Sultan Shihab-Ud Din established the first Madrasa-tul-Quran. Abdul Mashaikh Sheiki Sulatan, who was originally a Hindu, received his education in this school after his conversion and in course of time distinguished himself as an exponent of the Quran and was given the title of Imam-ul-Quran-Imam of Qari. Madrassas for the teaching of the Quran and Hadis were established, in all important villages, at the instance of Shah Hamadan. Sultan Qutb-ud-Din built a college and named it after himself in his headquarters at Qutb Uddinpura. Pir Haji Muhammad Qari was the head of the institution and the school continued its existence till the establishment of Sikh rule in the valley, when it closed for want of patronage. A long roll of distinguished professors and scholars were the products of this

institute. Mulla Jauhar 'Nath' was the head of this institution during the reign of Jahangir. Mulla Mohsin Fani, the eminent philosopher-poet and Mulla Abdus Sattar Mufti taught their pupils here. Sheikh Rahmatolla Tarabali, Mulla Tahir Ginmi Ashai the poet, Muhammad Zarnan Nafe, the historian and the younger brother of Ghani, Khwaja Qasim Tirmizi and Mulla Muhammad Kaosa were some of its distinguished alumni. { Information gathered from G.M. Sufis, Book Islamic Culture in Kashmir pp.146-48 Sufi records, {The information as given under this section has been collected from (Asrar-ul-A brat by Baba Daud Mishkawti, (2) Maqama(.i- diya by Khwaja Moin-ud-Din Naqshbandi. (3) Tazkiraf by Muhammad Mi Khan Matin, (4) Bavan-i-Waqa—a note on the Jami'Masjid. (5) Tahqiqat-i by Kbwa Amir-ud-Din Pakbliwal, (6)Tarik/z and (7) Tarikh-i-Hasan and from personal enquiries in Kashmir. }

9 Hargopal Koul: Guldasta, p. 116 Sufi p, 148

10 Sufi: Op.cit. Islamic Culture In Kashmir p149-50

11 Somnath Dhar: Jammu and Kashmir, p78,

12 Manmohan Dhar: Kashmiris Place in the Cultural Mosaic of India., Vitasta Annual No.1987

13 N.S.Shukla: Cultural Trends in Kashmir and Ksemendra; p 1

14 Dr. Surya Kant: His Ksemendra Studies, (Suniti Kumar Chaterji, Early Medieval History of Kashmir, pp 244-5)

15 Ibid. p 245

16 Suniti Kumar Chaterji: Early Medieval History of Kashmir, p246

Note the list of authors mentioned by Kshemendra is divided in three groups as quoted here:

1) The authors quoted in the Aucityacàracarca are: Amaraka,Anandavardhana, Karpatika, Kalidãsa, Kumaradasa, Gangaka. Gaudakumbakāra, Cakra, Candraka, Candaka, Dipaka, Dharmakirti, Parimal, Bhattanarayana, Bhataprabhakra, Bhattenduraja, Bhavabhuti, Magha, Matrgupta. Malavakuva!aya, Malavarudra, Muktapidaa, Yasovarmadeva, Rajasekhara, Latta, Lattana Varahamihira, Vyas, Syamala, Srimatupalaraja, and Sriharsa.

2) Authors quoted in the Kavikanlhabharana : are Amaraka, Aryabhatta, Indrabhanu, Utpalarājadeva, Cakrapala, Candraka, Bhattadāmodara gupta, Bhattanaraya Bhattabana, Bhatabhallata, Bhttamayura, Bhattamuktikalasa, Bhattavacaspati, Bhattasrisivasami, Bhattodyasimha, Rajasekhara, Laksmanaditya, Vidyananda, i a, Vyasa and Sriharsa.

3) Authors quoted in the Suvrttatilaka: are Abhinanda, Induraja, Ucpalaraja, Kalasaka, Kālidāsa, Gandinaka, Cakra, Tunjina, Dipaka, Narayanabhatta,

Parimala, Bana, Bhartrmenlha, Bhartrhari Bhavabhuti, Bhãravi, Muktakana, Yasovarman, Ratnakara, Rajasekhara, Rissu, Lãtadindara, Vallata, Vagbhata, Viradeva, Vysa Syamala, Sãhil, Harsa. (The above list has been prepared out of the index of verses quoted in the above works of Kshemendra, prepared by Dr. Suryakanta in his K Studies).

[17] Alberuni: India Trs. Sachau, Vol.1. p126

[18] Haider Malik Chadurah; Tarikh-I-Kashmir

[19] Shinya Fujiwara: Kashmir

[20] George Buhler Report of his tour in search of Sanskrit Mss 1817

[21] G.M.Sufi: Islamic Culture in Kashmir, p: 735

[22] G Lal: Kasheer. Sanskrit, p 171

[23] 'Calcutta University Calendar 1910, Part ii, Calcutta, 1910)

[24] Bernier; Travels of the Mogul empire Period under reference 1630

[25] Pandit P. N Bamzai: History of Kashmir D.U. (Desho, p. i7, Upadesa VI, Vers 8)

[26] Ibid. Manu chap., 1, vs. 88; chap. X, vs. 1, 75-76., ('Suryakanta, K Studies, p. I1, 'Supro, p. 178)

[27] Note for detailed study refer to the recent publication of Dr B.N. Sharga' six volumes, Kashmiri Panditon Ke Anmol Ratan, Sharga publication, 2000 A.D

[28] M.A.Stein, Kalhana: R.T Op.cit

[29] Ibid Vol.1 introduction, p46, note5

[30] Abul Fazal: Ain I Akbari, Vol.1, p108 (Sufi I.C.K. p.227

[31] Triloki Nath Dhar 'Kundan': In his Article on Batanya / Hindu Kashmiri lady, Panchtarni Annual No 1904

[32] Ibid

[33] Manmohan Dhar: Kashmir's Place in the Cultural Mosaic of India., Vitasta 1987)

[34] G.M. Sufi: Islamic Culture in Kashmir, p.224

[35] Ved Kumari: NP vol.1p.217

[36] Sufi: Op.cit, Kasheer P.206

[37] Kaumudi: Kashmir Cultural Heritage

NOTES AND REFERENCES

CHAPTER- 9 - PROMINENT CHRONICLERS

1 Asiatic Researches for transactions of the Society Vol, xv An Essay on The Hindu History of Casmir P3,. H.Wilson. 1825

2 Kalhana's Rajatarangini, trans. M.A.Stein bk. 1, v.7

3 Op.cit R.T. bk. I.v.8,

4 Moorcroft, William Mr. George Trebeck: Vol 1& 11 Moore Craft, 'Travels of Kashmir' 1825

5 Kalhana, Trans, M.A.Stein: R.T., vol., 1. p. xxiv

6 Krishna Mohan: Early Medieval History of Kashmir, p.9

7 Professor Buhler: Report p.40 {Stein Vol.11 p377

8 Winternitz: History of Sanskrit Literature, Vol, I, p. 583

9 R T., Kalhana: Stein:, Ancient India, p. 419

10 M.Y.Teng Secretary J&K.Academy of Art & Culture, N.P. Gai, Vol.1, publisher note, 1988

11 Dr. Ved Kumari: N.P Vol. 1.p.42

12 Kalhana. R.T.bk.1. v. 9, 10

13 R. S. Pandit: trs, Kalhana R.T. P. XIX

14 Stein., R.T trs, vol.1Book1, verse 11,-20

15 Ibid, R.T Vol 11, chap.11, sec, v, p 371

16 Ibid R.T. Stein, Introduction Vol. 1 p 14

17 Kalhana, R.T, Vol. 1. Trans. Stein, Introduction chap. IV, p.56

18 Ibid R.T. vol. 1, prelim, p 4

19 Ibid. Vol.1 Intro., p30 -p 35

20 Ibid p Intro. p 56, Para, 55

21 Stein Trans Vol., 11Notes, p 373

22 Prof. K.N.Dhar, Essay Hindu Historians and Muslim Kashmir, published in Heritage of Kashmir p. 76

23 Ibid, Heritage Kashmir, p., 89

24 Dutt Jogesh Chander: p.253; Dr.Kashinath, 111,443, J.L.Kelam, A History of Kashmiri Pandit p.56

25 Stein. R.T., vol.11 chap. 11 sec. v p 373-74

26 Ibid p., 374

27 Ibid. p., 378-9

28 Dr. Satish Ganju: Vitasta, Vol. xxxvii, y., 2005-6, P 109

29 Pir Hassan Shahs: Tarikh-I- Kashmir. Vol. II, p.20.

30 Stein Trans Vol., 11Notes, p 374

31 Kashmir Research Department Publications, Srinagar

32 Notes: There is a manuscript of this work in Srinagar Research Library. Professor A. Weber has published valuable excerpts from this work in the Indische Studies (Vol. XVIII pp.289-412.)

33 Kalhana, R.T, Vol. 11. Trans. Stein, chap. 11, sec., 1. P 351

Chapter- 10 - Foot Prints of KSP Architecture

1 Sir Alexander Cunningham:' Essays on the Arian Order of Architecture 'p241 Lawrence the Valley of Kashmir p 163:

2 Sir Walter Lawrence: The valley of Kashmir, Chapter Archaeology

3 Sir Alexander Cunningham:' Essays on the Arian Order of Architecture 'p243pub. 1848

4 Ibid: Essays on the Arian Order of Architecture 'p245pub. 1848

5 Lawrence: The Valley of K, P., 169

6 R C Kak: The Ancient Monuments of Kashmir, p 15

7 Kak: The Ancient Monuments of Kashmir, pp105-111

8 G.M. Sufi: Arts and Crafts under Muslim Rule, p 211

9 Ibid: p.211

10 Mirza Haider: Tarikh i-Rashidi (Eng. translation by Elias and Ross, p. 425.pub. 1895

11 Cunningham: 'Essays on the Arian Order of Architecture' pub. 1848

12 Mirza Haider: Tarikh i-Rashidi Op.cit

13 Cunningham: 'Essays on the Asian Order of Architecture'

14 Mrs Walter Tibbits: The Cities seen in East and West', chapter "The City of Sun"

15 Archaeological Survey Report 1906-07, p. 165

16 Ibid: p. 162-63

17 Mirza Haider: Tarikh i-Rashidi (Eng. translation by Elias and Ross, p. 424.pub. 1895

Chapter -11 - Language Single Link

1 Prof. Raj Nath Bhat: Vitasta Annual Number vol. xxxvii, p.81 (2005-6).

2 E.Pococke: India in Greece, p., 52

3 Prof.J.L.Kaul: Studies in Kashmiri, pub. Srinagar 1968-69

4 O.N.Koul and Peter Edwin Hook: Aspects of Kashmiri Linguistics, preface,

5 Dr Grierson: Linguistic Survey of India, Vol. Viii Indian Languages

6 Braj B Kachru: A History of, Kashmiri Literature 1981

7 O.N.Koul and Peter Edwin: Aspects of Kashmiri Linguistics edited

8 A.M.Ghatage; Historical Linguistics and Indo-Aryan languages.

9 M.F.Hasnain: Hindu Kashmir, p., 12

10 G.R. Gierson: Linguistic Survey of India, Vol. Viii, pt.2, p 235

11 Ibid: L.S.I. viii. Appendix, page 241,

12 Ibid. Page 251-253

13 Sir Herbert Risley,: Kashmir 1924

14 Ibid: Kashmir, P 6

15 J.C.Chaterji. Kashmiri Language, Report of the Archaeological & Research Department, J&K, Aug. 20, 1960

16 Fredric Drew: Language P. 466

17 Dr. Shashi Shekhar Toshkhani: Kashmiri Sahit Kaa Itihas, P.2.

18 Dr. Sedeshar Verma: The Antiquities of Kashmiri- An approach of the Linguistic scale of India, p.4

[19] Suniti Kumar Chaterji: Languages in India Introducing India, p. 2, Asiatic Society of Bengal

[20] Dr.Bhuler: The Archaeological Survey of' Kashmir, 1924.Language

[21] 'Dr. Buhler: Language and Glossary, P.455, Chap xix.

[22] Dr.Grierson: Op.cit, L.S.I., P234

[23] O.N.Koul, Peter Edwin Hook: Aspects of Kashmiri Linguistics; Preface

[24] Brij. B. Kachru:, Kashmiri Literature 1981

[25] Grierson, Essays on Kashmiri grammar

[26] Grierson: Essays on Kashmiri grammar

[27] Ashok R. Kelkar: Kashmiri A Descriptive Sketch

[28] Dr. Shashi Shekhar Toshkhani: Kashmiri Sahitya kaa Itihas P. 15, 16)

[29] Note Regarding the original text of Lal Deds Vaakh, D.N.Raina writes, "Philologists may have taken pains to study the original form of Kashmiri but the conclusion is accepted by all that Bhaskara's Lalla-vaakh in Sharda script is to be taken as authentic in modern Kashmiri. We owe it to a Brahmin Pandit Kesho Bhat of Rainawari Srinagar, who prepared the text of the Lal Vaakhs originally in Sharda, seen and revised by late Pandit Hara Bhat Shastri before these were published by Kasho Bhat himself."

[30] J.L. Koul: Kashir published in the year 1924.

[31] Note. The source of information about the authors and their publications from 1925 AD., onwards is mainly Braj B Kachru's work on Kashmiri literature

CHAPTER- 12 - POLITICAL CHRONOLOGY

[1] Earnest F.Neve: Beyond the Pir Panjal. London, 1915

[2] Jogesh Chander Dutt: Kings of Kashmira, (R.T. Kalhana trs., Vol., 11 (1887) Preface p. ii)

[3] M.A. Stein Trans, Kalhana RT book 1, p. 19 to 22

[4] Op.cit R.T. Book 1, p. 4 verse 19

[5] R.T. Book 1, p10 verse 48-49

[6] Tyndale Biscoe: Kashmir Ancient and Modern, 1922

[7] Diwan Kriparam : Gulab Nama, p. 52

NOTES AND REFERENCES

8 Jogesh Chander Dutt: (Translation Kalhana R.T.)Kings of Kashmira preface p. viii . . . ix,

9 Ved Kumari: trs. Nilamata Purana, Vol., II, verse 12, 13

10 Hymen Wilson: The Hindu History of Kashmir p. 10 (Bedia-Ud-Din Wakiat-I-Casmir.)

11 Ibid: The H.H.Of Kashmir p.13-14

12 Stein, trans. Kalhana R.T.Vol, 1 Bk. I p., 15, verse 86

13 Ibid: Op.cit R.T.1verse, 101-107)

14 Radha Kumud Mooker ji : Asoka Gaekwad lectures second edition 1955) P 30-34)

15 Walter's trs. Yuan Chwang P., 267

16 M.A. Stein Trans, Kalhana RT., Introduction page 74-75).

17 Op.cit R.T.Bk.1,p.,22,verse118-119

18 . . . Milindapanha (Ed Traenckner) pp.82-83)

19 Cunningham: Coins of the Indo-Scythian. P 44

20 Dr. Ray S.C: - Early History and culture of Kashmir. P 37-39.

21 Kalhana R,T Stein: Bk.1, Verse180-185).

22 Ibid. R T Book I, note 220, p36.

23 Ibid" Bk.1p.40-41 note 267

24 Hiuen -tsang in his book Si-Yu-Ki Records of Eastern countries, Bk IV p, 167 and 168

25 R.T. bk.1, p.46, verse, 306

26 Ibid bk. 1p.44, note 302

27 Kalhana: R. T. Trans. Stein Bk I. verse 322.

28 R.T.Bk.1 Verse.306-46

29 Ferguson: History of India Architecture Page 282

30 RT Vol., 1,-book III. P, 104

31 R.T. Vol., I, book3, p 113 note 460

32 Kalhana R.T. Bk.111 p 114 Verses, 472-73

[33] Ibid: R.T. Bk., IV, p 125, Verse, 60

[34] RT Bk. IV, Verse 45, notes, p 124

[35] RT 1V, verse, 94, notes p128 (Marco Polo in his memoirs page 24.

[36] K.S.Saxena: Political History of Kashmir, p. 51 pub. 1974

[37] (Chacha-nama chapter 111English translation in JASB no LXXIV and no.X, 1841{ Kelam, A History of Kashmiri Pandits, p.7,}

[38] Al' Beruni: India, trs Sachau, {Gwasha Lal Kaul: Kashmir through the Ages p. 29

[39] R.T. V1, Bk. IV, p 138, verse, 178-180

[40] Jon raja chronicle verse 599,

[41] R T., Bk. 1V p, 139 verse 181

[42] Ibid Bk. IV, p 154 verse345-348

[43] Stein R.T., Introduction p. 95

[44] Gwasha Lal Kaul: Kashmir through the Ages, p.33

[45] Kalhana V., P193-51-61.(Dutt R.C., A note on Kalhana's Rajatarangini I880)

[46] F.M. Hassnain: Hindu Kashmir Sun Rise p 63, (Dash_avatar_chjarita ms Research Library, Srinagar) R.T., V, verse 48- 49 {1989}

[47] Kalhana: R.T., trans. Stein, V, 44.)

[48] Dr. Goyal. Kashmir, p 48

[49] Kalhana: R.T., bk., v, verse72-109The "One day, when some people were grieving on account of the recent floods, he, Suyya, remarked that he had intellect but not money, and he could therefore give no redress. This speech was reported to the king by his spies, and the king wondered and caused him to be brought before him. The king asked him as to what he said. He fearlessly repeated that he had intellect but no money. The courtiers pronounced him to be mad, but the king, in order to try his intellect, placed all his wealth at the disposal of this man. Suyya took out many vessels filled with dinnaras, but went by boat of Madava. There in the village named Nandaka, which was under water, he threw a pot of dinnaras, and returned. Although the courtiers pronounced him to be undoubtedly mad, the king heard of his work, and enquired as to what he did afterwards. At Yakshadara in Kramarajya he began to throw dinnaras by handfuls into the water. The Vitasta was there obstructed by rocks which had fallen into its bed from both its rocky banks; and the villagers who were suffering from scarcity, began to search for the dinnaras, and in so doing removed the rocks which were in the bed of the river and cleared the passage of the water. No sooner had the water flowed out than Suyya

raised a stone embankment along the Vitasta, which was completed within seven days. He then cleared the bed of the river, and then broke down the embankments. The passage was now quite open, and the river flowed easily and rapidly towards the sea, as if anxiously and eagerly, after this long detention; and consequently the land again appeared above the waters. He then cut new canals from the Vitasta wherever he thought that the course of the river had been obstructed. Thus many streams issued out of one main river, even like the several heads of a serpent from one trunk. Sindhu which flowed from Trigrama to the left, and Vitasta on the right, were made to meet one another at Vainyasvami. And even to this day the junction made by Suyya, near this town exists; as also the two gods Vishnusvami and Vainyasvami at Phalapura and Parihasaura situated on either side of the junction; and the god Hrishikesha whom Suyya worshipped, just at the junction. And to this day may also be seen the trees which grew on the banks of the rivers. Ancient and Medieval Kashmir Rivers as it flowed before, distinguished by marks of ropes by which boats were tied to them. Thus Suyya diverted the course of rivers. He raised a stone embankment seven yojanas in length; and thereby brought the waters of the Mahapadma Lake under control.

[50] Ibid. Int. R.T. P.100)

[51] R.T. BK., V, p227, verse 354-389.

[52] R.T., Bk. VI verse 151-170

[53] R.T, Bk. VI p.263-64

[54] Al-Beruni': India Trs. Dr. E.C. Sachau p.206 (1888)

[55] R.T. Bk. VII p 287-88

[56] R. T. Bk VII, Verse 208),

[57] Rajatarangini, Taranga VII, Verse 364.

[58] Dr. Suryakanta Kshemendra Studies, (N. M, pp. 12-13, Parihasa I. Verses 128-140.)

[59] Ibid. (N. P. 8, Parihasa I, Verse 86.).

[60] Ibid

[61] Ibid

[62] Kalhana: R.T. Bk. vii Verse 461-485

[63] RT V-440, VII 1091-1094

[64] Ibid. R.T Vol, II., Viii, Verse 303-323

[65] R.T.Vol II, viii, 485, - 92, 498)

[66] R.T.,II. Viii, 1300-15)

[67] R.T. II, viii 3334,-35-36-38- 39- 41

[68] Waqiyat-I-Kashmir, p.24; Tarikh Hassan, II, p.153 (Dr. Saxena, Story of Kashmir P., 277}

[69] R.T Jonaraja verse, 50-55

[70] Dr. Saxena: History of Kashmir. p.282

[71] Ibid: History of K. p. 283

[72] Kahana: R.T Rajat Pandit. INVITATION

[73] "G.M.D.Sufi:, Islamic Culture in Kashmir, p. 54

[74] Jona Raja; Rajavali Pataka Trs. Dutt, Jogesh Chander, Kings of Kashmira

[75] D.J. F. Newall: An Abridgement of a Sketch of the Mohammadan History of Kashmir.1853-54 AD

[76] G.M. Sufi: L(Khwaja Muhammad Azam') Waqiat A Kashmir Page 60

[77] D.J.F. Newall: An Abridgement of a Sketch of the Mohammadan History of Kashmir p7, pub 1853-54 AD

[78] F.M. Hassnain: Hindu Kashmir, p 116 Light and Life pub. N.Delhi 1979

[79] Biggs: "Farista" Volume IV page 458

[80] Dr. Sufi: Kashir, vol.1, p.841

[81] Dr. Muhib-ul Hassan: Kashmir under the Sultans, p.65

[82] Ancient and Medieval Kashmir, How Sayyids gained access to the valley p55, 56,

[83] Pir Hassan Shah, Vol 1, p.180Fauq, History of Kashmir, Kelam J.L.,A history of Kashmiri Pandits, pp.31-32

[84] Rev Tyndale—Biscoe:Kashmir in Sun light and shade, page- 71

[85] Lieutenant Newall: Sketch of the Mohammadan History of Kashmir, J.A. S.B. No. 5 (1854) Page 415

[86] Fouq: Mukammal Tarikh-I-Kashmir vol. II Page-41

[87] Srivara: Kings of Kashmir Vol. 111,p 59& p 33

[88] Dutt, Jogesh Chander Op.cit,. p188 (Kilam J.L., A History of K.P. p50

[89] Ibid pp 195-96 {Kilam p. 50

NOTES AND REFERENCES

[90] G.M. Sufi: Op.cit Page-114

[91] Pir Hassan Shah,: Tarikh Kashmir Vol., 11, pp273-74

[92] J.C.Dutt: Kings of Kashmir, p., 371

[93] Fazal Allami: Ain-I-Akbari, V.1, p461, Trs.,H.Blochman M.A.

[94] Dr. Mahbub-ul-Hassan,:Kashmir under the Sultans, p.,143

[95] J.C. Dutt: Op.cit pp.420-21 Kilam A History of K P. p., 73

[96] Lawrence: Valley of Kashmir p 195

[97] Mr. M.R. Qanungo: in the Journal of Indian History for April 1929:

[98] Lawrence: The Valley of Kashmir p 195

[99] Pahalwan Anand Ram:, History of Kashmir, Kilam, H.K.P. p.,111

[100] William Moorcroft; Travels in the Himalayan Provinces Part II p293-294

[101] William Moorcroft:, Travels pp 235, 293-94

Selected Bibliography

- Abul-Fazl: *Ain-i-Akbari.* Translated by H. Blochmann and Col. H. S. Jarrett vols. Calcutta, 1894, 1927
- 1927
- Acharaya, Harisena : *Vrhat Katha Kosa (10th century)*
- Ahmad Maqbul S and Raja Bano: *Historical Geography of Kashmir.* Ariana Pub. House 1984
- Ahmed Dr S.D.: *An Account of Persian Literature in Kashmir* (2010)
- Alberuni: *India.* English edition by Dr. E. C. Sachau, vol I &ii London, 1910 Second edition, pub S Chand & co Delhi 1964
- Altekar, A.S,: *Position of Women in Hindu Civilization*, 2nd edition, Banaras, 1956
- Arrian: *Classical Accounts of India, III INDICA* (Megasthenes) P224
- Attaha F.M.: *Non Nominative Subject in Kashmiri*
- Bakaya N.L.: *Holidaying and Trekking in Kashmir*, pub., Srinagar
- Bamzai P.N.Kaul: *Kashmir and {Power Politics from Lake Success to Tashkent* Pub., Metropolitan Book Co. Delhi
- Bamzai P.N. Kaul: *History of Kashmir.* Delhi 1962
- Banerji S.C.: *Cultural Heritage of Kashmir*
- Barua Beni Madhab: *Asoka and His Inscriptions*, pub. New Age Publishers Calcutta 1946
- Bazaz, Prem Nath: *Daughters Of Vitasta*, Pub., Pamposh New Delhi, 1959
- Bazaz Prem Nath: *Kashmir in Crucible*, Pub., Pamposh New Delhi, 1967
- Beal Samuel: *Si-yu-Ki* (Buddhist records of the Western world, tr. from the Chinese of Hiuen Tsiang, AD629) London 1883

SELECTED BIBLIOGRAPHY

- Beal Samuel : (Translator) *The Life of Hiuen Tsiang by Shaman Hwuili* 1973
- Bernier François: *Travels in the Mogul Empire Including Kashmir* Translated By John Steuart Calcutta, 1826. (Earlier editions AD 1656-i668 London, latter editions 1891 1914 Bernier visited Kashmir in 1630)
- Bernier François: *Travels in Hindustan* pub., Calcutta 1684
- Bhat D. K: (1989), *Lithostratigraphy of Karewa group, Kashmir Valley, India and Critical review of its Fossil Record. Mem. GSI. Vol. 122*
- Bhatta Prajya and Shuka: *Rajavalipataka.* Translated by Jogesh Chunder Dutt., Calcutta, 1898
- Bisco Tyndel, C. E.: *Kashmir in Sunlight and Shade.* London, Mittal Publications New Delhi 1922.
- Bobb Monisha : *Kashmir*
- Breer Margaret F. *: Kashmir*
- Buhler: *A report on tour in search of Sanskrit MSS. in Kashmir*, Rajputana etc. 1877
- Buhler Francis: *Kashmir*
- Carter C.E.L. : *Memoirs of the Archaeological Survey of Kashmir No. 2 The Stone Age in Kashmir 1924*
- Charak Sukhdev Singh*: Maharaja Ranbir Singh*
- Chatterji Suniti Kumar: *Kashmiri Language* 1949
- Cunningham Sir Alexander: *Ladakh, Physical, statistical and Historica*l, London 1854
- Cunningham Sir Alexander: *Archaeological Report, Vol.*, 23, 1833-34.
- De Terra, H., (1936) *'Excavations at Burzahom'*, Miscellanea of the America Philosophical Society.
- De Terra and Paterson, (1939): *Studies on the Ice Age in India and associated Human culture.* Publication NO.43, Carnegie Institution, Washington
- Dhar Som Nath*: Jammu and Kashmir*, National Book Trust India New Delhi.
- Doughty Marion: *A Foot through the Kashmir Valley* pub. London,1902

- Drew (Fredrick): *Northern Barrier of India; popular account of Jammu and Kashmir territories.* London 1875, reprint 1971
- Doughlat, Mirza Muhammad Haidar, : *Tarikh-i-Rashidi*, 1837. A history of Central Asia, Edited by E. N. Elias and j by E. Denison Ross London, 1973
- Dutt, Jogesh Chunder(tr) *The Rajatarangini of Jonaraja Kings of Kashmira vol. 11, 1887*
- Dutt, Jogesh Chunder(tr) *Tarikhi-i-Kashmir* of Pir Hassan Shah
- vol. 23, 1927.
- Ferguson, James, P: *Tree and Serpent Worship*, 1873; Kashmir, pub. Centaur Press London 1961
- Feuerstein Georg, Subhash Kak and David Frawley (1995) *In search of the Cradle of Civilization.* Quest Books, Adyar, Madras, India
- Ganhar G.N. and P, N.: *Buddhism in Kashmir and Ladakh.*
- Gervis Pearce: *This is Kashmir* {Published by A.S. of Kashmir)
- Ghosh Dilip Kumar : *Kashmir in Transition* (1885-1893) 1975
- Gordon, D.H., *the Prehistoric Background of Indian Culture.*
- Goyal D. R.: *KASHMIR,* R & K Publishing House L-4, Connnaught Circus New Delhi. R & K 'Theme India' Series
- Grierson George*: Linguistic Survey of India, Vol., viii part ii* Calcutta. 1919
- Grierson George: *The Ethnology, Languages and Literature of India.*
- Griffith M.: *India's Princes and Heritage*. London 1894.
- Hassan Muhibbul: *Kashmir under Sultans*, pub. Calcutta 1959
- Hassnain F.M.:-*Hindu Kashmir*
- Hassnain F.M.: (Edited) *Heritage of Kashmir* Gulshan Publishers Srinagar Kashmir 1980
- Hassnain F.M. : (Edited*) Composite Cultural Heritage of Kashmir*
- Hugel Charles Baron Von, *Travels in Kashmir and the Punjab, Light and Life Jammu, 1845*
- Hugel Charles Baron Von: *Kashmir and Punjab, Light and Life Jammu* 1972

SELECTED BIBLIOGRAPHY

- Hugel Charles Baron Von: *Kashmir Under Maharaja Ranjit Singh* (Translated from German by Dr. D.C.Sharma Atlantic Publishers New Delhi.
- Hiuen Tsiang: *Si-yu-ki.: Buddhist records of the western World 'Translated from the Chinese of Hiuen Tsiang* (AD *629) by Samuel Beal.* London, 1890
- Hayman Wilson Horace: *The Hindu History of Kashmir*, London, 1841.
- Iqbal, S.M. & K.L. Nirash, *The Culture Of Kashmir*, Marwah Pub.,1978
- Jackson A.V. William: *History of India Vil. 1 Early Times to the sixth century B.C.* By Romesh Chander Dutt CI.E 1862
- Jaisingh Hari: *Kashmir a tale of shame*, Pub. UBSPD, New Delhi London
- Jonaraja: *Dvitiya Rajatarangini. Edited by Professor Peterso*n, Bombay, 1896.
- Jonaraja Rajatarangini: tr. *Dr. Ragunath Singh* 1962
- Jyoteeshwar Pathik: *Glimpses of the History of J&*K pub. Jay Kay Book House Jammu 1990
- Kachru Braj B: *Kashmiri Literature*
- Kak, R.C.: *Memoirs Of The Archaeological Survey of India*, Calcutta Govt. Press, 1923
- Kak, R. C.: *Ancient Monuments of Kashmir*, London, 1933.
- Kalhana: *Rajatarangini, a Chronicle of the Kings of Kashmir.* Trs, with an introduction, commentary and appendices by Mark Aural Stein, London 1892, 1960 Stein Vol II, London, 1900 (rpt) Delhi 1961
- Kalhana: *Rajatarangini, a Chronicle of the Kings of Kashmir. Trs. Ranjit Sita Ram Pandit, 1935*
- Kaul Gwasha Lal: *Kashmir through the Ages* (5000 B.C.-1967 A.D) 1960 Eighth edition 1967, pub. Chronicle Publishing House Srinagar Kashmir
- Kaul, J.L.: *Kashmiri Literature*
- Kaul, J.L.: *Studies in Kashmiri*, pub. Srinagar 1968
- Kaula Nath: *Kashmir Speaks.* London, 1950
- Kaumudi,: *Kashmir its Cultural Heritage*

- Kaw R.K. : *Contribution of Kashmir to Sanskrit Literature*
- Kilam, J.L. : *A History of Kashmiri Pandit*
- Kelkar Ashok R.: *Kashmiri a Descriptive Sketch*, Pune
- Khan Mohammad Ishaq: *History of Srinagar*. Aamir Publication Srinagar 1978
- Koul Anand (1924): *The Kashmiri Pandit*
- Koul Omkar N.: *Linguistic Studies in Kashmir*, Bahri Publications Pvt. Ltd. 1977
- Koul Omkar N, Petyer Edwin : *Aspects of Kashmiri Linguistics*, Bahri Publications Pvt. Ltd
- Krishna Mohan: *Early Medieval History of Kashmir*, Mehar chand Lachhman das Publications.
- Kulkarni S. R:, *The Truth and Kashmir*, Krishna Pub., N. Delhi 1957
- Lawrence, Sir Walter R:, *The Valley of Kashmir*, Oxford University press London, 1895
- Macauliffe M A.: *The Sikh Religion*. Oxford, 1909
- Maccridle John Watson: *Ancient India*
- Madan T.N: *Family and Kinship*, Asia publishing House, 1954.
- Majumder: *History and Culture of Indian People*
- Majumdar,R.C.(Editor)K.K.DasGupta(joint editor)*A comprehensive History of India vol., iii, part I*, pub., Peoples Publishing House.
- McCrindle, J.W. (1877). *Ancient India As Described By Megasthenes and Arrian*. Trubner & Co., London.
- Mishra, Kamalakar: *Kashmir Saivism* (The Central Philosophy of Tantrisim)
- Mookerji Radha Kumud:—*Asoka/(Gaekwad lectures)* Raj Kamal Delhi second edition 1955)
- Moorcroft, William, and George Trebeck: *Travels In Hindustan Himalayan Provinces of Hindustan and the Punjab; in Ladakh and Kashmir; in Peshawar, Kabul, Kunduz and Bokhara 1819 to 1825. Vol 1& Vol. 11,* Prepared for the press, from original journals and correspondence, by Horace Haymon Wilson, London, 1837 Sagar publications New Delhi 1971

SELECTED BIBLIOGRAPHY

- Moravian August Hermann (A missionary) :*Kashmir Antiquity*
- Naudou Jean: *Buddhists Of Kashmir, Agam Kala Prakashan* New Delhi
- Neve, Arthur: *Thirty Years in Kashmir*, London 1913
- Neve Dr. Ernest: *Beyond the Pir Panjal.* London, 1915
- Neve Dr. Ernest: *A. Crusader in Kashmir.* London, 1928
- Newall D.J.F: *An abridgement of a Sketch of the Mohammadan History Of Cashmir* 1853-54
- Oldham Dr C. F. : *Serpent Worship in India* in J.R.A.S.,1891
- Oppert Gustav: *The Original Inhabitants Of* Bharatvarsha or India 1836
- Pannikar K. M.: *The Founding of the Kashmir State.* London, 1953
- Pant Kusum: *The Kashmiri Pandit,* Allied publishers pvt., ltd.,India, 1978
- Parimu Dr., R.K.: *History of Muslim Rule in Kashmir* 1320-1819, Peoples Publishing House Delhi 1969
- Piggott Stuart: *Prehistoric India up to 1000B.*C Penguin Books, 1950
- Pithwalla Manick B.: *An Introduction to Kashmir, Its Geology and Geography*, Karachi 1953
- Pococke E.: *India in Greece* Oriental Publishers New Delhi 1972
- Rabbani G.M.: *Ancient Kashmir, A Historical perspective*, Gulshan Publishers 1981
- Radhakrishnan Dr. Sarvapali: *Introduction the Cultural Heritage of India, Vol.1* Ramakrishna Mission, Calcutta
- Raina Dianna : *Kashmir Distortions and Reality Reliance* Publishing House New Delhi
- Ray Dr. Sunil Chandra,: *Early History and Culture of Kashmir,* Munshiram Manoharlal New Delhi 1969
- Raza Monis: *The valley of Kashmir,* Ali Mohammad Pub., Vikas pub., N.Delhi 1978
- Razia Bano: (edited and trs.) *History Of Kashmir* by Haider Malik Chadurah, Bhavana Prakashan New Delhi, 1991

- Rev. H. Hosten: *Eulogy of Father Jerome Xavier, S.J., a Missionary in Mogor.*, (15 617). Translated from the Spanish by the, S.J. J.A.S.B., New Series,
- Risley Herbert, George Grierson, William Crook: *The Ethnology Of Language literature and Religion of India.* 1924- Academic press Gurgaon Haryana -1975
- Rothfeld Otto: *With Pen And Rifle in Kashmir*, Anmol Publications Pvt. Ltd.
- Rudrappa, J. : *Kashmir Saivism*
- Sankalia H.D.: *Prehistory of India*, Munshiram Manohar lal Publishers Pvt.India
- Saxena, Dr. K.S.: *The Political History Of Kashmir* 1974
- Schofield Victoria: *Kashmir in the Cross Fire*, Viva Books Pvt Ltd. Delhi, Mumbai Chennai
- Sharga Dr. B.N. : *Kashmiri Panditon Ke Anmol Ratan*, total vi volumes, Sharga Publications Lucknow, 2003-2005
- Sharma Suresh K. &S.R. Bakshi: Edited, *Kashmir Society And Culture* (Encyclopaedia of Kashmir series -9, Anmol publication, New Delhi
- Sharma Suresh K. &S.R. Bakshi Edited, *Nehru and Kashmir* (Encyclopaedia of Kashmir series -6, Anmol publication, New Delhi
- Sharma Suresh K. &S.R. Bakshi Edited, *Kashmir Art Architecture and Tourism* (Encyclopaedia of Kashmir series -2, Anmol publication, New Delhi
- Stein Aurel: *Archaeological Reconnaissance's in N.W*
- Srivara; *Jaina-RajaTarangni: translated by Jogesh Chander Dutt.* Calcutta 1898
- Sufi G.M.D. *Islamic Culture In Kashmir* Srinagar 1925
- Sufi G. M. D.: *Kashmir*. Lahore, 1948-49. 1974
- Sur Atul K: *Pre Aryan Elements In Indian Culture.*
- Swaroop S.K.: *Political History of Kashmir*
- Tikoo Prithvi Nath: *Story of Kashmir*
- Tikku Somnath: *Kashmir Speaking*

SELECTED BIBLIOGRAPHY

- *Ved Kumari: The Nilamat Purana (A Cultural and Literary study Vol 1 7& 11*Published by J&K academy of Art and Culture and Languages 1988
- Vigne, *G.T.:Travels in Kashmir Ladak, Iskardo.*, London 1842
- Vogel H.Ph: *Indian Serpent Lore*, 1926
- Vreese, K.D.: *Nilamata Edited* 1936
- Wadia, D.N. : *Geology of India* 3rd edition London 1953
- Wakefield: *Happy Valley History of Kashmir*
- Wani G.A: *Kashmir History and Politics* 1846-1983, Pub., Wani Srinagar 1986
- Watters Thomas M.R.A.S.: *On Yuan Chwang's travels in India* (AD629-645) Oriental Publishers India Delhi
- Younghusband Sir Francis: *Kashmir*. 1909 Edinburgh London, 1917
- Zadoo, Jugdhar and Kanji Lal : *Nilamat Puran*
- 1*Archaeological Survey of India: Annual Progress reports 1917-18-19-20-21, 1961-1965*
- *2Journals of Asiatic Society of Bengal*
- *3 Memoirs of Archaeological Survey of Kashmir*
- *Journal of the Rev. Jose ph Wolff.* Contains an account of his missionary labours from the years 1835 to 1839 IP London.
- *4 Recent Journals, Vitasta, Kashur Samachar, Kashmir Sentinel, Panchtarni*
- In addition books mentioned in the notes and references of individual chapters, and articles and documents published in various journals and pamphlets were referred to by the author while writing this book.